D1713259

Warmth of the Welcome

Warmth of the Welcome

The Social Causes of Economic Success for Immigrants in Different Nations and Cities

Jeffrey G. Reitz

WestviewPress

A Division of HarperCollins*Publishers*

Copyright © 1998 by Westview Press, A Division of HarperCollins Publishers, Inc.

Published in 1998 in the United States of America by Westview Press, 5500 Central Avenue, Boulder, Colorado 80301-2877, and in the United Kingdom by Westview Press, 12 Hid's Copse Road, Cumnor Hill, Oxford OX2 9JJ

Library of Congress Cataloging-in-Publication Data
Reitz, Jeffrey G.
    Warmth of the welcome : the social causes of economic success for immigrants in different nations and cities / Jeffrey G. Reitz.
        p.   cm.
    Includes bibliographical references and index.
    ISBN 0-8133-8346-3
    1. Immigrants—United States—Economic conditions.   2. Immigrants—Canada—Economic conditions.   3. Immigrants—Australia—Economic conditions.   4. United States—Emigration and immigration—Government policy.   5. Canada—Emigration and immigration—Government policy.   6. Australia—Emigration and immigration—Government policy.   7. United States—Social policy—1993–
8. Canada—Social policy.   9. Australia—Social policy.   10. United States—Race relations.   11. Canada—Race relations.   12. Australia—Race relations.   I. Title.
JV6471.R45   1998
304.8'2—dc21   97-50570
                                                                                                                    CIP

The paper used in this publication meets the requirements of the American National Standard for Permanence of Paper for Printed Library Materials Z39.48-1984.

10   9   8   7   6   5   4   3   2   1

Contents

Tables and Figures

Figures

Acknowledgments

In conducting the research reported in this book, I have received assistance, advice, encouragement, and support from a number of individuals and organizations, which I would like to acknowledge here. The research was supported by a grant from the Canadian Ethnic Studies Program of the Multiculturalism Branch of Heritage Canada, which was indispensable in launching the project. At the University of Toronto, both the Centre for Industrial Relations and the Department of Sociology provided important research support throughout the project. At the University of California at Los Angeles, my research was greatly advanced by the help I received as a visiting scholar for a year in the Department of Sociology. I also benefited from the professional hospitality of Elizabeth Stephenson and Martin Pawlocki of the Social Science Data Archive at UCLA's Institute for Social Science Research. At the University of Sydney, I enjoyed a period as visiting scholar in the Multicultural Centre, and at Australian National University, Roger Jones and Gina Roach of ANU's Social Sciences Data Archive provided much help in gaining access to Australian census data.

Raymond Breton, Ivan Light, and Suzanne Model provided extremely valuable substantive suggestions, and detailed and thoughtful commentary on a draft manuscript. Their help contributed greatly to the progress of the project. Support and advice also was received from a number of others including Ian Burnley, Stephen Castles, Jock Collins, Mariah Evans, Lois Foster, Jürgen Friedrichs, Ron Gillis, Donna Gray, Morley Gunderson, Christine Inglis, F. Lancaster Jones, James Jupp, Melvin Oliver, Vilma Ortiz, Frank Reid, Donald Trieman, Jonathan Turner, and Warwick Wilson. Research assistance throughout the project was provided by Richard Bernard, whose professional knowledge of the U.S. census microdata files was of considerable help particularly in the early stages, and also by Elaine Chan, Fatima Lee, Clay Mosher, and Stephanie Potter.

Jeffrey G. Reitz

PART 1

Explaining Immigrants' Economic Success in Different Destinations

1

Social Causes of the Economic Success of Immigrants

Overview

What has been called the "new immigration" has had a profound impact on all three countries that are traditional recipients of immigration—the United States, Canada, and Australia—but that impact has been very different in each case. The new immigration essentially is immigration from non-European sources. Such immigration has been numerically significant in the United States, Canada, and Australia in the past three decades, and it has raised similar issues in all three countries. Yet there have been very substantial differences in the place that the new immigrants occupy in the social and economic hierarchies of the three countries, and hence important differences in the impact that immigrants have had. What exactly are these differences? What are the reasons for them?

Some of the differences are due to external circumstances which affect immigrant flows, such as the U.S. border with Mexico and proximity to Latin America, the Canadian and Australian connections to the British Commonwealth, and Australia's Pacific location near emerging Asian economies. However, the thesis of this book is that to a much greater extent than has been recognized, the differences reflect fundamental characteristics intrinsic to the three societies. The impact of immigration is, in effect, a social product shaped by the three countries' various institutional structures. Furthermore, the relevant institutions are rapidly changing, partly in response to global economic change, and thus are creating forces which are changing the impact of immigration in all three countries.

The similarities among the issues raised in public debate about the "new immigration" in all three countries are striking. In each country, the issues have both economic dimensions and racial or cultural overtones, and the salience of these issues has grown. As the numbers of immigrants have increased, so too has concern over whether immigration is a net economic benefit, whether it undercuts native-born workers, whether social service utilization by immigrants is too costly, and whether the immigration program is properly managed to control abuses. In each country there are concerns about challenges posed by increased cultural diversity, and with whether any increase in racial tension can be successfully managed. In each country there have been complaints about the impact of racism and racial discrimination and about the vulnerable situation of immigrant women in particular. And in each country some obvious form of backlash has emerged against these complaints. Mainstream public opinion on immigration has turned sharply negative in each country, with substantial majorities wanting reductions in the numbers of immigrants. Immigration policy revisions to increase selectivity and enforce controls are ever more frequently introduced to deal with these issues of increasing domestic public concern.

The similarities of public debate among the three countries can be seen in the immigration best-seller. Popular books debating immigration in each country have tended to be inward-looking, seeing immigration as a domestic issue related only to domestic traditions and values; they hardly make reference to what the other countries experience. But the themes of economic burden and cultural tensions are common to each. Arthur Schlesinger's scholarly *The Disuniting of America: Reflections on a Multicultural Society* (1992) questions whether American individualism can survive the group-oriented politics of racial and cultural diversity. Peter Brimelow's more hard-hitting *Alien Nation: Common Sense about America's Immigration Disaster* (1995) invites drastic policy responses.

Race is a less traditional issue in Canada than in the United States, and Canada's highly touted policy of multiculturalism has been adapted in an attempt to meet the equity issues raised by the so-called visible minorities (a Canadian term referring to the perception of distinctive physical features of the new racial groups). Yet Canadian multiculturalism was formulated in the context of European immigration, and as racial conflicts have increased, multiculturalism is far from the universally accepted policy it once was. Reginald Bibby's *Mosaic Madness: The Poverty and Potential of Life in Canada* (1990) reflected growing popular disquiet. Minority groups are no more unified than is the mainstream in their support for traditional solutions to inter-ethnic relations in Canada, as evidenced by the enormous impact of Neil Bissoondath's *Selling Illusions: The Cult of Multiculturalism in Canada* (1994).

Race came to the surface quickly in Australia's less politically correct environment. Most symbolic of this difference was the debate sparked by Melbourne historian Professor Geoffrey Blainey's *All for Australia* (1984), which very early questioned the value of Asian immigration for Australia and the appropriateness of importing Canadian-style multiculturalism as a policy response. More recently, M.P. Pauline Hanson's fiery anti-immigration rhetoric has stirred the most controversy. Her One Nation party calls for an end to immigration altogether. Unlike Canada and the United States, Australia has enacted fairly drastic reductions in immigration quotas while aggressively attempting to control the selection process. Yet the debate in Australia about the economics and culture of immigration has continued almost as if immigration were unchanged.

These similarities in the politics of immigration should not, however, hide major differences in the actual place of immigrants and the impact of immigration in the three countries. In a nutshell, the economic role and status of the new immigrants—reflected in their initial employment earnings—has been substantially lower in the United States, particularly in certain high-immigration cities. Immigrant earnings have been higher in Canada and Australia, and there is less interurban variation in these two countries. The wide interurban variation in the status of immigrants in the United States, compared to relative uniformity in Canada, and even moreso in Australia, is an important cross-national difference.

Close examination shows that these differences—in both the cross-national and interurban dimensions—are not related only to differences in immigrant source countries. In fact, even among immigrants of particular origins, entry-level earnings have been substantially lower in high-immigration U.S. cities. For example, the census data examined in Chapter 2 show that Caribbean-born Black immigrants to the United States, particularly in certain cities, stand markedly lower in the economic hierarchy than their counterparts in Canadian cities. Chinese and other Asian immigrants also stand lower in U.S. cities than their counterparts in the cities of either Canada or Australia.

The fact that immigrants from the same or similar origins have markedly different entry-level earnings in different societies points toward characteristics of the societies themselves as a key cause. This essential methodological point has been emphasized by Charles Tilly (1994, 7), who considered how migrants from a particular town in Italy, Roccasecca, had different fates depending on their destinations in towns near Lyon (France), Mamoroneck (near New York), São Paulo, Buenos Aires, and Toronto. The similar source provides a kind of "control" for factors related to the international environment. Differences in the position of immigrants within a destination society may therefore be attributed to the society itself, including differences related both to selection and self-selection of immigrants having particular characteristics and to the experiences of immigrants with those characteristics within the institutions of that society. In this study, our controls for origins are at the level of the ethnic or racial group or country of origin and are not as precise as Tilly's (the particular town of origin). It is nevertheless useful to

consider how similar origins lead to different outcomes depending on
the destination. The approach helps identify *endogenous* causes of immigrant entry levels.

The institutional sources of immigrant entry levels turn out to be various. Previous work relevant to this international comparison has provided inadequate explanation primarily because it has focused on only a
limited range of institutional causes. One approach emphasizes immigration policy. This has been developed extensively in the work of the American economist George Borjas, for example in his book *Friends or
Strangers: The Impact of Immigrants on the U.S. Economy,* and other publications. Others point toward labor markets, their structure and regulation,
which certainly vary cross-nationally. These include Michael Piore in his
book *Birds of Passage* (1979), Stephen Castles (see Castles and Kosack
1985, and Castles 1989), and Alejandro Portes (1995). A particularly influential version of the labor market approach, put forward by Saskia
Sassen in *The Mobility of Labor and Capital: A Study in International Investment and Labor Flow* (1988), and *The Global City: New York, London, Tokyo*
(1991), emphasizes that distinctive labor markets in emerging "global
cities" such as New York assign immigrants to low-level service jobs.
Sassen suggests that economic globalization might be one of the forces
behind low immigrant standing in particular U.S. cities. In a very different vein, John Porter, in his classic work on Canadian society *The Vertical
Mosaic* (1965), suggested that the relative underdevelopment of Canadian
educational institutions framed the entry-level position of immigrants.
An analysis of Australia by Birrell and Birrell (1987) also pointed toward
the relevance of educational institutions. A number of writers in each
country recently have suggested, often somewhat angrily, that social welfare institutions may affect immigrant economic well-being.

These various institutional sectors—labor markets, education, social
welfare, and immigration policy—should not be examined in isolation
from each other. Rather, they should be considered as components of an
institutional system, components which are partly interdependent on
and partly autonomous from one another, and each of which might affect
immigrant standing in important ways. The interdependence is obvious
in the cultural themes which pervade the entire institutional system in
each country. American institutions generally tend to reflect a stronger or
more pronounced emphasis on the value of *individualism* than is found in
Canadian or Australian institutions. This has been emphasized by Seymour Martin Lipset in his comparative study of Canada and the United
States, *The Continental Divide* (1989), and in his more recent study of
American Exceptionalism (1996). Individualism permeates most American
institutions, particularly the economy and labor markets, as well as the
ideology of social welfare. It also has been a factor in the expansion of ed-

ucation and the development of mass postsecondary institutions channeling aspirations for individual mobility and pursuit of the "American Dream"—of success and individual accomplishment based on ability rather than on class or racial background. American immigration policy also reflects this individualistic approach in some ways. By contrast, Canada and Australian traditions reflect greater emphasis on the collective welfare as a societal goal.

Despite common themes, to a considerable extent the various institutions are also autonomous and function independently. This leads to the following very important questions. What is the relative importance of each institutional sector in affecting immigrants' entry-level status? How does each institution operate to affect immigrants? To what extent does the institution produce national uniformity of impacts on immigrants, and to what extent does it function differently at the national and urban levels, or produce varying outcomes at the urban level? And finally, why do the institutional systems operate and affect immigrants in the ways that they do?

The importance of an institutional analysis of immigration is underscored and magnified by the sweep of fundamental institutional change now underway. Labor markets, education, and social welfare all are undergoing more or less rapid change and restructuring. In all three countries, much of this restructuring is in the direction of increased emphasis on institutional individualism. However, change is occurring at different rates in each country, and in different ways depending on the institutional sector. For this reason, knowing the relative institutional effects will help project the impact of institutional change—past and future—on the economic performance of immigrants in each country.

This institutional approach also redefines and broadens the questions about how globalization is related to immigration. Sassen's 'global cities' analysis focuses primarily on labor markets. Yet globalization and global economic competition have been linked to a range of institutional changes. In each sector, the pace of change and its timing vary enormously from place to place. Moreover, often changes some promote as an inevitable feature of globalization have in fact been extremely divisive precisely because they have benefited some groups in society more than others. The future directions of change are far from certain. Hence the question of the impact of globalization must consider how and when specific changes might affect each institutional sector and how each sector affects immigrants.

The remainder of this introductory chapter outlines the framework and background of this study in greater detail. First, I examine the importance of immigrant entry-level earnings in relation to the overall impact of racial-minority immigration. I then consider how four institutional areas—immigration policy, labor markets, educational systems, and social welfare—may affect immigrant standing. I suggest how theory and research (mostly on single countries) previously have raised specific questions about the explanation of cross-national differences. The concept of an institutional system is discussed in this context. I also consider in somewhat more detail the possibility mentioned above, that cross-national variations in discrimination *within* institutions might be an important reason for cross-national differences in immigrant status. The chapter concludes with an outline of specific research methods and a description of the cross-national census microdata samples used in the analysis.

Immigrant Entry Levels and Race Relations

Since this study will argue that entry-level earnings of the new immigrants are as much determined by fundamental institutional structures as by racial attitudes or discrimination within institutions, it is important to emphasize that it is nevertheless a study in race relations. In fact, immigrant entry-level earnings take on increased importance precisely because of the racial dimension of immigration today.

To underscore how racial issues are intertwined with the themes of this study, it might be useful to examine three points. The first is the fact that the increased racial diversity brought about by contemporary immigration is an inevitable part of global economic change and that the trend toward greater diversity certainly will continue. The second point is that the ramifications of immigrant entry-level status are greater precisely because of patterns of race sensitivity and exclusion in society. And third, since increasing racial diversity will lengthen the immigrant integration process, the initial status of the new immigrants will have more lasting effects. Here I will expand briefly on these three points.

Immigration and Racial Diversity

It is the racial component of immigration today that most commands our attention; immigration today means increased racial diversity in the receiving societies. This increasing racial diversity should be recognized as part of a broader process of economic globalization. A centuries-old process now seems to be entering a new phase as worldwide labor mobility has become economically feasible, advantageous, and hence inevitable. Economic change and development now carry the virtually automatic implication, for most if not all advanced industrial societies, of progressive racial diversification.

Societies which participate in this global development cannot escape a profound human choice. Are entrenched global racial inequalities to be reproduced within the leading industrial societies, so that racial hierarchy emerges as a central feature of most? Or are we seeing the emergence of a new racial pluralism, in which the various strands of humanity find a positive new dynamic in intergroup relations within national societies? How do national policy decisions made in the new global economic environment affect emerging patterns of relations among the world's racial groups?

The worldwide sweep of migration has, in only a few decades, significantly increased the racial diversity of the United States and has created an essentially new racial diversity in Canada and Australia. The United States has the largest numbers of immigrants from non-European sources, having experienced an increase from less than 2 million in the 1960s to nearly 3.5 million in the 1970s and more than 6 million in the 1980s (see Table 1.1). In the context of the large racial minority population that exists in the United States, including more than 30 million African Americans, these new immigrants represent a progressive expansion and diversification of race in American society. Canada and Australia have smaller numbers of non-European immigrants, but the impact in those two countries is even greater for two reasons. One reason is obviously that the smaller absolute numbers represent a larger proportion of the Canadian and Australian populations. A second is that because of the small preexisting racial minorities in these countries even including aboriginal populations, Canada and Australia are encountering race as an important domestic issue within their mainstream institutions for the first time. Thus, whereas for the United States the new immigration is merely altering a scene in which race is the longstanding legacy of preindustrial migration, Canada and Australia are experiencing the issue of race more immediately in its complex industrial and postindustrial forms.

The specific origins of non-European immigrants has varied among the three reception countries. Diversity is greatest in the United States. Recent immigrants to the United States include substantial proportions of Mexicans, other Latin Americans, Blacks (mostly from the Caribbean), and Asians. The latter have widely disparate origins and include Chinese from Hong Kong, Taiwan, and the mainland; Southeast Asians from Vietnam, Cambodia, and elsewhere; Filipinos; Koreans; South Asians from India, Pakistan, Bangladesh, and Sri Lanka; and Japanese. Immigrants to Canada are less diverse primarily because there are so few Mexicans or Cubans among them. And diversity is least among immigrants to Australia, because Australia not only receives fewer Latin Americans but also receives only a very small number of Blacks from the Caribbean and other origins. The Asian composition of the immigrant flow to Canada and Australia is as diverse as that to the United States, though the mix is

TABLE 1.1   Numbers of Immigrants to the United States, Canada, and Australia, by Origins, 1961–1990

A. United States

Origins	*1961–1970* Number (,000)	Percent	*1971–1980* Number (,000)	Percent	*1981–1990* Number (,000)	Percent
Africa	39.3	1.2	91.5	2.0	192.3	2.6
Americas, total	1579.4	47.5	1929.4	42.9	3580.9	48.8
Mexico	443.3	13.3	637.2	14.2	1653.3	22.5
Canada	286.7	8.6	114.8	2.6	119.2	1.6
Central America, other North America	101.6	3.1	133.2	3.0	459.8	6.3
Cuba	256.8	7.7	276.8	6.2	159.2	2.2
Other Caribbean	262.7	7.9	483.0	10.7	733.5	10.0
South America	228.3	6.9	284.4	6.3	455.9	6.2
Asia, total	445.3	13.4	1633.8	36.4	2817.4	38.4
Hong Kong	25.6	0.8	47.5	1.1	63.0	0.9
China (including Taiwan)[1]	96.7	2.9	202.5	4.5	388.8	5.3
Macao						
Vietnam/Laos/ Cambodia	5.9	0.2	210.7	4.7	663.6	9.0
Philippines	101.5	3.1	360.2	8.0	495.3	6.7
Japan	38.5	1.2	47.9	1.1	43.2	0.6
Korea	35.8	1.1	272.0	6.1	338.8	4.6
South Asia	36.1	1.1	208.0	4.6	323.2	4.4
Other Asia	105.2	3.2	285.0	6.3	501.5	6.8
Oceania and Australasia, total	9.9	0.3	14.3	0.3	13.9	0.2
United Kingdom	230.5	6.9	123.5	2.7	142.1	1.9
Other Europe	1008.1	30.3	677.8	15.1	563.5	7.7
Unidentified countries	9.2	0.3	23.0	0.5	28.0	0.4
Total	3321.7	100.0	4493.3	100.0	7338.1	100.0

[1]Note for purposes of comparison with Canadian and Australian data that a substantial proportion of immigrants born in China may have Hong Kong as the country of last permanent residence.

Source: U.S. Bureau of the Census (1992, 11). Data exclude Puerto Rico. "Origins" in the U.S. data refers to country of birth.

(continues)

TABLE 1.1   (*continued*)

B. Canada

	1961–1970		1971–1980		1981–1990	
Origins	*Number (,000)*	*Percent*	*Number (,000)*	*Percent*	*Number (,000)*	*Percent*
Africa	14.0	1.0	64.8	4.5	68.4	5.1
Americas, total	246.8	17.5	401.7	27.9	280.4	21.1
Mexico	2.1	0.1	6.1	0.4	6.9	0.5
United States	161.6	11.4	178.6	12.4	75.7	5.7
Other North and and Central America	6.2	0.4	2.5	0.2	40.8	3.1
Cuba			0.3	0.0	1.1	0.1
Puerto Rico			0.0	0.0	0.1	0.0
Other Caribbean	52.8	3.7	131.4	9.1	87.2	6.6
South America	24.1	1.7	82.8	5.7	68.6	5.2
Asia, total	140.9	10.0	408.7	28.4	602.9	45.3
Hong Kong	36.5	2.6	83.9	5.8	129.3	9.7
Taiwan			9.0	0.6	14.3	1.1
China	1.4	0.1	10.6	0.7	36.2	2.7
Macao			0.3	0.0	2.0	0.2
Vietnam/Laos/ Cambodia			66.2	4.6	100.6	7.6
Philippines			54.1	3.8	65.4	4.9
Japan	0.3	0.0	6.0	0.4	4.2	0.3
South Korea			16.0	1.1	16.5	1.2
South Asia	30.4	2.2	92.1	6.4	108.6	8.2
Other Asia	72.3	5.1	70.5	4.9	125.8	9.5
Oceania and Australasia, total	33.2	2.4	31.2	2.2	17.4	1.3
Australia	26.4	1.9	14.7	1.0	5.1	0.4
New Zealand	6.8	0.5	5.2	0.4	2.4	0.2
Other			11.3	0.8	9.9	0.7
United Kingdom	341.9	24.2	216.5	15.0	92.3	6.9
Other Europe	618.9	43.8	314.8	21.9	269.2	20.2
Unidentified countries	15.8	1.1	2.7	0.2	0.3	0.0
Total	1411.5	100.0	1440.4	100.0	1330.9	100.0

Sources: Canada, Statistics Canada, *Canada Yearbook* (1963–1964, 203; 1967, 220; 1969, 208; 1970–1971, 267; 1973, 235; 1975, 188; 1976–1977, 212–213; 1978–1979, 186); Canada, Employment and Immigration Canada (1986, 28–30; 1992, 34–36). "Origins" in the Canadian data refers to country of last permanent residence.

(*continues*)

TABLE 1.1   (*continued*)

C. *Australia*

Origins	1961–1970 Number (,000)	Percent	1971–1980 Number (,000)	Percent	1981–1990 Number (,000)	Percent
Africa	53.0	2.8	54.2	3.4	57.1	5.2
South Africa	13.3	0.7	29.9	1.9	29.6	2.7
Other Africa	39.7	2.1	24.3	1.5	27.5	2.5
Americas, total	128.1	6.7	166.9	10.6	63.0	5.7
Canada	32.1	1.7	34.6	2.2	10.8	1.0
United States	78.8	4.1	89.3	5.7	19.3	1.7
Other America	17.2	0.9	43.0	2.7	32.9	3.0
Asia, total	169.7	8.9	302.3	19.2	423.7	38.4
China	3.4	0.2	2.2	0.1	21.9	2.0
Hong Kong	14.3	0.7	20.0	1.3	36.3	3.3
Taiwan					8.2	0.7
South Asia[1]	27.6	1.4	26.3	1.7	41.5	3.8
Kampuchea, Vietnam					54.0	4.9
Korea					7.9	0.7
Philippines	4.3	0.2	14.2	0.9	56.4	5.1
Malaysia, Singapore	46.4	2.4	88.4	5.6	66.1	6.0
Lebanon	23.2	1.2	34.3	2.2	22.3	2.0
Other Asia	50.5	2.6	116.9	7.4	109.1	9.9
United Kingdom and Ireland	773.8	40.5	465.4	29.5	239.8	21.7
Other Europe	589.6	30.9	263.2	16.7	152.1	13.8
Oceania, total	195.4	10.2	307.6	19.5	168.8	15.3
New Zealand	141.8	7.4	200.9	12.7	140.2	12.7
Other Oceania	53.6	2.8	106.7	6.8	28.6	2.6
Not stated	0.0	0.0	17.0	1.1	0.1	0.0
Total	1909.6	100.0	1576.6	100.0	1104.6	100.0

[1]For 1961–1978, data include India, Sir Lanka, and Pakistan; for 1979–1984, also Bangladesh; for 1985–1990, only India and Sri Lanka.

Sources: 1961–1978: Australia, Department of Immigration (1979, 51–55); 1979–1984: Australia, Commonwealth Bureau of Census and Statistics (*Yearbook Australia,* various issues); 1985–1990: Australian Bureau of Statistics (*Labour Statistics,* various issues). Origins in the Australian data refers to country of last permanent residence for 1961–1984, and country of birth for 1985–1990. For 1961–1978, 1985, 1989–1990, year ends June 30; 1986–1988, year ends December 31.

somewhat different. For example, the United States receives a larger proportion of its Asian immigrants from mainland China and Taiwan, whereas the flow to Canada and Australia more often has come from Hong Kong. The United States receives relatively more immigrants from Korea, the Philippines, and Southeast Asia, while Canada and Australia receive more from South Asia. It is obvious that sources of immigration are affected not only by physical proximity but also by historical connections to empire. Migration to Canada and Australia is affected by Commonwealth ties; migration to the United States seems to be based on the legacy of the country's past military involvements.

These various trends toward increased racial diversity are not temporary aberrations. They are harbingers of the future. It is not at all an exaggeration to say that they portend a major point of demarcation in human history, a new period in which global migration becomes as commonplace as domestic residential mobility has been in the past, and hence a period in which race is a major domestic issue in an ever increasing number of national societies. The implications of these trends require careful examination. Immigration is extremely unpopular at the moment, and the most recent policy decisions in all three countries call for reductions in new admissions of immigrants perceived as a burden. The volume of global migration will continue to fluctuate over time in response to specific economic and political events. The possibility that it will end is, however, remote. We continue to speak of "racial minorities" as marginal groups, but in the future, racial diversity increasingly will be recognized as a central feature of all industrial societies. This will be true not only in the United States, Canada, and Australia, but elsewhere as well. In Europe, the European Community labor pool will slow but not forestall this trend. Even Japan will not be exempt; in Tokyo today, illegal immigrants from elsewhere in Asia are settling in significant numbers. Global labor migration is increasing, and in the long run there will be no question of a racially homogeneous society participating in the global economy.

Race and the Multiple Impacts of Immigrant Entry-Level Earnings

Our emphasis on immigrant entry-level earnings reflects a prevailing contemporary discourse or conventional wisdom that when it comes to immigration, "higher is better" and higher immigrant earnings lead to a more positive impact. The view that immigration makes the most positive contribution and has the most positive impact when immigrants have the most favorable economic prospects has become quite well established in academic, journalistic, and government circles. Immigration policy defers to it. There is, in fact, international competition for the best-educated immigrants because of their expected beneficial effects.

The formula "higher is better" reflects a complex series of processes which are not only economic but also social, cultural, and political. The economic impact of higher immigrant earnings is substantial and multi-dimensional. Immigrants who earn high incomes make a positive net contribution to government balance sheets not only because of the higher taxes they pay but because their financial independence reduces any potential need for social services or unemployment compensation. It is an added advantage that their skills were acquired and paid for elsewhere. They constitute a source of stronger consumer demand, and through high rates of self-employment, they create jobs. The view that less skilled immigrants might become a source of cheap labor or undercut the position of domestic labor groups suggests a *redistributive* impact that is positive for some but negative for others. The net effect is less positive, however, partly because of the negative social and political fallout of the redistributive effects.

This immigrant economic calculus is routine today, and the numbers are closely watched. There has been a growing concern about the declining entrance status of immigrants. This concern is strongest in the United States, underscored by studies by George Borjas (1985, 1994) and Barry Chiswick (1986), which show that the economic performance of the non-European groups has been declining even in relation to educational levels. In Canada, a report on *The Social and Economic Impacts of Immigration* by the Economic Council of Canada (Swan et al. 1991) showed a positive impact on the economy. More recent analyses also have shown declining economic performance of recent immigrants (see Devoretz 1995). Similar concerns have been expressed in Australia, but the Centre for International Economics reports, including *Immigration and the Commonwealth Budget* (Centre for International Economics 1992) show that immigration is a cheap way to add to the nation's human capital and that negative budgetary effects appear in the short term, under ten years after arrival, and positive ones thereafter (see also Neville 1990). Furthermore, benefits from longer-term residents more than offset losses incurred by recent arrivals. These calculations are extremely precise, and effects are found to be sensitive to economic indicators.

It has not always been so. In the past the accountant's calculator was not focused so intently on the bottom line of the immigration balance sheet. Immigrant economic contributions and their presumed precise connection to high status and earnings have not always been monitored so carefully. Earlier, large populations of immigrants were valued as hardy workers who made a contribution by laboring in lowly occupations. This was true in all three countries during previous waves of immigration such as that in the early twentieth century. Even in the postwar period of the 1950s and early 1960s, when large numbers of European immigrants swelled the populations in Canadian and Australian cities, immigration enjoyed a greater popularity than it does today. The fact that many of these earlier European immigrants were less skilled did not seem to matter as much as does lack of skill today. Of course, the native-born population also was less skilled, so the gap was not huge, as Hill (1975) showed. But there was less focus on the precise status of immigrants as an indicator of their contribution.

Even fairly recent unskilled European immigration to Canada and to Australia did not generate these concerns so forcefully. For example, the several hundred thousand Italian immigrants arriving in Toronto in the 1950s and 1960s had an average eight years of formal education. A substantial group of Portuguese and Greek immigrants averaged even fewer years of education. Yet today, the perception is clearly that this comparatively unskilled immigration made an enormously positive contribution to the city and the country. When asking whether Toronto benefited from immigration during that period, no one looks toward any detailed economic cost-benefit analysis. The benefits are regarded as obvious. The fact that many of these immigrants took low-status jobs and labored for years to build a place for themselves is seen as a mark of their virtue as well as of their positive contribution. Similar comments apply to postwar southern European migration to Australian cities such as Melbourne.

Today, we demand more. A greater emphasis on the economic bottom line, on the "higher is better" formula, on immigrant "quality," may be a result of several factors. One is a changed labor market, in which skills are in greater demand and available jobs are fewer. Another factor might be increased social entitlements, which in Canada include virtually universal government-funded health care and larger expenditures on education. Finally, it is hard to ignore the possibility that increased anxiety about the social and cultural impact of immigration might in part stem from the fact that the sources have shifted from Europe to elsewhere. There might be a stronger demand for economic benefits to compensate for the anticipated social and cultural strains.

Positive social and political impacts of immigration would seem to be clearly threatened by low immigrant status and inequality, and the visibility of racial distinctions calls additional attention to these issues. The extent and nature of perceived inequalities, their sources, and their impact on various sectors of society are not precisely known. Perceptions vary, which gives occasion to social and political conflict. Immigrants in poverty create a perception of a social burden. Discriminatory treatment of immigrants leads to debate about social justice and underutilization of valuable skills. Claims for resources to combat or offset inequalities might be received with hostility. Inequality might breed discontent on the part of the minorities—if not immediately, then over time. This entire inequality/conflict scenario implies that equality, or higher status for immigrants, eases the process of immigrant social and political integration, particularly for racial minorities.

Equality also favors the cultural benefits of immigration. However, cultural benefits are cited more often as an immigration spin-off than as a primary rationale. Some say it is more important (see Jean Burnet et al. 1992). Those who hail cultural diversity as the hallmark of a modern, cosmopolitan society obviously assume that minority cultures are at least to some degree respected parts of the whole, and not consigned to a disreputable marginality. A degree of economic well-being is assumed. Those who fear cultural diversity often point toward negative cultural features of minority groups. Poor immigrants are more likely to find their culture negatively stereotyped. Where negative features do exist, they might at least arguably be products of poverty, demoralization, and social disorganization. They might have their ultimate source outside the minority group itself. Again, although the impact of immigration on indigenous culture is debated, the relevance of inequality to this impact seems quite clear.

Racial boundaries obviously complicate the disadvantages of low immigrant status and reinforce the "higher is better" formula. Race is a social construct which reflects the significance attached to intergroup boundaries. Hence, the importance of inequalities becomes magnified and the impact of low status has more telling consequences. So the question of immigrant equality and the determinants of immigrant status requires examination not only as a question of fairness but also as part of the more general appraisal and analysis of the impact of continuing immigration on society. It also seems clear that the conventional wisdom that "higher is better" has weight partly because of the racial sensitivity of society.

Long-term Impacts of Low Initial Immigrant Earnings

The entrance status of immigrants has significance not only for the present but for the longer term as well. Immigrants do experience mobility and success, with time. However, the evidence suggests that the process of immigrant integration will take longer for racial minority immigrants in all three countries. This is true for several reasons. New immigrant groups' progress in overcoming initial disadvantage is slower than has been the case for immigrants of European origins. Immigrants of European origins have had earnings trajectories roughly comparable to those in the mainstream populations, but analysis shows that the new racial minority immigrants earn between 15 and 30 percent less than might be expected based on such trends (based on studies by Chiswick 1986, Tienda and Lii 1987, Model 1991, and others). Whereas the European-origin groups can expect their earnings profiles to move toward those of the native-born population within a decade or two, the data suggest that while the earnings of the non-European-origin groups do increase, they do not reach a point of equity with the native born. In this respect, the new immigrant groups face significantly greater obstacles to economic integration than have the European-origin immigrants. Low entry-level earnings for them will be resistant to change. This means that the negative impact of lower entry-level earnings among new immigrant groups in the United States, particularly in certain urban areas, likely will extend and continue over the longer term.

Actually, studies of immigrant integration based on the usual "snapshot" surveys or on the census may underestimate how slow the immigrant integration process really is. Cross-sectional analyses comparing recent immigrants with earlier immigrants often are used to deduce the speed of the integration process. This is a mistake. In contrast, Borjas's (1985) analysis showing that the most recent immigrants have poorer economic trajectories than earlier immigrants even from the same source was based on a series of cross-sectional census data sets. This finding not only bodes ill for the future economic assimilation of these groups, it suggests that most projections of assimilation were overly optimistic. Bloom, Grenier, and Gunderson (1995) have found the same to be true in Canada. Over time, of course, there is a tendency for members of all groups to improve their position as they adjust to the new society and acquire new resources. However, because racial minority immigration is such a recent phenomenon, the extent of future mobility is uncertain.

Precisely what obstacles are slowing the advance of new immigrant groups over time—in particular, the extent to which discrimination is involved—is not yet known. Some argue that racial discrimination is one factor; others deny the importance of discrimination and point to other causes. This issue of discrimination will be taken up below, where we will examine institutional factors and other possible reasons for cross-national differences. However, slow immigrant integration has negative consequences regardless of its causes. Persistently poor economic performance in the extreme case tends to reinforce itself and to be reproduced over time. A below-par standard of living means less ability to provide basic necessities for oneself and one's family. Fewer resources will be available to find appropriate employment, to pursue economic opportunity, to gain necessary training, to provide education for children, and to secure a proper living environment for members of the community. Low entry-level earnings set a low starting point for subsequent efforts, increasing the distance that group members must cross in order to achieve equality and the time it will take, and limiting the resources they will have for the task. Members of some immigrant groups find themselves in positions at varying degrees of disadvantage but can expect significant improvements over time. Other groups are extremely disadvantaged. Their economic plight is so severe that they must concern themselves only with survival in the present, not upward mobility in the future. This is what is meant by an "underclass." The existence of an underclass represents a social problem, whatever its cause.

All these considerations underscore the fact that the formula "higher is better" is not only multidimensional but is also reinforced by a racial dimension. Low immigrant entrance status is particularly problematic in the case of recent racial minority immigrants because the negative effects of low status are compounded and because low entrance status tends to be a more enduring feature of the group.

Four Institutions Determining Immigrant Entry-Level Status

This is a study of how the new immigrants' place in society is shaped by the design of various social institutions. To emphasize institutional determinants of immigrant standing clearly does not mean that individual immigrant characteristics are not important; they are. The characteristics of individual immigrants—their level of education and knowledge of the host country language; whether they have prearranged jobs or specific skills that are in high demand; their financial resources, contacts, and sources of support back home or in the local community; their levels of ambition; or a number of other characteristics deemed desirable by the host society—all have a major impact on the position that the immigrants in question occupy within the host society. However, the object here is to explain differences in the position of immigrants from one country to another and from one city to another, and in this context the primary reference point for explanation is at the level of the country and its cities. This explanation, of course, would have to include an explanation for important differences in the characteristics of the immigrants themselves.

The institutional focus of this study encompasses institutional discrimination but is not limited to it. Institutional discrimination refers to discriminatory outcomes which are built into institutional arrangements. For instance, when the hiring policies of a local police force specify height or weight requirements even when these are not necessary to doing the job, and effectively block women or some minorities from access to jobs in policing, then the hiring policies can be said to constitute institutional discrimination. Nonrecognition of foreign credentials can also be a form of institutional discrimination when the foreign credentials actually provide valid indication of comparable professional knowledge and ability. In this chapter, our concern is with institutional causes of different outcomes, and we leave aside the question of whether the particular institutional arrangements in question are unfairly discriminatory. However, the latter issue also is important, and we will return to it in a concluding chapter.

The following discussion considers how each of four institutional sectors might be expected to affect cross-national differences in the economic status of immigrants. In this discussion, emphasis is placed on the interdependence of institutions in that the analysis of any one institution also considers pressures arising from the others. Some of the questions raised concern the functioning of the institutional system as a whole, in each of the three countries.

The Impact of Immigration Policy

In explaining cross-national differences in immigrant status, the most obvious place to begin is with national policy on immigration (Hing 1993). The express purpose of immigration controls is to regulate access to residence within a territory. Immigration policy defines the institutional devices which 'guard the doorway' of society. Great faith is placed in their ability to do so. The idea that the numbers and characteristics of immigrants can be controlled to suit particular economic needs defined by the collectivity through a democratic process is in many ways appealing and reassuring.

To what extent, if at all, do immigration policy differences explain lower entry-level earnings of immigrants from particular origins in certain U.S. cities compared to others, or compared to Canadian or Australian cities? The U.S. policy, in place since reforms in 1965 largely eliminated country-of-origin criteria, has provided for immigration primarily for the purposes of family reunion, with only small proportions allocated for occupational needs or selection on the basis of professional or other skills. By contrast, when Canada and Australia enacted parallel reforms to end selection based on country of origin, they were continuing to pursue expansionist immigration policies directed toward economic development. Each country developed a system of points for selecting immigrants on the basis of labor market criteria. These differences in the selectivity of immigration policy between the United States on the one hand and Canada and Australia on the other have been identified in virtually every commentary. Briggs (1984, xiii, 92–95) has suggested that by comparison to Canada and Australia, U.S. immigration policy "has been allowed to function without regard to its economic consequences." Briggs advocates greater control over numbers and skill levels of immigrants to the United States. Comparing Canada and the United States, Reimers and Troper (1992, 15) wrote that Canadian immigration is managed in relation to economic objectives, while U.S. policy is directed toward considerations of foreign policy, ethnic politics, and humanitarian aid (see also Boyd 1976; Keely and Elwell 1981). Comparing Australia and the United States, Freeman and Jupp (1992, 19) pointed to the greater "role of the state in immigration matters" in Australia.

The specific claim that the skill-selective immigration policies of Canada and Australia are a direct and primary cause of the higher relative levels of earnings of immigrants to Canada and Australia compared to the United States has been put forward most consistently by Borjas (1988, 1990, 1993, 1994a). He cites as the primary reason the Canadian and Australian system of points selecting "independent" immigrants.

> Both Australia and Canada now use a points system to screen visa applicants on the basis of such observable characteristics as education and occupation, and only those persons who pass the test are permitted to enter the country. This visa-allocation mechanism should ensure that immigrants admitted to these countries are relatively well educated and have a favorable demographic background (Borjas 1990, 208). . . .
>
> The Australian and Canadian points systems attracted a typical immigrant who is better educated, who has more favorable demographic characteristics, and who has higher (relative) earnings [which Borjas takes as an immigrant characteristic but is here considered as an outcome] than immigrants from the United States. The filtering of Australian and Canadian visa applicants, therefore, greatly increased the skill qualifications of the immigrant flow. . . . The almost complete absence of skill requirements in the awarding of U.S. entry visas would be expected to dilute the skill level of immigrants entering the United States. . . . The United States should . . . awaken to the notion that we are competing against other countries in the immigration market (Borjas 1990, 209–210, 216).

The idea that the United States has lost out to Australia and Canada in the competition for highly skilled immigrants because of the points systems in the latter countries carries the clear policy implication that the United States should adopt a more skill-selective policy.

A number of comparisons of immigration trends in the United States and Canada have sought to identify effects of policy differences, with varying results. An early study by Boyd (1976, 92, 94) used official immigration data on the intended occupations of immigrants to Canada and the United States between the mid-1950s and the early 1970s. She found that the proportion expecting professional employment increased in both countries, but earlier than might have been expected based on policy change.[1] Another study by Keely and Elwell (1981) confirmed various occupational trends for immigrant groups from different origins in both Canada and the United States, again without drawing definite conclusions about policy effects.[2]

By focusing on the precise year-to-year trends, Green and Green (1993) also have raised doubts that the increased educational levels of immigrants to Canada are a result of the points system. They (1993, 23–24 and Table 7) showed in 1986 Canadian census data that the average extent of education of immigrants to Canada was about 10 to 11 years for those arriving between 1946 and 1965, and increased by about one year for men and slightly less for women beginning with the 1966–1967 cohort and continuing on to 1986. The decisive year of shift came in the 1966–1967 cohort. Green and Green asserted that such a shift came too early to have been a reflection of 1967 policy changes unless the regulations were phased in prior to their announcement. This suggests that if the change is attributable to the points system, then the system must have been phased in prior to its official announcement. In an attempt to relate Canadian policy directly to immigrant flows, Green and Green (1993) also examined how year-to-year shifts in the point values allocated to certain occupations have been reflected in year-to-years changes in the occupational composition of the immigrant flow. They found that the impact of these changes has been limited, mainly because there are so many other variables in the points system. They also argued that "while the point system may have an effect on the independents, . . . that effect can be swamped by changes in the unassessed part of the inflow" (Green and Green 1993, 32). Thus, the effects of an increasingly rigorous points system seem to have been offset by a shift from points-assessed independent immigrants to family-class immigrants, who are exempt from points screening.

The most comprehensive study published to date is the review of Canadian and U.S. immigration statistics for nearly the entire century (1900–1992) by Alan Green (1995). Examining occupational patterns, Green found a post-1965 difference mainly at the bottom end of the skills distribution, not the top. "The most dramatic difference is with laborers. After the introduction of the points system, this class of workers virtually disappears from immigrant workers admitted to Canada, but soars in the United States" (Green 1995, 58).

"Soars" is probably an overly strong term. In Canada, the proportion of laborers was 1 percent or less during 1965–1992; but in the United States the proportion averaged only 4 percent in the period 1965–1980, and although this increased to 16 percent during the 1980s, it receded again to between 4 and 6 percent in the 1990s. Overall, the points system has not increased the proportion of professionals immigrating to Canada compared to the United States. As Green reported: "Since 1965, both countries have drawn from roughly the same sources, but the outcome in skills composition of immigrants has been very different, especially for unskilled workers. The remarkably close trend values for professional workers shows that, indeed, the Canadian points system has not attracted such workers, for the simple reason that it was never designed for that purpose" (1995, 59).

In other words, Green has argued, the result of the points system was to screen out the very least skilled workers, not to attract the most skilled.

Duleep and Regets (1992, 425–426) focused on a comparison of Canada and the United States, using 1980 census data distinguishing among immigrants originating from China, other Asian countries, Europe, and Great Britain and among four periods of immigration (1960–1964, 1965–1959, 1970–1974, and 1975–1980). Using a liberal coding of the Canadian education variable,[3] they found that in 11 of 16 comparisons, and in 6 of 8 comparisons for immigrants arriving since 1970, immigrant-origin groups in the United States had more education. "Despite what may be an upward bias in the Canadian schooling levels, the average schooling levels . . . show no clear-cut educational advantage for Canadian immigrants over their U.S. counterparts"(p. 426). When common source-pools are identified, the United States had the edge in the recruitment of highly educated immigrants during the 1970s—and before. Moreover, within these source-pools there is no clear trend difference between the two countries.

Analyses of trends in Australia also do not clearly show that the selection systems introduced in the 1970s had any major effects. Birrell and Birrell (1987, 100) show that during the early 1970s, with the initial systems in place between 1973 and 1982, the average skill levels of immigrant workers in Australia increased, but not because more skilled workers were recruited. Rather, declining immigration affected all groups, but professionals least. Birrell and Birrell attributed this trend to changes in the applicant pool rather than to changes in selectivity.

In Chapter 3, we provide a detailed analysis of the policy differences and a new analysis of their effects on immigration selection. We find first that immigration programs in Canada and Australia have been somewhat more *occupationally* selective than the U.S. system, but they are not necessarily more *skill* selective. And second, census data on immigrants shows that in virtually every origin category common to the three countries, the United States outcompetes both Canada and Australia for highly skilled immigrants. Duleep and Regets (1992) showed this for certain origin categories in their U.S.-Canadian comparison, and data in Chapter 3 confirm it for other origin categories across the three countries.[4] Immigrants to the United States from most specific sources are in fact better educated than those in Canada and Australia. Policy differences have affected the mix of family-class and independent immigrants in the three countries, but analyses of the effects of these categories suggest definite but rather modest effects on the overall skill mix of immigrants from particular source countries.

Chapter 3 also examines immigrant skill levels in particular urban areas. We find a difference in patterns of immigrant settlement across cities that might be related to immigration policy. Specifically, a tendency for immigrants in large urban settlements in the United States to be less well-educated applies much less to Canada and not at all to Australia. While we cannot be certain based on census data, patterns in the data strongly suggest that these differences in patterns of urban settlement might be related to the family-reunification emphasis of policy and the importance of family ties in the settlement decisions of the less skilled. In other words, immigration policy is an institutional sector which operates at the national level but might be relevant to interurban differences in the status of immigrants as well as to cross-national differences.

The limited extent of an immigration-policy difference effect requires explanation in terms of the institutional environment and the forces acting on policymakers in each country. Borjas gives no account of social forces in Canada or Australia which would lead them to be significantly more selective than the United States specifically on the basis of education-based skills. Our own examination of this issue shows the influence of the individualistic environment on U.S. immigration policy and identifies a number of pressures in Canada and Australia to select immigrants who will make a positive contribution to the respective collectivities. These pressures favor the selection of immigrants who will be self-reliant but not necessarily those who are specifically highly skilled.

In addition, there appear to be serious limits on the capacity of immigration policy makers in any liberal democracy to establish a high degree of control over immigrants' skill levels. Immigrants obviously are to a significant extent self-selected, influenced by conditions in the country of origin, in the country of destination, and in competing potential countries of destination. Moreover, immigrants are not units which can be selected individually. Individuals necessarily have family ties and various other social affiliations which can affect the selection and self-selection processes. Immigration policy can prove difficult to implement or administer effectively, and the history of immigration shows many instances in which carefully laid plans produced very unexpected results. Enforcement problems at the U.S.-Mexican border and litigation in the refugee determination process have received the most publicity, but the issue goes well beyond these special cases. A larger reality is that effective immigration control, as it is defined at present, might not be fully achievable. While immigration policy undoubtedly is important in affecting immigrant entrance status, it might be far less decisive than often believed. The capacity of the state to act in the field of immigration is declining, as Cornelius et al. have asserted (1994, 27–28), and "we must reconsider the classical, realist notions of the state as a sovereign and autonomous actor" (see also Duleep and Regets 1996).

Effects of Labor Market Structure

Immigrants, particularly those who are members of minority groups in the receiving country, are very often concentrated in jobs or labor market segments characterized by poor working conditions, unconventional hours, and lack of union representation or other formal protection as well as by low pay. Since labor markets control earnings directly, it is logical to look to features of labor markets to explain these different outcomes for immigrants. As a result, labor market structures have been the most heavily researched institutional sector in U.S. research on immigrant status.

One prominent theory is that unskilled immigrant labor can be exploited more readily in an environment lacking labor standards and regulation. Michael Piore (1979) suggested that segmented or stratified demand for unskilled labor explains why the United States is faced with the apparent paradox that as the educational and skill requirements in the mainstream labor force are increasing, there has been a resurgence of immigration, including immigration at low skill levels. He also suggested that segmentation is getting worse, because technological change and economic restructuring have produced new labor market structures altering traditional relationships and posing potential problems to vulnerable groups such as racial-minority immigrants. At the top end, skilled professionals such as engineers and technicians are needed to create and implement technological change; but at the bottom end, many skilled manufacturing jobs are eliminated at the same time as the demand for unskilled service work is expanding. The resulting polarized labor market creates a new and potentially more hostile economic climate for new immigrants. Similar arguments have been put forward by others, including Portes and Walton (1981), Castles and Kosack (1985), Cross (1987), and Castles (1989).

Immigrants who are concentrated in particular vulnerable industries also might find their economic prospects endangered if the industry encounters a downward trend. This possibility is suggested by William Julius Wilson's study (1978) of the Black underclass in the United States, which argued that economic restructuring had undercut unionized manufacturing jobs in which Blacks had a hard-won stake, offsetting the gains of the civil rights movement. Cross (1987) argued that this basic process affected immigrants in Britain, who became concentrated in automobile manufacturing and similar industries that were forced to shed jobs because of intensified international competition.

Labor market institutions are very region specific in the United States, and as has been mentioned, Saskia Sassen (1988, 1991) has argued that 'global cities' such as New York and Los Angeles have distinctive labor markets generating even greater low-wage employment demand for immigrants. These cities now play host to a corporate superelite which occupies the command-posts of the new global economy, and their affluence creates a demand for unskilled service workers, often immigrants. Sassen's analysis of immigration in the 'global city' follows many theoretical premises of segmented labor market theory, with the difference that the new corporate superelite has an expanding global reach. Its increased power makes it even more independent of national political institutions. As national boundaries fade in significance, the urban location of the global corporate headquarters—the global city—emerges as its key domain. This suggests an even less regulated and more polarized labor market, and a lower status for immigrant workers, compared to what might be expected elsewhere. Increasingly impervious to political control, this superelite gains effective control of immigrant recruitment and uses this control to weaken labor standards.

If labor market segmentation (or a related factor) has important effects on immigrants, then such segmentation could be significant not only for an interurban comparison but also a comparison between the United States and Canada or Australia, because of differences in the influence of the labor movement and in labor market structure among the countries. Both Canada and Australia offer greater labor market regulation and employment safeguards than is provided in the United States. The Canadian workforce is more heavily unionized, with over 30 percent of workers belonging to unions, compared with 17 percent in the United States (Kumar 1993). Immigrants to Canada might experience patterns of labor market concentrations (Seward and Tremblay 1989; Reitz 1990) different from those found in the United States. In Australia, not only have unionization rates been higher than those in the United States, but the Australian industrial relations structure with its wage bargaining system is comparatively highly centralized despite trends toward enterprise bargaining (Patmore 1991; Bamber and Lansbury 1993). Australian labor market institutions have prevented the development of a marked stratified labor market to the extent seen elsewhere (Kalleberg and Colbjørnsen 1990). The consequence might be higher relative earnings for immigrants to Australia. Lever-Tracy and Quinlan (1988) discount stratified labor market theory and secondary labor markets as applicable to immigrants in Australia. The authors argue that the immigrants have been concentrated in certain labor market sectors, but these are not necessarily disadvantaged, and that for Australia, "the pattern of occupational segmentation depicted does not accord either with the pronouncements of dual labor market theory or of those who see postwar immigrants serving as a reserve army of labor" (p. 306). Labor markets in all countries are undergoing rapid change, which could be affecting the status of immigrants.

Any serious examination of such questions on a comparative basis must confront the fact that even within countries, and despite the extensive research already conducted on labor market structures—including but not limited to their bearing on immigrants—labor market effects remain controversial, with no clear consensus reached even within a single society. The theoretical and empirical status of segmentation theory has been debated and is uncertain at best (Hodson and Kaufman 1982; Smith 1990). Though many immigrants are indisputably isolated in poorly paid labor market segments, disadvantaged labor market *location* does not necessarily translate into negative *effects* of labor market structures. The same points may be applied to Sassen's 'global cities' discussion (see Cohen 1987; Hjarnø 1996).

Furthermore, beyond the possibility of labor market segmentation, other features of labor markets in the countries under study here may affect the fate of their immigrants. One of these is the earnings distribution, the size of the gap between rich and poor. Overall earnings disparities, as measured in data assembled by the OECD and also for the Luxembourg Income Study, are significantly greater in the United States than in Canada, and are least in Australia. This cross-national difference is almost certainly affected by levels of regulation and unionization in the workforce, but may affect immigrants quite apart from any concentrations in specific labor market segments. If immigrants as workforce newcomers start in jobs near the bottom end of the earnings distribution, then it certainly matters to them just how low are these bottom extremes of earnings. By the same token, immigrants moving up toward the top of a distribution which reaches higher upper-end extremes could expect to benefit—but only when they arrive and not before. Entry-level effects would presumably be positive only for those starting above the midpoint.

Labor market competition between immigrants and natives could tend to drive down the price of labor even further, particularly in an unregulated market, where competition is greater and its effects more rapid. For example, Morales (1983) studied the use of undocumented workers in the auto parts industry of southern California, showing how it has lowered production costs and weakened unions in the area. At the same time, the magnitude of this effect clearly depends on the numbers of immigrants. Negative effects of lack of labor market regulation in the United States might be offset by the negative effect of larger numbers of immigrants in Canada and Australia. Local labor market conditions also must be taken into account, because immigrants are so unevenly distributed among cities.

In the cross-national context, Borjas (1988) suggested that overall earnings inequalities might have a positive effect on immigrant earnings. The opportunity structure in the United States, with its wider gap between

rich and poor, is expected to provide the best chances for high mobility–oriented immigrants to realize their goals. Immigrants who are less
ambitious or likely to do less well will be discouraged from coming to the
United States because the price of failure is higher there. They might be
expected to prefer Canada or Australia, which offer less opportunity at
the top end, while providing greater income security for those anticipat-
ing labor market difficulty. (These cross-national patterns of recruitment
due to labor markets are the reverse of what Borjas expected based on
immigration policy differences, hence his emphasis that policies offset
the expected labor market effects.) However, while Borjas's hypothesis
received some support from an analysis of migration between the United
States and Canada, its applicability to immigration from other sources,
and to racial minority immigrants whose earnings opportunities at the
top end may be far less meaningful and to whom labor market segmentation may be expected to apply, is much less clear.[5]

There have been several statistic-based interurban comparisons of immigrant and racial inequality within the United States. These have focused
primarily on the size of the immigrant and/or minority group as a main
independent variable, rather than on labor market structure (see Frisbie
and Niedert 1977), but the results are very suggestive nonetheless. DeFreitas (1988), for example, found that the size of immigrant labor supply ex-
erts a (slight) downward pressure on native-born wages, mainly for
Blacks. He argued that immigrant concentration in particular industries
isolated the competitive effects of the immigrant labor supply. This indirectly implies greater immigrant inequality as well. Borjas (1987) estimated
that an increase of 10 percent in the immigrant labor supply reduced immigrant wages by 10 percent while having no affect on native-born workers.
Tienda and Lii (1987) found that the larger size of a minority group reinforced minority group inequality, including immigrant inequality.

Chapter 5 examines the impact of both cross-national and interurban
variations in labor market structure on immigrant entry-level earnings.
The analysis considers effects of overall earnings distribution and of the
concentrations of immigrants within particular labor market segments.
These features of labor markets may affect entry-level earnings because
they influence *self-selection* at particular skill levels and affect earnings *allocation* for those with given levels of skill. The methodological possibilities are greater in the U.S. interurban analysis because of greater detail in
available measures of occupation and industry in the microdata samples.
This is important not only because interurban variations in the United
States are a salient cross-national difference but also because the analysis
of the United States might provide new information about labor market
effects that have not previously been examined on a comparative basis.
The results also add to our capacity to interpret cross-national differences.

Effects of Educational Institutions on New Immigrants

Educational institutions have powerful potential effects on immigrant status in two ways. First, they determine the educational levels of native-born workers with whom immigrants must compete, and second, they determine access and opportunities for immigrants to upgrade their own educational levels. Because of our concern with entrance status, the focus here will be on the first. Where the host population has amassed greater human capital resources and credentials, outsiders such as immigrants face correspondingly greater obstacles in the quest to gain an economic foothold (unless immigrant selection is highly responsive to native-born human capital accumulation, which we will see is definitely not the case, particularly in the United States).

Despite comparatively high educational levels of specific immigrant-origins groups in the United States, the *immigrant education gap* between those groups and the rest of the labor force there has been greater. This cross-national difference in the education gap is due not to less-educated immigrants in the United States. Rather it is a result of the more rapid expansion of education for the native-born in the United States compared to those in Canada or Australia. As will be seen in Chapter 4, the better-educated immigrants to the United States often fall behind the native-born workforce by an average of from one to two years of education or more, while immigrants to Canada and Australia have lower levels of education which are nevertheless comparable to—or often exceed—those of the native-born.

Why different industrial societies have different levels of aggregate investment in education, and with what consequences, are complex and poorly understood issues. In *The Coming of Post-Industrial Society*, Bell (1973) described how the increasing economic importance of theoretical knowledge was supposed to bring about a dramatic increase in the economic value of education; and some say it has (Reich 1991). Yet others have argued that educational credentials have become a critically important resource in U.S. society for reasons other than their value as "human capital" required by the economic system. For individuals, education is a means to pursue upward mobility and the "American Dream," even when that pursuit extends beyond realistic opportunities for mobility; and in any case, higher educational credentials confer social status and prestige as well as economic rewards, as Randall Collins argued in *The Credential Society* (1979). Employers might hire on the basis of educational credentials regardless of the objective levels of skill that they represent, if relative levels of education serve as a screen for basic individual ability or if the educational standing of the supervisory staff helps reinforce managerial authority in the workplace (Bowles and Gintis 1986). A society's aggregate investment in education is also partly a political decision rather than an individual decision, because government plays such a significant role in funding educational institutions at all levels.

These considerations suggest that education is to a considerable degree institutionally autonomous from labor markets. Its autonomy is further bolstered and strengthened by the fact that educational credentials attained early in life are the exclusive property of their individual owners, who maintain them throughout the life course. Because of this, there is a major lag between decisions to change the pattern of educational attainment in a society, and the redistribution of educational credentials across the workforce. Employers face the chronic problem that new requirements for workers with specific skills can be met only after educational institutions have responded and new cohorts of workers have been trained.

There clearly have been large cross-national differences in the growth of educational institutions, with implications for trends in native-born educational levels. In Canada, the main period of expansion of postsecondary education occurred about a decade or so later than in the United States. Canadian secondary school completion rates lagged substantially behind the U.S. rates for a time, but the gap closed in the 1970s and continued to close in the 1980s. University completion rates in Canada were only about one-third of the U.S. rates in 1960 but rose to about half in 1970 about 70 percent during the 1980s. Meanwhile, overall rates of postsecondary enrolment in Canada rose very rapidly during the 1980s, attaining parity with the United States. Today no U.S.-Canadian difference gap exists in education for the youngest generation, but differences in the older population mean that an overall education difference remains.

Canada's pattern of educational development had economic reasons, as Clark (1976, 28–29) described. Given that Canada's economy was based primarily in resource extraction, it had no need of an educated middle class; but later foreign investment in manufacturing created this need. The reasons for the underdevelopment of education in Canada up to 1965 were part of John Porter's classic analysis of Canadian society in *The Vertical Mosaic* (1965). It was Porter's view that Canadian elites designed Canadian institutions with the primary object of preserving their own privileged status, and they saw education as a potential minority mobility vehicle for competitors. Hence, they avoided the kind of commitment to mass education seen in the United States. As an alternative, they relied on immigration to fill specific occupational roles. It was, he argued, part of a 'colonialist' strategy for reducing social mobility within the country and protecting the position of the privileged. Their plan called for an ethnic stratification of immigrant sources. Some groups such as British and Americans were recruited to fill highly skilled professional and managerial positions; other groups, such as South and East

Europeans, were recruited to fill lower-level agricultural and industrial jobs. By providing minorities with fewer educational opportunities and encouraging ethnic community formation to isolate minorities from broader labor markets, elites expected that these minorities would be unlikely to challenge the upper levels of society. In Porter's view, several institutions in Canada interacted to limit the upward mobility of minorities, including the institutions of education, labor markets, and immigration policy. Minorities were to be excluded, creating greater ethnic inequality—a "vertical mosaic"—in Canada.

Subsequent researchers have criticized Porter's analysis but focused almost entirely on the mobility of minority-group immigrants after they arrived. This research essentially has disproved the hypothesis of lower mobility rates for non-WASP immigrants. There are no greater barriers to minority group mobility in Canada for those of European origins, at least by comparison to the majority population or to British-origin immigrants. This part of the strategy to maintain a 'vertical mosaic' seems to have failed.

However, Porter's other argument, about the design of Canadian institutions having implications for the ethnic hierarchy because of the effect on immigrant entrance status, might be valid. As Porter observed, the relative underdevelopment of educational institutions in Canada prior to 1965 made the Canadian middle class fairly accessible to highly educated immigrants. He also was right in arguing that this middle-class accessibility maintained ethnic exclusivity when most of the best-educated immigrants were British and American.

At the same time, key changes have occurred in Canadian society since 1965, changes which alter the patterns of social causation following from Porter's basic premises. First, immigration policy reforms of the mid-1960s removed country-of-origin criteria, replacing them with objective criteria related to employability. When the ethnic composition of highly educated immigrants changed, the ethnic and racial implications were transformed. Given the new immigration, the less developed Canadian educational system made the Canadian middle class more accessible to the new racial minorities. If there was an elite strategy to use immigration policy to maintain ethnic and racial exclusiveness in the middle class, it was defeated by the immigration reforms. The "vertical mosaic" was further undermined.

On the other hand, a second change, also under way as Porter was writing during the 1960s, was an upgrading of the Canadian educational system to match the U.S. system. There were many changes in education. Whereas in 1965 about twice as many Americans attended university as Canadians, today there is virtual parity between the two countries in that regard. The expansion process in Canada is now essentially complete.

The reasons for this change are many. One of the primary reasons may be the abandonment of the colonial reliance on foreign skills. Ironically, however, by seeking national autonomy, the Canadian educational system has been Americanized in some ways. Although the Canadian population remains less educated than that of the United States, this is primarily because of lower levels of education for those over 35 years of age, and particularly among those over 50. The impact of change is still being absorbed as new generations of better-educated Canadians slowly advance through the age-graded occupational structure. The consequence is that the entrance status for new immigrants declines as the educational credentials of the Canadian mainstream population accumulate, posing increased barriers to the advancement of newcomers.

The Australian case provides a useful contrast. Birrell and Birrell (1987, 49–51, 67) analyzed the underdevelopment of Australian education in terms not entirely different from Porter's analysis for Canada, but citing practical constraints on policy rather than a colonialist mentality as the primary cause. With the rapid development of the Australian economy after World War II, the demand for skilled workers simply rose too quickly to be met by the kind of "radical restructuring of Australia's educational and manpower training system" which would have been required (Birrell and Birrell 1987, 50). Educational expansion has occurred most slowly in Australia; the gap between Australia and North America only began to close in the 1980s. Distant from the North American environment, Australian educational institutions bear a closer resemblance to the European standard in terms of the numbers and levels of education expected of the population. Immigrants to Australia, like those in Canada, have faced fewer obstacles in the struggle for mobility. Expansion of higher education on a North American scale has become a priority for Australia only relatively recently (Dawkins 1988; Marginson 1993).

Clearly, educational standards in the native-born population reflect an institutional force to some extent independent of labor markets. Particularly in Canada and Australia, where all postsecondary education is in the public sector, the prevailing levels of education are largely the result of political decisions, with individual demand for education relevant to the extent that it affects such political decisions. The impact on immigrants also depends on patterns of settlement of highly educated native-born workers in particular urban areas, and the extent to which their decisions match those of the best-educated immigrants.

In Chapter 4, the implications of cross-national differences in educational systems are explored more closely. One important finding is the role of education in creating interurban differences in immigrant status within the United States. Differences in local educational institutions, and patterns of interurban mobility, have resulted in a very uneven distribution of native-born human capital across urban areas within the United States, creating regional patterns markedly different from those found in Canada or Australia. An extreme immigrant/native-born polarization of human capital endowments exists in the United States for reasons quite unrelated to labor market structures. Another significant finding is that the growth of educational institutions in Canada and Australia can be expected to move immigrant entrance status closer to that in the United States.

The Welfare State and Immigrant Adjustment

Social services and income redistribution adjust labor market outcomes to some extent. This institutional sector might be important in affecting how immigrants cope with initial problems of adjustment, and thus, might also have implications for their longer-term success in becoming integrated into the receiving society.

Canada and Australia share an ethos of public welfare that is stronger than that in the United States, and data on income redistribution both by taxation and by government transfer payments suggest that such redistributive forces are stronger in the first two countries. Hence, cross-national patterns of income redistribution actually exaggerate and magnify the extent of income inequality resulting from labor markets. What are the implications of these cross-national differences for immigrants? How do these implications depend on the earnings of the immigrant groups themselves, and how do these differ cross-nationally?

The analysis presented in Chapter 6 considers evidence on the joint impact of differences in social policy and in social welfare eligibility of immigrants. What we find is interesting and somewhat surprising, and certainly underscores the critical importance of institutional structures in determining the fate of immigrants. It is well known that in the United States, immigrants have been more frequent users of social welfare (Borjas and Trejo 1991; Borjas 1993, 1994a, 1994b; Borjas and Hilton 1996). In Canada and Australia, immigrants have less often been users of welfare (Baker and Benjamin 1995; Whiteford 1992). What is less well known is that these findings are not a result only of the poverty of Mexican Americans living in the United States; they also hold for other specific immigrant groups. This is true despite the fact that, again on a group-specific basis, immigrants to the United States are more highly skilled. What this seems to imply is that the institutional structures which lead to lower immigrant entry-level earnings in the United States also lead to higher rates of poverty and are a significant source of greater immigrant welfare use. The implications of these findings, further explored in Chapter 6, are far-reaching in demonstrating the overall impact of social institutions on immigrant economic success.

The Institutional System and the Relations Among Institutions

If societies differ systematically in the structure of each institutional sector, and if each sector can affect immigrants, then we might ask: Which cross-national institutional differences are most important, and why? This question is important not only to understand the past and present situation but also to project the future direction of change for immigrants presaged by widespread institutional restructuring. How is the restructuring of social institutions affecting immigrants? The pace of change varies not only from one country to another but also from one sector to another within a country. Implications for immigrants will vary accordingly, depending on the relative importance of particular sectors and on the way in which particular sectors change in each society.

To understand the relative importance of these various institutional sectors in affecting immigrant status, it will be necessary to understand how institutions function as a system in relation to each other and in relation to immigrants. Our framework for comparative study must include attention to a number of issues. These include (1) the interdependence and autonomy of institutions, (2) how distinctive features of the operation of each institutional sector may affect the position of newly arriving immigrants, and in particular, (3) how national and regional structures of each institution affect urban variation in immigrant entry-level status. Some comments on each will help establish our framework for analysis.

Interdependence and Autonomy of Institutions

Our institutional approach explicitly recognizes both the interdependence and the autonomy of institutional sectors. Interdependent institutions "fit" together because of a common cultural underpinning and because pressures arising within one institutional component generate constraints on others. For example, if individualistic labor markets generate inequalities, taxpayers might be reluctant to fund the correspondingly more expensive social safety net. The greater cost of economic failure generates pressures to create opportunities for mobility by such means as greater investments in education. And for reasons elaborated in Chapter 3, a laissez-faire immigration policy fits with laissez-faire social institutions. Still, a degree of institutional autonomy exists in that each sector is controlled in different ways and responds to different sets of internal pressures.

It might be useful to state where our own approach raises questions about previous analyses in terms of interinstitutional relations. Borjas's emphasis on immigration policy as a key institutional sector affecting immigrants contains two important assumptions about relations to other sectors. One is that immigration policy in the United States does not respond well to economic pressures such as those arising within labor markets. The relatively unselective U.S. immigration policy is seen as responding to humanitarian and other concerns which are counter-productive from an economic standpoint. On the other hand, the educational attainment of the native-born workforce is not seen as relevant to explaining the position of immigrants, possibly reflecting an assumption that labor market forces related to educational levels impinge upon immigrants and natives alike. In other words, education serves labor market forces in a way that immigration policy does not. In this view, what distinguishes education on the one hand from immigration policy on the other might be the extent to which political processes intervene to thwart economic requirements. The analysis presented here considers the possibility that educational institutions might be at least as autonomous from labor markets as is immigration policy.

Proponents of segmented labor market theory frequently depict the corporate sector as controlled by an elite which is influential in most institutional sectors (see Braverman 1974; Gordon 1972). This might be expected to create a situation in which U.S. labor markets, immigration policy, social welfare, and education reinforce one another in fostering a trend toward greater inequality. The data do fit this scenario, but only approximately. Each institutional sector appears to have been changing in the three countries at different rates, with potentially different outcomes for immigrants. While labor in Canada and Australia has remained stronger than that in the United States, educational institutions there, particularly in Canada, have become Americanized. Labor's interests regarding immigration might be accommodated in Canadian policy more than in U.S. policy, but it is difficult to find evidence for this. Immigration policies in Canada and Australia have diverged sharply in recent years, with severe cuts in Australia and higher targets in Canada.

Porter's approach is similar in portraying a single, dominant elite, but Porter suggests that elites in different countries might pursue different objectives in each institutional sector, explaining patterns of institutional difference across countries. Porter's colonialist Canadian elite deemphasize state-provided education while relying on immigration to recruit the needed workforce. Porter obviously differs from Borjas, however, in that Porter viewed education as autonomous from market forces and the average level of education for all workers as lower than required for economic development. The question raised by Porter's analysis is why did Canadian policy on education and immigration change so dramatically in the period following 1965? Did the Canadian elite maintain its power but change course, dropping its colonial tie to Britain and asserting its autonomy, like that of the United States? Or has the traditional Canadian elite been displaced by broader social and political forces in North America?

For our purposes it is not necessary to answer these questions, only to point toward their problematic nature. The interdependence of institutions means that the effects of each must be considered in light of its relations to others. The autonomy of institutions means that each institution can have independent effects. This also underlies the fact that patterns of institutional change can produce diverse impacts on immigrants.

Differences in Institutional Functioning and Effects on Immigrants

Each institution operates differently in its impact on immigrants, and the effects of one institutional sector might depend upon conditions in others. The analysis of each institution must reflect the specific pattern of potential effects.

Immigration policy traditionally has affected only the selection process and not income allocation following entry. Other institutional sectors have primary effects related to income allocation, though they also might influence self-selection. The impact of immigration policy is very much cohort specific: A policy in place at any particular time affects primarily the cohort arriving at that time. Later immigrants might be affected because of the ramifications of one cohort's family connections for subsequent immigrant eligibility. The composition of family-class immigrants arriving at any one time is a function of the characteristics of previous groups of immigrants.

Educational institutions have very different kinds of effects. Educational expansion affects new immigrants mainly because of a long-term process by which the educational levels within the native-born workforce are established. Institutional change in the educational sector produces effects that play themselves out slowly over decades and even generations. Educational institutions also might have direct effects on immigrants seeking opportunities for additional formal training, or education adapted to local labor markets, and on the second generation. More extensive education among the native born might create obstacles for immigrants, while the greater availability of educational opportunities might help immigrants' offspring. On the other hand, obstacles to education for first-generation immigrants might also reduce educational participation in the second generation, if severe economic hardships are imposed on their parents.

Labor market institutions have fairly immediate effects on immigrants who seek work upon arrival. Later effects are possible too, because specific patterns of labor market concentration have implications which appear only in light of later economic trends. Still, immigrants can affect these outcomes both by the strategies they pursue as individuals and because of the resources which might or might not exist in the immigrant community. This difference arises partly from the lack of central control in labor markets, compared to that in educational institutions or immigration policy.

Welfare institutions and the tax system obviously may affect immigrants by altering their location within an overall system of distribution, altering the impact of labor market inequality. One specific feature is the potential lack of accessibility of welfare to immigrants whose pattern of use seems to reflect social assimilation (Borjas 1991 and 1994a, 1700–1708; Borjas and Trejo 1993; Baker and Benjamin 1994).

There is a compounding or value-added aspect to these various effects. The impact of each institution on immigrants depends in part on the effects of other institutions on their position. Whether labor market inequality affects immigrants positively or negatively depends on whether they enter the distribution near the top or near the bottom; this entry-level position in turn is affected by immigration policy and by educational institutions. Whether welfare institutions have any effect on immigrants obviously depends on where their experiences in other institutions leaves them in the overall economic hierarchy.

National and Urban Structure of Institutions

Immigration today is largely an urban phenomenon, so it is important to see how institutional variation affects immigrant experiences at the urban level. Institutions vary by urban area, and national institutions also may have variable impacts in particular urban areas.

Urban and regional diversity in the United States is greater than that in Canada, and even moreso, than that in Australia. In other words, urban diversity is a cross-national variable. The functional specialization of cities is less pronounced in Canada because most major Canadian cities also serve as regional capitals, which constrains their functions. Major Australian cities all are regional capitals.

Each institutional sector presents a specific pattern of national-urban relationship. Immigration policy operates at the national level but can affect the settlement of different types of immigrants in different urban locations within a country. Immigration selection based on family connections might reinforce social networks in the settlement process, affecting specific areas of settlement. Settlement programs for particular groups such as the Vietnamese in the United States also might affect at least the initial destinations of immigrants.

The impact of educational institutions on particular urban areas depends on the locations of specific schools, colleges and universities and on domestic patterns of interurban mobility. These patterns of interurban mobility may follow labor market trends, but other forces operate as well. The factors which affect immigrant settlement and those which affect interurban mobility of the native-born might be different, leading to the possibility of more extreme skills disparities in particular urban areas.

Labor market structures also vary across cities, particularly in the United States. The "global cities" analysis suggests that institutional structures in cities with global responsibilities generate immigrant inequalities. Supporting this, as Chapter 2 shows, is the fact that immigrant entry levels are often lower in cities like New York, the prototypical global city. However, the institutional origins of this fact are open to question, given the lack of empirical confirmation that labor markets themselves differ substantially in global cities compared to others. More critically, immigration at the service of superelites in global cities clearly does not explain why immigration is so significant in nonglobal cities like Toronto and Sydney, to say nothing of Vancouver, Brisbane, or Perth. Nor does it explain higher immigrant entry levels in those places. Ironically, the global city theory does not provide an explanation for global patterns of immigration.

The independence of institutional variation can operate differently at the urban level than at the national level in a country like the United States because pressures constraining institutional design might operate differently at each level. Hence, the processes which cause cross-national differences in the status of immigrants might or might not be the same as those causing interurban differences.

Doubtful National Differences in
Racial Discrimination Within Institutions

To explain lower immigrant entry-level earnings in the United States or in particular U.S. cities, some might be tempted to suggest that there could perhaps be a more pervasive pattern of discrimination based on immigrant or racial minority status within labor markets and other institutional sectors in those places. Clearly, the fate of immigrants might be affected by discrimination. Host countries could differ in their predispositions toward treatment of specific groups. Castles and Miller (1993) distinguish folk (excluding), republican (assimilationist), and multicultural (culturally tolerant) models for the incorporation of immigrant groups. If the United States is considered assimilationist, and Canada and Australia multicultural (based on their own self-description), the difference could lead to differences in discriminatory treatment based on origins. Others debate whether American individualism might support equality of opportunity and hence less discrimination (Sniderman and Hagen 1985; Sniderman and Piazza 1993). Our focus here on institutions rather than on discrimination *within* institutions is based in part on evidence that the United States, Canada, and Australia do not differ dramatically in their

potential for discriminatory policies or practices within institutions such
as labor markets. What is the evidence?

For the U.S.-Canadian comparison, Reitz and Breton (1994) in *The Illusion of Difference: Realities of Ethnicity in Canada and the United States* assembled data on a range of indicators relevant to the potential for ethnic
or racial discrimination specifically against immigrants, such as attitudes
toward race, anti-Semitism, various components of social distance—attitudes toward immigration, racial integration in the workplace and in the
neighborhood, and intermarriage—and attitudes toward government intervention to assist racial minorities. Most of these indicators showed a
trend over time toward greater tolerance, but little cross-national difference. Americans and Canadians are equally opposed to racism. Similar
proportions of Americans and Canadians feel minorities impose disadvantage on themselves. They are equally likely to subscribe to negative
stereotypes of Jews, and equally likely to prefer excluding minorities
from private social encounters. Partly because of their attachment to individualism, Americans are more likely than Canadians to favor encouraging immigrants to maintain their own distinct cultures. On the other
hand, Canadians are more tolerant of interracial marriages.

Data also were examined on employment discrimination and the economic incorporation of minorities, again producing no evidence of a substantial difference. Earnings net of human capital are similar for racial
minority immigrants in the two countries (see also Baker and Benjamin
1995). Results of field surveys of racial discrimination in U.S. cities are
similar to results in Canadian cities.

The American emphasis on individualism implies a greater commitment to equal opportunity, whereas Canadians, being oriented toward
group rather than individual rights, are less concerned about equality of
opportunity and perhaps more likely to seek equality of outcomes. However, American individualism also supports related principles which
may work at cross-purposes. Individualism means also individual freedom, which in practice if not in theory might include freedom to discrim-
inate and freedom from regulations designed to combat discrimination.
Attitude data suggest that in the U.S. population at large, any link between commitments to individualism and to equal opportunity is weak.

In Australia, attitudes toward immigrants and minorities do not appear substantially more positive. A majority of between 50 and 60 percent
want immigration to be reduced, which is comparable to findings both in
the United States and in Canada.[6] Discrimination surveys also do not
support the hypothesis of less discrimination in Australia[7] (see also Foster et al. 1991). There are no substantial differences in other available indicators, such as the frequency of anti-Semitic incidents recorded by

B'nai B'rith.[8] Various comparisons of Canada with Australia (Holton and Lanphier 1994; Collins and Henry 1994), and Australia with the United States (see Freeman and Jupp 1992, 221), also do not support cross-national differences in the potential for discrimination. The relatively higher net earnings of immigrants in Australia could be a function of less discrimination, as might be suggested based on the studies by Evans and Kelley (1986, 1991). However, no empirical study has suggested substantial cross-national differences in the extent of employment discrimination against immigrants based on race or ethnic origins. The hypothesis that immigrant origin has a roughly similar effect on economic status in each country seems to be supported by existing data.

The quantitative significance of racial discrimination in the labor market is very difficult to measure. Some attribute the substantial earnings disadvantages of non-European immigrants, net of measured human capital such as education, to discrimination based on race. Net earnings disadvantages of Black immigrants to the United States are about 20 percent—comparable to what is observed for native-born African Americans, as Model has shown (1991; see also Jaynes and Williams 1989). Some attribute this disadvantage to "unmeasured human capital"—for example, the quality of education—or to less tangible individual characteristics, such as ambitiousness. Field surveys by job applicants from different racial groups show that some discrimination occurs, but they do not measure its significance in explaining the earnings disadvantages.

A main problem in measuring the extent of discrimination in the labor force is inherent in the concept of racial discrimination. Racial discrimination is defined as existing when the earnings of a racial minority group fall below what would be appropriate based on productive worth. Yet there is no consensus on how to measure productive worth in labor force data. What are the skills of immigrants, and what are they actually worth to employers? The relationship between conventional measures, such as years of education or experience, and organizational productivity is only assumed; there are no data on actual productivity to back it up.[9] So while some scholars, such as competitive labor market theorists, believe as a matter of faith that the market automatically reflects productive value, the more pessimistic remain skeptical but unable to prove their point. The debate goes on.

The cross-national similarity in the findings on the potential for racial discrimination probably reflects the fact that despite historical differences in experiences with race, the three countries share the same British and European cultural heritage. As a result, the populations of the three countries might exhibit the same attitudes toward non-Europeans and similar predispositions to racial intolerance and exclusion in specific social spheres including employment. Hence, the potential for discrimination hardly seems likely to provide the explanation for lower immigrant standing in the United States than in Canada or Australia.

The role of racial attitudes in the formation of immigration policy also does not appear to be markedly different among the three countries. The pressures to reform immigration policy during the 1960s (in Australia, during the early 1970s), were of a similar nature in each country, and had to do primarily with the politics of race. Immigration country-of-origin quotas increasingly were perceived as based on a morally unacceptable racial preference for Europeans. At the same time, the alternative immigration policies based on family reunification and on skill selectivity have been criticized as reflecting a continued agenda of racial exclusion in a new guise. So racial attitudes would not serve as a ready explanation for these differences in policy, in any case.

In each country, existing European-origin ethnic communities, and the desire to support continued European immigration, generated pressures to allow continued immigration of family members (Keely 1979a, 1979b; Kubat 1979, 59; Hawkins 1988, 346–353). All countries continued to "grandfather" these existing immigrant populations, allowing for family reunification. A motive for emphasis on family reunification, some suggest, might have been the desire by many groups to maintain the European orientation of immigration. Family reunification not only satisfies the domestic political pressures on the part of ethnic minorities, it ensures that migrants will continue to flow from the same racial stock. The family members of European immigrants would be European (Reimers and Troper 1992, 31; see also Birrell and Birrell 1987, 279). Jones has stated that Congress expected immigration following the reforms of 1965 to be predominantly European (from Italy, Greece, Portugal, and Yugoslavia), and was surprised when the backlog of relatives was disposed of so quickly (Jones 1992, 267–268).

The larger Canadian and Australian occupational selectivity component probably reflected the intention to maintain larger immigration programs for purposes of economic and population growth. Some have suggested that this selectivity also might serve a desire for racial exclusion. Skill-based selection criteria definitely guarantee a relatively smaller pool of potential immigrants from the less industrialized, non-European countries than from the highly educated populations of Europe. In Britain, the skill-based immigration criteria which replaced the open door to Commonwealth citizens also occasioned a heated debate about the possible racism implicit in such criteria (see Reitz 1988a). However, it is obvious that such measures did not in fact prevent substantial racial minority immigration in any of the three countries. Numerical targets have been adjusted in Canada and Australia, a move with racial overtones in both countries (Reitz 1988b; Hawkins 1989, 98–103).

Public opinion polls taken at about the time of the immigration policy reforms also show that the general receptivity to racial minority immigration probably was quite similar in the three countries, as well as more positive than it is now. In the mid-1960s and early 1970s, there was a common pattern of about 40 percent supporting the continuation of levels of immigration current at the time, up to 10 percent wanting more immigration, and only about 40 percent wanting less immigration, with the rest being undecided.[10] More people favored immigration than opposed it. Attitudes toward immigrant minority cultures did not differ substantially among the three countries, either.[11] The receptivity to refugees (many of whom have lower skill levels) also has been similar, although Canada and Australia have admitted significantly more refugees on a per capita basis than has the United States.[12] The recent backlash against immigration also has followed a similar pattern in all three countries; and while policies have deferred to such attitudes, the degree of skill selectivity has been affected only to a minor degree. All three countries have moved to increase such selectivity.

My hypothesis in this study is that the differences in immigrant inequality in the three countries, and differences in interurban variation, are affected far more by differences in the structure of specific institutions than by any differences in origin-specific treatment of racial minority immigrants. The latter is a comparatively minor aspect of the cross-national difference, if it exists at all.

The different histories of interracial relations among the three societies might affect immigrants more by the impact of those relations on the historical development of social institutions such as education, labor markets, and social welfare than by their impact on direct racial discrimination. It may be that American cultural and institutional individualism is in fact reinforced over time by the racial polarization of the society (see, for example, Quadagno 1994). The subject of the reciprocal relations between racial attitudes and institutional structures arises again when we consider the policy implications, including the implications for institutional restructuring today.

Data Sources and Outline of this Book

The analysis presented here focuses on the entry-level earnings of the first cohort of immigrants to arrive following the immigration reforms which effectively opened immigration to non-Europeans in the United States, Canada, and Australia. Census samples were drawn from the 1980 United States Public Use Microdata Sample (PUMS) 5-percent A-File (U.S. Bureau of the Census 1983), the 1981 Canadian Public Use Sample Tape (PUST) 2-percent Individual File (Canada, Statistics Canada 1984), and the 1981 Australian Census of Population and Housing File 1-per-cent Persons Sample (Australian Bureau of Statistics 1984). The sample includes 93 urban areas with populations greater than 500,000: 79 in the United States, 9 in Canada, and 5 in Australia. Within those urban areas, the sample includes men and women in the labor force with annual earnings greater than $100, aged 16–64, in urban areas greater than 500,000.[13] (The earnings analysis focuses on relative earnings within each country and thus ignores currency differences among countries.) The entire analysis compares the position of recently arrived immigrant groups, specifically immigrants arriving in the ten years prior to the censuses, with that of a benchmark, native-born population.[14] Immigrants arriving in the 1970s constitute the first major cohort following the changes in immigration policy in the late 1960s and early 1970s.

Chapter 2 describes the entry-level earnings of these immigrants in the major urban centers of each country. The substantial cross-national differences are even more pronounced when interurban variations, particularly those in the United States, are taken into account. The problem of explaining variations in entrance status between countries and variations within them are interrelated and are considered together.

Chapters 3 through 6 consider four institutional domains, respectively. Chapter 3 considers the importance of cross-national differences in immigration policy in affecting the educational levels and earnings potential of immigrants in each country. Chapter 4 deals with the impact of the U.S. emphasis on education and credentialism; Chapter 5, with the consequences of labor market structure for the position of immigrants; and Chapter 6, with the social welfare system.

Because each of the four institutional sectors operates differently, assessments of their effects on immigrants must be studied using various methods. Methodological issues will be considered as required, but it is important to realize that estimating the relative importance of institutional sectors in explaining cross-national or interurban variations will not be a simple matter of comparing the size of regression coefficients in a single equation. Regression equations are often used in the analysis, designed on an institution-specific basis to reflect processes within each. The larger comparative analysis will be less precise but will reflect the same concern with quantification. Establishing the most important institutional sectors requires this quantification, and therefore the latter is an important part of the theoretical conclusions and of related policy considerations.

The analysis utilizes the interurban variations not only because interurban differences in inequality are important but because interurban differences in the impact of institutional structures enable us to probe causal issues much more deeply than is possible in a simple three-country (three-case) analysis. In the United States, there is variation over 79 urban areas. The potential for interurban analysis is less in the other two countries, but we can see to what extent the processes identified in the United States are mirrored in Canada and Australia.

The conclusions of this analysis are presented in Chapter 7, and emerging policy issues, in Chapter 8.

2

Immigrant Entry-Level Status in Different Nations and Cities

When one looks at immigrant groups living in a particular urban area, as social scientists usually do, it is difficult to see how a group's social and economic position are affected by its institutional environment and context. In a given immigrant community, what we see is the location of the group in relation to the host population or to other specific groups. Our explanatory attention then focuses on what varies within this field of vision: on differences between immigrants and host population, among origin groups, or among individuals within groups. In this delimited frame, what does *not* vary is the social and institutional context in which the events play themselves out. So the impact of this context cannot be seen but only inferred.

Within a single setting, studies of particular immigrant origin groups, using both field observations and surveys, bring to light issues of how immigrants overcome initial disadvantages through processes of settlement, adaptation, integration, and mobility. These studies began in the United States with the Chicago series, including Thomas and Znaniecki's *Polish Peasant* (1920); the tradition continued with Gans's portrait of the Italian-born *Urban Villagers* (1962) in Boston; Wilson and Portes's (1980), and subsequent, studies of Miami Cubans; Ivan Light and Edna Bonacich's Korean *Immigrant Entrepreneurs* (1988) in Los Angeles; Jiobu's (1988) Japanese Americans in the Bay Area; Zhou's New York *Chinatown* (1992); Waters's (1994) West Indians in New York, and countless others. To a lesser extent, the same is true in other immigrant-receiving countries. In Toronto there are detailed studies of the Portuguese (Anderson 1974) and West Indians (Henry 1994). In Australia, Collins (1991) has provided a comprehensive overview. Much of our knowledge of the situation of immigrants is based on these studies. These studies show what is involved in the immigration experience from the vantage point of the immigrant community itself, clearly reflecting the gulf that often separates immigrants from their hosts.

Following in this same tradition, comparisons of different groups in the same location highlight the effect of the groups' characteristics, resources, and strategies in addressing the barriers they face. They show, for example, the effect of an entrepreneurial strategy—as do Portes and Bach's (1985) comparisons of Cubans with Mexicans—or the effect of occupational concentrations—as do Model's (1985) comparisons of Blacks, Italians, and Jews in 1910 New York. The study by Breton, Isajiw, Kalbach, and Reitz (1990) of eight groups in Toronto shows how variable is the intergroup pattern of community formation and social incorporation. In census studies, this comparative strategy may be extended to virtually all groups, such as the research by Treiman et al. (1986–1987) in Los Angeles, studies collected by Waldinger and Bozorgmehr (1996) in *Ethnic Los Angeles,* or Lieberson and Waters's (1988) study of the entire United States. Research emphasizing the different situations of different groups across an entire country is also available for Canada (e.g., Li 1988) and Australia (e.g., Evans and Kelley 1986, 1991).

Also of interest, however, are the nature and extent of the initial disadvantages and barriers that immigrant groups face. To see these initial conditions and to study their impact, it is necessary to compare different contexts and observe what happens to groups drawn from the same immigrant pool, following Tilly (1994), as was discussed in Chapter 1. Such contextual comparisons have been made relatively infrequently. However, a number of relevant studies have emerged in very recent years. One example is the work by Faist (1995), which although it compares different groups—Mexicans in the United States with Turks in Germany—argues that similarities are sufficient to allow the imputation of differences to context. The observation carries a strong implication that the different outcomes are a result of the characteristics of destination societies. Galster and Santiago (1994) examined varying rates of poverty for Puerto Ricans in 34 U.S. metropolitan areas.

This chapter provides a description of the relative earnings of specific groups of immigrants in the urban areas of the United States, Canada, and Australia. Comparative earnings data at the national level have been presented by Borjas (1988, 1990), Chiswick (1988), and Saunders and King (1994, 60–68). The description here is both cross-national and interurban, for groups intended to be comparable in terms of ethnic and cultural background. We will see that interurban variations in the position of specific groups in the United States, and the relative uniformity of the experience of specific groups among the urban areas of Canada and Australia, is an important part of the context-specificity of immigrant group status. To put it slightly differently, national contexts specify their own distinctive array of urban contexts. Hence, the relevant contexts are both national and urban.

The analysis focuses on the position of the first cohort of "new immigrant" groups arriving during the decade of the 1970s, showing their position at the beginning of the next decade (1980 for the United States, and 1981 for Canada and Australia). The entry-level earnings of a specific, recent (at the time) immigrant-origin group will be measured in terms of the average employment earnings of group members relative to average earnings in the dominant group. For purposes of this study, the earnings are measured within the labor force aged 16–64, for those earning at least $100 per year, and including wages and salaries plus self-employment income.[1] The description will show how entry-level earnings vary from one location to another. Employment earnings are a labor market outcome. The actual economic welfare of immigrant groups is determined by other items as well, including net family employment income, and nonemployment income, which also may vary by context. We will examine the impact of some of these other sources in Chapter 6, which focuses on the welfare state. Entrance status might also be measured in terms of occupational status relative to that of the dominant group. The focus here is on earnings because they are of strategic importance for newly arriving immigrants and because relative earnings vary more widely across contexts.

The dominant or mainstream ethnoracial group in each country is taken to be the native-born Whites (i.e., those of European origins). In the United States, the racial origins of the native born are a particularly important stipulation because of the size of native-born *non-White* groups in that country, among them Blacks, Asians, and Hispanics. These groups constitute about 20 percent of the native-born urban labor force population of significance for this study.[2] Many Hispanic Americans are of European origin, of course, but many are not. The group as a whole is usually considered a potentially disadvantaged cultural group in the U.S. context, in the same way as Blacks or Asians. Immigrant groups in the United States enter this complex racial hierarchy. Some might enter at higher levels than native-born Blacks, Asians, or Hispanics, and in this sense, experience a relative advantage. Others enter at a lower level. Overall, the competitive position of immigrants relative to the non-Hispanic native-born White group is somewhat lower than if immigrants are considered in relation to all native-born populations. However, in this study, the White native-born male group is regarded as the benchmark.[3]

The Canadian and Australian censuses measure ethnic and racial background differently from the U.S. census, and the results must be compared with care. In Canada, the relevant census question was posed in terms of ethnic origins rather than race, yet response categories clearly provide racial information. For Australia, the relevant question concerned birthplace; but given the fact that this question was asked both for respondents and for each of their parents, and given the traditional ethnic composition of the Australian population, the responses also provide racial information. Specific operational definitions will be discussed as the presentation unfolds.

Gender and race interact in the labor market, requiring special analytic treatment. Because men are the dominant group in the workforce, immigrant men are compared to dominant group men. Immigrant women are compared *both* to dominant group women and to dominant group men. A double comparison for immigrant women is important for two reasons. First, a comparison of immigrant women with dominant-group women ignores gender as a source of common disadvantage. All groups of women share workforce positions which tend to be marginal compared to those of men, and comparing minority-group women only with majority-group women ignores the position that both occupy in the workforce as a whole. The reality is that native-born non-Hispanic White males are the dominant group in relation to all other workforce groups, and the description should reflect this benchmark comparison. Second, the degree of disadvantage based on gender itself varies from one context to another. The position of immigrant women cannot be described without reference to the degree of gender disadvantage in the particular setting.

National Variations in Immigrant Group Entry-Level Earnings

Let us begin by describing entry-level earnings for a number of recently arrived immigrant groups within the United States. Table 2.1 shows that entry-level earnings vary widely by origins for both men and women. Immigrant men of European origins have entry-level earnings that are 90 percent of the earnings of the dominant group.[4] Non-European immigrant men enter at a wide variety of levels. For those of Asian origins, there is an enormous variability. Japanese American immigrant men initially average 124 percent of the earnings of the dominant group; the figure for Asian Indian men is 90 percent; for Koreans, 78 percent; for Filipinos, 68 percent; for Chinese, 63 percent; and for Vietnamese, 55 percent. Entrance levels for Black and Hispanic immigrants are at the low end of the scale. Black immigrant men initially earn 54 percent of the earnings of native-born White men, while for Mexican immigrant men the figure is even lower, at 46 percent. Other Latin American immigrants have entry-level earnings in this same range, averaging 55 percent of the earnings of the dominant group.

Immigrant women enter the workforce at levels varying within a narrower range circumscribed by gender. The overall impact of gender in the United States is revealed in the earnings of dominant-group women, which in this sample is 48 percent of the earnings of dominant-group males. Immigrant women of European origins initially earn 44 percent of

TABLE 2.1 Entry–Level Earnings of Recent Immigrants (Arriving 1970–1980) in the U.S. Urban Labor Force, by Origins and Gender, 1980

	Men				Women			
Origin	Mean Earnings $	Relative Mean Earnings[1]	(N)	Origin	Mean Earnings $	Relative Mean Earnings[1]	Earnings Relative to Native-Born White Men[2]	(N)
Native-born non-Hispanic White	18,646	1.00	(112218)	Native-born non-Hispanic White	8,945	1.00	0.48	(80107)
All native-born races	17,872	0.96	(130901)	All native-born races	8,889	0.99	0.46	(98736)
Immigrants:				Immigrants:				
Japanese	23,085	1.24	(1117)	Filipino	10,508	1.17	0.56	(3759)
White (Europe-born)	16,774	0.90	(10567)	Asian Indian	9,956	1.11	0.53	(1677)
Asian Indian	16,727	0.90	(3049)	White (Europe-born)	8,118	0.91	0.44	(6608)
White (other)[3]	14,907	0.80	(4068)	Korean	8,092	0.90	0.43	(1911)
Korean	14,501	0.78	(2105)	White (other)[3]	7,962	0.89	0.43	(1663)
Filipino	12,636	0.68	(3094)	Japanese	7,874	0.88	0.42	(479)
Other Asian	12,022	0.64	(1102)	Other Asian	7,785	0.87	0.42	(663)
Chinese	11,658	0.63	(3470)	Chinese	7,397	0.83	0.40	(2763)
Cuban	11,305	0.61	(1869)	Black[4]	7,346	0.82	0.39	(4308)
Other Latin American	10,305	0.55	(7079)	Vietnamese	7,179	0.80	0.39	(1104)
Vietnamese	10,185	0.55	(1570)	Cuban	6,607	0.74	0.35	(1534)
Black[4]	10,013	0.54	(4985)	Other Latin American	6,101	0.68	0.33	(5033)
Mexican	8,606	0.46	(15049)	Mexican	5,588	0.62	0.30	(5798)

[1]Mean earnings as a proportion of the mean earnings of White non-Hispanic persons of the same gender.
[2]Mean earnings as a proportion of the mean earnings of White non-Hispanic men.
[3]Persons reporting White race born in Asia, Africa, and Central and South America (including the Caribbean).
[4]Blacks include Hispanic Blacks.

Source: 1980 U.S. Census Public Use Microdata Sample 5 Percent File. For a description of the urban labor force sample used in this and subsequent tables, see Chapter 1, note 14.

the earnings of the dominant White male group, or 91 percent of the earnings of dominant-group women. As with the immigrant men, there is great earnings variability among Asian immigrant women depending on specific origins. Filipino immigrant women initially earned a high of 56 percent of the earnings of dominant-group men (117 percent of the earnings of dominant-group women). For Asian Indian immigrant women the figure is 53 percent (111 percent), for Koreans, 43 percent (90 percent); for Japanese, 42 percent (88 percent); for Chinese, 40 percent (83 percent); and for Vietnamese, 39 percent (80 percent). Black and Hispanic immigrant women have the lowest entry-level earnings: 39 percent for Black immigrant women (80 percent), 30 percent for the Mexican immigrant women (62 percent), and 33 percent for immigrant women of other Latin American origins (68 percent).[5]

Entry-level earnings in Canada and Australia tend to be higher than in the United States, even for immigrants of similar origins. Table 2.2 provides cross-national comparisons of entrance statuses for broad origin groups. For recent White[6] immigrant males in Canada and Australia, the entry-level earnings are on par with those of the dominant group—100 percent—compared to only 90 percent in the United States

White immigrant women to Canada and Australia also enter the earnings hierarchy at a relatively higher level—50 and 65 percent of native-born White male earnings—compared to their U.S. counterparts, at 44 percent. Part of this difference is due to cross-national differences in the impact of gender as well as of immigrant status. When compared with mainstream women, White immigrant women in Canada enter the workforce at roughly the same level, 89 percent, as White immigrant women in the United States, 91 percent. The higher overall entrance earnings of the White Canadian immigrant women relative to dominant group men (50 percent of the earnings of dominant group males, compared to 44 percent for their counterparts in the United States) is due to the better position of women in general in Canada. The entry level of White immigrant women in Australia is, at 65 percent of the earnings of the male benchmark group, substantially higher than for their counterparts in Canada (50 percent) or the United States (44 percent). This is due both to the fact that the entire female segment of the labor force placed more favorably in Australia as well as to the relatively better initial earnings of White immigrant women in Australia.

Non-European immigrant groups also have higher entry-level earnings in Canada and Australia. Black immigrants to the United States and Canada are primarily of Caribbean or West Indian origins. The initial relative mean earnings of Black immigrant men in the United States was 54 percent, while in Canada it was 70 percent. This is a substantial difference, larger than the cross-national difference for European-origin immigrant

TABLE 2.2   Entry-Level Earnings of Recent Immigrants in the Urban Labor Force, by Host Country, Origins, and Gender, ca. 1980

Gender and Host Country	Native-Born Whites, Mean Earnings[1]	(N)	Immigrants, Mean Earnings Relative to Native-Born Whites									
			White[2]	(N)	Black[3]	(N)	Asian, Total	(N)	Chinese only	(N)	Latin American	(N)
Men												
United States	18,646	(112218)	0.90	(10567)	0.54	(4985)	0.75	(15507)	0.63	(3470)	0.50	(23997)
Canada	18,752	(43880)	1.00	(2024)	0.70	(341)	0.76	(1754)	0.77	(658)	0.71	(251)
Australia	14,140	(3884)	1.00	(1281)	4		0.84	(354)	0.72	(79)	4	
Women												
United States	8,946	(80107)	0.91	(6608)	0.82	(4308)	0.99	(12356)	0.83	(2763)	0.66	(12365)
Canada	10,582	(32787)	0.89	(1361)	0.81	(324)	0.85	(1396)	0.86	(584)	0.74	(205)
Australia	9,058	(2520)	1.01	(829)	4		1.00	(267)	0.89	(58)	4	
Earnings Relative to Native-Born White Men												
United States	0.48		0.44		0.39		0.47		0.40		0.32	
Canada	0.56		0.50		0.46		0.48		0.48		0.42	
Australia	0.64		0.65		4		0.64		0.57		4	

[1]Mean earnings are in the respective national currencies.
[2]In this and subsequent tables, White immigrants include only those born in Europe, or, in the case of Canada, the United States.
[3]Blacks include Hispanic Blacks in the United States.
[4]Too few cases.

Sources: 1980 U.S. Census Public Use Microdata 5-Percent File; 1981 Canadian Census Public Use Sample Tape 2-Percent Individual File; 1981 Australian Census of Population and Housing 1-Percent File. For further details on these sources, see Chapter 1, note 14. For more specific definitions of origins used for each country, see Chapter 2, pp. 46–47 and notes 4–6.

males and roughly equivalent to the difference between Filipino and Black immigrant men within the United States. In other words, in these data, entry earnings for Black immigrant men in Canada are roughly the same as for Filipino immigrant men in the United States. This difference is certainly large enough to produce a substantial difference in the process of integration of Black immigrant men in the two countries.

For Black immigrant women, entry-level earnings also are higher in Canada: 46 percent of the male earnings, compared to 39 percent in the United States. As with White immigrants, the explanation for this difference is the higher relative position of women in general in Canada; the position of Black immigrant women relative to mainstream women is the same in both countries. What this means for Black immigrant women in Canada is that their actual entry level is approximately equal to the entry level for *White* immigrant women in the United States (about 45 percent of the earnings of native-born White males in each case).

Entry-level earnings for Chinese immigrants and for Asians in general can be compared across the three countries. Chinese immigrants, both men and women, enter the earnings hierarchy in a more favorable position both in Canada and in Australia than do their counterparts in the United States. Whereas for recent Chinese immigrant men the relative mean earnings in the United States is 63 percent, in Canada it is 77 percent and in Australia 72 percent. The initial earnings of Chinese immigrant women is 40 percent of the earnings of the native-born White males in the United States, 48 percent in Canada, and 57 percent in Australia.[7]

The figures for Chinese immigrants in Australia are admittedly based on small numbers of cases (79 and 58 for men and women, respectively). The comparison for Asian-origin immigrant men in general shows relative mean earnings of 75 percent in the United States, 76 percent in Canada, and 84 percent in Australia. The comparison for Asian-origin immigrant women is 47, 48, and 64 percent respectively. In these data, it is important to keep in mind the difference in composition, and the fact that earnings are related to specific origins. Some Asian groups with higher earnings within the United States are substantially represented in Canada and Australia (South Asians), while others are less represented (Koreans). Recent Asian immigrants to Australia have higher entry-level earnings than do Asian immigrants to either Canada or the United States.

The cross-national differences in entry-level earnings—lower in the United States, higher in Canada and Australia, are consistent across groups for immigrant men and women both. These differences constitute only part of the cross-national patterns we seek to explain. There are substantial interurban variations as well. The next part of the chapter describes urban concentrations of immigrants in each country and follows with an examination of entry-level earnings across these urban areas.

Urban Concentrations of Immigrant Groups

In all three countries, recent immigrants have been concentrated in a comparatively small number of very large cities. In the past, New York was virtually identified with immigrants; Ellis Island and the Statue of Liberty in New York harbor evoke images of immigrants. Today, not only New York but also Los Angeles, San Francisco, and Miami to a significant extent symbolize immigrants and the new immigration. The same is true for Toronto and Vancouver in Canada, and Sydney and Melbourne for Australians. All these cities have large proportions of immigrants. In 1980, each had a population of which between 7 and 14 percent was made up of immigrants arriving in the preceding 10 years. For New York, the percentage was 10.0 percent; Los Angeles 13.5 percent; San Francisco 6.9 percent, Miami 12.9 percent, Toronto 14.3 percent, Vancouver 11.7 percent, Sydney 10.1 percent, and Melbourne 7.9 percent. In each country, other cities also have a lot of immigrants, but these are clearly the ones with the greatest immigrant concentrations.

Having said this, it is important to point out a very significant cross-national difference. The degree of concentration of immigrants in particular urban centers is more extreme in the United States than in either Canada or Australia. Immigrants to Canada and Australia are spread more evenly among major cities, and this is particularly true in Australia. This difference is not simply a result of differences in the total volume of immigration, in other words, because there are more immigrants to Canada and Australia on a per capita basis, in some way requiring them to spread out more. Nor is it a result of any differences in the degree of urbanization or concentration of economic activity attracting immigrants in the three countries. Rather, it seems to be a result of differences in the institutional context of immigration in each country, differences that might affect immigrant entrance statuses. It is the heavy degree of urban concentration of immigrants in the United States which has led Sassen (1991) to speculate on the existence of "global cities" with special attractiveness to immigrants. We will offer an explanation of this phenomenon in later chapters. Here, let us look at the urban concentration of immigration in a bit more detail before examining the specific entry-level earnings of groups in the urban areas of the three countries.

The concentrations of recent immigrants in the major cities[8] of the three countries are shown in Table 2.3. The 28 urban areas with 4 percent or more of their populations consisting of recent immigrants include all 5 of the largest Australian cities, and 8 of the 9 largest Canadian cities, but only 15 of the 79 U.S. cities of comparable size. In fact, after New York, Los Angeles, San Francisco-Oakland, and Miami, and setting aside outly-

TABLE 2.3 Immigrant and Other Population Characteristics, by Urban Area and Host Country, ca. 1980

Urban Area[1]	Host Country	Recent (1970–1980)	Earlier	Total	Total Population	Unemployment Rate
Toronto	Canada	14.3	29.6	43.9	2,998,947	3.9
Los Angeles–Long Beach	United States	13.5	10.9	24.4	7,477,503	6.0
Miami	United States	12.9	25.8	38.7	1,625,781	4.8
Jersey City	United States	12.9	17.0	29.9	556,972	8.5
Vancouver	Canada	11.7	20.9	32.6	1,268,183	5.0
Perth	Australia	10.6	27.6	38.2	1,001,800	7.1
Sydney	Australia	10.1	22.8	32.9	3,391,600	4.8
New York	United States	10.0	13.7	23.8	9,120,346	6.8
Calgary	Canada	9.3	13.5	22.8	592,743	2.8
Edmonton	Canada	8.1	12.6	20.7	657,057	3.7
Honolulu	United States	7.9	7.1	15.0	762,565	3.8
Melbourne	Australia	7.9	28.3	36.2	2,916,600	5.2
Winnipeg	Canada	7.3	13.1	20.4	584,842	5.5
San Francisco–Oakland	United States	6.9	9.4	16.3	3,250,630	5.7
Orange County[2]	United States	6.9	7.3	14.2	1,932,709	4.0
San Jose	United States	6.8	8.1	14.9	1,295,071	4.3
Brisbane	Australia	6.3	15.3	21.5	1,157,200	5.3
Adelaide	Australia	5.9	28.5	34.3	987,100	7.8
Montréal	Canada	5.8	13.3	19.1	2,828,349	8.7
Oxnard-Ventura	United States	5.7	9.2	14.9	529,174	5.0
Hamilton	Canada	5.6	24.8	30.4	542,095	5.6
San Diego	United States	5.5	6.9	12.4	1,861,846	6.0
Chicago	United States	5.3	6.4	11.8	7,103,624	6.8
Newark	United States	5.3	7.8	13.1	1,965,969	6.2
Houston	United States	5.3	3.2	8.4	2,905,353	3.4
Fresno	United States	5.1	6.6	11.7	514,621	9.3
Washington, D.C.	United States	4.5	4.5	9.1	3,060,922	3.9
Ottawa–Hull	Canada	4.5	11.8	16.3	717,978	6.6
Riverside–San Bernardino	United States	3.8	6.4	10.2	1,558,182	7.2
Providence	United States	3.7	5.2	8.9	919,216	6.7
Ft. Lauderdale	United States	3.3	5.7	9.0	1,018,200	4.1
Boston	United States	3.3	5.8	9.0	2,763,357	4.4
New Brunswick	United States	3.0	6.1	9.1	595,893	5.5
West Palm Beach	United States	2.9	5.7	8.6	576,863	3.7
Hartford	United States	2.9	6.9	9.8	726,114	4.0
Dallas	United States	2.8	9.4	12.2	2,974,805	3.0
Sacramento	United States	2.5	4.9	7.4	1,014,002	8.8
San Antonio	United States	2.7	4.7	7.4	1,071,954	4.6
Seattle	United States	2.4	4.5	6.9	1,607,469	5.7
Nassau	United States	2.1	6.8	8.9	2,605,813	5.4
Austin	United States	2.1	2.0	4.1	536,688	3.5

(*continues*)

TABLE 2.3 (*continued*)

Urban Area[1]	Host Country	Percent Immigrant Recent (1970–1980)	Earlier	Total	Total Population	Unemployment Rate
Phoenix	United States	2.1	3.4	5.5	1,509,052	5.2
Springfield	United States	1.9	4.6	6.5	530,668	5.7
Tucson	United States	1.9	4.5	6.3	531,443	6.2
Denver	United States	1.8	2.6	4.4	1,620,902	4.2
Portland	United States	1.8	2.9	4.6	1,242,594	5.9
Salt Lake City	United States	1.7	2.7	4.5	986,255	5.3
New Orleans	United States	1.6	2.4	4.1	1,187,073	5.6
Orlando	United States	1.6	3.3	4.9	700,055	4.0
Detroit	United States	1.6	4.3	5.8	4,353,413	11.7
Philadelphia	United States	1.5	3.2	4.7	4,716,818	7.6
Tampa	United States	1.5	3.8	5.3	1,569,134	5.2
Long Branch	United States	1.5	4.5	6.0	503,173	6.3
Oklahoma City	United States	1.5	1.2	2.7	834,088	3.6
Norfolk	United States	1.4	2.4	3.8	806,951	5.3
Cleveland	United States	1.4	4.2	5.6	1,898,825	6.8
Rochester	United States	1.3	4.5	5.7	971,230	6.4
Baltimore	United States	1.2	2.2	3.4	2,174,023	6.5
Gary	United States	1.1	3.7	4.8	642,781	8.8
Albany	United States	1.1	2.4	3.5	795,019	6.6
Atlanta	United States	1.1	1.5	2.6	2,029,710	5.0
Minneapolis–St. Paul	United States	1.1	1.7	2.8	2,113,533	3.9
Raleigh	United States	1.0	1.3	2.3	531,167	3.6
Milwaukee	United States	1.0	2.6	3.6	1,397,143	5.6
Columbus	United States	1.0	1.5	2.5	1,093,316	5.9
Allentown	United States	1.0	2.9	3.9	635,481	5.1
Syracuse	United States	0.9	3.0	3.9	642,971	8.1
Jacksonville	United States	0.9	2.1	3.0	737,541	5.6
Kansas City	United States	0.9	1.4	2.3	1,327,106	5.4
Grand Rapids	United States	0.9	2.1	3.0	601,680	6.2
Charlotte	United States	0.8	1.3	2.2	637,218	4.2
Buffalo	United States	0.8	3.8	4.6	1,242,826	9.6
Richmond	United States	0.8	1.3	2.1	632,015	4.0
Québec	Canada	0.8	1.7	2.5	576,075	10.8
Tulsa	United States	0.8	1.1	1.9	689,434	3.6
Omaha	United States	0.8	1.5	2.3	569,614	4.5
Toledo	United States	0.8	1.6	2.4	791,599	11.1
Wilmington	United States	0.7	2.4	3.1	523,221	5.9
Greenville	United States	0.7	0.9	1.6	569,066	4.9
St. Louis	United States	0.7	1.5	2.2	2,356,460	7.6
Akron	United States	0.7	2.1	2.7	660,328	8.8
Pittsburgh	United States	0.7	1.7	2.3	2,263,894	7.4
Cincinnati	United States	0.6	1.3	1.9	1,401,491	6.9
Nashville	United States	0.6	0.8	1.4	850,505	5.6

(*continues*)

TABLE 2.3 *(continued)*

Urban Area[1]	Host Country	Percent Immigrant			Total Population	Unemployment Rate
		Recent (1970–1980)	Earlier	Total		
Memphis	United States	0.6	1.0	1.5	913,472	7.6
Indianapolis	United States	0.6	1.1	1.7	1,166,575	6.4
Dayton	United States	0.6	1.3	1.9	830,070	8.4
Greensboro	United States	0.5	0.9	1.4	827,252	4.9
Youngstown	United States	0.5	2.2	2.7	531,350	11.3
Flint	United States	0.4	1.7	2.1	521,589	13.3
Birmingham	United States	0.4	0.8	1.2	847,487	6.8
Louisville	United States	0.4	0.7	1.1	906,152	7.7
Northeast Pennsylvania[3]	United States	0.4	1.4	1.7	640,396	8.6

[1]SMSAs in the United States, CMAs in Canada, and Statistical Divisions in Australia.
[2]Anaheim-Santa Ana-Garden Grove SMSA.
[3]Wilkes Barre-Scranton area.

Sources: See Table 2.2.

ing areas,[9] the U.S. immigration leaders include only Honolulu, San Diego, Chicago, Houston, Fresno, and Washington.

Some fairly large U.S. cities have smaller but nevertheless significant immigrant populations—Boston, for example, or Texas cities such as Dallas—but there are a number in which immigration constitutes only a minor part of the local demographic landscape. These include Detroit and Philadelphia, where the absence of immigrants is attributable in part to the absence of jobs. It also includes St. Louis, Pittsburgh, Baltimore, Minneapolis-St. Paul, and Atlanta. Each of these cities, in 1980, had a population of more than 2 million, and both Minneapolis and Atlanta had above-average local job demand (unemployment rates below the national average). About 1 percent of the population in these cities in 1980 was made up of recent immigrants. Among other U.S. cities with more than 1 million in population, low immigrant populations in Cleveland, Cincinnati, or Buffalo seem attributable to the local economy, but in Denver, Seattle, Tampa, Phoenix, Milwaukee, Kansas City, and Portland, they do not.

In Canada, large numbers of recent immigrants have settled in virtually every urban area with more than 500,000 in population. This includes not only Toronto and Vancouver, but also Calgary, Edmonton, and Winnipeg, in which, like San Francisco and New York in the United States, more than 7 percent of the 1981 populations consisted of immigrants who had arrived in the previous decade. The absolute numbers of immigrants in these cities are less than in Toronto and Vancouver, but they are far from negligible. Montréal, Hamilton, and Ottawa-Hull follow closely, with between 4 and 6 percent recent immigrants. Québec City is unique in having very few recent immigrants, only 0.8 percent of its population. By contrast, in the United States, recent immigration has had very little impact indeed on many cities comparable in size to Hamilton, Calgary, Edmonton, or Winnipeg.

Immigrants are distributed much more evenly across urban areas in Australia. Sydney and Melbourne are the leaders, but Perth actually had a recent immigrant population proportionately larger than that of New York (that is, 10.6 percent of total population); and Brisbane and Adelaide both had about 6 percent of their populations consisting of recent immigrants.

A correlational analysis of recent immigrant settlement shows that city size and labor demand appear to have independent effects on immigrant settlement in all three countries.[10] Many of the major immigrant-reception areas in the United States in recent years have had growing economies, with populations growing because of internal migration as well as immigration. This was true, at least in the 1970s, of southern California (particularly Orange County) and San Jose, Houston, Dallas, and Miami, for example. By contrast, certain very large cities, among them Detroit and Philadelphia, were in economic decline. Only a few immigrants would be attracted to such cities, mainly on the basis of specific situations.

There is a continuity over time in which cities are the primary immigrant reception areas. Existing immigrant populations appear to serve as magnets for further immigrant settlement. This can be seen in the fact that the size of immigrant populations prior to 1970 is associated with *subsequent* immigration, quite apart from urban area size or economic conditions. Once an urban area is established as an immigrant settlement area, further immigration to that city occurs. Certain cities, such as New York, are, for particular reasons, attractive to large numbers of foreign settlers over time, regardless of the specifics of the job market at any given moment. Most likely there are features of urban areas which attract immigrants and do so over time. No doubt chain migration plays a role. But it is also obvious that immigration does no damage to local economies. To the contrary, the data strongly suggest a "virtuous cycle" whereby immigration at one point in time is associated with employment growth, which boosts subsequent immigration.

Further, established immigrant communities may serve as a "social safety net" for immigrants, offering them security and support during periods when the job market is weak. Cities where few immigrants have settled in the past seem riskier as settlement sites. The protection afforded by established immigrant communities might be as important as labor demand in determining the migration decisions of immigrants.

The same factors operating to affect immigrant settlement in the U.S. appear also to operate in Canada and Australia. However, in Canada, immigration settlement is more strongly related to employment growth than to population size. On the one hand, Toronto and Vancouver have a history of significant immigration, and a lot of recent immigration. In these cities, immigration has been highly significant in the past, and these cities also have good employment growth records during the 1970s. Thus, they attract many recent immigrants. However, at the same time, the reason for high immigration to Alberta, mainly Edmonton and Calgary, by comparison to Ottawa-Hull, Winnipeg, or Hamilton, would seem to be the record of employment growth primarily, because these cities are about the same size, with comparable histories of immigration.

Montréal has one of the largest immigrant populations in Canada but has attracted fewer recent immigrants than would be expected based on its size. This might be partly due to the lower employment growth, though the language issue has reduced immigration over many years. Very likely, the intensified debate over immigration, and new language policies, also had a particular effect in Montréal. Québec has the smallest immigrant population, because of the joint effect of all these factors.

In Australia, with just five major urban areas, the effects of urban size and employment growth are less consistent. The high proportion of recent immigrants in Sydney reflects the impact of high employment growth, large size, and the history of immigration. Similar conditions apply to Melbourne. The impact of previous immigration in Perth would seem to explain why in 1981 the city had more immigrants than Brisbane. Certainly its economy has been in better shape than Adelaide's. Adelaide had substantial previous immigration, but its economic downturn and its relatively smaller size make it the least attractive Australian city for immigration.

Historically, in all three countries, immigrants of European origin have been spread out into a larger number of urban areas than have more recent immigrants. And among recent immigrants, it is those of non-European origins who are most concentrated in a small number of urban areas. This is why the story of immigration in each country tends to be the story of specific groups in specific cities: Jamaicans in New York, Cubans and Haitians in Miami, Koreans in Los Angeles and New York, and Chinese in New York, San Francisco, and Los Angeles. In Canada, it is Jamaicans in Toronto, Haitians in Montréal, and Chinese in Toronto and Vancouver. In Australia, Sydney and Melbourne are the main destinations for Asian immigrants more than European immigrants. Still, although urban concentration is a striking feature of racial-minority immigrant settlement in all three countries, there is a lot of variation, and the greater concentration in the United States holds. There is a tendency for racial-minority immigrants to concentrate in certain cities in the United States to the exclusion of others.

Black immigrants both in the United States and in Canada are highly concentrated in just a few cities (see Table 2.4, panel A). New York has about half the U.S. urban Black immigrants. Of the rest of the Black immigrants, about half settled in one of just six other cities: Miami, Washington, Boston, Los Angeles, Newark, and Chicago. These seven cities account for 75 percent of the recent urban Black immigrant population in the United States in 1980. In Canada, Black immigrants are concentrated in two cities: Toronto and Montréal. Almost 60 percent were in Toronto, and another 25 percent in Montréal. So just these two cities account for 85 percent of the urban Black immigrant population of Canada. One might say that the pattern of settlement for Black immigrants in the United States is somewhat more selective than in Canada, since so many large U.S. cities which were possible destinations for Black immigrants were not chosen. The seven cities which account for the 75 percent of Black immigrants in the United States contained only 27 percent of the urban population, whereas the two Canadian cities with large numbers of Blacks had 54 percent of the urban population in Canada.

For Chinese immigrants, there is also greater concentration in key cities in the United States than in either Canada or Australia. In the United States, New York and San Francisco-Oakland account for 39 percent of Chinese immigrants, though together they have only 10 percent of the total urban population (Table 2.4, panel B). Toronto accounted for the same percentage of Chinese immigrants to Canada, but Toronto by itself is 30 percent of the urban Canadian population. Sydney has over half the Chinese immigrants in urban Australia, but Sydney is 36 percent of urban Australia. So for the United States, the emphasis on New York and the Bay Area as destinations for Chinese immigrants represents a greater concentration than for either Australia or Canada. Another 30 percent of the Chinese are spread out more evenly over six other cities: Los Angeles (which received half of the 30 percent), Chicago, Boston, San Jose, Houston, and Washington. In Canada, 30 percent of the Chinese went to Vancouver. The eight cities in the United States with 70 percent of the Chinese immigrants represent 31 percent of the total urban population, while Toronto and Vancouver have 70 percent of the Chinese immigrants to Canada and represent 40 percent of urban Canada. In Australia, Melbourne received most of the Chinese immigrants not going to Sydney.

Other groups represented mainly in the United States are also heavily concentrated in particular areas. More than half the Cubans in the U.S. ur-

TABLE 2.4   Size of Recent Immigrant Groups in the Urban Labor Force, for Men
in Major Urban Areas, by Origins and Host Country, ca. 1980

	Size (Sample N)	Percent of Total	Cumulative Percent
A) Black Immigrant Men			
United States (N = 4985)			
New York	2393	48.1	48.1
Miami	354	7.1	55.1
Washington, D.C.	281	5.6	60.7
Boston	202	4.1	64.8
Los Angeles–Long Beach	182	3.7	68.4
Newark	181	3.6	72.1
Chicago	162	3.2	75.3
Philadelphia	99	2.0	77.3
Nassau-Suffolk	99	2.0	79.3
Canada (N = 341)			
Toronto	200	58.7	58.7
Montréal	87	25.5	84.2
B) Chinese Immigrant Men			
United States (N = 3470)			
New York	785	22.6	22.6
San Francisco	587	16.9	39.5
Los Angeles–Long Beach	531	15.3	54.8
Chicago	128	3.7	58.5
Boston	118	3.4	61.9
San Jose	111	3.2	65.1
Houston	100	2.9	68.0
Washington, D.C.	97	2.8	70.8
Orange County	78	2.2	73.1
Honolulu	74	2.1	75.2
Canada (N = 658)			
Toronto	258	39.2	39.2
Vancouver	202	30.7	69.9
Calgary	59	9.0	78.9
Edmonton	50	7.6	86.5
Australia (N = 79)			
Sydney	43	54.4	54.4
Melbourne	27	35.5	88.6

(*continues*)

TABLE 2.4   *(continued)*

	Size *(Sample N)*	*Percent of Total*	*Cumulative Percent*
C) Cuban Immigrant Men			
United States (N = 1869)			
Miami	1051	56.2	56.2
Jersey City	160	8.6	64.8
Los Angeles–Long Beach	130	7.0	71.7
New York	114	6.1	77.8
Newark	94	5.0	82.9
Chicago	51	2.7	85.6
Tampa	42	2.2	87.9
West Palm Beach	32	1.7	89.6
D) Mexican Immigrant Men			
United States (N = 15049)			
Los Angeles–Long Beach	6824	45.3	45.3
Chicago	1926	12.8	58.1
Houston	1214	8.1	66.2
Orange County	1017	6.8	73.0
San Diego	673	4.5	77.4
Dallas–Ft. Worth	660	4.4	81.8
San Francisco–Oakland	413	2.7	84.6
San Jose	293	1.9	86.5
Oxnard-Ventura	263	1.7	88.3
San Antonio	256	1.7	90.0

Sources: See Table 2.2.

ban areas are in Miami, and more than half the urban Mexicans are either in Los Angeles-Long Beach or Chicago (see Table 2.4, panels C and D).

Urban Variations in Immigrant Group Entry-Level Earnings

The labor market position of immigrant groups is most directly experienced in specific urban areas, and the cross-national comparison of entry-level earnings for immigrants looks quite different when specific urban areas are considered. Entry-level earnings of specific immigrant groups vary much more markedly from one urban area to another in the United States than in the other two countries. For some groups, entry-level earnings in the United States reach lows which contrast as much with the position of the same group elsewhere in the United States as with its position in the other countries. To some extent, the cross-national variations are related to extremely low entry-level earnings for particular groups in specific U.S. cities.

Consider first the immigrants of European origins in specific urban areas across the three countries, shown in Table 2.5, panel A.[12] The cross-national variations can be seen as they appear at the level of specific urban areas. Whereas recent White immigrant men to the U.S. earned an average of 90 percent of the earnings of the dominant group, this figure varies from a low of 76 percent in Chicago, 77 percent in New York, and 79 percent in Los Angeles to 90 percent in San Francisco, and is at virtual parity (101 percent) in Washington, D.C. For Canada, the entry-level earnings of White immigrants also vary somewhat, but in a much narrower range. In Toronto, White immigrants earn 95 percent of the earnings of the dominant group, and in Vancouver, they earn 102 percent. In Australia, there is even less variation, and the entry-level earnings of the White immigrants hover right around the parity level for both Sydney and Melbourne

There is a nearly parallel situation for recent immigrant women of European origins. In the United States, the entry-level earnings of White immigrant women vary about 20 points—between a low of about 30 percent of dominant male earnings in Newark to a high of nearly 50 percent in Boston. In Vancouver, Montréal, and Toronto, there is much less variation in the relative entry-level earnings of these immigrant women; they earn between 47 and 57 percent of what dominant-group males earn. In Australia, European-origin immigrant women in both Sydney and Melbourne earn 65 percent of the earnings of the native-born White men, which is virtual parity with the position of native-born White women.

What this means is that differences in immigrant entry-level earnings between the United States and the other two countries are even more extreme if particular urban areas are considered. The gap between the status of these immigrants in the three largest U.S. cities—New York, Los Angeles, and Chicago—and the general pattern for Canadian and Australia cities is not 10 percent, as we saw in the overall cross-national averages, but rather more like 20 to 25 percent. The overall cross-national variation masks the variations within the United States and the extent to which there are contextual variations in entrance statuses. To put it differently, one key feature of the U.S. context is extreme immigrant inequality in particular locations. To explain this pattern will require attention to institutional forces which vary in their impact on specific urban areas.

What holds for the White immigrants also applies to racial minority immigrants. This means that the entry earnings for specific groups of racial minority immigrants in certain U.S. cities is far below what it is in other cities, and also below the more uniform levels in Canada and Australia. However, the specific city in which racial minority immigrants reach their lowest entry levels varies; it tends to be the city in which the group is most heavily concentrated.

TABLE 2.5   Entry-Level Earnings of Recent Immigrants in the Urban Labor
Force, for Major Urban Areas, by Origins, Gender, and Host Country, ca. 1980

A. White Immigrants

	Men			*Women*		
Urban Area	*Relative Mean Earnings*	*(N)*	*Urban Area*	*Relative Mean Earnings*	*(N)*	*Earnings Relative to Native-Born White Men*
Vancouver	1.02	(299)	Melbourne	1.04	(227)	0.66
Sydney	1.02	(520)	Sydney	1.03	(309)	0.65
Washington, D.C.	1.01	(326)	Vancouver	0.97	(186)	0.54
Melbourne	0.99	(327)	Montréal	0.96	(169)	0.57
Toronto	0.95	(869)	Boston	0.91	(288)	0.48
Detroit	0.95	(290)	Chicago	0.90	(630)	0.41
Montréal	0.93	(329)	Los Angeles–Long	0.90	(578)	0.46
San Francisco– Oakland	0.90	(385)	Beach			
			Washington, D.C.	0.88	(242)	0.45
Boston	0.80	(417)	Toronto	0.84	(673)	0.47
Los Angeles–Long Beach	0.79	(861)	San Francisco– Oakland	0.84	(247)	0.43
Newark	0.77	(434)	Philadelphia	0.80	(178)	0.38
New York	0.77	(2373)	New York	0.76	(1341)	0.43
Chicago	0.76	(1010)	Newark	0.71	(287)	0.29
Total, Australia	1.00	(1281)	Total, Australia	1.01	(829)	0.65
Total, Canada	1.00	(2024)	Total, Canada	0.89	(1361)	0.50
Total, United States	0.90	(10567)	Total, United States	0.91	(6608)	0.44

B. Black Immigrants

	Men			*Women*		
Urban Area	*Relative Mean Earnings*	*(N)*	*Urban Area*	*Relative Mean Earnings*	*(N)*	*Earnings Relative to Native-Born White Men*
Toronto	0.70	(200)	Toronto	0.84	(195)	0.46
Boston	0.61	(202)	Newark	0.79	(172)	0.32
Chicago	0.55	(162)	Boston	0.75	(165)	0.40
Newark	0.51	(181)	Washington, D.C.	0.71	(262)	0.36
New York	0.49	(2393)	Los Angeles–Long	0.70	(155)	0.36
Washington, D.C.	0.49	(281)	Beach			
Los Angeles–Long Beach	0.48	(182)	New York	0.68	(2375)	0.38
Miami	0.48	(354)	Miami	0.63	(280)	0.32
Total, Canada	0.70	(341)	Total, Canada	0.81	(324)	0.45
Total, United States	0.54	(4985)	Total, United States	0.82	(4308)	0.39

(continues)

TABLE 2.5   (*continued*)

C. Chinese Immigrants

	Men			Women		
Urban Area	Relative Mean Earnings	(N)	Urban Area	Relative Mean Earnings	(N)	Earnings Relative to Native-Born White Men
Toronto	0.77	(258)	Toronto	0.90	(256)	0.50
San Jose	0.74	(111)	Vancouver	0.84	(171)	0.46
Vancouver	0.73	(202)	Los Angeles–Long Beach	0.78	(446)	0.40
Chicago	0.71	(128)				
Houston	0.67	(100)	Boston	0.71	(103)	0.38
Los Angeles–Long Beach	0.60	(531)	San Francisco–Oakland	0.66	(499)	0.34
Boston	0.55	(118)	New York	0.61	(652)	0.34
San Francisco–Oakland	0.51	(587)				
New York	0.44	(785)				
Total, Canada	0.77	(658)	Total, Canada	0.86	(584)	0.48
Total, United States	0.63	(3470)	Total, United States	0.83	(2763)	0.40

D. Asian Immigrants

	Men			Women		
Urban Area	Relative Mean Earnings	(N)	Urban Area	Relative Mean Earnings	(N)	Earnings Relative to Native-Born White Men
Detroit	0.92	(261)	Detroit	1.29	(166)	0.57
Sydney	0.86	(162)	Chicago	1.17	(1017)	0.54
Melbourne	0.85	(123)	Philadelphia	1.14	(254)	0.54
Philadelphia	0.83	(319)	Newark	1.05	(185)	0.43
Newark	0.82	(197)	Sydney	1.02	(126)	0.64
Chicago	0.78	(1243)	San Jose	0.94	(475)	0.44
Toronto	0.77	(717)	Orange County	0.93	(388)	0.41
Vancouver	0.75	(364)	Los Angeles–Long Beach	0.90	(2035)	0.46
New York	0.72	(2302)				
Houston	0.70	(534)	Houston	0.90	(327)	0.41
Los Angeles–Long Beach	0.69	(2587)	Montréal	0.90	(118)	0.53
			Toronto	0.86	(631)	0.47
Boston	0.69	(203)	New York	0.84	(1582)	0.47
Dallas	0.67	(257)	Vancouver	0.83	(306)	0.46
Montréal	0.66	(205)	Dallas	0.83	(159)	0.39
Washington, D.C.	0.64	(617)	Boston	0.82	(174)	0.43
San Jose	0.64	(543)	Honolulu	0.81	(581)	0.45

(*continues*)

TABLE 2.5 *(continued)*

D. Asian Immigrants (continued)

	Men				Women			
Urban Area	Relative Mean Earnings	(N)		Urban Area	Relative Mean Earnings	(N)	Earnings Relative to Native-Born White Men
Orange County	0.64	(497)		San Diego	0.79	(367)	0.43
Honolulu	0.63	(603)		San Francisco–Oakland	0.78	(1410)	0.40
San Diego	0.62	(380)					
San Francisco–Oakland	0.58	(1519)		Washington, D.C.	0.78	(509)	0.40
Total, Australia	0.84	(354)		Total, Australia	1.00	(267)	0.64
Total, Canada	0.76	(1754)		Total, Canada	0.85	(1396)	0.48
Total, United States	0.75	(15507)		Total, United States	0.99	(12356)	0.48

E. Mexican Immigrants

	Men				Women			
Urban Area	Relative Mean Earnings	(N)		Urban Area	Relative Mean Earnings	(N)	Earnings Relative to Native-Born White Men
San Francisco–Oakland	0.48	(413)		Chicago	0.70	(709)	0.32
				Orange County	0.62	(435)	0.27
New York	0.48	(109)		San Diego	0.59	(232)	0.32
Chicago	0.47	(1926)		Dallas	0.58	(203)	0.27
Houston	0.45	(1214)		Houston	0.55	(288)	0.25
San Diego	0.45	(673)		San Francisco–Oakland	0.55	(168)	0.28
San Antonio	0.45	(256)					
Dallas	0.44	(660)		Los Angeles–Long Beach	0.54	(2935)	0.28
San Jose	0.44	(293)					
Los Angeles–Long Beach	0.41	(6824)		San Jose	0.48	(128)	0.23
Orange County	0.41	(1017)					
Total, United States	0.46	(15049)		Total, United States	0.62	(5798)	

Sources: See Table 2.2.

Table 2.5, panel B, shows entry-level earnings of Black immigrant men and women in various cities where they have settled in large numbers. In New York and Miami, Black immigrant men earn less than 50 percent of the earnings of the dominant male group; in Boston, they average 61 percent of the earnings of the dominant group. This is closer to the Toronto, and the overall Canadian, average of 70 percent of native-born White male earnings. A similar patterns holds true for Black immigrant women. The entry level of these women varies between a low of 32 percent in Miami, to 40 percent in Boston; this compares with 46 percent in Toronto, the national Canadian average. Differences in the origins of members of these Black communities may account for some of these variations. Black immigrants in Miami are mainly Haitians, whereas large proportions of Black immigrants in Boston, New York, and Toronto are Jamaicans. But note that the difference between entry levels for Black immigrant men in New York and Toronto—21 percent—is substantially greater than the difference in Black male entry levels between the U.S. and Canada generally—16 percent. The larger interurban differences cannot easily be attributable entirely to specific origins.

Chinese immigrants in New York and San Francisco-Oakland have entry-level earnings as low as for Blacks in New York and Miami, while the entry levels for Chinese immigrants in Los Angeles, Houston, and especially San Jose are substantially higher, in the latter case about comparable to what they are in the Canadian cities (Table 2.5, panel C). So again, cross-national differences are much greater when we take account of the internal U.S. variation. For the Chinese, the difference in entry-level earnings between New York or San Francisco-Oakland and Toronto is on the order of 20–30 percent for men, compared to 14 percent at the national level. For Chinese women at the urban level, the variation is of the order of 12–16 percent, compared to 8 percent at the national level.

The interurban variation for the entry-level earnings of Asian groups in general is more difficult to interpret, because of the variation in specific Asian origins. However, the data (Table 2.5, panel D) enable a portrayal of Australian cities in racial minority comparisons. We observe the general pattern of virtually no variation among Australia areas, somewhat greater variation in Canada, and wide extremes in the United States, with some areas showing Asian entry earnings nearly 20 points below the national average for men and nearly 10 points below the national average for women.

There is no cross-national comparison for Mexican immigrants, but interurban variation in their entry levels within the United States is interesting nonetheless (Table 2.5, panel E). For men, the entry-level earnings of recent Mexican immigrants varies between 41 and 48 percent, and for women between 23 and 32 percent. The entry level of Mexican immigrants is rather low throughout the major areas of their concentration within the United States, but there are meaningful variations nonetheless.

Toward an Institutional Explanation
for Immigrant Entry-Level Status

In summary, while origin groups vary in entry levels, the contextual variations in entry-level earnings of specific origin groups are also very significant. Entrance earnings are substantially lower in the United States than in Canada and Australia, including for particular groups such as Blacks, Chinese, and Asians in general. Moreover, the actual cross-national differences are greater than suggested by the national figures, when the much greater interurban variation in the United States is taken into account. Recent immigrants are more heavily concentrated in particular urban areas in the United States, and their entry level reaches lower extremes there. For Blacks, the Canada–United States contrast is greater when account is taken of the fact that entry-level earnings of Blacks are lower in New York and Miami than in Boston, though in Boston the entry level of blacks is still lower than in Toronto or elsewhere in Canada. For Chinese, the Canada–United States contrast is greater when account is taken of the fact that the entry-level earnings of Chinese are lower in New York and San Francisco than in Los Angeles, though in Los Angeles they are lower still than in Toronto or Vancouver, or elsewhere in Canada. The comparisons with Australia cannot be so specific because of the smaller size of the Australian census sample, but the data indicate that entrance statuses for both White and Asian immigrants are higher and more uniform in Australian cities than in either Canada or the United States.

These national and interurban variations require explanation. The fact that the variations in entry-level earnings affect all groups, and not just particular cases, suggests that the explanation should be couched in terms of the attributes of the context rather than only the particularities of specific groups. This reinforces the point that the entrance status of immigrants is, to a degree, a social product. The fact that the variations affect Whites as well as racial minorities suggests that race and racial discrimination are not the key to explanation, though of course varying statuses of racial minorities is the result.

The next chapter considers the importance of immigration policy in the explanation. Immigration policy operates at the national level, but we will see that it can play a role in determining settlement patterns of immigrants in particular urban areas, and thus have an impact on the interurban variations in entry-level earnings. However, we will also see that immigration policy is far from the only determinant of either the interurban differences or the cross-national differences.

PART 2

Four Institutional Areas Affecting the Terms of Immigrant Entry

3

The Skill Selectivity
of Immigration Policy

This chapter examines cross-national differences in immigration policy to assess the significance of policy in explaining differences in the entry status of immigrant groups. The specific questions explored are these: (1) What exactly are the policy differences related specifically to skill selectivity? When the specific provisions of policy are examined, we find that Canadian and Australian policies give more attention to the *occupational* backgrounds of immigrants (whether their specific work experiences are in occupations such as chef or welding, which might be in demand), but not necessarily more attention to skill levels per se (such as years of education or university degrees). (2) What are the actual effects of these policy differences on the skill levels of immigrants in specific origin groups? Data on actual policy effects suggest that the effects are real but very limited. The attempt to place a numerical estimate on this effect must remain tentative, but policy differences cannot be expected to explain more than a small part of the cross-national difference in immigrant group entry levels.

We also ask, (3) how may immigration policy affect *where* less-skilled immigrants settle within a country, and hence entry levels in particular urban areas? The specific urban concentration of less-skilled immigrants in the United States could be a policy effect related to chain migration and family reunification. We find that in Canada and Australia, where immigration policy has created relatively smaller family reunification categories, there is much less tendency for less-skilled immigrants to be heavily concentrated in particular urban areas.

The Relative Priority of Skill Selectivity
in Immigration Policy, 1965–1990

When the United States, Canada, and Australia reformed their immigration policies in the 1960s and early 1970s, they established new selection criteria, and these criteria moved each country in a somewhat different direction. The U.S. policy called for immigration as required primarily to meet humanitarian concerns such as family reunification and refugee asylum, with only a small component to be admitted based on specific occupational and labor force needs. By contrast, the Canadian and Australian policies envisioned immigration as continuing to make a larger contribution to economic and population growth. To ensure that immigrants meet labor market needs, Canada and Australia spelled out selection systems requiring immigrants to qualify on the basis of points which are awarded for particular human capital endowments.

The Canadian and Australian policies specify larger categories of immigrants based on economic criteria, and include educational levels and occupational skills among their selection criteria. But the selectivity hurdles are low, and while selection criteria have been upgraded somewhat over time, the size of the skill-selected immigrant pool has shrunk. Even in the most recently announced policies, moderately educated immigrants can easily satisfy the points criteria. To see this, it is necessary to examine the policies of all three countries in greater detail.

Immigration Policy in the United States, 1965–1990

Formal U.S. immigration policy specifies a very small skill-selected component, but with fairly high skill levels. The preference system in place since the reforms of 1965 (see Table 3.1),[1] which has defined the basic approach to skilled immigration since that time (Keely 1979a, 1979b; Gardner and Bouvier 1990; Jones 1992), specified a category of preferred professionals to be certified by the Department of Labor, the Third Preference category, which would constitute just 10 percent of those admitted under the preference system. An additional category, the Sixth Preference, was designated for skilled and unskilled workers, for whom Labor Department certification also was required. This group, constituting another 10 percent, was not prescribed to be highly skilled, but Labor Department policy could make it so, depending upon its assessment of labor demand. Thus, potentially 20 percent of those selected under the preference system might be skill selected.

The professionals category, though small, at least ensures that one group of immigrants to the United States will be very highly skilled. According to Reubens (1987), many of these immigrants become professionals in inner-city hospitals and clinics, and in nursing homes. He wrote that foreign medical graduates are "about 30 percent of the resident medical staff in all hospitals in the United States and over half in New York City's municipal hospitals" (p. 14). Statistics from Sorensen, Bean, Ku, and Zimmerman (1992, 50), derived from a 0.4-percent sample of the

TABLE 3.1   U.S. Immigration Policy

A. 1965

As of December 1, 1965, new immigration regulations were in effect for immigration to the United States. Between that date and June 1968, the quota system of the 1952 McCarran-Walter Act was phased out. The Act of 1965 contains regulations on numerical limitations, labor certification, and a preference system for visas.

A. *Annual Numerical Limitation:* 170,000 for the Eastern Hemisphere and 20,000 per country. 120,000 for the Western Hemisphere with no country limitation. The following persons are exempted from numerical limitations: parents of U.S. citizens over 21 years, spouses, minor unmarried children of U.S. citizens, permanent resident aliens returning from abroad; certain former citizens applying for reacquisition of citizenship; certain former U.S. government employees.

B. *Preference System* (applied to aliens from the Eastern Hemisphere only):
1. First Preference: Unmarried sons and daughters of U.S. citizens—20% maximum of the 170,000 person ceiling
2. Second Preference: Spouse and unmarried sons and daughters of an alien lawfully admitted for permanent residence—20%
3. Third Preference: Professionals. Labor certification required—10%
4. Fourth Preference: Married sons and daughters of U.S. citizens—10%
5. Fifth Preference: Brothers and sisters of U.S. citizens—10%
6. Sixth Preference: Skilled and unskilled workers. Labor certification required—10%
7. Seventh Preference: Refugees—6%
8. Nonpreference: Other aliens from Eastern Hemisphere

C. *Labor Certification:* Required of all Eastern Hemisphere aliens in third, sixth, and non-preference categories. Required of all Western Hemisphere aliens except parents, spouses, and children of U.S. citizens and permanent resident aliens.

Source: Monica Boyd (1976, 86). "Immigration Policies and Trends: A Comparison of Canada and the United States," *Demography* 13, no. 1. Based on Hohl (1974, 73–75), and U.S. Department of State (1972).

B. Visa Allocation System for U.S. Immigrants, ca. 1987

Immigrants Exempt from Numerical Limitations
- Immediate relatives of U.S. citizens: spouses, unmarried minor children (including orphans), parents of U.S. citizens at least 21 years old
- Refugees and asylees adjusting to permanent status[a]
- Special immigrants: certain ministers of religion; certain former employees of the U.S. government abroad; certain persons who lost U.S. citizenship; certain foreign medical graduates
- Babies born abroad to legal, permanent resident aliens

(continues)

TABLE 3.1   (continued)

Immigrants Subject to Worldwide Numerical Limitations

Preference Category	Type of Immigrant	Percent and Number of Visas	
First	unmarried adult children of U.S. citizens	20%	54,000
Second	spouses and unmarried adult children of permanent resident aliens	26%	70,200[b]
Third	members of professions or persons of exceptional ability in the arts and sciences and their spouses and children	10%	27,000
Fourth	married children of U.S. citizens and their spouses and children	10%	27,000[b]
Fifth	brothers and sisters of adult U.S. citizens and their spouses and children	24%	64,800[b]
Sixth	workers in skilled or unskilled occupations in which laborers are in short supply in the United States and their spouses and children	10%	27,000
Nonpreference	Other qualified applicants	Any numbers not used above[c]	

[a]These are limited annually under separate legislation

[b]Numbers not used in higher preferences may be used in these categories

[c]Nonpreference visas have been virtually unavailable in recent years

Source: Robert W. Gardner and Leon F. Bouvier (1990, 343). "The United States." In *Handbook on International Migration,* edited by William J. Seron, Charles B. Nam, David F. Sly, and Robert H. Weller. Copyright © 1990 by Greenwood Press. Reproduced with permission of Greenwood Publishing Group, Inc., Westport, CT.

Alien Address Registration Program, showed that of those admitted in the professional category in 1980, 75.7 percent were employed as professionals in the United States, and of those in the skilled and unskilled worker category, 45.7 percent were employed as professionals.

The proportion of immigrants who were skill selected under this policy turned out to be less than 20 percent, however, for two reasons. First, immediate family members were to be admitted without numerical limitation, and the number coming in under this provision was substantially larger than expected. The number of immediate family members was expected to range in the neighborhood of 50,000 (Reimers and Troper 1992, 32), but actual numbers varied up to 300,000. Hence, the expected proportion of immigrants in the skill-selected categories (Third and Sixth Preferences) fell from 20 percent to about 10 percent. In 1980, for example, of 530,639 immigrants arriving in the United States, 157,743 arrived as immediate family members and another 75,835 as refugees.[2] Another reason why the skill-selected categories were small was simply that there were significant quota shortfalls. Of the 289,479 who entered under numerical limitations, only 18,583 were in the most highly skilled professional category. This was only 6.4 percent of those in the numerically limited category, not the planned 10 percent. The net result is that the professional category made up only 3.5 percent of the total number of immigrants. Another 25,786 entered under the skilled and unskilled worker category (Sixth Preference). This is 8.9 percent of the numerically limited immigrant pool (again, less than the quota of 10 percent), and 4.9 percent of all immigrants. So in 1980, only 8.4 percent of all immigrants entered under one of the employment preference categories.[3] Furthermore, it should also be kept in mind that as Sorensen et al. (1992, 46) have shown, about half of those arriving in these categories are immediate relatives, rather than the skilled workers themselves (see also Borjas 1993, 23). If illegal immigrants are added, the proportion of immigrants who are selected on the basis of occupational skills is seen to be even smaller.[4]

Compared to earlier policy in place since 1952, which called for 50 percent of immigration based on employment-related criteria (Briggs 1984, 68), this 1965 policy, designed to open immigration to more non-Europeans, represented a reduction in such emphasis. Over time, as it became clear that immigration was shifting toward individuals of non-European origins, there have been only limited attempts to upgrade immigrant skill levels. The precise numerical limitations specified by law have been adjusted periodically. However, only two legislative changes have sought to limit unskilled immigration. The Immigration Reform and Control Act of 1986 was intended to curb illegal immigration, and it could have an important effect on immigrant skills to the extent that illegal immigration is actually reduced. The basic plan for skill-selected immigration has been modified only by the Immigration Act of 1990. In 1990, allocations based on occupational criteria were increased and overall ceilings on immigration were established (Jones 1992, 289–290). Of annual immigration in the range of 700,000, 140,000 (20 percent) were to be selected on the basis of skills, representing a tripling of this emphasis. Still, the basic orientation of U.S. immigration toward humanitarian ob-

jectives, with a small contingent required to meet specific, mostly highly
skilled employment requirements, remains. (Oddly, a form of quota for
certain European immigrants also was reintroduced. Family reunification requirements in place since 1965, originally intended to benefit the
Europeans, now worked against them. Provisions were made for 40,000
visas, increased later to 55,000 visas, for persons from "traditional source
countries.")

Immigration Policy in Canada, 1962–1993

Unlike the United States, where abolition of country-of-origin immigration quotas was not expected to have a major demographic impact,
Canada expected to maintain a fairly large-scale immigration which had
been under way since the end of World War II. Canada's new immigration policy in the 1960s clearly represented an upgrading of skill requirements for immigrants (see Table 3.2, panel A). As the previous policy had
operated, immigration produced the settlement across urban Canada of a
fairly large number of persons, many of Italian and other southern European origins, who often had very little formal education. The thinking
was that if new immigrants coming from anywhere in the world might
face an uncertain prospect for integration into Canadian society, then selection criteria favoring labor force requirements might help in this regard. The reunification of immediate family members, implemented
without points-based screening, would continue to produce settlement of
Europeans on a significant scale; but unlike the situation in the United
States, this source would not provide enough persons to meet the
planned population and labor force targets. So the points system was
planned to select immigrants from around the world most likely to be
successfully integrated into Canadian society. Canadian policy also differs from U.S. policy in placing emphasis on the location of settlement
within countries. It does this by assigning points to persons willing to go
where the labor demand is greatest. More-distant family members would
be required to meet at least part of the points-based criteria. As in the
United States, in Canada there is a separate category for persons sponsored by immediate relatives who are citizens or permanent residents,
and they are exempt from assessment. The system was spelled out in regulations without requiring an amendment to the 1952 Immigration Act.
The system is still in effect, although there have been various revisions to
the points categories, and new enabling legislation.[5]

The Canadian skill-selected immigrant categories certainly were larger
than those in the United States. The more substantial labor market orientation of Canadian immigration policy is reflected in the greater total
proportion of immigrants screened on the basis of points: Between 1968

TABLE 3.2   Canada's Immigration Policy

A. Policy and Points System, 1967–1973

On October 2, 1967, Canada adopted new immigration regulations; there are three main categories of immigrants:

A. Independent.

B. "Sponsored" dependents—husband, wife, fiancée, generally close relatives.

C. "Nominated relative"—apply likewise to close relatives; responsibilities of nominator include willingness and ability to provide care, maintenance for the person, to otherwise assist him in becoming established.

The independent immigrant must obtain 50 out of 100 assessment points based on the system described below. Nominated relatives also are assessed on the basis of education, age, personal assessment, occupational skill, and occupational demand criteria discussed below.

The assessment system for potential immigrants is based on:

1. *Education and Training:* up to 20 assessment points to be awarded on the basis of one year of school per unit.

2. *Personal Assessment:* up to 15 points on the basis of the immigration officer's judgment of applicant's adaptability, motivation, and initiative.

3. *Occupational Demand:* up to 15 units if demand for applicant's occupation is strong in Canada.

4. *Occupational Skill:* up to 10 units for professionals, ranging down to one unit for the unskilled.

5. *Age:* 10 units for applicants under 35, with one unit deducted for each year over 35.

6. *Arranged Employment:* 10 units if the candidate has a definite job arranged.

7. *Knowledge of French/English:* up to 10 units depending on degree of fluency.

8. *Relative:* up to 5 units if applicant has relative able to help him become established.

9. *Employment Opportunities in Area of Destination:* up to 5 units when applicant intends to go to area of Canada where there is a strong demand for labor.

Source: Monica Boyd (1976, 85). "Immigration Policies and Trends: A Comparison of Canada and the United States," *Demography* 13, no. 1. Based on Canada, Manpower and Immigration (1974), Hawkins (1971), and Parai (1974).

(*continues*)

TABLE 3.2 *(continued)*

B. The Points System, ca. 1985

Factor	Units of Assessment	
	Previous	*Revised*
Education	12 maximum	12 maximum: no change
Specific Vocational Preparation	15 maximum	15 maximum: no change
Experience	8 maximum	8 maximum: no change
Occupation	15 maximum: a score of zero; automatic processing bar	10 maximum: a score of zero; automatic processing bar
Arranged employment	10: 10 unit penalty if not obtained	10: no penalty if not obtained
Location	5 maximum 5 unit penalty if designated as not in need	eliminated
Age	10 maximum: 10 units if 18 to 35 years. If over 35, one unit subtracted for each year up to 45	10 maximum: 10 units if 21 to 44 years. Two units subtracted per year if under 21 or over 44
Knowledge of French and English	10 maximum: Five units to a person who reads, writes, and speaks English or French fluently; 10 units if fluent in both languages	15 maximum: up to 15 units for fluency in official language(s)
Personal Suitability	10 maximum	10 maximum: no change
Levels Control	N/A	10 units maximum: set at 5 to start
Relative	5	eliminated
TOTAL	100	100
PASS MARK	50	70
Bonus for Assisted Relative Applicants	15–30	10 if accompanied by an undertaking of assistance

Source: Freda Hawkins (1989, 296). *Critical Years in Immigration: Canada and Australia Compared.* Kingston, Ont.: McGill-Queen's University Press.

and 1974, about 70 to 75 percent of immigrants in Canada were "independent" immigrants or "assisted relatives" (Wright and Maxim 1991, 5–6, 12), compared with less than 10 percent in the United States. This labor market orientation is also reflected in the usual bureaucratic location of the immigration control function in ministries charged with employment issues.[6] In the United States, primary responsibility for immigration is located in departments associated with legal rights and foreign affairs.[7]

However, this difference in labor market emphasis did not guarantee a difference *specifically in skill levels*. The skill-selected categories were larger, but the actual skills required to meet the criteria in those categories were quite limited. The result is that based on the policy itself, the expected average skill levels for immigrants to Canada compared to the United States would not be easily projected one way or the other. The points system as initially formulated in 1967 was indeed a very weak screening mechanism, presenting a very low hurdle in skill levels, and in no way comparable to the United States' Third Preference professionals category. This can be seen by simply counting points. The 1967 system required applicants to score 50 points out of a possible 100. Of 100 possible points, only 30 were based on skill level specifically, and since points were earned for every year of schooling and for even low levels of occupational skill, the priority actually given to high skill level was less than 30 points. Another 30 points depended upon general and specific labor demand, which could be for work at any skill level. The remaining 40 points were based on age, knowledge of English or French, having a relative in a position to help, and the personal assessment of the immigration officer. An independent immigrant not only did not have to have a university education, he or she was not required even to have a high school education. Other criteria were given substantial weight. Some of these criteria might be related to skill, but this was not assured by the system itself. The points system by no means guaranteed that only highly educated applicants were selected, even for independent immigrants.

As an example, an applicant for landed immigrant status in Canada in 1967 might have scored 50 points by the following formula: 35 years old (10 points), speak English (10 points), have job offer (10 points), promise to go to an area with strong demand (such as Toronto for most of the 1970s, 5 points), and get the maximum personal assessment (15 points). This hypothetical applicant might have *no formal education whatsoever*, not even one year, no particular skill (other than impressing the immigration officer), and could even have a job in an occupation in which labor is not in short supply within Canada. Under the points system, whether a person with no education actually gets admitted to Canada depends to a considerable degree on the discretion of the individual immigration officer.

Policy changes since 1967 have attempted to increase control of immigration, but the changes do not clearly lead to an upgrading of required skill levels. Over time, the points system has been tightened up only to a limited degree. The independent immigrant category remains a far cry from the U.S. professional (Third Preference) category. By 1985, the number of required points for independent immigrants had increased from 50 to 70, with minimum requirements in the job experience and occupation categories (see Table 3.2, panel B). Compared to the earlier version, the later points system increases the importance of occupational qualifications and reduces the importance of age and "personal suitability" requirements. And yet even the most recent revisions of the points system do not specify really high skill levels in objective terms. Regulations introduced in January 1993 reduced points awarded to relatives who are not immediate family members, and increased the number awarded to persons in occupations with high skills.[8] The version in place in 1996 maintains the same 12 points for education. The most significant change is the increase in points for knowledge of English or French from 10 points to 15 (Canada, Citizenship and Immigration Canada 1996, 13).

Offsetting the potential effects of the points-system upgrades are the very dramatic declines in the proportion of immigrants admitted under points. As mentioned above, from the time the points system was introduced in 1967 until 1974, over 75 percent of immigrants were independent immigrants or assisted relatives. By 1984 this number had declined to less than 30 percent—about 24 percent independent immigrants, and less than 6 percent assisted relatives. Note that the category of independent immigrants includes not only the principal applicant but also accompanying dependents who constitute about half of the total. This means that perhaps as few as 15 percent were actually selected on the basis of points.[9] The main factor in the decline in points-selected immigrants seems to have been a decline in the total numbers admitted. In 1974, immigration totaled over 218,000, but this was reduced to between 80,000 and 90,000 during the period from 1983 to 1985, and this reduction seems to have been realized mainly by a reduction in independent immigrants. Family-class immigration remained comparatively steady, at about 50,000 per year. In percentage terms, clearly, family-class immigration rose over time as a proportion of total immigration; it rose from about 20 percent in 1968 to between 40 and 50 percent from the later 1970s to 1984. Refugees also became significant—as many as 20 percent or more of the total—after 1978.

More recently, Canada has again increased the size of the occupationally selected categories. This is possible in part because of increases in the total numbers of immigrants admitted, which reached about 250,000 by 1993. This increase allowed the proportion of independent immigrants to climb back to 35 percent and that of assisted relatives to about 10 percent. However, family-class immigrants also began to increase, reaching 112,000 by 1993 (Canada, Citizenship and Immigration Canada 1993).

The fluctuating proportions of independent-class immigrants reflect a chronic problem in Canadian immigration policy. The root of the problem is that policymakers seek to choose immigrants as individuals, based on human capital considerations, but immigrants come as members of families. Family connections mean that each independent immigrant represents a potential source of perhaps three or four subsequent family-class applicants. The only way to avoid the implications of this fact is to reduce or delay family-class eligibility, which policymakers are reluctant to do because of pressures from resident immigrants and because of the risk of reducing the attractiveness of Canada as a destination. If each independent immigrant is associated with three subsequent family-class applicants, then over the long term, independent immigrants cannot rise above one-quarter of the total, 25 percent. To maintain a high proportion of independent immigrants is difficult without continually increasing total immigration. Any circumvention of this arithmetic in the short term will be corrected in the longer term.

In order to strengthen the economic component of immigration, in the 1980s Canada created new categories of independent immigrants called business-class immigrants, which include the self-employed, entrepreneurs, and investors. Persons who meet certain criteria in these categories are awarded points credited toward potential admission, 55 points for the entrepreneurs and investors, and 30 for the self-employed. In 1993, business-class immigrants numbered about 33,000 of the 90,000 independent immigrants (in turn, 35 percent of the 256,000 total immigration). However, in the business class, the dependents are more prominent than among independent applicants generally. In the business class, the dependents outnumber the principal applicants by 3 to 1. So the principal applicants in the business class were only about 8000.

The comparison of policy suggests that Canada's point system is oriented toward labor force integration but not necessarily toward high skills and that Canada, like the United States, has a strong family-reunification component in its immigration program. This suggests that the effects of policy differences on the entry status of immigrants in Canada compared to the United States might not be large.

Immigration Policy in Australia, 1973–1990

A close look at the Australian points system reveals that like Canada's, the Australian selection process does not necessarily imply the selection of very highly skilled persons. It is important to look at the system as it was initially introduced and developed, to show that skill levels are by no means upgraded in any dramatic way simply because immigrants were screened on labor market demand.

Australian immigration law in place during the 1970s (Migration Act of 1958; see Freeman and Betts 1992, 75) was actually less specific than Canada's, making policy-substance-based estimates of its impact even more hazardous. There was even more administrative discretion (see Birrell 1984, Birrell and Birrell 1987; Hawkins 1989; Wooden et al. 1990; Jupp 1991; Collins 1991; Freeman and Jupp 1992). Major changes were announced regularly. The abolition of quotas by country of origin, which had been rather pointedly called the "White Australia" policy (though it was no more racially exclusionary than the U.S. and the Canadian policies prior to their reform), was announced by the Labor government of Prime Minister Gough Whitlam after it took office in December 1972. Australia's occupational preference system also was brought in, initially as in Canada, by regulation. It was even less formalized. The government simply issued an approved list of occupations that were experiencing high labor demand (Birrell and Birrell 1987, 100). The selection procedure had a high-tech name, Structured Selection Assessment System (SSAS), but compared to Canada's points system it left even greater discretion to migration officials. These officials used a two-part schedule which included an economic part related to employment, which might be compared to the initial Canadian points system. Officers were instructed to use the approved list of occupations to rate applicants on a five-point scale from 'very good' to 'not favorable'. A second part of the assessment considered personal and social factors, including attitudes, lifestyle, and appearance. Again, the immigration officer used the same simple five-point scale (Hawkins 1989, 105–106).

The list of approved occupations contained categories without formal definitions and thus did not select any specific group on the basis of particular skills. Occupations in demand often tended to be *low* in skills. In fact, the selection criteria based on occupational demand resulted in many highly skilled and professional applicants *not* meeting the test. Many professional categories in Australia were in a state of oversupply. On paper, the immigrants admitted by this SSAS system seem even farther from the U.S. Third Preference professionals than Canada's independent immigrants, given that education played no role whatsoever in the criteria of their selection.

The SSAS system was replaced by a more detailed points system called the Numerical Multi-factor Assessment System (NUMAS), in 1979 (Birrell and Birrell 1987, 103). NUMAS was intended to give greater weight to absolute skill levels. It retained the two-part list of priorities and employed numerical ratings on all criteria. The NUMAS system encountered severe criticism for being too formalistic, for not giving enough attention to family reunion (Birrell 1984, 75–79), and for being too restrictive of non-European immigration (Hawkins 1989, 143). But in fact, even the NUMAS system was also quite unselective and gave only a few points for high skill levels or education. Out of 100 points, only 10 were based on skills and education. The effective range was only 5 points, really, because under NUMAS, a university-educated professional would receive 10 points for these qualifications, while a person who attended but did not complete secondary school, working in a clerical occupation, would receive 5 points—a difference of only 5 points.

NUMAS was replaced only two years later, in 1982, by a new Migrant Assessment System (Hawkins 1989, 299). Hawkins (1989, 145) described the Migrant Assessment System as "closer to the Canadian points system than NUMAS was and shares its major emphasis on family migration and labor market needs" (see her summary of the Australian points criteria in Table 3.3, which may be compared with the second section of Table 3.2, panel B). It is easy to see that the importance of particular criteria may vary depending on the specific officer using the system. In addition, the specific selection criteria are formally changed from time to time.

Again, it is useful to count points. In the Migrant Assessment System, skill-based points increased to 18. Still, an applicant for admission to Australia could receive the required 60 points if they: were sponsored by a noncitizen resident of Australia (25 points), aged 30 (8), semiskilled (6) but without having completed secondary school (5), in an occupation with a labor shortage (10), and with a good (not outstanding) employment record (8). The trade-offs for professionals with recognized qualifications such as a university degree are such that while more points are given for being professional (4) or having a university education (2), persons with these qualifications might not get in if they had a poor employment record (0 points rather than 8) or if they were not willing to live in a designated growth area (6 points).

This scheme was definitely still a very weak screen. Persons with better qualifications than in this example would get in, but not because the selection system required it. So the Australian policies in place as non-European immigrant communities were established hardly assured the selection of any significant group of elite applicants according to the standards of the U.S. professional preference category.

The proportion of immigrants selected on the basis of labor market criteria in Australia has been high—comparable to, or even more often, higher than that in Canada. In most years, immigrants selected on the basis of labor market criteria constituted more than half of the total (Collins 1991, 262). Refugees made up about 15 to 20 percent, and family reunification accounted for 20 to 30 percent. Partly for geographic reasons, and

TABLE 3.3   Australia: The Points Table

Factor		Points
Skills	Professional, technical, and skilled workers	
	whose qualifications are recognized in Australia	10
	whose qualifications have been assessed but are not fully recognized in Australia (these points are granted only in exceptional circumstances)	6
	Service occupations	6
	Clerical, commercial, and administrative	6
	Semi-skilled	6
	Rural and unskilled	2
Employment	Employer nominees	16
	Other arranged employment	10
	Occupation in shortage or minor shortage	10
Age	25–35	8
	23–24 and 36–37	6
	20–22 and 38–39	4
	Under 20 and from 40–45	2
	Other	0
Education	Completed tertiary	8
	Full secondary	6
	First part secondary	5
	Some education	3
Employment record	Outstanding	10
	Good	8
	Satisfactory	5
	Poor	0
Economic prospects	Full sponsorship by an Australian citizen	28
	Labor shortage and business migration	25
	Full sponsorship by a non-citizen	25
	Good	15
	Satisfactory	10
	Minor problems	5
	Major problems	0
Growth area	Intention to settle in a designated growth area	6

Note: To pass, eligible applicants must score 60 points or more.

Source: Freda Hawkins (1989, 299). Critical Years in Immigration: Canada and Australia Compared. Kingston, Ont.: McGill-Queen's University Press.

to an extent even greater than in Canada, enforcement of immigration policy has been less of a problem for Australia than for the United States. Whether the Australian policy is in fact more vigilant against violation than U.S. policy is difficult to say. Overall, the specific provisions of Australia's immigration policy suggest that the impact on immigrant skills will be even less than in Canada. A larger proportion are screened for occupational criteria, but skills play a less important role in this screening than in Canada.

In sum, Canadian and Australian policies have given more emphasis to labor market criteria than has U.S. policy, but not necessarily more emphasis to education-based skill levels. Employment-related categories in Canada and Australia have been larger than those in the United States, but the specific skills criteria have been much weaker. And as the skill-related criteria have been upgraded over several years, the size of the categories shrank. The official prescriptions of policies in the three countries really do not ensure cross-national differences in the educational or skill levels of immigrants. In terms of *change* in policy content since the late 1960s or early 1970s, the Canadian and Australian policies appear to represent an upgrading in the skills area, while the U.S. policy moved in the other direction. Based on the substance of the policies themselves, we expect that skill levels might be only slightly higher, if at all, in Canada and Australia.

The Institutional Context for Immigration Policies

The fact that policy differences relate more to occupational selectivity than to skill selectivity can be understood in terms of the comparative institutional context and the social, cultural, and political forces impinging on immigration policy makers in each country. The relatively laissez-faire U.S. immigration policy seems to fit with American individualism. In the popular American conception, the immigrant is closely linked to the 'land of opportunity' imagery. The belief was that anyone, from any origins, no matter how destitute or lacking in social breeding, could with hard work and a practical bent of mind, 'make it.' The immigrant success story is the quintessentially American parable, a validation and exemplification of opportunities for social and occupational mobility available in the United States. This explains why the Statue of Liberty is such an important national symbol, welcoming immigrants in New York harbor with its message to the world: Give me your tired, your *poor* [emphasis supplied], your huddled masses yearning to breathe free! This historical idealization of immigrants as brash adventurers persists in contemporary times, as reflected in this 1965 quotation from Hubert Humphrey: "The most energetic, hard-working people of each generation of Americans have been those newest to our country. So when we want to put a little more zest into America, add a little more flavor to this great Republic, give it a little more drive, just let there be a little infusion of new blood, the immigrant. He is restless, he seeks to prove himself" (quoted in Keely 1979b, 40).

Even when immigration is advocated as a contribution to the country as a whole, it is the individual immigrant's entrepreneurial spirit that is valued. Careful selection of immigrants based on preexisting middle-class credentials and human capital endowments would seem to do violence to this heroic imagery. Given that Americans assume self-reliance, there is little need to be picky about immigrants.

Canada and Australia, with their extensive immigration histories, might easily lay claim to a similar immigration mythology, but do not, at least not to the same degree. In Canadian and Australian minds, the image of immigrants as symbols of a "rags-to-riches" scenario is less deeply ingrained. Perhaps because of their small size and secondary international standing, neither Canada nor Australia is as prominent an immigration destination as is the United States. The size and power of latter promotes heroic images. By contrast, Canada was, as Reimers and Troper (1992, 18) wrote, "less a land of second chance than a land of second choice." Australia's location dictated at times that grants be given to encourage immigrants to make the journey. Being second choice, or having to woo immigrants from afar, could lead to concerns about ending up with second-best, when it comes to immigrants. This could promote a desire for a bit of planning, regulation, and selectivity, but hardly suggests that the two countries have been in a position to try to skim the cream off the immigration pool.

Interest-group politics and pressures related to immigration also may differ among the countries, but the implications of group interests for skill selectivity are not clear-cut. One view is that business groups want unskilled immigrants as cheap labor to undercut the domestic workforce. Unrestrictive immigration policies serve business interests, if immigrants represent a 'reserve army of labor', depressing wages and undermining class solidarity (Castells 1975, 49; Castles and Kosack 1985; Castles 1989; Piore 1979). In the United States, a main example has been the promotion of unskilled Mexican immigration by California agribusiness interests. Robert Bach (1978) pointed out that the perverse practice of legislating immigration controls and then not enforcing them in effect "ensures submissiveness by dealing with undocumented immigrants as criminals" (Bach 1978, 537). The general public as consumers generally has shared this interest because the arrangement helps keep food prices low. The same forces may be evident in more recent proposals to legalize "cross-border" workers.

Following this logic of class interests, that business groups favor unskilled immigration to undermine labor, it may be expected that labor groups might be more inclined toward skilled immigration. Historically, unions in the United States indeed have opposed unregulated and less-skilled immigration in an effort to protect the wage position of domestic labor (see Rosenblum 1973; Parmet 1981). In debating immigration reform in the United States in the 1960s, the Democratic and labor-oriented presidential candidate John F. Kennedy (1964, 102–107) emphasized the priority of immigrant skills. Business interests were described as aligning themselves with ethnic organizations and humanitarian groups in an 'unholy alliance' (Keely 1979b, 40) to promote family reunification and other policies which would promote the influx of an unorganized and comparatively docile labor pool.[10]

If labor is more influential in Canada and Australia, then following the class-interests analysis outlined above, one would expect more pressure for highly skilled immigrants. Yet while Hawkins's (1988, 1989) comparison of immigration policy in Canada and Australia confirmed that unions were a key interest group in immigration policy formation in both countries, she did not attribute any particular position to them regarding immigrant skill levels. Canadian unions have sought consultation, and were not in any way instrumental in designing the points system. In fact, Hawkins argued, during the period when reforms and the points system were introduced, Canadian businessmen also seemed little interested in immigration. "No one could possibly say, for example, that Canadian employers and their organizations have really applied themselves to . . . substantive issues in immigration. They have certainly submitted briefs on appropriate occasions. But there has been nothing like a campaign or a sustained effort to influence the direction of policy" (Hawkins 1988, 348).

Australian unions have exercised greater power in immigration policy making, but their efforts have been toward incorporating immigrants within the labor fold. This has led to a greater receptivity to immigrants by Australian unions, reflected also in the significant services provided by unions to immigrant workers (Bertone and Griffin 1992). The incorporation of Asian immigrants into the Australian union movement reportedly has helped offset anti-Asian sentiment within those Australian unions (Quinlan and Lever-Tracy 1990). At the same time, Freeman and Betts (1992) suggest that compared to the United States, the lack of illegal immigration into Australia is a result of union power and not only geography. "It is inconceivable that the Australian Council of Trade Unions would tolerate widespread illegal entry into the country of the kind that has occurred in the USA for decades" (Freeman and Betts 1992, 87).

Business groups argue that their interest today is in more highly skilled workers (Borjas 1990).[11] Highly skilled professionals are the source of the most rapidly increasing labor costs, and employers' groups have been credited with supporting increased emphasis on skills in the 1990 immigration reforms (Freeman and Betts 1992, 84). However, businessmen may prefer domestic sources for the most highly skilled jobs, not immigrants.

Preference for foreign as opposed to domestic sources of skilled workers may be greater when there is a less-developed domestic educational system, which was the argument about Canada made in Porter's *Vertical Mosaic* (1965), and about Australia by the Birrells (1987), as discussed in Chapter 1. Regarding the education-immigration policy link in the Canadian case, Boyd (1976, 84) agreed with Porter's view.[12] However, it is difficult to find evidence confirming that skill selectivity in Canadian or Australian immigration policy was influenced by lower domestic educational levels. To the extent that the pursuit of skilled immigration arises from deficiencies in domestic education, then it may be expected that skill-mix requirements will be identified in relation to the lower prevailing domestic standard. Given the lower standard, and even though the occupational distributions of Canada and the United States may have differed little (McRoberts and Selbee 1981), educational requirements typical in many professional and managerial occupations in Canada were lower (Lipset 1989, 160). Similarly, given the overall size and expansionist objectives of Australian immigration, the relative size of the skilled and unskilled components that would be perceived as meeting the Australian workforce needs would reflect the domestic standard.

In considering Porter's hypothesis, it must be emphasized that the policy potentially most affected by educational underdevelopment would have been the one in place *prior to the introduction of the points system.* Porter's discussion of Canada, as well as the Birrells' for Australia, focused on the 1950s. Even though one-third of Canada's professional and skilled workforce at the time was supplied through immigration (Porter 1965, 45), the unskilled component was larger. Overall average educational levels of immigrants at that time were actually lower than in the United States. By the time the points system came into place, Canada had already begun to expand postsecondary education to match the U.S. standard. Lower domestic educational standards as a source of pressure for skilled immigration would apply less in more recent times. The domestic educational standard which frames immigration policy has risen sharply in both countries, and particularly in Canada. There has been a gradual convergence of Canadian and Australian educational institutions with those of the United States, so this source of immigration policy differences has been declining over time. So as educational levels have risen, the impetus to use skilled immigration to offset lower levels of domestic education would be declining in significance during the time of the development of the points system.

Welfare institutions also frame immigration policy formation. Today, the Canadian or Australian approach to immigration could be affected by their comparatively generous provisions of social entitlement. The more generous the entitlement, the greater the potential concern about the impact of newcomers. Public funding for all manner of services increased dramatically over several decades to include not only primary and secondary education but also low-tuition university education, increased unemployment benefits, and government-funded health insurance. This could raise concerns about whether immigrants will be net contributors to social services or net users. Will they carry their weight? Will they contribute in economic terms? Will they be a burden on society? And an immigration policy which manages selection in relation to economic criteria may therefore resonate with the ideology of collective welfare. The motto is not so much "give me your tired, your poor" as it is "give me your self-sufficient, your well-heeled." It is ironic, perhaps, that the society most compassionate toward its own citizens has the greatest incentive to be exclusive in admitting newcomers. Incidentally, business or labor interests in immigration may be as often articulated in relation to social policy issues as to employment.

This Canadian and Australian emphasis on self-sufficiency would not necessarily lead to pressures to select highly skilled immigrants, however. What would be most important is employability, and employability may be ensured by selecting immigrants above a minimum occupational skill level required by the labor force, not necessarily very high. Moreover, immigrants with the closest family ties to those already resident within the country might represent the greatest probability for self-sufficiency. So again, the more collectivist context such as might prevail in Canada or Australia would be expected to lead to a more carefully managed immigration policy but not necessarily to a more skill-selective one.

More recently, the relatively small scale of U.S. immigration might have reduced interest in immigration on both sides, business and labor, leaving the field to humanitarian sentiments, ethnic politics, or foreign relations. By contrast, Canada and Australia, countries with small populations spread over huge territories, still pursue immigration as a national goal of primary importance. Through immigration, both countries have achieved high population growth rates. Large-scale immigration inevitably requires more attention to its economic impact but not necessarily to any particular skill mix.

None of these considerations of cultural values, labor market interest groups, educational institutions, or social policies produce a clear basis for expecting that Canadian and Australian policymakers are under greater pressures to select highly skilled immigrants. Institutional differences among the three countries lead us to expect policies which may favor more *regulated* immigration policies in Canada and Australia compared to the United States, with perhaps some—but by no means heavy—emphasis on selecting immigrants on the basis of skills. The greater strength of labor groups in Canada and Australia may serve primarily to reinforce the avoidance of immigrants at the lowest skill levels. So we should not be surprised to find, as we did, that there is not much actual difference in the substance of policy, and we should examine carefully the evidence of its actual effects on immigrant characteristics. It is to these effects that we now turn.

Analysis of Actual Policy Effects on Immigrant Skill Levels

The empirical analysis of effects of immigration policy differences has been fairly primitive, though a few studies have employed better data and techniques. Testing policy effects by means of a simple cross-national comparison of immigrant skill levels is a very crude start. It helps to add a time-series "before-and-after" analysis, to see if differences in policy change lead to differences in trends. However, because of differences in the pre-1960s policies, a before-and-after analysis with only this one reference point might capture the effects of before rather than after. The time-series must tap more than just the mid-1960 changes, if the goal is to determine the effects of the post-1960s Canadian and Australian points systems. The best analysis would be one which examines selections under specific policy categories in each country, compared cross-nationally. While a definitive analysis is not yet available, there is a basis for drawing some conclusions about policy effects.

Different origin groups do make different use of the employment categories, affecting the likely impact of policy provisions on skill levels of specific groups of immigrants. Moreover, the group-specific pattern has changed over time. Following the 1965 policy reforms in the United States, family-reunification categories were used by Europeans, while employment and refugee categories were used by non-Europeans. Disproportionate use of employment categories by non-Europeans would favor higher skills in those groups. However, later, family-reunification applied to a larger number of non-Europeans, who followed their relatives previously selected on the basis of occupation. By the 1980s, immigrants from the United Kingdom or Canada were being selected on occupational criteria more often than immigrants from other sources including Asia, Africa, or Latin America (see Table 3.4, panel A). For example, in 1986, 268,248 immigrants arrived who were born in Asia, and nearly 150,000 of those entered as immediate family members exempt from numerical control. Only about 25,000 were admitted under occupational selection. In the same year, about 100,000 persons born in the Caribbean immigrated to the United States, with only about 3,000 having been selected on the basis of occupational criteria and nearly half admit-

TABLE 3.4 Percentages of Immigrants Admitted to the United States and
Canada Under Labor Market Criteria, by Origins and Year

A. United States: Occupational Preferences

Origins	1981 Total Immigrants	1981 Percentage Third and Sixth Preference	1986 Total Immigrants	1986 Percentage Third and Sixth Preference
United Kingdom	14997	30.3	13657	32.5
Europe	51698	9.7	48855	12.5
Canada	11191	29.5	11039	24.8
Mexico	101268	2.0	66533	3.8
Caribbean	73301	3.7	101632	2.9
Central and South America	60422	6.8	70254	9.8
Asia	264343	7.5	268248	9.5
Africa	15029	12.1	17463	10.9
Other	4193	21.7	3897	13.4
Total	596442	7.4	601578	8.9

B. Canada: Independent Immigrants

Origins	1981	1984	1987	1991
Europe	50.2	32.2	42.7	27.1
Africa	47.7	23.8	54.4	26.3
Asia	16.4	19.7	43.5	36.0
Australasia	61.1	29.9	48.4	37.5
United States	[1]	37.7	46.5	33.9
Caribbean	36.2	18.1	30.9	12.3
Other North and Central America	49.9	11.3	21.8	8.9
South America	26.6	18.3	47.8	22.6
Oceania	10.6	11.0	43.9	25.6
Not stated	47.1	64.0	69.2	38.6
Total: All regions	35.0	23.7	42.5	29.8

[1]No separate figures exist for the United States in 1981.

Sources: Data for the United States come from United States, Immigration and Nationalization Service (1985, Tables 5 and 6; 1989, Tables 5 and 6). Totals include those admitted as immediate family members. Origins data for total numbers of immigrants are based on country of birth; origins data for persons admitted under occupational preferences are based on "foreign state of chargeability" which in most cases is the same. For the United Kingdom and colonies, the Hong Kong portion has been assigned to the Asia category; other colonies assigned to the "other" category. Data for Canada are from Canada, Employment and Immigration Canada (1983, 1986, 1989, 1992). Independent immigrants include investors, entrepreneurs, the self-employed, and retirees.

ted as immediate family members exempted from numerical control. Duleep and Regets (1992, 417) also point out that a much larger proportion of immigrants from developed countries such as the United Kingdom or Japan are admitted on the basis of occupational skills. The Canadian points system potentially affects the skill distribution in specific groups, because although it affects most immigrant origin groups, it is not applied equally to all of them (see Table 3.4, panel B). In Canada, the proportions of Caribbean and Asian immigrants selected on the basis of points is larger, although it fluctuates substantially from year to year.

Comparison of Trends in Immigrant-Group Skill Levels

Borjas based his claim that the Canadian and Australian policies produced more highly skilled immigrants on a simple before-and-after comparison, for immigrants from all origins combined, focusing on the mid-1960s as a reference point. Based on census data, immigrants arriving in Canada between 1960 and 1964 had about one-half year less education than their counterparts entering the United States, while immigrants arriving between 1975 and 1980 had nearly one year more education (Borjas 1994a, 1694). The trend over time appears to be toward progressively less-well-educated immigrants in the United States, and toward better-educated immigrants in Canada and Australia. The educational levels of immigrants to the United States declined by almost one year on average, while the educational levels of immigrants both to Canada and to Australia rose by nearly one year. During the 1970s, and relative to Canada, the United States increased its proportion of less-educated immigrants somewhat more than it increased its proportion of highly educated immigrants (Borjas 1993, 26).[13]

This pattern of cross-national differences is largely due to relative changes in the origins-mix of immigrants, and much less to changes in the selection of immigrants within origin groups. Trends based on specific origin groups have been more similar among the three countries. As discussed in Chapter 1, Duleep and Regets (1992) showed that for Chinese, other Asian, European, and British-origin immigrants, those settling in Canada did not have more education. In Table 3.5, we extend Duleep and Regets's analysis in two ways. In our urban census sample, we use a finer breakdown of origin groups, including specific European origins, Blacks, and specific Hispanic origins. We also extend the analysis to include Australia, and we consider men and women separately. Two periods of immigration are distinguished: before 1970 and after. This approximately compares immigrants arriving before and after the policy changes. Before 1970, we find, in every origins category where comparisons are possible except Black men, other Asian women, and Hispanics,

TABLE 3.5 Mean Years of Education of Immigrant Groups in the Urban Labor Force, and Proportional Size of Group, by Host Country, Period of Immigration, Origins, and Gender, ca. 1980

A. Men[1]

	United States, Immigrants Arriving…					Canada, Immigrants Arriving…					Australia, Immigrants Arriving…				
	Before 1970		1970–1980			Before 1970		1970–1980			Before 1970		1970–1980		
Origins	Yrs. Educ.	Propor-tion[2]	Yrs. Educ.	Propor-tion	Education Change	Yrs. Educ.	Propor-tion	Yrs. Educ.	Propor-tion	Education Change	Yrs. Educ.	Propor-tion	Yrs. Educ.	Propor-tion	Education Change
Immigrants, total	12.25	36345	11.50	61711	-0.75	11.42	12195	12.27	5210	0.85	10.16	2000	10.93	1869	0.77
White, total	12.47	27.2	12.59	17.1	0.12	11.07	84.1	11.65	38.8	0.58	9.66	67.6	10.74	63.9	1.08
United Kingdom	13.83	2.4	14.77	2.1	0.94	12.68	20.3	12.74	11.6	0.06	10.05	29.4	10.35	32.2	0.30
North, West Europe	13.45	7.4	14.94	2.3	1.49	12.10	14.4	13.43	3.6	1.33	10.11	9.2	10.69	3.9	0.58
East Europe	12.59	4.1	13.17	2.1	0.58	11.36	10.1	13.14	2.6	1.78	10.38	3.2	11.57	2.7	1.19
South Europe	10.37	7.3	9.63	6.2	-0.74	9.01	31.3	8.66	13.7	-0.35	8.56	23.3	9.46	10.5	0.90
Black, total	12.53	11.7	12.22	8.1	-0.31	12.69	2.2	11.94	6.5	-0.75	–	–	–	–	–
Asian, total	14.83	21.9	14.38	25.1	-0.45	13.53	7.4	13.00	33.7	-0.53	12.79	13.1	11.98	18.4	-0.81
Chinese	14.00	8.9	13.19	5.6	-0.81	12.96	3.7	12.68	12.6	-0.28	13.92	3.4	11.51	4.2	-2.41
Filipino	13.96	5.6	14.50	5.0	0.54	–	–	–	–	–	–	–	–	–	–
Indian	17.85	3.2	16.21	4.9	-1.64	–	–	–	–	–	–	–	–	–	–
Korean	16.98	1.4	14.41	3.4	-2.57	–	–	–	–	–	–	–	–	–	–
Vietnamese	16.08	0.1	13.08	2.5	[3]	–	–	–	–	–	–	–	–	–	–
Japanese	14.61	1.7	15.23	1.8	0.62	–	–	–	–	–	–	–	–	–	–
Other Asian[4]	14.51	1.0	13.67	1.8	-0.84	14.11	3.7	13.18	21.0	-0.93	–	–	–	–	–
Hispanic, total	10.59	31.3	8.68	38.9	-1.91	13.44	0.6	12.05	4.8	-1.39	12.41	9.8	12.12	14.2	-0.29
Mexican	8.74	16.5	7.42	24.4	-1.32	–	–	–	–	–	10.88	1.3	9.82	4.1	-1.06
Cuban	12.12	6.1	10.75	3.0	-1.37	–	–	–	–	–	–	–	–	–	–
Other Latin American	11.87	8.6	10.80	11.5	-1.07	13.44	0.6	12.05	4.8	-1.39	10.88	1.3	9.82	4.1	-1.06

(continues)

TABLE 3.5 (continued)

B. Women[5]

Origins	United States, Immigrants Arriving...					Canada, Immigrants Arriving...					Australia, Immigrants Arriving...				
	Before 1970		1970–1980			Before 1970		1970–1980			Before 1970		1970–1980		
	Yrs. Educ.	Propor-tion[2]	Yrs. Educ.	Propor-tion	Education Change	Yrs. Educ.	Propor-tion	Yrs. Educ.	Propor-tion	Education Change	Yrs. Educ.	Propor-tion	Yrs. Educ.	Propor-tion	Education Change
Immigrants, total	12.04	28151	11.43	38902	-0.61	11.19	8064	11.44	3950	0.25	10.01	1028	10.73	1228	0.72
White, total	12.21	26.4	11.94	17.0	-0.27	10.91	80.4	11.21	34.5	0.3	9.72	69.3	10.55	62.9	0.83
United Kingdom	12.89	3.5	13.48	2.0	0.59	12.14	23.8	12.37	10.3	0.23	10.14	30.4	10.28	29.6	0.14
North, West Europe	12.96	8.3	13.84	2.6	0.88	11.76	13.0	12.55	3.5	0.79	10.27	9.2	10.60	4.2	0.33
East Europe	12.05	3.4	12.44	2.4	0.39	11.50	9.4	12.65	2.6	1.15	10.92	4.3	11.03	2.7	0.11
South Europe	9.92	5.0	8.4	5.0	-1.52	8.69	26.2	8.02	11.4	-0.67	8.46	22.8	8.75	9.1	0.29
Black, total	12.22	16.6	11.77	11.1	-0.45	11.89	3.2	11.21	8.2	-0.68	–	–	–	–	–
Asian, total	13.35	24.1	13.25	31.8	-0.10	12.38	7.8	12.27	35.3	-0.11	11.63	13.3	11.63	21.3	0.0
Chinese	12.26	8.6	11.95	7.1	-0.31	11.53	4.1	11.48	14.8	-0.05	11.37	3.0	10.47	4.6	-0.09
Filipino	14.63	7.0	14.61	9.7	-0.02	–	–	–	–	–	–	–	–	–	–
Indian	15.66	1.3	14.48	4.3	-1.18	–	–	–	–	–	–	–	–	–	–
Korean	13.63	1.7	12.53	4.9	-1.10	–	–	–	–	–	–	–	–	–	–
Vietnamese	13.73	0.2	11.81	2.8	[3]	–	–	–	–	–	–	–	–	–	–
Japanese	12.67	4.4	13.41	1.2	0.74	–	–	–	–	–	–	–	–	–	–
Other Asian[4]	12.94	0.8	12.09	1.7	-0.85	13.31	3.7	12.84	20.6	-0.47	11.7	10.3	11.96	16.6	0.26
Hispanic, total	10.88	26.0	9.04	31.8	-1.84	12.68	0.7	11.44	5.2	-1.24	10.32	1.4	9.56	2.7	-0.76
Mexican	9.29	11.0	7.58	14.9	-1.71	–	–	–	–	–	–	–	–	–	–
Cuban	12.05	6.0	11.01	3.9	-1.04	–	–	–	–	–	–	–	–	–	–
Other Latin American	11.32	9.0	10.11	12.9	-1.21	12.68	0.7	11.44	5.2	-1.24	10.32	1.4	9.56	2.7	-0.76

N's for mean years of education are implicit in the data on proportional size of each group.

[1] Native-born White male educational levels are: United States, 13.49 years (N = 112075); Canada, 11.87 years (N = 43865); Australia, 11.27 years (N = 3824).

[2] The basis for proportions reported below is the total number of immigrants.

[3] Insufficient data to establish a trend.

[4] For Canada and Australia, Other Asian includes all Asians except Chinese.

[5] Native-born non-Hispanic White female educational levels are: United States, 13.22 years (N = 79997); Canada, 11.93 years (N = 32776); Australia, 11.22 years (N = 2483).

Sources: 1980 U.S. Census Public Use Microdata 5-Percent File; 1981 Canadian Census Public Use Sample Tape 2-Percent Individual File; 1981 Australian Census of Population and Housing 1-Percent File. For further details on sources, see Chapter 1, note 14. For more specific definitions of origins used for each country, see Chapter 2, pp. 46–47 and notes 4–6.

immigrants to the United States were better educated than immigrants to either Canada or Australia.[14]

What is even more striking, however, is that even *after* the policy changes, immigrants to the United States tended to be better educated than those to Canada or Australia, from every origin category except Hispanics. The finding holds true for Blacks, Chinese, other Asians, the British, and most specific European regions of origin (for East European men, the difference between Canada and the United States is negligible, and for East European women there is a slight trend toward higher levels of education in Canada). Furthermore, even the decline between the 1960s and the 1970s in the educational levels of immigrants to the United States compared to Canada and Australia does not hold within most origin groups—such as immigrants from the United Kingdom and Northwest Europe, Blacks, and Asians in the aggregate. For Asians, the decline in educational levels was greater in Canada and Australia than in the United States, and for Blacks, the decline in educational levels was greater in Canada than in the United States (there were too few Blacks in Australia to measure).

These data suggest that policy effects on immigrant educational levels are not powerful enough to offset any potential countervailing trends in immigrant self-selection. Duleep and Regets concluded that "Canadian policy does not appear to have a consistent effect on the educational levels of immigrants" (p. 431). Our data extend the basis of this conclusion to include Blacks and specific European origins, and indicate that the conclusion also applies to Australian policy. These small effects are consistent with what we expected based on a detailed analysis of the specific provisions of the points systems as implemented in Canada and Australia. The policies have been labor market oriented, but not especially skill oriented.

The Issue of an "Origins-Mix" Effect of Policy

In recent publications, Borjas (1993; 1994a, 1694–1695) has attempted to deal with the apparent failure of policy to produce cross-national differences in the skills of immigrants from particular origins by arguing that lower and more rapidly declining educational levels of U.S. immigrants in the aggregate, compared specifically to Canada, is a policy effect which works by changing the origins-mix of immigrant populations. This origins-mix-effect argument is not really relevant to the present analysis, because our focus is on the entry levels of particular groups. However, it is worth pointing out that even this argument is doubtful. The reasons are important because they underscore the limitations of immigration policy.

In the first place, based on formal policy, origins-mix effects are possible only as a result of skill selection within origins-group applicant pools. The points system could result in disproportionate selection of immigrants from origin groups with higher skill levels. However, an origins-mix effect which actually *drives* skill selectivity would have to be based on a policy which discriminates on the basis of origins. Neither Canada nor Australia has such policies.

In any case, we can observe in Table 3.5 that the origins-mix differences attributed to policy by Borjas do not in fact raise skill levels of immigrants in Canada or Australia. In comparing Canada and the United States, Borjas pointed to the fact that immigrants to Canada are more often from Europe (Borjas 1993a, 24; 1994a, 1695), which is true. However, Europe is not the source of the best-educated immigrants. In Canada and for immigrants arriving in the 1970s, Europeans are actually the least-well-educated group. Best educated are the Asians (13.00 years for men, 12.27 for women), followed by the Hispanics (12.05 years for men, 11.44 for women), and Blacks (11.94 years for men, 11.21 for women), with Europeans last (11.65 years for men, 11.21 for women).

Further, among European immigrants, there are two important origins-mix differences between the United States and both Canada and Australia; one favors higher skills in Canada and Australia and the other favors higher skills in the United States. Canada and Australia select more heavily from Southern Europe, which is a less-educated origins group, and from the United Kingdom, which is a better-educated group. In neither case is this likely a result of the points system. Southern European immigrants in Canada and Australia are more often family-class immigrants, the relatives of the large groups of immigrants who arrived after World War II.

U.K. immigrants in Canada and Australia may often be selected based on points, but the success of Canada and Australia with this group probably relates to the traditional Commonwealth links, not to the points system itself. Further, it is hard to see how the points system could cause continued immigration to Canada and Australia from the United Kingdom but not from other parts of Europe where educational levels are as high as they are in the United Kingdom. It is also worth noting that the educational levels of those U.K. immigrants who went to the United States actually rose more rapidly than did the educational levels of their counterparts going to Canada and Australia.

The most distinctive origins shift negatively affecting the educational level of immigrants to the United States is the big increase in immigration by poorly educated Mexicans. Increased Mexican immigration in the United States accounts for about half of the relative decline in the overall educational levels of immigrants there compared to Canada or Australia.

This trend is obviously exogenous and can hardly be attributed to immigration policy. More Mexican immigration to the United States than to Canada or Australia is almost certainly related primarily to factors other than differences in selection criteria.

Impact of Immigration Selection Categories on Educational Levels

Only a few studies have been able to introduce policy categories into the analysis of effects on skill levels. If these studies are compared, they suggest that U.S. skill-selected preference categories are far more distinctive in skill levels than Canadian or Australian points-selected categories. This is consistent, again, with the comparative analysis of the policies themselves: The U.S. Third Preference professionals category is a true high-skilled category, but independent immigrants selected by the Canadian and Australian points systems are much less so.

For the United States, Sorensen, Bean, Ku, and Zimmerman (1992) used a unique data set comprised of a sample of legal aliens (formally admitted permanent residents) from the 1980 Alien Address Registration Program, supplemented with INS data on admission category, and (using a link based on Social Security Numbers) Social Security Administration data on earnings. They found that among immigrants who arrived after 1965, only 5.5 percent were admitted in either of the two employment preferences (Sorensen et al. 1992, 42). A disproportionate share of these, particularly in the professional category, were from Asia. Eighty-three percent of professional category immigrants were born in Asia, and only 7.7 percent in Europe. By contrast, of those in the family preference category, one-third were born in Europe, and 45 percent in Asia.

Employment rates in family preference categories and employment preference categories were about equal overall, though immigrants in the family preference categories earned less. Employment rates were calculated separately for principal beneficiaries (the immigrants who had actually qualified under the category) and derivative beneficiaries (those brought in as immediate family members of persons admitted in the category). Among principal beneficiaries, employment rates were understandably much higher in employment-preference categories (more than 90 percent, compared to 69 percent for the family-preference categories; see Sorensen et al. 1992, 47). However, the derivative beneficiaries of those in employment-preference categories were half of all those admitted in these categories, and those derivative beneficiaries were much *less* likely to be employed than derivative beneficiaries in the family-preference categories (29 percent, compared to 42 percent).

Family-category immigrants earn less, however. Employment-preference immigrants are far more likely to be in high-status occupations and to earn high incomes than are immigrants in the family-class categories. The difference in the proportion of professionals or managers is, as expected, far more pronounced for the Third Preference category, professionals. Seventy-six percent of these are employed in the professional/managerial category, compared to 26 percent of the native-born employed. By contrast, 46 percent of the Sixth Preference, skilled and unskilled workers, were professionals (Sorensen et al. 1992, 50). In addition, the earnings of those in the employment-preference categories were greater—in the $16,000–18,000 range, compared to $10,000–11,000 for those in the family-preference categories or immediate relatives (Sorensen et al. 1992, 52).

In Canada, where independent immigrants are not necessarily as skill-selected as those in the high-skill preference categories in the United States, the skills difference between independent and family-class immigrants may be less than in the United States (even though skill selection of immigrants in Canada has became more rigorous over time). In recent cohorts, the skill levels of independent immigrants were only somewhat higher than for family-class immigrants. For 1992 Hong Kong immigrants, for example, of independent immigrants, 40 percent had at least some university education, compared to 28 percent of the family-class immigrants. Sixty-six percent of independent immigrants spoke an official language of Canada, compared to only 45 percent among family-class immigrants. The higher skill levels of independent immigrants may or may not offset the trend toward more family-class immigrants. Close family ties are not necessarily an indicator of low skill levels.

The Canadian government has compiled a data set parallel to the one used by Sorensen et al., but it is not available for direct comparison. The best available study for Canada is the one by Wright and Maxim (1991). This team used pooled regression techniques to link Department of Employment and Immigration data on the class mix of immigrants (independent vs. family-class or refugees) from 16 source countries over 18 years (1968–1985) to indicators of entry-level earnings potential as estimated in census data (1971 and 1986 microdata samples). Their analysis showed that each increase of 1 percent in the proportion of immigrants who were independent class (and selected based on points) resulted in a 0.5 percent increase in net earnings. About half of this increase was related to trends over time, possibly including increased restrictiveness in the points system itself. Interestingly, the family-class proportion had little effect (the reference category in the analysis being refugees). This analysis suggests that the points system is not without effects on the earnings capacity of immigrants. However, its effects seem small, compared to other sources of variation.

Based on all available sources—the previous research reviewed in Chapter 1, the cross-national comparison of the education of immigrants from particular origins, and studies of the direct impact of selection categories within each country—our most general conclusion is that cross-national differences in immigration policy have produced some differences in the educational levels of immigrants to the three countries, but most likely the impact has not been large. Year-to-year trends in policy do not produce sharply defined effects on the composition of immigrant groups. While skill-selected immigrant categories in the United States are substantially more highly skilled, there are comparatively few of these. The effects of skill-selected categories in Canada and Australia are offset mainly by their weaker selectivity but also by the limits on their size, both in numbers and in proportions of the total. The net result is that within origins categories, except for Hispanic immigrants, U.S. immigrants are better educated. The more selective immigration policies in Canada and Australia have effects which are not strong enough to overshadow other processes affecting immigrant selection, such as self-selection.

To attempt a precise measure of the immigration policy-difference effect would be hazardous. Still, on the basis of this evidence, one might conservatively suggest that lack of selectivity of U.S. immigration policy compared to Canada and Australia might have lowered mean educational levels within particular groups of immigrants to the United States by no more than one-half year. This is surely an upper-limit estimate; the true number is very likely less than this. Obviously, an estimate like this must be treated with caution; but it is one which makes sense based on the data, and it will give us a benchmark for comparing the impact of immigration policy with other influences.

Urban Concentrations of Less-Skilled Immigrants in the United States: A Policy Effect?

The skill levels of many immigrant groups in the United States are lower in the urban areas where immigrants are most heavily concentrated, often in New York, Los Angeles, Chicago, San Francisco, and Miami. Bartel (1989) demonstrated this fact in census data for European, Asian, and Hispanic immigrants examined in aggregate categories. It is of considerable importance in explaining the lower immigrant earnings in those cities. Here, we will extend Bartel's analysis to more specific origin groups and consider whether the pattern of urban concentration of the less-skilled may be the same or different in Canada and Australia, and what might be the role of policy in any differences. Does the family-reunification emphasis of U.S. immigration policy create greater concentrations of immigrants when families tend to settle together? Does the related process of chain migration operate differentially by educational levels?

The U.S. pattern whereby the largest immigrant concentrations are on average less-skilled might have various explanations. One is that an immigrant community might form an informal social safety net, which is most important for the relatively less skilled. It might provide job opportunities based on ethnic ties, as suggested by research on the 'enclave economy' (Light 1972; Portes and Bach 1985), and it might be the primary locus for immigrant settlement services and sources of aid. By contrast, immigrants selected on the basis of skills or occupational criteria would choose areas of settlement based on those skills and would be less influenced by where other members of the same origin group have settled. The result might be that immigrant inequalities are far less in areas where immigrant communities are small.

A more specific process involved here as well is that of chain migration. Chain migration is a process whereby initial settlers recruit additional settlers from the same source (Massey et al. 1987; Massey 1990; Boyd 1989; Portes and Rumbaut 1990; Tilly 1994). Family-class immigrants are most likely to settle near their families, and this may be particularly true if they lack highly salable occupational skills. In other words, chain migration also might be negatively skill selective. Research on chain migration suggests that the process operates most extensively to recruit less-educated migrants (see Anderson 1974). Persons at high occupational levels may choose to relocate when they have already found a job, often based on professional contacts or "weak ties" (Granovetter 1983). The presence of a large number of immigrants in an urban area may be irrelevant to these decisions. By contrast, immigrants at lower levels of education may more often choose to settle near their families, expanding on existing immigrant communities.

These processes of differential selection by educational levels may be reinforced by immigration regulations. While this is the case in all three countries, it might be more prominent in the United States, for two reasons. First, the United States recruits a much larger proportion of family-class immigrants. Thus, immigrants to the United States are more likely to be exposed to the forces which attract individuals to immigrant communities that already have formed. The self-selective processes by educational level have greater scope for operation. Second, the skill gap between the family-class and occupationally selected immigrants is likely to be greater in the United States. This is because the Third Preference category focuses on professional skills alone. There may be very few immigrants in this category likely to make settlement decisions based on immigrant community proximity.[15]

The Canadian and Australian points systems give priority not only to skills such as educational level or professional training and experience but also to having a job offer, working in an occupation in high demand, and intending to live in a community where there is labor demand. These latter may influence areas of settlement even without being necessarily related to skills. This could lead to a process whereby independent immigrants who are nevertheless comparatively less skilled may be likely to settle in areas with comparatively small immigrant communities. This could lead to an even more homogeneous pattern of immigrant community characteristics and entrance status across the country, compared to the United States. So in countries like Canada or Australia, where family reunification is less prominent as an exclusive priority in immigration policy, concentrations of less-skilled immigrants also may be less prominent.

Our analysis expands Bartel's to include more detailed origin categories and to permit cross-national comparison. Table 3.6 examines the relations between immigrant-origin community size (logged) and educational levels for various origin groups within each country. The results are presented as metric regression coefficients, to more effectively display the size of the effect. A metric coefficient of 1.0 means that an increase in the number of recent migrants from a particular origin group of one order of magnitude is associated with a increase in the average educational levels of those immigrants by one year.

The statistical analysis shows that in the United States, larger origin-community size leads to lower educational levels for most immigrant groups, including Whites, Blacks, all three Hispanic groups, and most Asian groups. The largest effect is for the Chinese. Among men, a significant negative effect of community size on educational levels of recent immigrants holds for every group except the Koreans and Vietnamese. This Vietnamese exception is interesting. Vietnamese refugees have settled according to a process very different from the settlement of other groups. The settlement process was managed so that destinations for particular immigrants were facilitated by local non-Vietnamese volunteer groups. Ethnic networks probably played a much smaller role in the settlement of Vietnamese refugees than for other immigrant groups, and it may be this fact which is reflected in the departure of the Vietnamese from the general settlement pattern.

Among immigrant women in the United States, a negative community size effect also holds for Whites, Blacks, Hispanics, and some Asian groups, though fewer than is the case for men. As for men, the negative community size effect does not hold for Koreans or Vietnamese, but it also does not hold for Filipinos, Japanese, or non-Chinese Asians in general.[16] The recruitment patterns for men and women, particularly in certain Asian groups, seem to differ.

In Canada and Australia, the negative effect of greater immigrant community size is far less consistent than in the United States. It does not hold for Asian immigrants—either Chinese, other Asians, or all Asians

TABLE 3.6   Effects[1] of Recent Immigrant Community Size (Logged) on Years of Education for Urban Labor Force, by Host Country, Origins, and Gender, ca. 1980

Immigrant Origins	United States		Canada		Australia	
	Metric B	(N)	Metric B	(N)	Metric B	(N)
Men						
White	−0.544 [2]	(10567)	−1.852 [2]	(2024)	0.783 [4]	(1261)
Black	−0.563 [2]	(4985)	−0.481 ns	(341)	−	
Asian, total	−0.766 [2]	(15507)	0.925 [2]	(1754)	2.068 [2]	(343)
Chinese	−2.116 [2]	(3470)	0.799 [4]	(658)	2.533 ns	(78)
Non-Chinese Asian, total	−0.151 [3]	(12037)	0.853 [3]	(1096)	2.266 [2]	(265)
Filipino	−0.415 [2]	(3094)	−		−	
Asian Indian	−0.979 [2]	(3049)	−		−	
Korean	0.028 ns	(2105)	−		−	
Vietnamese	0.499 [3]	(1570)	−		−	
Japanese	−0.632 [2]	(1117)	−		−	
Other Asian	−0.497 [4]	(1102)	−		−	
Mexican	−0.327 [2]	(15049)	−		−	
Cuban	−0.548 [2]	(1869)	−		−	
Other Latin American	−1.027 [2]	(7079)	−0.517 ns	(251)	−2.780 [4]	(76)
Women						
White	−0.355 [2]	(6608)	−1.511 [2]	(1361)	0.640 ns	(820)
Black	−0.348 [2]	(4307)	0.032 ns	(322)	−	
Asian, total	−0.082 ns	(12287)	1.343 [2]	(1396)	1.362 [4]	(261)
Chinese	−1.737 [2]	(2761)	0.772 [4]	(584)	−1.329 ns	(57)
Non-Chinese Asian, total	0.633 [2]	(9526)	1.186 [2]	(812)	1.766 [4]	(204)
Filipino	−0.055 ns	(3727)	−		−	
Asian Indian	−0.819 [2]	(1676)	−		−	
Korean	0.478 [2]	(1902)	−		−	
Vietnamese	0.965 [2]	(1102)	−		−	
Japanese	0.263 ns	(467)	−		−	
Other Asian	1.121 [2]	(652)	−		−	
Mexican	−0.504 [2]	(5794)	−		−	
Cuban	−0.443 [3]	(1530)	−		−	
Other Latin American	−1.009 [2]	(5027)	−1.123 [4]	(205)	−3.140 [4]	(33)

1. A separate regression equation, with recent immigrant community size as the only independent variable, is estimated for each origin-gender group in each country. The metric regression coefficients represent the change in mean years of education in the immigrant group for each 10-fold increase in the number of immigrants arriving in the urban area.

2. $p < 0.001$

3. $p < 0.01$

4. $p < 0.05$

Sources: See Table 3.5.

together. This constitutes a significant departure from the U.S. pattern. On the other hand, the opposite holds for Black and White immigrants in Canada and Hispanic immigrants in both countries. The data for these groups do fit the negative community-size hypothesis. So the negative community-size hypothesis applies less consistently in Canada and Australia than in the United States.[17]

Can the intergroup variability in Canada and Australia be explained in terms of immigration processes (as we suggested may be the case of the Vietnamese in the United States)? Immigrant groups in Canada which fit the negative community size effect—Blacks, Whites, and Hispanics—are no less likely to be selected under economic criteria, at least as suggested by the Canadian data for 1981 in Table 3.4, panel B. Nevertheless, the larger proportions in all groups selected based on economic criteria rather than family ties potentially affects the consistency of the community-size effect across groups.

The pattern linking immigrant group size and educational level applies to the major U.S. immigrant settlement areas as shown in Table 3.7, which highlights immigrant men in specific origin groups. The largest Black immigrant communities are in New York and Miami, and they are clearly the least well educated. Black immigrants in New York average 11.9 years of education, and those in Miami average 10.3. The educational levels of the smaller Black immigrant communities in the United States are higher, particularly in Washington, Los Angeles, and Chicago, where the average level of education is nearly 13 years or higher. These differences reflect a significant community size effect in lowering Black immigrant educational levels, and hence entrance status, among four major Black communities in the United States.

The largest recent Chinese immigrant communities in the United States are in New York and San Francisco, and again the average educational levels of Chinese immigrants in these cities are, at 10.6 and 12.3 years, respectively, well below the overall urban average. This again suggests the operation of a community size effect.

The Chinese community in Los Angeles is comparatively large and nevertheless better educated. The average educational level of recent Chinese immigrants in Los Angeles is 13.6 years, above the 79-SMSA average. The level of education of the Los Angeles Chinese community is higher than that in the smaller Boston Chinese community, for example. Waldinger and Tseng (1992, 96) compared the Chinese in Los Angeles and New York and found that the differences in educational levels were partly related to specific origins (mainland Chinese in New York, other origins in Los Angeles), and partly to other causes. They point out that the Los Angeles Chinese community was originally concentrated in a small Monterey Park enclave and was more affluent, and that networks

TABLE 3.7   Size of Recent Immigrant Groups and Mean Years of Education, for Men in Major U.S. Urban Areas, by Origins and Urban Area, 1980

Urban Area	Size (Sample N)	Mean Years of Education	Urban Area	Size (Sample N)	Mean Years of Education
A) White			**B) Black**		
New York	2988	12.3	New York	2393	11.9
Los Angeles–Long Beach	1627	13.5	Miami	354	10.3
Chicago	1278	12.3	Washington, D.C.	281	13.7
Detroit	568	11.7	Boston	202	12.0
San Francisco–Oakland	560	14.3	Los Angeles–Long Beach	182	12.9
Boston	511	11.8	Chicago	162	12.9
C) Chinese			**D) Filipino**		
New York	785	10.6	Los Angeles–Long Beach	641	15.0
San Francisco–Oakland	587	12.3	San Francisco–Oakland	533	14.4
Los Angeles–Long Beach	531	13.6	Chicago	318	15.6
Chicago	128	14.6	Honolulu	277	11.2
Boston	118	11.7	New York	215	15.8
San Jose	111	16.0	San Diego	202	12.9
E) Asian Indian			**F) Korean**		
New York	627	15.1	Los Angeles–Long Beach	578	14.5
Chicago	414	16.4	New York	271	14.8
Los Angeles–Long Beach	179	15.8	Chicago	181	14.9
Houston	166	15.8	Washington, D.C.	136	14.2
Washington, D.C.	155	16.9	San Francisco-Oakland	78	13.9
Detroit	117	16.6	Philadelphia	76	13.9
G) Vietnamese			**H) Japanese**		
Los Angeles–Long Beach	188	13.4	New York	263	15.5
Orange County	171	13.8	Los Angeles–Long Beach	261	14.8
Houston	138	12.8	San Francisco–Oakland	78	14.7
San Jose	125	13.4	Chicago	73	14.6
Washington, D.C.	105	13.9	Honolulu	66	13.5
San Diego	67	13.6	Orange County	38	14.2
I) Mexican			**J) Cuban**		
Los Angeles–Long Beach	6824	7.3	Miami	1051	10.5
Chicago	1926	7.7	Los Angeles–Long Beach	130	11.7
Houston	1214	7.3	New York	114	10.6
Orange County	1017	7.2	Newark	94	10.6
San Diego	673	8.2	Chicago	51	11.7
Dallas	660	6.4	Tampa	42	11.7
San Francisco–Oakland	413	8.3			
San Jose	293	8.2			
San Antonio	256	7.4			

Source: 1980 U.S. Census Public Use Microdata Sample 5-Percent File. For a description of the urban labor force sample used here, see Chapter 1, note 14.

shaped its subsequent development. Thus this community may represent a variation consistent with the broader pattern. The concentration of less-well-educated mainland Chinese in New York might also be a consequence of chain migration.

The phenomenon of internal ethnicity (Light et al. 1993) is relevant here: That is, ethnic diversity *within* immigrant communities may affect their effective size. Our analysis would be improved by more precise measures of ethnic origins. This same point is relevant to the Black community. In Miami, for example, most Black immigrants are francophone Haitians. In other cities, the major group is Jamaican, but in those cases there are other anglophone West Indians such as Trinidadians and members of other groups. If there is less internal ethnic variety within the Black community of Miami, the negative community size effect might be intensified there.

For Mexicans, the community size effect would be expected to be strongest in Los Angeles, and strong also in Chicago, Houston, and Orange County. In fact, the educational level of the Mexican immigrants in Los Angeles (7.3 years), Houston (7.3 years), and Orange County (7.2 years) is slightly lower than the 79-area average (7.4 years). Other, smaller Mexican communities have higher levels of education, not only in the Bay Area (in San Francisco-Oakland, 8.3 years, and in San Jose, 8.2 years), but also close to the Mexican border, in San Diego (8.2 years) In terms of this analysis, the case of Dallas is an anomaly. The Mexican community in Dallas is small, about half the size of the one in Houston. And yet the level of education of Mexican immigrants in Dallas is significantly lower. Other factors must play a role in explaining the educational levels of recent Mexican immigrants in Dallas.

The community size effect for Cuban immigrants would be expected to apply most strongly in Miami. And in fact, the Miami Cuban community has comparatively less education (10.5 years) than the 79-area average (10.8 years). Sanders and Nee (1987, 753) compared Cuban immigrants in Miami-Hialeah with those settling elsewhere in Florida, where there are fewer immigrants, and found (inter alia) much lower educational levels for Miami Cubans. Only about half the employed immigrants in Miami-Hialeah had four years of high school, and only 12 percent had four years of college. By contrast, 70 percent of the employed Cuban immigrants elsewhere in Florida had four years of high school, and almost one in four had four years of college. The impact on entrance status is clear in the Sanders and Nee data, in that Miami-Hialeah Cubans earned only 72 percent of the earnings of Whites, while Cubans living elsewhere in Florida had earnings virtually equal to those of Whites.

The contrast with Los Angeles Cubans is also interesting. In Los Angeles, Cuban immigrant education averages 11.7 years, higher than in Miami by 1.2 years, and consistent with a community size effect. On the other hand, New York Cubans are a small group, and New York Cubans are no better educated than those in Miami. Other factors must play a role in New York.

Conclusions

The findings of this chapter suggest that policy is important but is only one part of the explanation for the different entry-level status of immigrants in U.S., Canadian, and Australian cities. A lack of occupational selectivity and a greater orientation toward family reunification in U.S. immigration policy compared to Canada and Australia may help explain the lower entry-level earnings of immigrant groups in the United States, particularly in certain urban areas. An examination of policy content shows that immigration in Canada and Australia is intended to be more carefully regulated than in the United States, but the regulation is oriented toward occupational selectivity more than toward skill selectivity. This fits with the institutional environment of immigration policy in the three countries. There is no mandate in Canada and Australia for an immigration policy which would be expected to select immigrants more highly educated than immigrants to the United States. The data on the educational levels of immigrants in the 1970s are fully consistent with this policy aspect—educational levels are higher in the United States for every significant origin category except Hispanics.

Possible effects of immigration policy in directing immigrants to certain areas on a skill-selective basis are noteworthy, however. The most significant effect of the U.S. emphasis on family reunification on immigrant entrance status may be that family networks bear upon the settlement process. Less-educated family-class immigrants may be more likely to utilize these networks. Occupationally selected immigrants, more numerous in Canada and Australia, may have fewer networks of contact, and intended area of settlement is a formal selection criterion in itself. In this way, immigration policy differences may affect the impact of immigrants on particular urban areas within countries.

Differences in immigration policy reflect other differences in institutional and cultural contexts, and these other differences may have a direct impact on immigrants and their entry-level status. The significance of these direct effects is considered in the following three chapters.

4

Education and the Accumulation of Credentials by the Native Born

In part, lower entry-level earnings for immigrants in the United States result from the larger skills gap faced by immigrants in that country, as was pointed out in Chapter 1. Yet as has been shown in Chapter 3, apart from the case of Hispanics, who are in any case relatively small groups in Canada and Australia, the skills of immigrants to the United States from particular origin groups are actually as high as, or higher than, those of their counterparts in either Canada or Australia. Very clearly, higher native-born education in the United States is a primary cause of the lower entrance earnings for immigrant groups there. Borjas (1990, 209) referred to this fact, without emphasizing its significance.[1] This significance derives from the fact that native-born educational levels reflect a powerful and autonomous institutional force in society. Aggregate levels of education in a population result from a complex set of processes which are social and cultural as well as economic, and which are retained by individuals to significant economic effect throughout the life course. Educational levels are not a simple function of contemporary labor market demand. Furthermore, educational institutions do not affect the native born and immigrants in the same way.

This chapter explores the impact of native-born education further in three respects. First, we examine overall trends in educational attainments in the three countries. Rates of growth in educational attainment have been different in the three countries, and temporal changes only slowly work their way through the age-graded occupational hierarchy. The overall competitive environment for immigrants varies by the age of the native-born comparison group. Furthermore, past and contemporary changes in educational attainment can be projected into the future. Progressive narrowing of cross-national differences in native-born educational standards seems inevitable, with important implications for future immigrant entry-level status.

Second, we examine how these cross-national differences affect immigrants, by determining the size of the immigrant education gap and establishing the average entry-level earnings. What part of the lower entrance earnings for specific immigrant groups in the United States, observed in Chapter 2, can be attributed to the emergence of a more extensively credentialed native-born U.S. workforce? To answer this question, we will provide a quantitative estimate using earnings-determination equations from each country.

A third objective of the chapter is to examine the impact of variations in educational credentials among urban areas *within* countries. Certain urban areas, particularly in the United States, have comparatively high levels of education among the native born—New York and San Francisco are two examples. High native-born educational levels do not, however, lead to the recruitment of better-educated immigrants. In fact, at least at the urban level in the United States, we find that the reverse is actually the case. It is precisely the high-education cities which have the largest concentrations of immigrants, and as we saw in Chapter 3, cities with high immigrant concentrations tend to have *lower* immigrant educational levels. Hence, there is a *polarization of immigrants' skills* in the major immigrant settlement areas in the United States. This same pattern is somewhat less evident in Canada, and very little in Australia.

Such interurban and cross-national differences are very helpful in explaining the interurban and cross-national differences in immigrant entry level described in Chapter 2, and it will be important to examine the underlying reasons. If *less*-educated immigrants are attracted to urban areas with *better*-educated native-born workers in the United States, why is this the case? And why are these patterns different in Canada and Australia? What can interurban patterns in the United States tell us about the reasons for cross-national differences? How are future immigrants likely to be affected by the evolving convergence in levels of educational attainment between Canada and the United States, and to a lesser extent, Australia? Considering answers to these questions will bring us a step closer to the goal of this study.

Cross-national Trends in Mainstream
Educational Credentials, 1960–1994

Higher educational levels in the United States than in the Canadian population and workforce are to a significant extent a result of a historical pattern of slower educational development in Canada rather than of continuing contemporary differences in educational institutions. Today, rates of educational attainment are comparable in the two countries. Differences in educational attainment in the two countries tend to be most pronounced in the older population. This means also that a closer convergence of educational attainment levels in the two countries is virtually inevitable with the passage of this older generation. Furthermore, the better-educated younger population in Canada is approaching its peak earning years, and its impact on the earnings distribution is growing.

In Australia, by contrast, while educational attainment rates are also rising, they still lag substantially behind U.S. standards. Hence, years of native-born education in Australia will be fewer than in Canada and the United States, for some time to come.

Comparative Trends for Young Cohorts

To see the time-series dimension of educational change, it is useful to compare the educational attainments of a young cohort with those of the entire population. Attainment rates for a young cohort reflect contemporary educational development; changes there are reflected in overall population figures as generational replacement occurs. Table 4.1 presents educational profiles for the three countries: young cohorts (old enough to have completed their education) on the left side of table, and aggregate educational levels in the entire adult population on the right side. The table includes both men and women, and all racial groups.[2]

Data from young adults show that educational expansion in the United States advanced between 1960 and 1980 but slowed considerably after that. The proportion of young adult Americans having completed secondary school rose from 61.7 percent to 84.5 percent over the period 1960 to 1980, but then leveled off. The proportion completing four years of university increased from 11.1 percent in 1960 to 22.1 percent in 1980, but remained fairly constant thereafter until 1990. After 1980, American postsecondary enrollment ratios compiled by UNESCO continued to rise slowly, perhaps reflecting a shift toward nonuniversity vocational institutes.

Canadian enrollment rates at all levels lagged far behind U.S. rates before the 1960s, but expansion was comparatively rapid after that time. In the 1960 young adult cohort, while 61.7 percent of the Americans had completed secondary school, only 28.2 percent of Canadians had done so. While 11.1 percent of Americans had completed a university degree, only 3.6 percent of Canadians had done so. Postsecondary enrollment ratios for Canada in that year were half of the U.S. ratios. However, for subsequent cohorts, Canadian enrollment and attainment rates rose more rapidly than did the U.S. rates, and the Canada-U.S. gap began to nar-

TABLE 4.1 Education of Population: United States, Canada, and Australia, 1960–1990

| | Age-Specific Enrollment/Attainment Rates (Young Adult Cohort) | | | | | | | | | Education of Population over 25 Years of Age | | | | | |
| | Percent Completing Secondary School | | | Postsecondary Enrollment Ratios[5] | | | Percent Completing University Degree | | | Percent Completing Secondary School | | | Percent Completing University Degree | | |
Year[1]	U.S.[2]	Can.[3]	Aus.[4]	U.S.	Can.	Aus.	U.S.[6]	Can.[7]	Aus.[8]	U.S.[9]	Can.[10]	Aus.[11]	U.S.[12]	Can.[13]	Aus.[14]
1960	61.7	28.2	–	32.1	16.0	13.1	11.1	3.6	–	41.1	22.1	–	7.7	3.4	–
1965	–	–	–	40.2	26.4	16.0	–	–	–	49.0	–	–	9.4	–	–
1970	73.8	38.9	–	49.4	34.6	16.6	16.3	7.8	–	52.3	27.1	–	10.7	5.3	–
1975	–	61.7	–	57.3	39.3	24.0	–	13.3	–	62.5	39.2	–	13.9	7.6	–
1980	84.5	71.7	56.6	56.0	42.1	25.4	22.1	14.9	10.3	66.5	52.6	43.5	16.2	9.6	6.7
1985	86.1	72.0	59.3	57.9	53.6	27.6	22.2	14.6	11.8	73.9	56.2	46.2	19.4	11.1	8.0
1990	85.7	77.0	62.9	65.6	61.7	31.3	23.2	16.0	11.9	77.6	63.0	54.5	21.3	12.8	9.7

[1]Approximate years; see notes below. Canadian census data are for one year later than indicated; Australian data are for years indicated in notes.

[2]Percent of persons aged 25–29 completing secondary school; U.S. Bureau of the Census (1993 Table 230, p. 152; 1988, Table 215, p. 133).

[3]Percent of persons aged 25–34 with secondary school graduation certificate; 1961 (Canada, Statistics Canada 1963, Table 102, includes grades 12 and 13 and persons aged 25–29); 1971 (Canada, Statistics Canada 1974, Table 5); 1976 (Canada, Statistics Canada, 1978, Table 29); 1981 (Canada, Statistics Canada, 1984, Table 3); 1986 (Canada, Statistics Canada 1989, Table 2); and 1991 (Canada, Statistics Canada, 1993, Table 2).

[4]Percent of persons aged 25–34 attending highest level of secondary school available; Australian Bureau of Statistics (1982, Table 1.5, p. 5, 1982 data reported for 1980; 1985, Table 1.10, p. 11; 1990, Table 5, p. 10).

[5]Ratio of the number enrolled in all postsecondary schools and universities (including vocational schools, adult education, two-year community colleges, and correspondence courses) to the number of persons aged 20–24; UNESCO (1975, for 1960–1965; 1985, for 1970–1975; and 1993, for 1980–1988). The 1990 figures are for 1988; after that date, the Canadian data changed in contents.

[6]Percent of persons aged 25–29 with four years of college or more. See note 2.

[7]Percent of persons aged 25–34 with university bachelor's degree. See note 3.

[8]Percent of persons aged 25–34 with post-school degree. See note 4.

[9]Percent of persons 25 years or older completing four years of high school. U.S. Bureau of the Census (1993, Table 233, p. 154).

[10]Percent of persons 25 years or older with secondary school graduation certificate. See note 3.

[11]Percent of persons 25 years or older attending highest level of secondary school available. See note 4.

[12]Percent of persons 25 years or older completing four years of college or more. See note 9.

[13]Percent of persons 25 years or older with university degree. Canada, Statistics Canada (1989, Table 1); Canada, Statistics Canada (1993, Table 1).

[14]Percent of persons 25 years or older with post-school degree. See note 4.

row. At the secondary level, Canadian completion rates increased from about half the American rate in 1960 to almost 85 percent of the American rate in 1980, and 90 percent of the American rate by 1990.

The Canada-U.S. gap in university degree completions also narrowed very considerably, particularly for the cohort reaching young adulthood between 1960 and 1975. During that period, existing universities in the government-funded system expanded greatly, and many new universities were founded. University completion rates in Canada were only about one-third of the U.S. rates in 1960, but rose to about half in 1970, and to about 70 percent during the 1980s. Government-funded, vocationally oriented community colleges also expanded in Canada. A comparison of postsecondary enrollments shows that as enrollment rates rose in both countries, the 1960 gap of more than two to one (32.1 percent compared to 16.0 percent) was virtually eliminated by 1990.[3]

Recent Canadian and American educational data assembled by the OECD (Center for Educational Research and Innovation [CERI], 1992) show that as of 1989, for the most recent cohorts of young adults, Canadians have caught up to or even passed Americans. Current rates of university graduation relative to the size of the population cohort were about the same in both countries—one in four (CERI 1992, 99). Both full-time and part-time enrollment rates in both university and nonuniversity institutions are higher in Canada than in the United States (p. 79). The international data on the current quality of education, at least at the lower secondary school level, also seem to favor Canada.[4]

In Australia, where educational expansion has been slower, convergence with the United States or Canada is less striking. The fact that education has not been a priority even in the recent past is reflected in the lack of good data on education in Australia before 1980. Since 1980, there has been a gradual upward trend in education. For example, the secondary school completion rate for young adult Australians in 1980 was only 56.6 percent, compared to 71.7 percent in Canada and 84.5 percent in the United States. During the 1980s, this Australian rate remained at about 80 percent of the Canadian rate, while both rates rose relative to the American rate. The Australian rate rose from about two-thirds of the American rate in 1980, to three-fourths of the American rate in 1990. University completion rates in Australia also rose relative to American rates during the 1980s, but were still lagging in 1990. The OECD data cited earlier show that the rate of university completion, which in Canada and the United States had converged to one in four, in Australia was still only one in five (CERI 1992, 99). Rates of enrollment in nonuniversity postsecondary education in Australia were about one in three, compared to nearly one in two in Canada and the United States (CERI 1992, 14). UNESCO data on postsecondary enrollment ratios for recent cohorts of

young adults (Table 4.1) show that while increases in Australia are occurring at a steady rate, they are only very slowly converging with those in
Canada or the United States.

Comparative Educational Levels of the Adult Populations

Despite increases in the educational attainment rates of the young cohorts, there are substantial differences in the educational levels of the
adult populations of the three countries. In 1990, the proportion of the
population with secondary school education was 77.6 percent in
the United States, 63.0 percent in Canada, and only 54.5 percent in Australia. The proportion with university degrees was 21.3 percent in the
United States, 12.8 percent in Canada, and 9.7 percent in Australia.[5]

As educational institutions expand, the educational level of the entire
adult population lags behind that of its youngest cohorts. Despite a trend
toward U.S.-Canadian convergence in educational enrollments, a significant cross-national difference in the educational levels of the adult populations still exists because of the generational lag. This lag is demograph-
ically specific to older segments of the population, many of whom are
still in prime employment years. The impact of contemporary trends on
the overall distribution of skills in the workforce is felt immediately on
the youngest cohorts, but accumulates over time. In fact, the more rapid
the change, the greater the generational lag. So although Canadian educational attainment rates for young cohorts have moved toward convergence with U.S. rates, educational levels in the entire adult population of
Canada were still significantly below the American levels in 1980. And
while the gap had narrowed by 1990, convergence for the entire population still lies in the future. On the basis of changes in the Canadian educational system in the 1970s and 1980s, one might expect the distribution of
skills in Canada and the United States gradually to converge and to become equivalent by the year 2010 or 2020.

Generational lags in educational attainment rates are seen in Table 4.1
by examining the extent to which rising educational levels for the entire
adult population lag behind those of its youngest cohort. In the United
States, this generational lag was substantial during the period of most-
rapid educational growth, the 1960s and 1970s, which was also the time
of the famous 'generation gap' in politics. The generational lag in education declined in the 1980s as growth slowed and the better-educated
young people entered the adult population. For the United States, the
proportion of the population over age 25 having completed high school,
at 41.1 percent in 1960, lagged behind its youngest cohort by 20 percentage points. As the proportion completing high school increased to 52.3
percent in 1970, and to 66.5 percent in 1980, the lag remained close to 20

percent. Only in 1990, when the overall percentage increased still further to 77.6 percent, did the slower growth in the youngest cohort allow the lag to decline to 8 percent.

In the Canadian case, the expansion of secondary school education for the younger Canadian cohorts was slower in 1960. The overall high-school completion rate of 22.1 percent lagged behind the younger cohort by only 6 percent. However, while the overall completion rate rose to 52.6 percent in 1980, the rate for the young cohort had risen much faster, to 71.7 percent, creating a lag of 19 percent. This lag declined to 14 percent by 1990 but was still higher than the United States' 8 percent. Thus, the secondary school completion rates for the adult Canadian population are not only still catching up with the prevailing standard for the younger population, they have farther to go in this regard than is the case in the United States. Current Canadian young-adult completion rates are 90 percent of the U.S. rates for the young cohort in 1990, while overall Canadian completion rates are only 80 percent of the U.S. rates.

The same story can be told at the university level. During the period from 1960 to 1990, the proportion of the U.S. population with four years of university education or more increased from 7.7 percent to 21.3 percent. University completion rates for young cohorts had risen rapidly in the 1980s, so the lag for the general population of 3.4 percent in 1960 rose to 5.6 percent in 1970 and 5.9 percent in 1980. Then, because university completion rates for the young cohort leveled off, by 1990 the lag was reduced to only 1.9 percent.[6]

In the Canadian case, university degree completion for the adult population rose from 3.4 percent to 12.8 percent during the same period. There was virtually no generational lag in 1960 (when the young cohort figure was only 3.6 percent), but a lag of over 5 percent had emerged by 1980; by 1990 the lag declined only to just over 3 percent. Hence, the more rapid expansion of university degree attainment in Canada during this period—the cohort rate doubled in the 1960s and doubled again in the 1970s—has produced a situation in which the general population lags farther behind the young cohort in Canada than in the United States. By the same token, as generational replacement proceeds in the future, the university completion rates across the adult Canadian population can be expected to increase relative to the American.

The bottom line is that the underdevelopment of education in Canada, discussed by Porter and others as a reason for Canada's greater emphasis on immigrant selection, no longer applies, but it has its residue in the older Canadian age cohort. This cohort is in its prime earning years but is also being displaced rapidly in the contemporary world. This historical trend is an important force affecting immigration and the status of immigrants in Canada, as we shall see later.

For Australia, the general population also appears to be catching up to the younger cohorts, but at lower levels. This indicates that the present differences in educational attainment between Australia and North America are likely to prevail for some time. The secondary school completion rates for the total adult population—62.9 percent—are only 8.4 percent behind the young cohort. Thus, the generational lag is less than for Canada, and closer to what is found for the United States. Smaller changes in overall educational attainment numbers can be expected for Australia compared to Canada. At the university level, the Australian adult completion rate of 9.7 percent lags behind the young cohort by only 2.2 percent, less than for Canada but greater than for the United States. Australian educational levels are changing less rapidly than are Canadian levels and will not converge toward North American levels in the near future.

Cohort-Specific Cross-National Differences in Educational Levels

A more detailed cohort-specific comparison of educational levels across all age groups confirms that the Canada-U.S. differences are more prominent in the older age cohort, while Australia-U.S. differences span age cohorts to a greater degree. A Canada-U.S. comparison of adult age cohorts for 1973 is possible, based on surveys undertaken for the analysis of occupational mobility (see Wanner 1986, 52). The U.S. source is the 1973 "Occupational Change in a Generation Replicate Study" (Featherman and Hauser, 1978); for Canada it is the 1973 "Canadian Mobility Study" (Boyd et al. 1985). Mean years of education rose in both countries, but for the cohorts turning 25 between the 1930s and 1961, the Canada-U.S. difference remained between 1.2 years and 1.6 years (see Table 4.2). Educational levels grew more rapidly in Canada in the 1960s, however, so that for the group turning 25 in 1962–1966, the Canada-US difference declined to 0.8 years. For the cohort turning 25 in 1967–1971, the difference declined to only 0.2 years. Similarly, regarding the most highly educated (those with 16 or more years), for the cohorts turning 25 between the 1930s and 1961, the growth in both countries maintained about a two-to-one U.S. advantage. When we reach the cohort turning 25 in 1967–1971, however, the U.S. advantage had declined to only 17 percent.

The cohort-specific comparison can be made across all three countries in our urban labor force sample. It shows that even by 1980, the convergence of education in Canada and the United States has narrowed the educational disparity for the youngest cohorts, while the same did not happen in Australia. For the oldest cohorts, the Canadian population has educational levels closer to those of Australians; for the youngest cohorts, the Canadian population has educational levels closer to those of

TABLE 4.2 Comparison of Mean Years of Education for Men in the United States and Canada, by Age Cohort, 1973

Age in 1973	Year Turned 25	Mean Years of Education			Percent with 12 Years or More			Percent with 16 Years or More		
		United States	Canada	Differ-ence	United States	Canada	Difference Index[1]	United States	Canada	Difference Index[1]
62–66	1932–1936	10.2	8.6	1.6	42.1	18.0	2.75	11.2	4.7	2.46
57–61	1937–1941	10.8	9.5	1.3	52.8	26.9	2.40	11.6	5.5	2.17
52–56	1942–1946	11.3	9.8	1.5	61.7	29.1	2.79	13.1	6.7	2.03
47–51	1947–1951	11.7	10.1	1.6	64.4	29.9	2.91	17.9	7.9	2.40
42–46	1952–1956	11.9	10.6	1.3	68.8	36.1	2.60	20.1	10.5	2.02
37–41	1957–1961	12.2	11.0	1.2	73.0	36.9	2.84	22.9	12.5	1.95
32–36	1962–1966	12.5	11.7	0.8	77.5	48.3	2.26	22.4	16.4	1.37
27–31	1967–1971	12.8	12.6	0.2	82.6	62.0	1.81	24.3	21.1	1.17

[1]Index values may be interpreted as the relative probabilities of attaining the given level of education. An index value of 1.00 indicates no difference between the two countries. For a detailed description of the index, see Reitz (1977).

Source: Wanner (1986, Table 1, p. 54). U.S. data are from the 1973 Occupational Changes in a Generation Replicate Study, 1973 (N = 33,600 civilian men aged 20–64). Canadian data are from the 1973 Canadian Mobility Study, conducted by Statistics Canada as a supplement to a labor force survey (N = about 45,000 men and women; only men included here).

the Americans. In Table 4.3, comparative census data on educational levels are presented on a cohort-specific basis (and by gender), for 1980 and (in Canada and Australia) 1981, in our urban labor force sample. For the older age cohorts, among men the gap between the United States on the one hand, and Canada and Australia on the other, is between two and three years. Among young adult men, the gap for Canada narrows to about 1.5 years; for Australia the gap is reduced only slightly.

These data reinforce the point that educational standards have changed for Canada relative both to the United States and to Australia. Immigrants in the United States face the greatest obstacles in establishing their credentials on a competitive basis in the workplace. Immigrants to Canada face less competition. The younger cohort offers more competition at the entry level, but older workers at the peak of their earning years have less education and are less likely to be able to maintain a position of domination. On the other hand, the parameters of change are in place. A rapidly expanding population of credentialed workers will pose a greater challenge for immigrants, as the younger population gains ascendance in the occupational world. The same is less true in Australia, since the education gap with the United States has remained at a higher level there—over two years in the young adult population of 1981.

For women, labor force trends are somewhat different, owing to the selective effect of education in labor force participation. Cross-national trends in educational attainment apply to women, but these trends are not as salient in our labor force samples. Thus, the impact of changing educational levels on labor market processes in the three countries interact with forces affecting women's labor market participation.

The trend toward convergence of Canadian and U.S. native-born educational levels suggests that one source of higher entry-level earnings for immigrants in Canada may be fading. When the implications of current educational trends in Canada are fully played out, the entrance earnings of immigrants in the two countries will be more similar than has been the case in the past. By contrast, the fact that educational levels have remained lower in Australia suggests that the immigrants in Australia will continued to enjoy a comparative advantage.

Explaining Cross-National Differences in Education

What are the forces behind the more rapid rise in educational levels in the United States, compared to Canada and Australia? What is changing these relative educational levels? Research based on the human-capital perspective suggests that from an economic standpoint, Canada and Australia have underinvested in education (or perhaps the United States has overinvested). Since economic theory normally implies optimal investments, the

TABLE 4.3 Mean Years of Education of Native-Born Whites in the Urban Labor Force, by Age Cohort, Gender, and Country, ca. 1980

Gender Country	Age Cohort[1]						Intercohort Gain in Years of Education (25–34 Cohort over 50+ Cohort)
	25–34	(N)	35–49	(N)	50+	(N)	
Men							
United States	14.29	(32222)	13.82	(31782)	12.82	(24714)	1.47
Canada	12.73	(13083)	11.70	(11618)	10.68	(7641)	2.05
Australia	11.97	(1103)	10.98	(1010)	10.22	(706)	1.75
United States lead over Canada	1.56		2.12		2.14		
United States lead over Australia	2.32		2.84		2.60		
Women							
United States	14.06	(22655)	13.21	(21044)	12.45	(15846)	1.61
Canada	12.64	(9764)	11.39	(7797)	10.81	(4626)	1.83
Australia	11.74	(629)	10.62	(670)	10.24	(297)	1.50
United States lead over Canada	1.42		1.82		1.64		
United States lead over Australia	2.32		2.59		2.21		

[1]Persons under 25 were omitted from this analysis.

Sources: 1980 U.S. Census Public Use Microdata 5-Percent File; 1981 Canadian Census Public Use Sample Tape 2-Percent Individual File; 1981 Australian Census of Population and Housing 1-Percent File. For further details on these sources, see Chapter 1, note 14. For more specific definitions of origins used for each country, see Chapter 2, pp. 46–47 and notes 4–6.

research in effect suggests that differences in the aggregate investment in education in the three countries must have a noneconomic explanation— but it does not attempt to provide such an explanation.

Human-capital theory examines the decision to get an education as a purely economic calculation made by individuals. In these terms, individual investments in education are based on the value of education in labor markets. This value is set by employers who operate in competitive product markets. Employers are assumed to base wage offers on their own perceptions of the relevance of education to the economic productivity of job applicants. They pay a premium for education, based on the extra contributions that education makes to the production of salable products in a competitive marketplace.

In this analysis, educational upgrading reflects both changing occupational distributions and changing educational standards within occupations. The proportions of persons employed in professional or managerial occupations in the United States, Canada, and Australia have been rising for many years, and of course these are the occupations with the highest educational requirements (Bell 1973; Featherman and Hauser 1978, 48–52; Jones and Davis 1986, 20). At the same time, the standards of education in most occupations have been rising. Although there are few systematic studies of the link between education and the economic value of goods and services produced, Hunter (1988) and Hunter and Lieper (1993) have shown that increases in educational requirements are linked to increases in the complexity of work tasks. Daly (1986) has shown cross-nationally (comparing the United States with Britain) that a given industry is more productive in the country in which its workers are better educated. Educational expansion generally has been linked to increased economic productivity (Walters and Rubinson 1983). The human capital perspective suggests that the industrial and occupational structure determine the educational requirements of work, because they set the technological foundation for production, including the relevance of individual worker skills. Increased educational requirements reflect increases in the technical complexity of work and the increased relevance of education to the competent and productive performance of work tasks.

This human capital analysis points to two alternative scenarios related to higher levels of education in the United States and to differences in patterns of change over time. In one, education has had more economic value to employers in the United States, because of a closer relation to production. The additional time and money invested in education there would be explained by the fact that education paid off more for individual workers and for their employers. Substantial upgrading of educational standards in Canada or Australia to the U.S. level could reflect rapid economic change. In a second scenario, education has been equally relevant to economic production in the United States, Canada, and Australia, but either the latter countries have been underinvesting in education for reasons exogenous to the economy or Canada may be overinvesting now. Available data support the underinvestment analysis for both Canada and Australia. Canadian and Australian underinvestment in education can be seen in comparative studies showing that the marginal return to education has been higher there than in the United States, and higher than necessary to motivate investment. This would imply that the Canadian and Australian economies are similar to the U.S. economy in terms of the productivity relevance of education, and that increases in the educational levels of workers in Canada and Australia would yield significant income benefits. In 1959, in the United States, the social rate of return, or in other words, the pre-tax earnings yield to individuals, taking account of income foregone while education is undertaken, in relation to the total cost of education and related expenses (see Hicks 1987, 104) was 10.1 percent for secondary education and 11.3 percent for postsecondary education (Psacharopoulos 1985, 600). The latter figure just barely exceeds the standard for advanced industrial societies (see Psacharopoulos 1981, 1985). In Canada, in 1961, the corresponding figures were 11.7 percent and 14.0 percent (Psacharopoulos 1985, 599). Thus, secondary education yielded returns which were 1.3 percent higher in Canada than in the United States, and postsecondary education yielded returns of 2.7 percent more in Canada than in the United States (see also Dooley 1985, 1986).[7] Hicks (1987, 104) presented data suggesting that in 1960, Canada suffered 8.1 percent lower per capita income because of a lower standard of educational attainment (see Krueger, 1968, for further details). There also has been a pent-up demand for education in Australia, not met by the publicly-funded educational system. The social returns to higher education in Australia in 1976 were still 16.3 percent. This is a full 5.0 percent higher than in the United States in 1959, and 2.3 percent higher even than in Canada in 1961.[8]

Instead of considering Canadian or Australian underinvestment in education, many have worried about the possibility that Americans have been "overeducated" (Freeman 1976), or have overinvested in education for various social or cultural reasons unrelated to economic production. After all, increases in educational standards have occurred within all occupational groups, even for unskilled occupations. In fact, in the United States, the increase in mean years of education between 1962 and 1973 for laborers was 1.81 years, from 7.98 to 9.79, which was actually greater than the increase in mean years of education for self-employed professionals, 0.34 years, from 15.55 to 15.89 years (Featherman and Hauser 1978, 26). As Shockey (1989) and Bills (1992) have shown, although there are many overeducated individuals in the United States, those individuals still have higher earnings. But these earnings advantages seem less than in Canada or Australia.

A number of explanations for the American emphasis on education have been offered, exogenous to economic explanations. One argument is that high levels of education in the United States arise from its emphasis on individualism and a consequent national obsession with mobility and achievement (Lipset 1989). Education symbolizes individual progress toward a social ideal of upward mobility, and rising standards of living. As the size of the middle class expands, the more ambitious the population, and the greater the emphasis on competition and individual success, the greater the educational attainment. Cultural determination of human capital investment is readily recognized in the case of certain minority groups (Jews, for example, or certain Asian groups). Such an orientation toward education also may characterize a society as a whole, affecting its perceptions of the social or economic value of education.

Credentialism is another exogenous explanation for educational expansion. This term refers to the use of education as a job qualification when in fact the education is technically unnecessary (Berg 1971). Collins's analysis in *The Credential Society* (1979) pointed out that credentialism emerged in part as a response to ethnic and racial diversity, and served to reinforce group boundaries. Collins argued that as ethnic diversity in the United States reached a peak just before World War I, the Anglo-Protestant elite response included the development and expansion of the importance of education not only to Americanize immigrants but to reinforce a "contest-mobility" system (1979, 102). Later, as Blacks succeeded in increasing rates of high school completion, Whites found that to secure high-status jobs required more advanced education. "Easier passage through lower or intermediate levels of the educational system has had the aggregate effect of devaluing those levels of the credential currency and mounting pressures for yet higher levels of attainment" (p. 130). So in a credentialist society, rising educational levels may serve to maintain group inequality.

Others have suggested as well the possibility that education might affect hiring because of organizational factors not directly related to production, such as its impact in legitimating authority or ensuring compliance from lower-status workers (Wright 1979, Bowles and Gintis 1986). Black and Myles's (1986) comparative study suggested the possibility that this factor may play a greater role in management in the United States than in other countries. Education could be perceived as related to social skills required in the exercise of authority (Holzer 1996). If social capital in the United States has declined (Putnam 1993), higher levels of human capital may be required, to offset the potential negative effects.

Another approach is to ask, Why would Canada and Australia underinvest in education? Porter's theory pointed to a colonialist Anglo dominance, and Birrell and Birrell (1987) pointed out that Australian decision-makers demurred from the radical changes that would have been involved. Given the major role of government in postsecondary education in those countries, the exogenous factors would be filtered through political decisionmaking. Because Canadian and Australian universities are public, the expansion of university education has been largely a social and political decision which only indirectly reflects economics and which may respond to many other factors. According to Pike (1988), the expansion of education in Canada was occasioned not only by its economic value but also in part by the proximity of the United States, the impact of U.S. labor markets in Canada, and the U.S. cultural influence in Canada. In effect, Canada was forced to align its labor market forces with those in the United States. Pike also suggested that the growing nationalism in Canada in fact demanded that jobs requiring high skills be filled by Canadians and not by immigrants. Perhaps the focus of colonial status, Porter's point, was shifting. Perhaps the colonialism that Porter had suggested was at the root of the use of immigrants in high-skill jobs was beginning to abate.

In Australia, the political pressure to develop domestic educational institutions was not enhanced by the close proximity of a dominant power such as the United States. While some attribute the expansion of education in Australia at least in part to U.S. influence (Gross and Western 1981, 1), the slower expansion of the Australian educational system may have been occasioned in part by its isolation from other sources of social pressure for advanced education. The same explanation may have relevance for Québec, which is more isolated from U.S. labor markets than are other parts of Canada.

Recent rapid expansion of postsecondary education in Canada seems to have lowered the earnings advantages of those with such education, compared to their counterparts in the United States. Freeman and Needels (1993) showed in an analysis of males between the ages of 25 and 64 that the ratio of college graduates to men with high-school training rose more rapidly in Canada during 1979 to 1987 than in the United States. Their time-series analysis for this period points to this trend as the most significant cause of the more modest rise in college/high-school earnings differentials in Canada compared to the United States. So perhaps Canada is no longer underinvesting. In fact, by the mid-1980s, analysts had begun referring to the "overeducated Canadian" (Dooley 1985, 1986); there seem to have been fewer references, however, to an overeducated Australian.

It seems clear that the educational levels of the native born are a powerful independent force in labor markets, that they have an enormous impact on earnings in all three countries, and that their impact may vary for economic and other reasons. Hence, our analysis treats education as an autonomous institutional force and examines the impact of educational levels on the earnings of the native born and immigrants as potentially differing from one country to another.

Impact of Native-Born Education
on Immigrant Entry-Level Earnings

Higher native-born educational levels in the United States in 1980 increased the skills gap for all immigrants, regardless of origins. In Table 4.4, the mean educational levels of recent immigrants in the urban labor force (from Table 3.5) can be compared to educational levels of the native-born White workforce[9] for each country, on an origins- and gender-specific basis. Consider immigrants from Europe. European immigrants to the United States from every national origin category are generally better educated than their counterparts in Canada or Australia, but they experience a greater skills gap with native-born Whites. This gap for immigrants arriving in the United States during the 1970s was 0.90 years for men and 1.28 years for women. This can be compared to 0.22 years for men in Canada and 0.72 years for women; and to 0.53 years for men in Australia and 0.67 for women. Looked at differently, if White Canadian native-born workers had the U.S. standard of education but the same European immigrants, the skills gap for this immigrant group in Canada would have been 1.84 years for men, twice as high as in the United States, and 2.01 years for women. Similarly, if White, native-born Australians had the U.S. standard of education, but the same White immigrants, the skills gap would have been 2.75 years for men, over three times higher than in the United States, and 2.67 years for women. So for White immigrants, the larger skills gap in the United States is entirely due to the higher native-born educational levels, not to lower immigrant skills.

Similar comparisons apply to non-European immigrant groups. Cross-national differences in skills gaps for Black and Chinese immigrant men are illustrated in Figure 4.1. Black immigrant men in the United States have lower skills than the native-born White workforce, by 1.27 years. By striking contrast, Black immigrants in Canada are actually slightly better educated than the native-born White workforce. If Canada had the U.S. standard of education for the native-born Whites, but the same Black immigrants, those immigrants would have confronted a major skills gap in Canada, 1.55 years, significantly higher than the one faced by Black immigrants in the United States. Similarly, Black immigrant women in the United States, despite being better educated than their counterparts in Canada, experience a greater skills gap of 1.45 years of education in the United States.

TABLE 4.4 Comparison of Mean Years of Education for Native-Born and Recent Immigrant Groups,[1] by Host Country, Origins, and Gender, ca. 1980

A. Men

Origins	United States		Canada			Australia		
	Mean Years of Education	Relative to Native White	Mean Years of Education	Relative to Native White	Relative to U.S. Native White	Mean Years of Education	Relative to Native White	Relative to U.S. Native White
Native-born White	13.49[2]		11.87			11.27		
Immigrants, total	11.50	-1.99						
White, total	12.59	-0.90	12.27	0.40	-1.22	10.93	-0.34	-2.56
United Kingdom	14.77	1.28	11.65	-0.22	-1.84	10.74	-0.53	-2.75
North, West Europe	14.94	1.45	12.74	0.87	-0.74	10.35	-0.92	-3.14
East Europe	13.17	-0.32	13.43	1.56	-0.06	10.69	-0.58	-2.80
South Europe	9.63	-3.86	13.14	1.27	-0.35	11.57	0.30	-1.92
Black, total	12.22	-1.27	8.66	-3.21	-4.83	9.46	-1.81	-4.03
Asian, total	14.38	0.89	11.94	0.07	-1.55	–	–	–
Chinese	13.19	-0.30	13.00	1.13	-0.49	11.98	0.71	-1.51
Filipino	14.50	1.01	12.68	0.81	-0.81	11.51	0.24	-1.98
Indian	16.21	2.72	–	–	–	–	–	–
Korean	14.41	0.92	–	–	–	–	–	–
Vietnamese	13.08	-0.41	–	–	–	–	–	–
Japanese	15.23	1.74	–	–	–	–	–	–
Other Asian	13.67	0.18	–	–	–	–	–	–
Hispanic, total	8.68	-4.81	13.18	1.31	-0.31	12.12	0.85	-1.37
Mexican	7.42	-6.07	12.05	0.18	-1.44	9.82	-1.45	-3.67
Cuban	10.75	-2.74	–	–	–	–	–	–
Other Latin American	10.80	-2.69	12.05	0.18	-1.44	9.82	-1.45	-3.67

(continues)

TABLE 4.4 (continued)

B. Women

Origins	United States Mean Years of Education	United States Relative to Native White	Canada Mean Years of Education	Canada Relative to Native White	Canada Relative to U.S. Native White	Australia Mean Years of Education	Australia Relative to Native White	Australia Relative to U.S. Native White
Native-born White	13.22³		11.93			11.22		
Immigrants, total	11.43	-1.79	11.44	-0.49	-1.29	10.73	-0.49	-2.00
White, total	11.94	-1.28	11.21	-0.72	-2.01	10.55	-0.67	-2.67
United Kingdom	13.48	0.26	12.37	0.44	-0.85	10.28	-0.94	-2.94
North, West Europe	13.84	0.62	12.55	0.62	-0.67	10.60	-0.62	-2.62
East Europe	12.44	-0.78	12.65	0.72	-0.57	11.03	-0.19	-2.19
South Europe	8.40	-4.82	8.02	-3.91	-5.17	8.75	-2.47	-4.47
Black, total	11.77	-1.45	11.21	-0.72	-2.01	–	–	–
Asian, total	13.25	0.03	12.27	0.34	-0.95	11.63	0.41	-1.59
Chinese	11.95	-1.27	11.48	-0.45	-1.74	10.47	-0.75	-2.75
Filipino	14.61	1.39	–	–	–	–	–	–
Indian	14.48	1.26	–	–	–	–	–	–
Korean	12.53	-0.69	–	–	–	–	–	–
Vietnamese	11.81	-1.41	–	–	–	–	–	–
Japanese	13.41	0.19	–	–	–	–	–	–
Other Asian	12.09	-1.13	12.84	0.91	-0.38	11.96	0.74	-1.26
Hispanic, total	9.04	-4.18	11.44	-0.49	-1.76	9.56	-1.66	-3.66
Mexican	7.58	-5.64	–	–	–	–	–	–
Cuban	11.01	-2.21	–	–	–	–	–	–
Other Latin American	10.11	-3.11	11.44	-0.49	-1.76	9.56	-1.66	-3.66

¹Data for recent immigrant groups from Table 3.5.

²Mean education for native-born Black men: 12.05; mean education for all native-born men: 13.24.

³Mean education for native-born Black women: 12.57; mean education for all native-born women: 13.07.

Sources: See Table 4.3.

FIGURE 4.1   Education, Native-Born Whites and Recent Immigrants, Men, ca. 1980

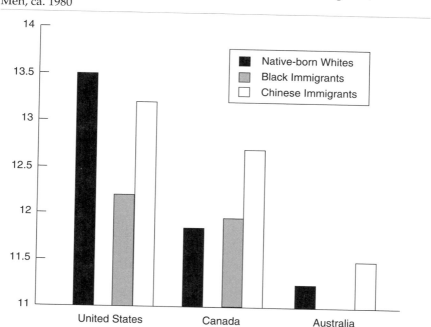

Source: Table 4.1

The same holds true for Chinese immigrants and for Asian immigrants, in general. If the Canadian and Australian native-born White workforce were as highly educated as the American, there would have been a skills gap for Chinese immigrants in those countries, and it would have been larger than the one faced by Chinese immigrants in the United States. For both men and women, the gap would have been larger by 0.5 years in Canada, and by 1.5 years in Australia.

The only real exception to this general pattern is for the Hispanic immigrant groups, which cannot be directly compared across countries. Mexicans and Cubans do not migrate in substantial numbers to either Canada or Australia, and the other Latin American origins are dissimilar in the three countries. For all origins which can be directly compared, the higher skills gap for immigrants in the United States is shown to be entirely a function of higher educational standards for the native born.

Earnings Determination Equations for Each Country

It is conventional to analyze the earnings effects of the immigrant skills gap by means of regression equations, with human capital variables entered along with immigrant origins. The usual procedure is to focus attention on the extent to which immigrant disadvantage arises from human capital deficits compared to the native born. Here, attention is given to the human capital of the native born as a variable. There is no formal difference in the earnings determination equations, however, specified as Equations 4.1 and 4.2.[10] Estimates for two basic equations, the first (4.1) with only immigrant origins entered, and the second (4.2) with human capital variables including education, work experience, hours worked, and language knowledge,[11] are provided for men and women in our urban census samples for each country in Table 4.5. The regression effects are expressed as proportions of mean White male earnings, both for men and for women.[12]

Coefficients in the first equation reflect essentially the same entry-level earnings data presented in Chapter 2, in Tables 2.1 and 2.2, but here they set up the human capital regressions to follow. In the United States, the average earnings of Black immigrant men, $8633 below the earnings of the White, native-born urban workforce, represent a deficiency of 46 percent. (Table 2.1 showed that Black immigrant men earned 54 percent of the earnings of the native-born White benchmark.) Black immigrant women earn $1600 less than native-born White women, which represents a deficiency of 18 percent. (Table 2.1 showed that Black immigrant women earn 82 percent of what native-born White non-Hispanic women earn.) The figures for women are consistently compared to the male benchmark. The $1600 deficiency for Black immigrant women compared to native-born White women becomes a deficiency of $11,300 when compared to the White male benchmark. Recent Black immigrant women earn 61 percent less than native-born White males. (Table 2.1 reported their mean earnings as 39 percent of native-born White males.) Table 4.5 shows how earnings for immigrant groups in Canada and Australia are higher than for their U.S. counterparts, again repeating in a different form the information in Table 2.2.

Results for the second equation (4.2) include the measured effects of the six human capital variables listed. These results correspond roughly to Borjas's (1988, 48) comparable analyses of the same data at the national level.[13] Years of education have been standardized to represent differences from the mean, so the coefficients show how earnings vary with education at about the mean value. At the mean, education has stronger effects in Canada and Australia than in the United States. In the United States, at the mean, each year of education boosts male earnings by $1440, or about 7.7 percent of mainstream mean earnings. The effect of an additional year of education has been higher (in proportional terms) in Canada than in the United States, at 8.5 percent, and higher in Australia than in either country, at 9.2 percent.[14] The non-zero coefficient for educa-

TABLE 4.5 Regression Effects[1] of Immigrant Origins on Entry-Level Earnings, for Recent Immigrants in Urban Labor Force, by Gender and Host Country, Overall (Eq. 4.1) and with Human Capital Controls (Eq. 4.2), ca. 1980

	United States		Canada		Australia	
	a_i/K (Eq. 4.1)[2]	a'_i/K (Eq. 4.2)	a_i/K (Eq. 4.1)	a'_i/K (Eq. 4.2)	a_i/K (Eq. 4.1)	a'_i/K (Eq. 4.2)
Men						
Intercept K (Native-born Whites)	$18,646	–	$18,752	–	$14,140	–
Immmigrant Origins						
White	–0.1003	–0.0731	–0.0044	–0.0868	–0.0023	+0.0129
Black	–0.4630	–0.3312	–0.3028	–0.3483	–	–
Chinese	–0.3748	–0.3313	–0.2295	–0.2905	–0.2781	–0.2250
Filipino	–0.3223	–0.3683	–	–	–	–
Asian Indian	–0.1029	–0.2973	–	–	–	–
Korean	–0.2222	–0.3293	–	–	–	–
Vietnamese	–0.4537	–0.3091	–	–	–	–
Japanese	+0.2381	+0.1071	–	–	–	–
Other Asian	–0.3552	–0.2878	–0.2470	–0.3585	–0.1297	–0.1388
Mexican	–0.5384	–0.1146	–	–	–	–
Cuban	–0.3937	–0.2329	–	–	–	–
Other Latin American	–0.4473	–0.2237	–0.2898	–0.3209	–0.1871	–0.0853
Human Capital						
Education, Years[3]	–	0.0772	–	0.0852	–	0.0921
Education, Yrs. Sq.	–	0.0036	–	0.0044	–	0.0006
Experience, Years	–	0.0636	–	0.0733	–	0.0541
Experience, Yrs. Sq.	–	–0.0010	–	–0.0012	–	–0.0009
Hours	–	0.0068	–	0.0064	–	0.0096
Language Knowledge (Yes/No)	–	0.1335	–	0.1229	–	0.1242
(N)	(167274)		(48238)		(5324)	
Women[4]						
Intercept (Native-born Whites)	$8,946	–	$10,582	–	$9,058	–
Immigrant Origins						
White	–0.5646	–0.5463	–0.4953	–0.5249	–0.3554	–0.3612
Black	–0.6060	–0.5631	–0.5445	–0.5366	–	–
Chinese	–0.6033	–0.5969	–0.5142	–0.5557	–0.4318	–0.4202
Filipino	–0.4364	–0.5366	–	–	–	–
Asian Indian	–0.4661	–0.5375	–	–	–	–
Korean	–0.5660	–0.5750	–	–	–	–
Vietnamese	–0.6149	–0.5799	–	–	–	–
Japanese	–0.5777	–0.5951	–	–	–	–
Other Asian	–0.5824	–0.5720	–0.5279	–0.6104	–0.3400	–0.3956
Mexican	–0.7003	–0.5587	–	–	–	–
Cuban	–0.6457	–0.6011	–	–	–	–
Other Latin American	–0.6728	–0.5893	–0.5802	–0.6090	–0.4165	–0.4347

(*continues*)

TABLE 4.5   *(continued)*

	United States		Canada		Australia	
	a_i/K	a'_i/K	a_i/K	a'_i/K	a_i/K	a'_i/K
	$(Eq.\ 4.1)^2$	*(Eq. 4.2)*	*(Eq. 4.1)*	*(Eq. 4.2)*	*(Eq. 4.1)*	*(Eq. 4.2)*
Women (continued)						
Human Capital						
Education, Years	–	0.0381	–	0.0518	–	0.0547
Education, Yrs. Sq.	–	0.0024	–	0.0027	–	0.0007
Experience, Years	–	0.0164	–	0.0302	–	0.0233
Experience, Yrs. Sq.	–	–0.0003	–	–0.0005	–	–0.0004
Hours	–	0.0079	–	0.0070	–	0.0129
Language Knowledge (Yes/No)	–	0.0408	–	0.0231	–	0.0643
(N)	(115744)		(36062)		(3441)	

[1]Regression effects expressed as proportions of mean earnings for native-born White men represented by the intercept K; see note 10 in text. Earnings data for each country are in the respective national currencies.

[2]For specification of the regression equations, see note 10 in this chapter.

[3]Education is measured as a deviation from the mean.

[4]For men and women, the coefficients are estimated in gender-specific equations but are expressed here as a proportion of the mean earnings for men, K.

Sources: See Table 4.3.

tion-squared in the United States means that the effect of education is greater above the mean and less below the mean. At one year above the mean, each year of education boosts earnings by $1574, while at one year below the mean, each year of education boosts earnings by $1305. For women, all human capital endowments have substantially smaller impacts on earnings, but cross-national differences in the impact of education remain. Of work-related human capital measures, only hours worked matters more for women, a fact which perhaps is as significant a measure of female disadvantage as the lower increments for other human capital endowments.

For most immigrant-origin comparisons, cross-national differences in the earnings coefficients are much smaller after taking account of human capital. This indicates that cross-national differences in the skills gap are a very large part of the differences in entry-level earnings. Consider the comparison of Black immigrants in the United States and Canada. In 1980, the entry-level status of recent Black immigrant men in the United States was 16 percent lower than in Canada, but after taking account of human capital, the relative earnings of black immigrants were virtually the same in the two countries. Hence, virtually all of the cross-national difference in entry levels for Black immigrant men is due to the difference in the human capital gap. For Black immigrant women, entry-level earnings are higher in Canada by 6 percent, but when human capital is taken into account, the difference in relative earnings becomes 3 percent. So about half of the higher earnings of Black immigrant women in Canada are human-capital related.

To see the impact of differences related specifically to the education gap, it is necessary to examine regression coefficients for education. In the United States, a year of education at the mean level increases earnings by 7.72 percent. The education gap for Black immigrant men of about 1.3 years, therefore, can be estimated to generate an earnings gap of about 10 percent of native-born male earnings (about $1900 in 1980). In Canada, there is no Black immigrant education gap for men, so none of the disadvantage of Black male immigrants can be attributed to this source. Hence, of the 16 percent lower entrance earnings for Black male immigrants in the United States, about two-thirds, 10 percent, can be attributed to the greater education gap.

For Black immigrant women, a comparable situation exists. In the United States, a year of education at the mean level increases women's earnings by 3.81 percent. The education gap for Black immigrant women of about 1.4 years is therefore estimated to generate an earnings gap of about 5.5 percent of native-born male earnings. In Canada, the Black immigrant women's education gap was only 0.7 years, which at Canadian rates would lower earnings by 3.6 percent, or 1.9 percent lower than in the United States. So of the approximately 6 percent lower entrance earnings for Black immigrant women in the United States, about one-third (32 percent) can be attributed to the greater education gap. There is a smaller cross-national difference in the education gap, accounting for a smaller part of the difference in entry-level earnings.

The comparisons for recent Chinese immigrants include Australia. For men, the origins coefficients show smaller differences after taking account of human capital, again implying the extent to which differences in the human capital gap help explain differences in entry-level earnings. However, for Chinese immigrant women, the human capital gap varies less in the cross-national comparison, and in the regression results it can be seen that it is responsible for less cross-national difference in entry-level earnings (more of the Canada-U.S. difference than the Australia-U.S. difference).

Generally, for immigrant women, the size of the impact of human capital differentials is less than for men, because human capital matters less in the determination of earnings for women. It is also important to note that in many cases, significant penalties for immigrant status still remain, despite the low levels of earnings among women in general and immigrant women in particular. There are significantly negative impacts of immigrant minority status for Black, Chinese, Korean, Vietnamese, Mexican, Cuban, and other Latin American women.

Cross-National Earnings Decomposition

Next we repeat the cross-national comparisons, this time focusing attention on the impact that differences in native-born White educational levels have on immigrant earnings in each country. A more explicit and direct method of measuring the impact of cross-national differences in native-born educational levels on immigrant earnings can be provided by means of an earnings decomposition. The earnings decomposition method developed by Oaxaca (1973) is be applied here to answer two parallel questions based on regression results. First, what would be the entry-level earnings of immigrants in Canada and Australia if their native-born workforces were as highly educated as the U.S. native workforce?[15] And, reversing the logic, what would be the entry-level earnings of immigrants in the United States if the mainstream U.S. workforce had lower educational levels, comparable to those of Canadian or Australian native-born workers? To answer these questions, we will calculate the expected earnings of the native-born Whites in one country, assuming educational levels prevailing in another. This estimation will be based on earnings determination estimated separately for the native-born Whites.[16]

Table 4.6 presents cross-national comparisons of the entry-level earnings of selected immigrant origin groups, based on this assumption of equivalent native-born White male educational levels. Baseline entrance earnings data for the selected groups (from Table 2.2 and Table 4.5) are presented in the first three left-hand columns in Table 4.6. These figures compare the entrance earnings of selected immigrant origin groups in the United States (first column) with those of the same group in Canada (second column, top half of table) and in Australia (second column, bottom half of table). The signs in the third, "difference" column, all negative, indicate the extent to which proportional earnings of the group are lower in the United States than in Canada and Australia.

What the comparisons would look like if educational levels of U.S. native-born White males were adjusted to Canadian or Australian levels can be seen in the middle three columns of Table 4.6 (both panels). The assumption underlying this particular estimation is that educational levels for U.S. workers continue to be translated into earnings in the same way after adjustment to Canadian levels. In the U.S. earnings equation for the native-born benchmark group, Canadian and Australian educational levels are substituted for the U.S. level (see note 1 to Table 4.6). The position of all immigrant groups in the United States is relatively improved by this downgrading of native-born educational levels. Cross-national differences are all much less. While the figures in the difference column are almost all still negative, indicating greater inequality in the United States, the scale of the differences is substantially reduced.

TABLE 4.6 Estimated Effects of Native-Born Education on Cross-national Differences in the Entry-Level Earnings of Immigrants in Urban Labor Force, by Origins and Gender, ca. 1980

U.S.-Canadian Comparison

Origins and Gender	Relative Mean Earnings (Observed: Tables 2.2, 4.5)			Estimate for U.S. Native-Born Men with Canadian Native-Born Education[1]			Estimate for Canadian Native-Born Men with U.S. Native-Born Education[2]		
	United States	Canada	Difference	United States	Canada	Difference	United States	Canada	Difference
Men									
White	0.90	1.00	−0.10	1.03	1.00	+0.03	0.90	0.87	+0.03
Chinese	0.63	0.77	−0.14	0.72	0.77	−0.05	0.63	0.67	−0.04
Other Latin American	0.55	0.71	−0.16	0.63	0.71	−0.08	0.55	0.62	−0.07
Black	0.54	0.70	−0.16	0.61	0.70	−0.09	0.54	0.61	−0.07
Women									
White	0.44	0.50	−0.06	0.50	0.50	0.00	0.44	0.43	+0.01
Chinese	0.40	0.48	−0.08	0.45	0.48	−0.03	0.40	0.42	−0.02
Other Latin American	0.33	0.42	−0.09	0.37	0.42	−0.05	0.33	0.37	−0.04
Black	0.39	0.46	−0.07	0.44	0.46	−0.02	0.39	0.40	−0.01

(continues)

TABLE 4.6 (continued)

U.S.-Australian Comparison

Origins and Gender	Relative Mean Earnings (Observed: Tables 2.2, 4.5)			Estimate for U.S. Native-Born Women with Australian Native-Born Education[3]			Estimate for Australian Native-Born Women with U.S. Native-Born Education[4]		
	United States	Australia	Difference	United States	Australia	Difference	United States	Australia	Difference
Men									
White	0.90	1.00	-0.10	1.09	1.00	+0.09	0.90	0.82	+0.08
Asian	0.75	0.84	-0.09	0.91	0.84	+0.07	0.75	0.69	+0.06
Women									
White	0.44	0.65	-0.21	0.53	0.65	-0.12	0.44	0.53	-0.11
Asian	0.48	0.64	-0.16	0.58	0.64	-0.06	0.48	0.52	-0.04

[1]Native-born White White Canadian men have a mean education of 11.87 years compared to 13.49 years for U.S. native-born non-Hispanic White men. When this Canadian figure (and the mean of education squared, 149.92) is substituted into the earnings equation for U.S. non-Hispanic White men ($Y = -285.1(ED) + 68.0(ED^2) + 1201.1(EXP) - 19.6(EXP^2) + 128.0(HOURS) - 6962.0$), U.S. benchmark earnings are predicted to decline from $18,646 to $16,364, 87.8 percent of the former figure.

[2]When the educational level of U.S. native-born non-Hispanic White men (and the mean of years of education squared, 190.49) is substituted into the corresponding Canadian earnings equation ($Y = -331.4(ED) + 83.88(ED^2) + 1408.1(EXP) - 23.0 (EXP^2) + 121.3(HOURS) - 7515.7$), the earnings of native-born White Canadian men are predicted to rise from $18,752 to $21,600, up 15.2 percent.

[3]Native-born White Australian men have a mean education of 11.27 years. When this figure (and the mean years of education squared, 133.37) is substituted into the earnings equation for U.S. non-Hispanic White men (see note 1), U.S. benchmark earnings are predicted to decline from $18,646 to $15,409, the latter being 82.6 percent of the former figure.

[4]When the educational level of U.S. native-born non-Hispanic White men is substituted into the earnings equation for Australian native-born White men ($Y = 1660.0(ED) - 9.6(ED^2) + 782.4(EXP) - 13.0(EXP^2) + 133.3(HOURS) - 15519$), the earnings are predicted to rise from $14,139 to $17,280, up 22.2 percent.

Consider first how the U.S.-Canadian comparison is affected. In most cases, the estimates show that half or more of the lower entry-level earnings of these immigrants in the United States is a result of the higher educational level of the native-born U.S. benchmark group. All immigrant minorities are affected, but the higher the entrance earnings of the immigrant group, the greater the proportional impact of lowering native-born education to Canadian levels. For White immigrants, lowering native-born education explains virtually all of the U.S.-Canadian difference in entrance earnings. White immigrants enter at 90 percent of native-born earnings in the United States, and at levels equal to native-born earnings in Canada. Since adjusting U.S. native-born educational levels downward to the Canadian standard completely offsets the native-born advantage in the United States, virtually no cross-national difference remains.

The situation is somewhat different for minority group immigrants, whose observed entry earnings are lower. In those cases, entrance earnings are still lower in the United States after adjustment. For example, the before-adjustment (observed) entrance earnings of recent Chinese immigrant men in the United States is 14 percent below that of their counterparts in Canada. After adjusting the U.S. native-born White educational level to the lower Canadian standard, we find that the entrance earnings of Chinese men in the United States are higher but are still 5 percent below what they are in Canada. Hence, the higher education of native-born White men in the United States accounts for about two-thirds of the cross-national difference in entry-level earnings for Chinese men. In the case of Black immigrants, the observed entrance earnings in the United States are 16 percent below those of Black immigrants in Canada but only 9 percent lower after the U.S. native-born White educational level is adjusted downward to the Canadian standard.

For the analysis of immigrant women, we still use the native-born White male benchmark. The 8 percent lower entrance earnings of Chinese immigrant women in the United States are only 3 percent lower after adjustments. The 7 percent lower entrance earnings of Black immigrant women in the United States are only 2 percent lower after adjustments.

In the final right-hand three columns of Table 4.6, the adjustment is reversed: Canadian native-born White male educational levels are assumed to rise to U.S. levels, with earnings implications assumed this time to be determined by the existing Canadian earnings equations (see note 2 to Table 4.6). The impact of this adjustment is to lower the entrance earnings of immigrant groups in Canada, shown in the second of the three columns, leaving a residual difference with the United States, shown in the third column. This adjustment produces estimates which are virtually the same as the previous ones, despite the cross-national difference in the earnings equations. Clearly the estimates are not highly sensitive to variations in the earnings impact of education such as exist between the two countries.[17]

The estimated impact of native-born education is somewhat different in the U.S.-Australian comparison, for two reasons. First, the difference in native-born education is greater, so the adjustment alters the comparison more significantly. Adjusting native-born U.S. educational levels down to Australian levels would so reduce native-born earnings that the entry-level earnings of both White and Asian immigrant males actually would be higher in the United States than in Australia (reflected in the fact that the difference figures are positive for men). The cross-national differences are reversed. The second reason for the difference affects women, and is related to the lower earnings position of women in general in the United States compared to Australian standards. For Asians, the entrance statuses of immigrant women in the United States are 16 percent lower than in Australia; for Whites, the difference is 21 percent. The adjustment for the impact of native-born education offsets only about half of this cross-national difference. A substantially higher entrance status for immigrant women in Australia exists even after the adjustments. Again, as with Canada, the reversed logic considering the comparison with Australian native-born males having the U.S. levels of education leads to roughly the same result.

In sum, the higher average educational level of mainstream white men in the United States accounts for up to one-half or more of the lower entry-level earnings of immigrant groups in the United States compared to the status of the same immigrant groups in Canada or Australia. This substantial effect deserves serious attention, given the absolute and relative changes in native-born educational levels in the three countries. The importance of these changes is underscored in the concluding chapter, Chapter 7.

'Education Cities,' Immigrant Concentrations, and Skills Polarization

An important aspect of the cross-national variations in native-born educational levels are the interurban variations *within* countries. U.S. cities are highly diverse in this regard. The best-educated members of the U.S. workforce tend to be more heavily concentrated in certain urban areas than in others. Canada also has a degree of urban variability in native-born education, but in Australia there is virtually none. There is, in short, cross-national variation in the extent of interurban variation. How do interurban variations in native-born educational levels affect immigrant entry-level earnings, and what is the bearing of these interurban patterns on cross-national differences?

This section of the chapter describes interurban variations in native-born White educational levels, and shows that because immigrants tend to be concentrated within the 'education cities,' particularly in the United States, and because these immigrant concentrations tend to have a *negative* impact on immigrant educational levels, as was seen in Chapter 3, there is *an immigrant skills polarization* which produces low entrance status for immigrants in such cities. The analysis considers the implications of these patterns, and why they may be different from what is seen in Canada and especially Australia.

Interurban Variations in Native-Born Educational Levels

Table 4.7 lists, for the largest urban areas of the three countries, the mean years of education for native-born White men.[18] In the United States, the range of variation is very wide, from a high of nearly 15 years in Washington, D.C., to 14 years in New York and several cities in California, down to 13.5 years in heartland cities like Chicago, Minneapolis-St. Paul, Atlanta, and Houston, and only 13 years or less in Cleveland, St. Louis, Detroit, Cincinnati, Pittsburgh, and Baltimore.

Obviously, these variations are related in part to the occupational and industrial mix in each urban area. What might be called 'education cities' tend to be the headquarters and nerve centers of major sectors of societal activity. Washington is the capital of politics, New York of business and finance; both have heavily bureaucratic workplaces. Places like the Bay Area, Orange County, and Boston are capitals of high-tech industry, education, and medicine. By contrast, those cities at the opposite extreme represent centers of implementation rather than innovation, of production rather than planning. Noyelle and Stanback (1983) identified a complex urban typology in the United States, distinguishing city specialties even within the general categories of manufacturing, service, and consumer-oriented cities. This typology affects the skills composition of the population. Work in these areas typically requires less formal education.

The link between occupational structure and educational levels can be measured by the correlation coefficient between the proportion of the workforce engaged in professional or managerial occupations, and the mean years of education of the workforce. This coefficient is a huge r=0.79. Occupational structure measured in this simple way explains nearly two-thirds of the variation in educational levels of the native-born workforce (R^2=0.62). The managerial-professional sector in Washington is the largest in the United States, 38.6 percent of the workforce. Several other cities have high proportions: Boston (33.1), both Bay Area SMSAs (33.6 in San Jose, and 30.5 in San Francisco-Oakland), Orange County (30.9), Minneapolis-St. Paul (29.5), Seattle (29.2), Newark (29.6), and New York (28.8).

TABLE 4.7 Mean Years of Education of Native-Born White Men in the Urban Labor Force, for Major Urban Areas in the United States, Canada, and Australia, ca. 1980

14.00 Years or More	Mean	(N)	13.00 to 13.50 Years	Mean	(N)
Washington, D.C.	14.73	(2732)	Dallas	13.49	(3238)
San Jose	14.40	(1220)	Riverside–San. Bern.–	13.35	(1011)
San Francisco	14.30	(2936)	Ontario		
New York	14.05	(5650)	New Orleans	13.33	(908)
Los Angeles–Long	14.05	(4986)	Philadelphia	13.30	(4687)
Beach			Kansas City	13.22	(1505)
Denver	14.05	(1863)	Milwaukee	13.21	(1554)
Orange County	14.00	(2092)	Columbus	13.20	(1233)
			Buffalo	13.15	(1363)
			Tampa	13.12	(1399)
			Cleveland	13.10	(2019)
			St. Louis	13.08	(2266)
			Ft. Lauderdale	13.06	(931)
			Detroit	13.05	(4196)

13.50 to 13.99 Years	Mean	(N)	Less than 13.00 Years	Mean	(N)
Newark	13.98	(1754)	Cincinnati	12.94	(1297)
Sacramento	13.89	(1089)	Pittsburgh	12.91	(2654)
San Antonio	13.87	(580)	Baltimore	12.91	(2140)
Miami	13.80	(765)	Indianapolis	12.84	(1347)
Boston	13.78	(2451)	Toronto	12.40	(10088)
Seattle	13.77	(1986)	Ottawa-Hull	12.36	(3558)
Houston	13.73	(2616)	Calgary	12.23	(3063)
Nassau	13.69	(2783)	Vancouver	12.15	(5041)
Salt Lake City	13.68	(1051)	Edmonton	11.88	(3379)
Minneapolis–St. Paul	13.58	(2623)	Hamilton	11.69	(2185)
San Diego	13.56	(1887)	Winnipeg	11.63	(2670)
Chicago	13.55	(6378)	Québec	11.47	(3143)
Phoenix	13.54	(1514)	Melbourne	11.46	(4607)
Atlanta	13.51	(1795)	Sydney	11.37	(5754)
Portland	13.51	(1503)	Adelaide	11.34	(1602)
			Montréal	11.16	(13038)
			Perth	11.01	(1476)
			Brisbane	10.91	(2061)

Sources: See Table 4.3.

However, as important as occupational structure is, it is not the only explanation. Education cities have other characteristics which also may contribute to a higher level of education for native-born workers. Statistically they tend to be large cities (r=0.34 with population size) and have strong labor demand (r=−0.45 with the unemployment rate). These factors may affect interurban migration of native-born Americans. In addition, cities like New York, Los Angeles, and San Francisco are regarded as the most attractive places to live, prizes in the competition for residential location. New York is culturally the most cosmopolitan city in the United States, and California is its lifestyle leader. Workers compete nationally for managerial or professional jobs in those areas. Employers in those areas may have the pick of potential workers, and the winners would likely be those best qualified for employment. The local populations living in centers of high-skill work may be affected most strongly by the competitive drive to qualify for these occupations. They may be the ones most caught up in the 'credential disease.'

Canada also has substantial interurban educational variation, but the range of variation is less than in the United States. The top-to-bottom range is 1.3 years, compared to about 2.4 in the United States; statistically, however, the variation is as great (s.d.=0.4 in both countries). Toronto and Ottawa-Hull are two leading 'education cities' in Canada, partly reflecting their status as corporate and political capitals. Toronto and Ottawa-Hull have large professional-managerial sectors (27.0 and 33.9 percent, respectively). Hamilton is a manufacturing center, with lower levels of education among the native born. Occupational structure is relevant to educational levels, and while this is true in Canada, it is less so than in the United States (r is only about 0.2). One reason is lower educational standards in Québec. Montréal and Québec have mean educational levels about a year less than Toronto and Ottawa-Hull, despite similar occupational structures (27.7 and 32.4 percent in professional-managerial jobs, respectively). In Canada, educational levels are more strongly related to employment demand (r=0.7) than in the United States (r=0.4).

In Australia, interurban variations in educational levels are much less marked. Melbourne, Sydney, and Adelaide lead Perth and Brisbane in mean educational levels, but the differences are only about one-half year. These cities have a fairly homogeneous industrial and occupational structure. Each is the capital of an Australian state, and each is the metropolitan center for a specific region. In Australia, occupational mix determines educational levels as greatly as in the United States (r=0.8 based on the five cases), but the diversity on this dimension is less.

Interurban variations in mainstream educational levels are bound to have an impact on the entrance status of immigrants in particular locations. Moreover, the cross-national differences in interurban variations in educational levels are intriguing, raising the question of how they may be related to the parallel cross-national differences in interurban variations in immigrant status. In both respects, American heterogeneity stands in marked contrast to the homogeneity of Australia; Canada is in between. A key issue, of course, is the location of immigrants within each country's urban pattern, a question to which we now turn.

The Concentration of Immigrants in 'Education Cities'

Recent immigrants in the United States are heavily overconcentrated in high-education cities. This was already clear from an informal inspection of Table 4.7. Of the top seven 'education cities,' all but one—Denver—attract a lot of immigrants. The high-education cities of Washington, San Jose, San Francisco-Oakland, New York, Los Angeles, and Orange County all are major immigration cities. Other major immigrant-reception areas, such as Newark, Miami, Boston, and Seattle, are above average on the native-born White education scale as well. By contrast, low-education cities like Cincinnati, Baltimore, and St. Louis, have fewer immigrants. Table 4.8 provides quantitative information on the degree of concentration of immigrants in high-education cities. The left-hand side of the table shows, for the United States, the percentage distribution of the workforce across cities classified by mean educational level, comparing the native-born Whites and various immigrant groups. Over half of all recent immigrants (52.8 percent of males and 54.3 percent of females) reside in cities that fall into the highest education categories, compared to only about 20 percent of the native-born Whites. Only about 15 percent of all recent immigrants live in areas in the two lowest education categories, compared to nearly half of all native-born Whites.

The pattern of immigrant overconcentration in education cities holds for all origin groups. There are significant group-to-group variations, however. Overconcentration is heaviest for Blacks, among whom about 60 percent live in the highest category of education city. Similar proportions of Chinese, Japanese, Korean, Mexican, and other Latin American immigrants live in high-education cities. The degree of concentration is less for Asian Indians and for white immigrants, though it is substantial for them as well. Among all groups, only the Cubans are not overconcentrated in the highest-education category, a consequence of their heavy concentration in Miami, which happens to fall into the second-level category in this analysis. But even Cubans are substantially underconcentrated in the two lowest categories. Only about 18 percent of Cubans live in such cities.

Education cities attract immigrants for several reasons. The simplest reason is that education cities tend to be large and have the most dy-

TABLE 4.8 Recent Immigrant Concentration in High-Education Urban Areas, by Origins, Gender, and Host Country, ca. 1980[1]

Origins and Gender	Percent Residing in Urban Areas at Each Native-Born White Mean Level of Education by Origins and Gender, United States Only				Mean,[2] Years of Education of Native-Born White Labor Force in Urban Area of Residence, by Origins, Host Country, Gender		
	High 14.00+	13.50– 13.99	13.00– 13.49	Low <13.00	United States	Canada	Australia
Men							
Native-born White	19.8	32.2	31.6	16.4	13.48	11.85	11.26
Immigrant, total	52.8	31.5	11.1	4.5	13.82	12.06	11.27
White	43.8	31.1	17.8	7.2	13.73	12.04	11.25
Black	59.1	27.0	10.0	3.9	13.88	12.02	–
Asian, total	52.9	29.9	12.2	5.0	13.84	12.09	11.30
Chinese	63.8	23.3	9.8	3.0	13.92	12.16	11.33
Non-Chinese Asian	49.8	31.8	9.8	3.0	13.81	12.05	11.30
Filipino	53.6	34.6	6.9	4.9	13.78	–	–
Asian Indian	39.0	34.0	18.7	8.3	13.71	–	–
Korean	58.1	23.9	11.4	6.5	13.84	–	–
Vietnamese	45.2	33.2	18.2	3.4	13.82	–	–
Japanese	61.9	27.1	8.1	2.9	13.89	–	–
Other Asian	46.4	35.7	13.7	4.2	13.80	–	–
Mexican	58.8	33.8	7.0	0.4	13.87	–	–
Cuban	15.2	67.7	7.8	9.3	13.69	–	–
Other Latin American	63.7	24.9	5.6	5.8	13.88	12.03	11.36
Women							
Native-born White	21.0	32.3	30.9	15.7	13.5	11.87	11.26
Immigrant, total	54.3	30.7	10.4	4.6	13.8	12.10	11.26
White	42.6	32.7	17.7	7.0	13.7	12.09	11.25
Black	66.1	24.0	7.1	2.8	13.9	12.09	–
Asian, total	52.9	31.5	11.1	4.5	13.9	12.12	11.30
Chinese	66.6	23.3	7.6	2.4	14.0	12.17	11.29
Non-Chinese Asian	49.0	33.9	12.1	5.1	13.8	12.08	11.30
Filipino	52.2	34.9	8.2	4.7	13.9	–	–
Asian Indian	40.9	35.6	16.9	6.7	13.8	–	–
Korean	52.2	28.8	13.2	5.8	13.8	–	–
Vietnamese	45.2	33.0	18.2	3.6	13.8	–	–
Japanese	49.1	39.9	7.1	4.0	13.9	–	–
Other Asian	48.1	35.0	13.1	3.8	13.8	–	–
Mexican	64.9	29.0	6.0	0.2	13.9	–	–
Cuban	15.1	67.4	7.5	10.0	13.7	–	–
Other Latin American	67.0	21.8	5.2	6.0	13.9	–	–

[1]For N's, see Tables 2.2 (for native-born Whites), and 3.6 (for recent immigrant groups).
[2]The entries below show the means, across each category of origins, host country, and gender, of the measured level of education of the native-born White labor force, which is itself a mean value.

Sources: See Table 4.3.

namic economies. Immigrants—like the native-born—prefer such cities, as we saw in Chapter 3. High levels of native-born education obviously are not a deterrent to settlement by less-educated immigrants. Immigrants choose urban destinations on the basis of economic opportunity and family ties and networks of contact, without seeking to match native-born educational levels. Research on internal migration of the native born within the United States suggests that such migration may reinforce skills polarization involving immigrants. Barff, Ellis, and Reibel (1995) used census data to show that highly educated native-born migrants are attracted to expanding cities. Such internal migration reinforces the pattern observed here, linking high native-born education to economic expansion. At the same time, the presence of immigrants in these cities may actually discourage internal migration of the less educated, who seek to avoid immigrant competition.

How much greater the skills gap is for immigrants who settle in a high-education city can be seen in the right-hand half of Table 4.8, which allows comparisons also with the corresponding situation in Canada and Australia. For each of the groups indicated, the figures represent the average native-born White male educational level encountered in the local area of residence. For recent immigrant men in the United States, the figure is 13.82, indicating that the average immigrant man lives in a city where the mean years of education of the native-born White male population is 13.82 years. Since the average native-born white male educational level across all cities is 13.48 years, overconcentration in education cities implies that the average immigrant faces a skill gap which is higher than at the national level by 0.34 years.

The group most concentrated in high-education cities in the United States is the Chinese. The average Chinese immigrant man lives in a city in which the native-born White male has 13.92 years of education. This raises the effective skills gap by 0.44 years. For Black immigrant men, concentration in high-education cities increases the skills gap by 0.40 years, for Mexicans by 0.39 years, and for Koreans by 0.34 years. The group with least representation in high-education cities is the Cubans, and even they face a higher skill gap of 0.21 years on average.

In Canada, the concentration of recent immigrants in high-education cities is less than in the United States. In Australia, it is virtually nonexistent. The right-hand columns of Table 4.8 facilitate this comparison by showing the average native-born educational level faced by immigrants in their particular city of residence, for immigrants in Canada and Australia as well as the United States. These educational levels can be compared to the overall average for the native-born across all cities in the particular country. In Canada, the concentration of immigrants in high-education cities is consistent for all groups, but the resulting increase in the skills gap faced by immigrants in Canada is less. The average recent immigrant in Canada lives in a city in which the native-born population has a mean of 12.06 years of education. This figure is higher than the native-born, all-city average of 11.85 years, and hence the city-specific skills gap is higher as well, by 0.21 years, less than the comparable U.S. figure, 0.34. For Black immigrants in Canada, the skills gap due to concentration in high-education cities is increased by 0.17 years, less than half the corresponding amount for Black immigrants in the United States (0.40). For Chinese immigrants, the skills gap is higher by 0.31 years, again substantially less than in the United States (0.44 for Chinese). For each group for which a measurement is possible, immigrants in Canada are less concentrated in high-education cities, with the result that they face a lesser skills gap.

The main reason immigrants in Canada are less concentrated in high-education cities is that immigrants to Canada are generally less concentrated in specific urban areas. This was seen in Chapter 2. Though recent immigrants to Canada are more concentrated than earlier immigrant groups, compared to those in the United States, immigrants in Canada are spread relatively evenly across urban areas. There is a tendency for immigrant settlement in Canada to occur where local educational standards are higher, just as in the United States. But all of the Canadian cities have a substantial representation of immigrants, so the attractiveness of areas of settlement to new immigrants is less clearly linked to higher educational levels of the native-born population than is the case in the United States.

In Australia, immigrants are not significantly concentrated in high-education cities. Data in Table 4.8 show that the local educational levels of dominant populations are virtually the same for the immigrants and the native-born. The reasons are twofold. First, the concept of education cities applies less to Australia, because of the lack of variation in this regard. Urban areas in Australia are more homogeneous in terms of education and the occupational distributions of the native born, compared to both Canada and the United States. So there is less opportunity for urban location to affect the skills environment for immigrants. But secondly, immigrants are less concentrated in specific urban areas than in either the United States or Canada. Even though Australians are acutely aware of recent immigrants being heavily concentrated in Sydney, especially, and in Perth and Melbourne more than in Adelaide or Brisbane, on a comparative basis, these concentrations are less than in the United States or Canada. By North American standards, even Adelaide and Brisbane have a lot of immigrants, nearly as many on a percentage basis as San Francisco–Oakland and Orange County, and more than San Diego, Chicago, or Washington. The economic and social homogeneity of Australian cities compared to those in Canada or the United States is reflected in this distribution of immigrants. Few urban characteristics in Australia—other than sheer city size—are strong predictors of immigrant settlement.

Because immigrant concentration in high-education cities is greater in the United States, the cross-national differences in the immigrant skills gap on a city-specific basis are somewhat greater than the differences in the skills gap computed on a national basis. At the national-level comparison, for men (the figures for women are similar) the native-born educational level was higher in the United States by 1.63 years compared to Canada. However, because the immigrants in the United States are more heavily concentrated in high-education cities, the effective difference in the immigrant skills gap is greater. The average male immigrant faces an urban-level native-born education standard which is 1.76 years higher in the United States than in Canada—8 percent more than in the national comparison. This overall number applies also for Chinese male immigrants in particular. For Blacks, the average male immigrant in the United States faces a local-level native-born education standard which is in fact 1.86 years higher than that faced by the average Black male immigrant in Canada—14 percent more than in the national comparison.

Compared to Australia, there are greater differences in the concentration of immigrants in education cities in the United States, and the urban-level analysis makes an even greater difference in the skills gap. For men, the native-born educational level was higher in the United States by 2.22 years compared to Australia. However, the average male immigrant faces an urban-level native-born education standard which is 2.55 years higher in the United States than in Australia, 15 percent more than in the national comparison. Similar numbers apply to specific groups, such as Chinese immigrants.

Educational Polarization for Immigrants in U.S. Cities

Educational polarization represents the combination of two forces at work. One is the effect of immigrant concentration in education cities; the other is the effect of immigrant concentrations in producing lower immigrant educational levels. Our findings on immigrant concentrations in high-education cities in the United States, when combined with the findings in Chapter 3 that large immigrant communities tend to have lower educational levels, again particularly in the United States, point clearly to a consistent pattern of educational polarization for U.S. immigrants. Less-skilled immigrants to the United States tend to be concentrated in urban areas where the dominant native-born White male population is relatively highly educated, opening up a substantially higher skills gap for immigrants in those areas. Both patterns were somewhat less pronounced for racial minority immigrants in Canada, and virtually absent in Australia. So not only is the skills gap for immigrants higher in the United States than in the other two countries, but distinctive patterns of immigrant urban settlement in the United States create an even greater locally-effective skills gap. Urban skills polarization for immigrants in the United States contributes to the much lower entry-level earnings of immigrant groups in U.S. cities.

The distinctively American educational polarization can be seen on a group-by-group basis in Table 4.9. The three left-hand columns show mean educational levels for immigrant groups to the United States, according to the mean educational level of the dominant population. The polarization is more pronounced for many of the minority immigrant groups than it is for White immigrants. As the mean educational level for native-born White males rises across categories of cities, the mean educational level for White immigrants rises slightly for men and falls slightly for women. For White immigrant men, an education gap of about 0.4 years in the low-education cities increased to 0.7 and 1.1 years in the high-education cities. This is a moderate degree of polarization.

For racial minorities, polarization is more pronounced. Consider Black immigrants. As the native-born White educational level rose across urban categories, Black immigrant educational levels for men *fell* from 12.5 years to 12.2 years, and for Black immigrant women they also fell from 12.2 to ll.8 years. Hence, an education gap for Black immigrant men of 0.6 years in the low-education cities rises to become to 1.9 years in the high-education cities; and an education gap for Black immigrant women of 0.7 years in the low-education cities rises to become 2.0 years in the high-education cities.

It is useful to consider comparisons of immigrant communities in specific cities.[19] Skills polarization applies for Black immigrants in New York, by far the largest Black immigrant community in the United States, and also in Boston and Miami. Each of the three cities have native-born White educational levels above the national average, and in each of them, the educational level of Black immigrants falls below their national average. In New York and Boston, this polarization is fairly moderate. The native-born education level is about 0.3 years above the national average, and the Black immigrant educational level is about 0.3 years below the Black immigrant average. So for those two cities, the skills gap for Black immigrants is about 0.6 years higher than for Black immigrants nationally—1.9 years in New York and 1.8 years in Boston, compared to 1.3 years nationally. In Miami, the skills polarization is greater—3.5 years— mainly because of the lower level of education of Black immigrants (mostly Haitians) there, at only 10.3 years on average. Even in Miami, however, skills polarization is boosted by the fact that native-born White education is higher than the national average.

TABLE 4.9 Effect of Native-Born White Level of Education on Years of Education of Recent Immigrants in the Urban Labor Force, by Origins, Gender, and Host Country, ca. 1980

Origins and Gender	Mean Years of Education,[1] by Native-Born Education Level in the Urban Area, by Origins and Gender, United States Only			Metric Regression Coefficients for Effect of Native-Born Education in Urban Area on Immigrant Years of Education (Equation in Chapter 4, note 20)		
	Low <13.0	Moderate	High 13.5+	United States	Canada	Australia
Men						
Native-born White	13.1	13.7	14.1	+1.038 [2]	+1.082 [2]	+1.142 [2]
Immigrant, total	12.1	10.8	12.3	-0.611 [2]	-0.918 [2]	-0.312 ns
White	12.7	13.0	13.0	-0.766 [2]	-1.393 [2]	-0.480 ns
Black	12.5	12.2	12.2	-1.058 [2]	-0.860 [4]	–
Asian, total	15.2	14.4	13.9	-2.217 [2]	-0.354 ns	+0.511 ns
Chinese	15.2	14.1	12.1	-4.383 [2]	+0.491 ns	+3.600 ns
Non-Chinese Asian, total	15.2	14.5	14.7	-1.376 [2]	-0.454 [4]	+0.136 ns
Filipino	15.3	14.2	14.7	-1.369 [2]	–	–
Asian Indian	16.7	16.4	15.6	-1.930 [2]	–	–
Korean	14.4	14.5	14.4	-1.120 [3]	–	–
Vietnamese	12.6	13.0	13.5	+0.111 ns	–	–
Japanese	16.4	14.8	15.4	-1.246 [4]	–	–
Other Asian	14.5	13.2	14.0	-1.124 ns	–	–
Mexican	7.2	7.4	7.8	-0.488 [4]	–	–
Cuban	10.8	10.7	11.1	-0.572 ns	–	–
Other Latin American	11.4	10.6	10.9	-1.422 [2]	-1.735 [2]	-7.458 ns
(N)				(167281)	(46250)	(5504)

Women

Native-born White	12.9	13.3	13.8	+0.834 [2]	+0.860 [2]	+0.679 [2]
Immigrant, total	12.0	11.0	11.8	-0.761 [2]	-0.645 [2]	-0.360 ns
White	11.9	12.1	12.4	-0.281 ns	-1.240 [2]	-0.594 ns
Black	12.2	11.6	11.8	-0.877 [2]	0.045 ns	–
Asian, total	13.6	13.6	12.8	-1.788 [2]	-0.399 [4]	-0.390 ns
Chinese	13.5	13.1	11.0	-3.918 [2]	-0.114 ns	-3.557 ns
Non-Chinese Asian, total	13.6	13.6	13.6	-0.881 [2]	-0.113 ns	+0.290 ns
Filipino	15.0	14.6	14.6	-1.251 [2]	–	–
Asian Indian	15.0	14.7	13.9	-1.792 [2]	–	–
Korean	12.1	12.6	12.7	-0.463 ns	–	–
Vietnamese	11.4	11.8	12.2	+0.316 ns	–	–
Japanese	13.3	13.2	13.7	-0.265 ns	–	–
Other Asian	12.2	12.0	12.2	-0.256 ns	–	–
Mexican	8.1	7.5	7.7	-1.287 [2]	–	–
Cuban	11.3	10.9	11.3	-0.488 ns	–	–
Other Latin American	10.8	9.8	10.2	-1.154 [2]	-0.359 ns	+0.022 ns
(N)				(115722)	(36073)	(3597)

[1]N's for mean year of education are implicit, derivable from the N's in Table 3.6 and the data in Table 4.8.

[2]$p < 0.001$.

[3]$p < 0.01$.

[4]$p < 0.05$.

Sources: See Table 4.3.

Washington also has a fairly large Black immigrant community, but polarization is less. This is because although Washington is the premier U.S.
education city, Black immigrants in Washington are also highly educated,
at 13.7 years, on average. High Black immigrant education levels in Washington may relate to distinctive origins of these persons compared to the
communities in New York or Boston, for example. The Black immigrant
skills gap in Washington is only 1.0 years. Smaller Black immigrant communities in Los Angeles and Chicago also are less skills-polarized. The reason is a higher level of education of the immigrants, possibly related to recruitment patterns associated with smaller immigrant communities.

Higher skills polarization in education cities also affects Chinese immigrants. For them, the national skills gap is smaller than for Blacks—only
0.3 years, compared to 1.3. However, polarization is stronger because
Chinese immigrants are as concentrated in education cities as are Blacks,
and there is an even stronger community size effect reducing the educational levels of the Chinese immigrants in those cities. The result is that
Chinese immigrant men in high-education cities have on average 2.0
years *less* education than the native born, while Chinese immigrant men
in low-education cities have 2.1 years more education than the native
born. Chinese immigrant women in the high-education cities are 3.1
years less educated than native-born White males, while those in low-education cities are 0.4 years better educated than the native-born White
males. Higher native-born education coupled with lower immigrant education conspire to produce a skills gap for Chinese immigrants in particular cities of concentration, which is similar to that faced by Black immigrants in their largest communities.

Skills polarization applies to two of the three largest Chinese communities in the United States—New York and San Francisco—but not to Los Angeles. Actually, all three are high-education cities, and a skills gap exists for
all three that is greater than the 0.3 years skill gap for Chinese Americans
nationally. In New York and San Francisco, the large Chinese immigrant
communities have educational levels below their national averages, so the
polarization is due both to this and to the higher education of the native-
born Whites in those cities. In those cities, the skills gap for recent Chinese
immigrants is 3.2 years and 2.0 years, respectively, compared to only 0.3
years nationally. In Los Angeles, by contrast, the educational level of the recent Chinese immigrants is above the national average. But because of the
high level of education of the native-born Whites in Los Angeles, a skills
gap of 0.5 years exists; still, it is just barely above the national average.

There is a degree of urban-area educational polarization for most major
recent immigrant groups in the United States. In fact, among the groups
examined, all show educational polarization in high-education cities, with
the sole exception of the Vietnamese group. Recall from Chapter 3 that the

Vietnamese were the only group for whom concentrations (as of 1980) were not associated with lower levels of education. Now we see that although the Vietnamese are concentrated in high-education cities, this concentration does not lead to any significant skills polarization. For males, the skills gap is about 0.5 years in the low-education cities and 0.5 years in high-education cities. For females, the skills gap is about 1.5 years in cities at varying levels of native-born education.

Comparative Educational Polarization for Immigrants in Canadian and Australian Cities

To provide a summary analysis of polarization and to facilitate cross-national comparison, the right-hand columns of Table 4.9 present regression coefficients indicating how immigrant educational levels vary as native-born educational levels vary. (The coefficients are for the interaction of immigrant status with native-born education level in the determination of immigrant educational levels.[20]) For the United States, all but the Vietnamese coefficients (males and females) are negative. Negative coefficients indicate that immigrant educational levels do not keep pace with rising native-born educational levels. The coefficients are metric, measuring the average number of years that immigrant educational levels change with a one-year rise in the educational level of the native-born workforce. Negative figures below –1.0 indicate that as native-born education rises one year, immigrant education actually falls. For White immigrants, the figures are negative between zero and minus one. This indicates that as mainstream educational levels rise one year, White immigrant educational levels rise but not as fast. For Black immigrants, the figures are about minus one. For Chinese immigrants, they are about minus four. Figures for most groups are below minus one. The only positive coefficients are for male and female Vietnamese immigrants, and these coefficients are not significant. Urban immigrant educational polarization is pervasive in the United States.

In Canada, there is urban-area educational polarization for immigrants, but it follows a different pattern and is less consistent among racial minority immigrants than in the United States. The inverse relationship between native and immigrant education in Canada is strongest for European immigrants (the figures are minus one or lower for both men and women). Among the non-European groups, polarization is substantial for Black men but not Black women, and for Latin American men, but not for Asians, and particularly not for Chinese. The situation of the latter stands in sharp contrast to that in the United States. The high-education cities in Canada have less-educated White immigrants, but the relation to the education of racial minorities is less consistent.

Black immigrants in Canada are concentrated heavily in Toronto, with a smaller community in Montréal. These two Black communities fit differently into the overall national picture than do their U.S. counterparts. The concentration of Black immigrants in Toronto creates polarization, because Toronto is an education city (by Canadian standards), and Black immigrants to Toronto are no better educated than Black immigrants in Canada generally. So for Toronto, the situation of Black immigrants is most like that in U.S. cities like New York and Boston, with regard to polarization, as distinct from the size of the skills gap, which is far less. The skills gap in Toronto is 0.5 years, compared to the national norm in which Black immigrants are better-educated by 0.1 years. The skills gap in New York is 1.9 years, compared to the urban norm of 1.3.

Montréal, in contrast, is completely different from the U.S. situation. There is no polarization at all for Black immigrants in Montréal, and in fact the educational levels of Black immigrants there are farther above the native-born average than is the national norm. The main reason is that Montréal is not an education city; the mean level of education there is 0.7 years below the Canadian urban norm. Black immigrants are only slightly less well educated in Montréal compared to the national norm. So because of the lower native-born standard, Black immigrants are one-half year better educated than the mainstream population in Montréal. The case of the Black community in Montréal accounts in part for why Black immigrants in Canada are slightly less skills polarized than their counterparts in the United States. Many Black Haitians come to Montréal because of its French-speaking environment, making their pattern of recruitment quite distinctive.

The Chinese communities in Canada also are far less skills polarized than their U.S. counterparts, mainly because of the weaker community size effect, but also because of somewhat less concentration in high-education cities. The largest Chinese communities in Canada are in Toronto and Vancouver. In the case of Toronto, the mean educational level of Chinese immigrants is higher than the native-born norm, as much so as is the case nationally. The reason is that although Toronto is a relatively high-education city by the Canadian standard, Chinese immigrants in Toronto are positively selected on education. Vancouver's educational standards are below Toronto's but still higher than the national norm. The Chinese community there is less educated than the national norm, but only slightly so. Hence, Vancouver Chinese still have educational levels above the local native-born standard. Compared to the Chinatowns in the United States, particularly in New York and San Francisco, these Chinese Canadian communities are not at all skills polarized.

For Australia, the data show no consistent urban-area skills polarization for immigrants. We have seen that educational levels in Australian cities are fairly uniform, that immigrants are not particularly concentrated in high-education cities, and moreover (as shown by data reviewed in Chapter 3) that the larger immigrant communities did not tend to have lower levels of education. In Table 4.9 for Australia, many coefficients are actually positive, including for Asian men both Chinese and non-Chinese, and for Chinese women. The negative coefficients are close to unity, or more, only for Latin American men and for Chinese women.

Overall, the analysis of the concentration of immigrants in education cities confirms the importance of native-born education as an independent variable affecting the entry-level earnings of immigrants, and demonstrates clearly how immigrant recruitment can be quite independent of native-born educational levels. The concentration of immigrants in education cities lowers the relative skill levels of immigrants mostly in the United States but also to some extent in Canada, compared to Australia. Such concentrations contribute to a widening skills polarization, which because of the stronger negative community effect on immigrant education, is greater for minority immigrants in the United States. The locally effective entry level is reduced.

Conclusions

This chapter has evaluated the importance of native-born education as an independent variable affecting immigrant entry-level earnings, and has presented data leading to the following two main conclusions.

First, the level of educational participation in a society has a major impact determining the competitive environment faced by new immigrants. When the situation of immigrants in the United States is compared with those of immigrants in Canada and Australia, it is clear that at least half or more of the lower earnings by immigrants in the United States are explained by the higher levels of education of the mainstream population. The entry level of immigrants is highest in Australia mainly because the level of investment in the skills of the mainstream population there is the lowest. Industrial societies vary in their investment in work-related skills, often for reasons quite exogenous to the economy. This affects the status of newcomers by determining the size of any skills gap they face.

High educational standards could affect immigrant recruitment, but we know little about this potential effect. It could be that high educational standards in the United States attract the better-educated immigrants and create obstacles and barriers which discourage and deter less-educated immigrants, causing them to prefer Canada or Australia instead, and that this may be one reason why the United States outcompetes Canada and Australia for the best-educated immigrants. But this effect does not appear strong. The interurban analysis in the United States suggests that the presence of a highly educated native-born population does not deter low-skilled immigrant settlement. Whatever market forces might cause immigrant educational levels to match native-born education in destination cities are very weak forces. Just as at the urban level, it may be that immigrants are attracted to a particular country because of economic opportunity, and they accept the fact that the average level of education is often much higher there than in their country of origin. In seeking the best job opportunities, it may in fact be natural for immigrants to be drawn to those areas where, as it happens particularly in the United States, the dominant native-born workforce is the best educated.

The second conclusion is that the impact of a highly educated mainstream workforce is magnified when it is concentrated in those particular urban areas which happen also to attract the most immigrants, and where the immigrants themselves often have comparatively low levels of education. Such educational polarization between the native born and immigrants is pervasive in the United States. It is also evident in Canada, but there it is not so pronounced, mainly because immigrants are less concentrated in particular cities. In Australia, by contrast, there is much less educational polarization, partly because immigrants are still more evenly distributed, but also partly because of the relative homogeneity of the Australian cities themselves and the more equal distribution of the highly educated native born across cities. Educational polarization in the United States and Canada increases the effective skills gap for immigrants in their main immigration centers, while the lack of such polarization in Australia eases the economic adjustment for immigrants there.

This chapter has examined native-born educational levels as one consequence of educational institutions which operates independently of labor markets. The next chapter looks specifically at labor markets, and shows that effects of labor markets are in fact quite independent of the effects of educational polarization demonstrated in this chapter, not only cross-nationally but also on an interurban basis.

5

Labor Market Segments
and Earnings Disparities

The average immigrant enters the earnings distribution in its bottom half. This is true for most immigrant groups in all three countries. Hence, the overall shape of the earnings distribution in that bottom half can have a major effect on actual amounts of money that individual immigrants earn. Wider and more polarized earnings distributions such as exist in the United States mean simply that the best-paid jobs there are actually paid more in relative terms than the best-paid jobs in Canada or Australia. By the same token, the worst-paid jobs in the United States are paid less than the worst-paid jobs in Canada or Australia. Given the low level at which most immigrants enter the distribution, greater U.S. earnings inequalities are bound to affect them on the negative side, at least initially. These effects of earnings distributions actually compound the effect of the greater immigrant skills gap in the United States. In addition, immigrants are concentrated in specific labor market locations which may place them at further risk of exploitation and disadvantage.

This chapter explores these issues empirically and quantitatively, attempting to estimate the effect of labor markets on immigrant entry levels in each country. The chapter proceeds as follows. First, we describe recent trends in labor market institutions in each country, showing that the most important differences probably have to do with earnings distributions and the power of organized labor in affecting them. Second, based on differences in earnings distributions, we attempt to provide rough estimates of effects on immigrant entry-level status for specific groups. Although different labor market theories imply different processes, it is argued that the assumptions necessary for this estimate are reasonable from all theoretical standpoints. Impacts on immigrants also can be projected over time, to take account of the country-specific way that earnings distributions may be changing over time.

Third, we present an analysis of very important interurban differences in labor markets within the United States, which is useful for two reasons. The interurban analysis provides an important window on how variations in labor markets may affect the cross-national differences, and shows the substantial independence of labor market polarization from the educational polarization identified in Chapter 4. And equally important, because so many more labor market variables can be measured in the interurban U.S. census microdata, it is possible to examine the impact of both the overall structure of labor markets (and resulting income distribution) and the specific location of immigrants within that structure. The results show, interestingly, that the major effects of labor market structure on immigrants seem to operate regardless of their specific location or niche within that structure. Labor market structures have their effect not so much because they force immigrants into particular kinds of jobs as because of their effects on overall earnings distributions. The findings generally support the assumptions behind our estimates of cross-national labor market effects as well as the estimates themselves.

All of these results will contribute to the overall objective of this study, which is to compare the effects of different institutional sectors in determining immigrant standing. Generally, the results indicate that while greater earnings inequalities such as exist in the United States do in fact contribute to lower immigrant entry-level earnings for minority groups, particularly in certain urban areas and for the least skilled, the magnitude of these effects in explaining the cross-national differences is less than the magnitude of those produced by differences in educational institutions.

Comparative Labor Market Structures and Earnings Inequality

Labor markets have their most immediate effects on inequality by determining the distribution of earnings from employment and self-employment, measured before taxes. This section begins by describing the overall earnings distribution in each country. Then we consider how specific labor market structures and processes are related either to overall earnings distributions or to the earnings of immigrants specifically.

Income and Earnings Inequality

Before considering earnings data for the urban samples prepared for this study, it is useful to consider related data on the three countries from other sources. Some of these studies have measured inequality of disposable incomes, after taxes, and at the household or family level. This approach would include the impact of government policy in the form of taxation and social programs, which is a separate institutional sector and which significantly modifies the labor market outcomes. If the household or the family is a unit of redistribution or consumption, then family structure (size, or labor force participation rates of members) might also determine the outcome for individuals. While our concern is with individual earnings, family earnings might also reflect labor market structure if individuals make labor market decisions based on their position within the family.

Actually, all data sources indicate that economic inequality is greater in the United States than in either Canada or Australia, almost regardless of the measure used. Inequality is greater in the United States, whether the focus is on income or earnings inequality; whether measured at the individual, family, or household level; whether measured before or after taxes; and whether measured using an index sensitive to extremes at the top or bottom. However, the extent of the cross-national differences depends on the specific component or dimension of inequality that is the focus of interest. In particular, data on inequalities of earnings point toward a clear ranking of greater inequality in the United States, less in Canada, and least in Australia.

Three previous comparative sources are most relevant for our purposes:[1] a report from the Organization of Economic Cooperation and Development (OECD) on ten industrial countries, including the United States, Canada, and Australia, prepared by Sawyer (1976); the Luxembourg Income Study (LIS, an ongoing comparative project producing national microdata sets which at the time of the first report by Smeeding, O'Higgins, and Rainwater (1990), included the United States and Canada among seven countries, and which has since been expanded to include Australia (in studies by Saunders and King [1994] and by Bradbury [1993], among others[2]); and a trend report from OECD (1993). All sources for the United States, Canada, and Australia use data originally collected by the respective national census bureaus.

The OECD study by Sawyer (1976, 14) for the late 1960s–early 1970s includes a comparison of pretax household income distribution (see Table 5.1, panel A). It shows a clear ranking with the United States having the most inequality, Canada somewhat less, and Australia considerably less. The Gini index, measuring inequality across the entire distribution,[3] is 0.41 in the United States, 0.38 in Canada, and only 0.31 in Australia. These cross-national differences in inequality apply both at the top and at the bottom. In the United States, the 20 percent of households with the highest income (i.e., the top quintile) received 44.8 percent of the total, compared to 43.3 percent in Canada and only 38.9 percent in Australia. In the bottom part of the distribution, we see that in the United States, the lowest-income quintile received 3.8 percent of the total, compared to 4.3 percent in Canada and 6.6 percent in Australia. To put these figures in

TABLE 5.1   Pretax Household Income, Family Income, and Individual Earnings Inequality in the United States, Canada, and Australia

Index		United States	Canada	Australia
A. OECD, 1966–1972				
Household Pretax Income Inequality[1]	Share of:			
	top quintile	44.8	43.3	38.9
	bottom quintile	3.8	4.3	6.6
	Gini index	0.41	0.38	0.31
B. Luxembourg Income Study, 1985–1987[2]				
1. Family Pretax Income Inequality[3]	Share of:			
	top quintile	45.9	42.4	44.4
	bottom quintile	3.9	4.9	4.4
	Gini index	0.423	0.380	0.406
2. Male Pretax Full-time, Full-year, Wage Inequality[4]	Percentiles as percent of mean:			
	90th	163.1	148.9	144.0
	10th	45.7	53.8	62.5
	Coefficient of variation	0.561	0.483	0.447
	Gini index	0.286	0.234	0.196

[1]*Sources:* Sawyer (1976, 14). U.S. data from Bureau of the Census, Current Population Survey, 1972; Canadian data derived from two Statistics Canada surveys: Income Distribution by Size in Canada, and Family Expenditure Survey for 1969; Australian data from N. Podder (1972), and Commonwealth Bureau of Census and Statistics, Income Distribution, 1968–1969.

[2]*Sources:* Data for the Luxembourg Income Study come from the following: U.S. data are from the Bureau of the Census, Current Population Survey, 1986; Canadian data are from the Statistics Canada Survey of Consumer Finances, 1987; Australian data are from Australian Bureau of Statistics, Household Income Survey, 1985–1986.

[3]*Source:* Saunders and King (1994, 63).

[4]*Source:* Bradbury (1993, 9).

perspective, note that the poorest households in Canada receive a 13 percent larger share of the total income than do their U.S. counterparts, and the poorest in Australia earn a 74 percent larger share of the total. And whereas the bottom quintile has only 8.5 percent of the income of the top quintile in the United States, they have 9.9 percent in Canada, and 17.0 percent in Australia. Overall, the most striking difference is between the United States and Canada on the one hand and Australia on the other.

The Luxembourg Income Study (LIS) data include both family income and individual earnings, thus permitting a comparison of the two. Saunders and King (1994) provided cross-national data on inequalities of pretax family income (Table 5.1, panel B). They found greater inequality in the United States than in Canada, but the observed relative position of Australia was different. The Gini index for the United States was 0.423 compared to 0.380 for Canada. However, for Australia, the index value was 0.406, indicating greater inequality in Australia than in Canada, though still less than in the United States. These patterns were reflected both at the bottom and the top of the distribution. Looking at the bottom quintile, the share of income received in the United States was 3.9 percent; and while in Canada it was 4.9 percent, in Australia it was only 4.4 percent. Whereas the bottom quintile in the United States still had about 8.5 percent of the earnings of the top quintile, in Canada they had 11.5 percent, and in Australia 10.0 percent (see also Saunders, Stott, and Hobbes 1991, 67). These findings of somewhat greater family income inequality in Australia than in Canada are different from what is found regarding individual earnings inequality, and may reflect a distinctive pattern of women's labor force participation in Australia (see Chapter 6, note 4).

When these same LIS data are analyzed in terms of individual earnings, the results are different, however. They clearly indicate least inequality in Australia, more in Canada, and most in the United States. Bradbury (1993) compared inequality of male wages in the LIS data (see Table 5.1, panel B2). In terms of individual male wages, Australia has the least inequality of the three countries. The Gini index is 0.196 for Australia, 0.234 for Canada, and 0.286 for the United States. Other indexes used by Bradbury show the same pattern in different ways. One such index is the statistical variance of earnings, standardized on the mean.[4] This measures the range of earnings received by the middle two-thirds of the distribution, and by implication, the range of earnings received by the bottom and top one-third combined. This index shows that the range of earnings required to encompass two-thirds of the workforce in the United States is about 0.56 above and below the mean, while the comparative range in Canada is only 0.48 above and below the mean, and in Australia only 0.45 above and below.

Bradbury also presented his LIS results in the form of earnings percentiles. Earnings percentiles measure an individual's earnings which would place them above a given percentage of the workforce in each country. The percentiles, also shown in Table 5.1, panel B2, show that in the United States, those in the 90th wage percentile (whose wages are higher than 90 percent of the workforce in the United States) earn 163.1 percent of mean earnings; in Canada, those in the 90th percentile earn 148.9 percent of mean earnings; and in Australia, 144.0 percent of mean earnings. Looking at the bottom end of the distribution, those in the 10th percentile (whose wages are higher than only 10 percent of the workforce, and below the other 90 percent) earn 45.7 percent of the mean earnings; in Canada, a person in the 10th earnings percentile earns 53.8 percent of mean earnings (almost 18 percent higher than in the United States); and in Australia, that person earns 62.5 percent of mean earnings (almost 37 percent higher than in the United States). In other words, those in a high or low percentile are farther from the mean in the United States, closer to the mean in Canada, and closest in Australia.

A recent OECD (1993) report, summarized in Table 5.2, shows the same ranking of earnings inequality—the United States with the most inequality, Canada with less, and Australia with the least.[5] Table 5.2 adds three other points. First, the United States-Canada-Australia ranking is observed for both men and women and at both the bottom and the top of the distribution. Second, the trend over time, from 1973 through about 1990, is toward greater inequality in all three countries. And third, the changes over time are less than the absolute differences among the three countries.[6]

Other trend studies on a country-specific basis also have shown progressively greater earnings inequality over time, or earnings polarization, within each of the three countries. Grubb and Norton (1989) analyzed pretax wages and salaries of individuals in the United States, using census data for 1960, 1970, and 1980, showing a progressive trend toward greater inequality. The index they used, Theil's T (similar to the Gini index), increased from 0.35 in 1960 to 0.37 in 1970 and 0.39 in 1980. Since 1980, inequality has continued to increase. Harrison and Bluestone (1990, 7) show, using census data, that family income inequality had increased more rapidly since 1980 than before (see also Burtless 1990; Bound and Johnson 1992). For Canada, Morissette, Myles, and Picot (1995) used data from the Canadian Survey of Consumer Finances (the same source used for the LIS data base) to examine trends in earnings from 1969 to 1991. They showed increases in individual inequality of earnings in Canada during the 1980s. Saunders, Stott, and Hobbes (1991, 75) likewise found increases in inequality of family pretax earnings for Australia.

Our own data on earnings inequality for men and women, from the 1980–1981 urban labor force microdata census samples, are presented in Table 5.3. These earnings data differ from earnings data reported above in that they include only the urban areas with a population of more than 500,000 (rather than the entire country), and they cover the entire workforce with non-zero earnings, so part-time and part-year workers are included (not only full-time, year-around employees). Nevertheless, the data show the same pattern found in other data sources: greater inequality in the United States, somewhat less in Canada, and still less in Australia, for both men and women.

What has been found may be summarized as follows. First and foremost, earnings inequality has been consistently found to be greater in the United

TABLE 5.2   Earnings Distributions by Gender and Year: The United States, Canada, and Australia, 1973–1991

Gender and Year	United States		Canada		Australia	
	Ratio of Top Decile Earnings to Median	Ratio of Bottom Decile Earnings to Median	Ratio of Top Decile Earnings to Median	Ratio of Bottom Decile Earnings to Median	Ratio of Top Decile Earnings to Median	Ratio of Bottom Decile Earnings to Median
Men						
1973			1.67	0.52		
1975	1.93	0.41			1.50	0.75
1979	1.93	0.41			1.48	0.74
1980	1.95	0.41			1.49	0.74
1981	1.98	0.41	1.67	0.48	1.54	0.74
1985	2.10	0.38			1.54	0.72
1986	2.08	0.37	1.68	0.42	1.58	0.71
1987	2.09	0.37			1.53	0.71
1988	2.10	0.38	1.71	0.45	1.56	0.70
1989	2.14	0.38			1.54	0.69
1990			1.75	0.44	1.56	0.70
1991					1.59	0.70
Average 5-year change	+0.10	−0.01	+0.04	−0.02	+0.03	−0.02
Women						
1973			1.70	0.55		
1975	1.97	0.47			1.37	0.77
1979	1.96	0.49			1.40	0.80
1980	1.96	0.50			1.43	0.78
1981	2.01	0.50	1.76	0.47	1.44	0.78
1985	2.09	0.47			1.48	0.78
1986	2.12	0.45	1.76	0.41	1.48	0.77
1987	2.10	0.44			1.47	0.76
1988	2.11	0.44			1.48	0.75
1989	2.15	0.44			1.48	0.74
1990			1.75	0.44	1.47	0.75
1991					1.49	0.75
Average 5-year change	+0.11	−0.03	−0.01	−0.02	0.02	−0.02

Source: OECD (1993, 159–161).

TABLE 5.3   Earnings Inequality in the Urban Labor Force,[1] by Gender, for the United States, Canada, and Australia, ca. 1980

		United States	Canada	Australia
Men				
	Percentiles as percent of mean			
	75th	131.1	131.3	118.9
	25th	48.7	52.8	64.9
	Coefficient of variation	0.765	0.708	0.537
	(N)	(266,354)	(61,390)	(7,877)
Women				
	Percentiles as percent of mean			
	75th	135.8	136.8	124.4
	25th	45.2	47.2	55.6
	Coefficient of variation	0.771	0.706	0.570
	(N)	(192,309)	(44,776)	(4,846)

[1]The analyses in this table were performed on the entire urban area labor force samples, including native born and immigrants from all periods of immigration. Subsampled populations were weighted, but N's are unweighted.

Sources: 1980 U.S. Census Public Use Microdata 5-Percent File; 1981 Canadian Census Public Use Sample Tape 2-Percent Individual File; 1981 Australian Census of Population and Housing 1-Percent File. For further details on these sources, see Chapter 1, note 14. For more specific definitions of origins used for each country, see Chapter 2, pp. 46–47 and notes 4–6.

States, less in Canada, and least in Australia. This rank-order has been found in all previous studies which have focused on earnings inequality, such as the OECD reports and the Luxembourg Income Study, and it is found for the urban labor force census samples used in this study. Second, cross-national differences in overall *income* inequality may be different. Income patterns reflect government taxation and social transfers, and these too may affect the relative economic welfare of immigrants and others (this factor is considered separately in Chapter 6). Finally, the trend is toward greater earnings inequality in each country. Any effects of earnings inequality, such as on immigrants, are likely to become magnified over time.

Labor Market Bases of Earnings Inequality

What are the labor market structures and processes which account for the cross-national differences in earnings distributions? How might these be expected to affect the relative position of immigrants? Observed differences and trends in earnings inequality may be related either to the size of specific industrial or occupational segments, or to variations in the wages paid for essentially the same types of jobs within industries and occupations, or both. Institutional factors such as the overall strength of the labor movement might affect either of these two dimensions. Research suggests that it is sometimes quite difficult to link overall earnings trends to specific types of employment, but that unionization has a consistent impact. This is also true on a cross-national basis.

Industrial and Occupational Sectors and Strata. There is substantial similarity among the United States, Canada, and Australia in the distribution of employment across the major sectors of manufacturing, services, and agriculture (Bamber and Whitehouse 1993; see Table 5.4). Over the past several decades, these three countries have posted the highest employment growth among major industrial nations, due to the combined impact of population growth (partly from immigration), and labor force entry by women (Godbout 1993, 3–6). The service sector has been the major source of job growth, and increased its proportion of the total from 58 percent in 1963 in the United States, 56 percent in Canada, and 52 percent in Australia to about 70 percent in all three countries in 1990. Agricultural employment dwindled, and manufacturing employment shrank from about 35 to 25 percent.

There are minor cross-national differences in specific subsectors which might be associated with high- or low-wage employment, but evidence suggests the effects of such differences are small. The service sector is very far from uniform, as Browning and Singelmann (1978) pointed out. Their fourfold division between social services (health, education, and government), producer services (financial, insurance, business services), distributive services (trade, transportation, and storage), and personal services (hotels, restaurants, retail trade), though imprecise in some ways, nevertheless captures an important component of this variation. Service sector expansion in the United States was concentrated in subsectors most characterized by high-skill and professional employment, namely social and producer services, and not in the personal-services subsector characterized by low-wage employment.

Across the three countries, there are only minor differences in employment by subsector within services. Australia employs a slightly larger proportion in wholesale and retail trade and in restaurants and hotels; Canada and the United States employ a slightly larger proportion in community, social, and personal services (including health, education, and public administration). However, the differences in the proportions employed in these sectors in the three countries are small.[7] Employment in high-tech sectors of manufacturing is not large in percentage terms or rising quickly (Riche et al. 1983; Etzioni and Jargowsky 1984), and differences among countries are small. Substantially higher levels of education in the United

TABLE 5.4 Civilian Employment by Sector, for the United States, Canada, and Australia, 1963–1990

	Agriculture					Industry					Services				
	1963	1973	1983	1988	1990	1963	1973	1983	1988	1990	1963	1973	1983	1988	1990
Australia	10	7	7	6	5	38	35	28	26	25	52	57	65	68	69
Canada	12	7	6	5	4	33	31	26	26	25	56	63	69	70	71
United States	7	4	4	3	3	35	33	28	27	26	58	63	68	70	71

Source: Greg J. Bamber and Gillian Whitehouse (1993, 283). "Employment Economics and Industrial Relations: Comparative Statistics." In *International and Comparative Industrial Relations: A Study of Industrialised Market Economies,* Second Edition, edited by Greg J. Bamber and Russell D. Lansbury. London: Routledge. Reproduced by permission of Routledge.

States than in Canada are associated with higher educational standards *within* job categories, rather than higher proportions of workers in professional and technical categories themselves (Lipset 1989, 162).

Grubb and Wilson (1989) analyzed the industrial sources of the trend toward greater wage inequality in the United States over the period between 1960 and 1980. Using a detailed industrial classification, they decomposed inequality trends into those which occur within sectors, those which arise from employment shifts to sectors with greater inequality, and those which arise from employment shifts to sectors with lower earnings. They found that the first two of these are most operative. First, there was an increase in inequality within sectors, for example within manufacturing industries. And second, there was an important shift to the social service sector (particularly health and education), where there are high skill levels and high wages but also greater inequality. There was no shift to the poorly paid consumer-services sector. Hence it seems unlikely that greater inequality in the United States compared to Canada or Australia has its source in any greater shift to low-wage service sector employment.

Overall, there is no evidence to support the view that the cross-national differences in earnings inequality are related to differences in the size of industrial or occupational sectors. Rather, it would appear that the differences are related to the nature of employment or the wage-setting process within sectors.

Part-Time Employment and Underemployment. The potential for low earnings might also be indicated by the proportion employed part time, the proportion underemployed or unemployed, or the proportion with periodic spells of such experiences. However, rates of unemployment and part-time employment show inconsistent differences among countries. In 1980, unemployment rates varied far more among areas within countries than between countries. In our urban labor force samples, unemployment averaged 6.1 percent across the 79 urban areas in the United States, 5.8 percent across the 9 in Canada, and 6.1 percent across the 5 in Australia. More recently, unemployment rates have been higher in Canada and Australia. As an instance, the proportions unemployed in 1993 in the United States were 7.3 percent, compared to 11.3 percent in Canada and 10.6 percent in Australia (International Labor Office 1993, 20). This does not necessarily imply lower rates of employment marginality in the United States, however. Card and Riddell (1993) suggest that the U.S.-Canadian difference in unemployment is due less to differences in employment than to differences in unemployment benefits in Canada. They argue that in the United States, persons losing their jobs may report themselves as out of the labor force earlier than in Canada, because unemployment benefits run out sooner than would be the case for a person in the same situation in Canada. This implies that marginal attachment to employment might not be so different between the two countries as the unemployment figures suggest.

Measures of rates of part-time employment might be even less reliable because of problems of definition, and the cross-national comparisons seem to depend on data sources. In an urban labor force census sample for 1970 (1971 for Canada and Australia), average levels of part-time employment across urban areas were almost identical for each country: 12.07 percent in the United States, 12.05 percent in Canada, and 12.07 percent in Australia. In the comparable 1980 (1981) data, the figures had gone up in each country, more in Australia and less in Canada. They were 16.68 percent in the United States, 14.96 percent in Canada, and 18.60 percent in Australia. Data from de Neubourg (1985, 563) show that in 1973, rates of part-time employment in the United States were higher than in Canada (14.3 percent compared to 12.4 percent, respectively), but they were rising more rapidly in Canada. By 1983, in the United States they were still at 14.1 percent, but they were up to 15.3 percent in Canada. Consistent with this, Godbout (1993, 14) found in OECD data that increases in part-time employment as a proportion of all employment were higher in Canada and Australia than in the United States. On the other hand, Gornick and Jacobs (1996, 10), using the perhaps more comparable Luxembourg Income Study data, showed that part-time employment was clearly higher in the United States in 1986, particularly among men (whose demand for full-time employment might be greater). The percentage of male workers employed part time was 9.8 in the United States (0.8 percent of these worked 1–9 hours per week, and 9.0 percent worked 10–34 hours), compared to 5.6 percent in Canada (0.6 percent worked 1–9 hours, and 5.0 percent, 10–34 hours), and 4.4 percent in Australia (0.6 percent worked 1–9 hours, and 3.8 percent, 10–34 hours). For women, all rates were higher, and on a cross-national basis they were higher in Australia (41.8 percent) than in either Canada (29.6 percent) or the United States (28.2 percent). Rates of part-time employment appear to be increasing more rapidly in Canada and Australia, perhaps partly as an employer strategy to evade unionized employment. But we cannot conclude that part-time employment in these countries is necessarily higher than in the United States. Certainly there is little basis here for suggesting that lower entry-level earnings for immigrants in the United States are related to a greater incidence of part-time employment.

Morissette, Myles, and Picot (1993) suggested that a recent trend toward increased earnings inequality in Canada has more to do with increased reliance on marginal and part-time employment, compared to the United States, where it is related more to changing earnings distributions among the full-time employed. If Canadian employers now rely on part-time employment as a nonunion alternative, then this analysis suggests that the impact of unionization in reducing earnings inequality might be offset where part-time employment is feasible. This may be increasingly the case in the industrial and occupational mix now emerging in all countries, including Canada and Australia.

Self-Employment.   Self-employment is increasing in the United States partly because of immigration but also partly as the result of a shift toward reduced organizational size. This trend, which seems to contradict the rise of huge multinational conglomerates (Mills 1951, Steinmetz and Wright 1989) could alter the earnings prospects of immigrants. Data from our urban labor force samples show that self-employment rates for males in the United States are higher (at 9.56 percent) than in Canada (8.77 percent) but lower than in Australia (12.05 percent). These fairly small differences seem unrelated to other labor force factors and probably have little impact on overall earnings distributions.

Unionization.   Low and declining rates of unionization in the United States clearly might play a role in the increased earnings inequality within manufacturing industries and the higher rates of inequality in the social-service sector (Freeman and Medoff 1984, Asher and DeFina 1997). Figure 5.1 presents trend data on unionization rates in the three countries (see also Visser 1992; International Labor Office 1993, 34–35; Lipset 1996, 86–108). In 1970, union strength was comparable in the United States and Canada, at about 30 percent of the workforce. A variety of forces have reduced union membership in the United States since then to about half of what it is in Canada. These reasons include reduced employment in unionized industries as well as reductions in union membership within industries (Kochan et al. 1986). Canadian unions have been relatively insulated from these trends (Meltz 1989; Kumar 1993) not only because (at least until recently) employment losses in unionized industries have been less but also because the Canadian legal environment is more conducive to unionization, and because Canadian unionization has been more heavily invested in the public sector. In the most recent years, the prospects for unions in Canada are less than they have been, because the North American Free Trade Agreement (NAFTA), since the late 1980s, has exposed Canadian industries to employment trends in manufacturing which are closer to those in the United States (Verma et al. 1996:437–440), and because of recently-declining employment in the heavily-unionized public sector in Canada.

    The Australian industrial relations system for many decades has given a very prominent role to unions in setting wage levels across many employment sectors (Patmore 1991). The 1970 unionization rate of over 50 percent reflects a broader system within which unions affected wage awards in many sectors of the workforce. Wage awards have been made

FIGURE 5.1   Union Membership in the United States, Canada, and Australia

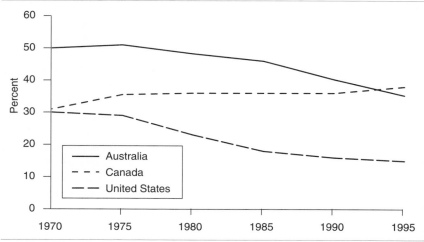

Sources: For 1970–1990, the figures are from OECD (1991, 101; 1994, 184). The 1970 U.S. figure is derived from Dickens and Leonard (1985, 326); see also Bamber and Whitehouse (1985, 326). For 1995, the figure for Australia is from *The Australian* (Feb. 20, 1995, p. 8); for Canada and the U.S. the figures reported are for 1993 (Lipset and Meltz 1993, 1).

at the national levels, and workers, even those in marginal employment situations such as in the personal-service sector, could apply to a national body for wage awards which would establish higher minimum standards than might be available in a wide-open, competitive marketplace. This system has undergone many changes in recent years, however, mainly in the direction of introducing greater market competition into wage determination. In place of the national wage-award system, for example, Australia has moved toward enterprise-level collective bargaining. And along with these changes has come declining union membership. Today, union membership rates in Australia are similar to those in Canada, and they might fall still further in the years to come.

Union power may be the most important cross-national variable affecting the earnings distribution. In labor market segmentation theory, lack of union representation is the most salient feature of disadvantaged labor market segments. Lemieux (1993, 97) shows that "differences in the patterns and extent of unionism in Canada and in the United States explain 40 percent of the difference in [overall] wage inequality of men in the two countries," and that unions reduce the within-sector variance of wages for both men and women, in both countries. Where occupational and industrial shifts seem to have their impact on earnings distributions within the United States, the most likely explanation is related to unionization rates in the affected employment group. Similar employment shifts in Canada and Australia may not produce the same earnings distribution effects precisely because the position of unions is different. The decline in union membership in Australia had produced little change in the earnings distribution by 1991, judging from the OECD data in Figure 5.1. The power of unions in the wage determination process in Australia remains greater than for their counterparts in Canada, despite the decline in Australian union membership to Canadian levels. However, the seeds of change in Australia have been sown. It seems likely that the more recent changes in Australian inequality are related to changes in the industrial relations system or the position of unions in collective bargaining.

Summary

This section has compared national labor markets in two respects: earnings distributions and underlying labor market structures and processes. Earnings inequality is clearly greatest in the United States, a fact which is probably related at least in part to the weakness of the labor movement there in protecting workers from the impact of industrial and workplace restructuring. Earnings inequalities have increased most in the United States, again partly as a result of the comparatively dramatic decline in union power in that country. By contrast, differences in employment by industry or occupation are small and seem to have little to do with differences in the earnings distributions. On the other hand, greater exposure to marginal and part-time employment in Canada might to some extent offset the impact of Canadian union strength compared to that of unions in the United States. Opportunities for self-employment may provide alternatives to low-wage employment in the United States, but the aggregate impact on earnings distributions compared to Canada and Australia is likely very small.

Cross-national Labor Market Differences and Immigrant Earnings

Expected Effects of Distributions and Structures

An estimate of how entry-level earnings of immigrants in the United States, Canada, and Australia are affected by labor market differences ideally should take account of (1) the effect of differences in the earnings distribution itself (the fact that the Canadian and Australian distributions are collapsed, or 'squeezed', compared to the wider U.S. distribution), and (2) the effect of differences in the sectoral location of immigrants within the labor market (for example, differences in the concentration of immigrants in particular kinds of jobs). For the cross-national comparison, as a first approximation, we will make a calculation taking account only of (1), differences in the shape of the overall distribution. This analysis would include any effects of labor market structure on the overall earnings distribution, short of those that alter the position of immigrants within the earnings hierarchy. If the less-regulated U.S. labor markets permit greater exploitation of immigrants, then immigrant inequality there would be greater than what would result from the wider earnings distribution alone. Hence, the first-approximation estimates here are very likely minimum estimates of the effects of labor markets. Some of the effects of labor market concentrations are tested in the interurban analysis later in the chapter.

Focusing only on the earnings distribution for our estimation is most clearly justified from the point of view of human capital theory. Human capital theory assumes that labor markets contain no structural barriers which might affect immigrants differentially. Borjas (1990) applied a human capital analysis to suggest that labor market inequality could have positive effects on immigrant standing because inequality attracts those immigrants with the greatest potential to take advantage of high earnings opportunities and the least risk of enduring extremely low earnings. Given that the average *entry*-level earnings of all major minority immigrant groups is below the mainstream average in each country, Borjas's analysis clearly assumes that immigrants are making decisions based on their perceptions of long-term earnings prospects rather than on what happens to them in the first ten years. In any case, as was pointed out in Chapter 1, the empirical basis for Borjas's analysis was very limited, consisting primarily of U.S. and Canadian migrants, most of whom were of European origins, English-speaking, and with similar educational backgrounds; yet Borjas's human capital analysis was based on the impact of the overall earnings distribution.

An analysis focusing only on earnings distributions does capture some of the effects examined by labor market stratification theory, but not all of them. The theory applies mainly to minority-group immigrants and emphasizes the exploitative potential of unregulated and inegalitarian labor markets particularly for the less skilled and the culturally different. From the standpoint of stratified labor market theory, there are two labor market effects which produce disadvantages for immigrants. In one, unregulated labor markets drive down wages for all unprotected workers. Immigrants are differentially affected because they are more often in the unprotected position. This effect is reflected in the overall earnings distribution. In another, less regulated labor markets allow employers greater opportunities to exploit the vulnerability of immigrant labor in particular types of jobs that are unwanted by mainstream workers and that offer lower pay. This segmentation effect of laissez-faire labor markets on immigrants would be in addition to any effect of greater overall earnings inequality.

Data on the concentration of immigrant groups in particular labor market strata are available for each country, but unfortunately, it is not possible to establish the basis for cross-national comparison. Immigrant group concentrations in specific industries, occupations, and work settings is a matter of common observation in all three countries. Immigrant histories always point to types of work done by immigrants. However, each country-specific study uses a different classification. And in any case, the impact of such segmentation is controversial in the analyses which have been performed within countries. The following considerations should be taken into account in assigning weight to this effect crossnationally.

DeFreitas (1988) showed that in the United States by far the most pronounced immigrant concentrations are in very specific industries which are difficult to characterize in terms of any of the standard broad classifications such as those related to segmented labor market theory. One of these standard classifications is "peripheral" industries, which as defined by Oster (1979) include light industries such as food products, textiles, printing, leather, wood products, stone products, and parts of various other industrial sectors (but few within heavy metal, machinery, or transportation equipment), plus parts of transportation (buses, taxis, and trucks, but not rail or air services), communication (radio broadcasting but not telephones) and utilities (water but not gas or electricity). Another standard classification is the so-called secondary labor markets such as the low-end service sector, which includes retail trade, personal services, and entertainment and recreational services. Only a few concentrations in these sectors show up in census data: Koreans and Chinese men (but not women) in personal services, Latin American men and women in peripheral industries. To capture immigrant concentrations in specific industries, DeFreitas developed an index of what he called "immigrant-intensive" industries, essentially an ad hoc collection of 101 three-digit code industries distinguished simply by the fact that immigrants are concentrated in them. Many of these are within the so-called peripheral industries, but only a selection. Within the food sector, meat, bakery, and sugar products are immigrant intensive, but dairy and beverages are not. Most of textiles is immigrant intensive, but not the thread and fabric mills. None of the printing industry is immigrant intensive, but all of the stone products industries are. At the same time, certain socalled core industries are immigrant intensive: plastics, glass products, office machines, household appliances, radio and other communication equipment, ship and boat building, and watches and clocks. Furthermore, some sectors of wholesale trade are immigrant intensive (furniture, lumber and construction materials, sporting goods, clothing, groceries), as are some sectors of retail trade (bakeries, food stores, and restaurants, for example), parts of finance (banking and real estate, but not insurance), auto and electrical repair, and personal services. In the professional services category, doctors' and dentists' offices, hospitals, and colleges and universities are immigrant intensive, but legal services, elementary and secondary schools, business and trade schools, and libraries are not. In DeFreitas's analysis, while each immigrant group displayed a different pattern of industrial location, both men and women in all immigrant groups were substantially overrepresented in immigrant-intensive industries.

DeFreitas's classification of immigrant-intensive industries cannot be duplicated in Canadian or Australian census microdata samples, because the sample data do not contain adequately detailed industrial classifications. Studies of detailed patterns of immigrant and ethnic occupational concentrations have been done in Canada and Australia, but the results are difficult to compare quantitatively with DeFreitas's. Reitz (1990, 166; see also Seward and Tremblay 1989) showed in survey data for Toronto that immigrants are concentrated in occupations which can only be identified in very detailed occupational classifications, and that these occupations differ very substantially by specific origin group, both European and others, as well as by gender within groups. West Indian Black immigrant men were concentrated in medical and health occupations, including that of physician, and were also commonly welders, clerks, guards, and taxi drivers. West Indian Black immigrant women also were concentrated in medical and health occupations, specifically as nurses and nurse's aides. They also worked in personal services and in data processing. The concentrations of German immigrant men were in tool and die making, metal machining, food processing, and mechanical repair occupations. German immigrant women were concentrated in electrical products, hairdressing, food preparation, and in commercial and file art. The impact on earnings varied enormously among the various cases considered. It was sometimes positive in the case of established immigrant groups. For example, Italian male occupational concentration, often in construction trades, was associated with very positive net earnings outcomes (net of human capital) for them. The impact was usually negative in the case of groups that had arrived more recently, such as Portuguese men and women. The occupational concentrations of the latter group, for example in cleaning occupations, were associated with negative net earnings outcomes. Reitz's findings about the patterns of concentration were similar to DeFreitas's in the sense that they were finely graded and varied from group to group. However, the findings cannot be compared in terms of the size of effects on immigrant earnings, even in the case of specific cities, because the classifications are different (industries in DeFreitas's case, occupations in Reitz's).[8] Similar comments apply to less detailed studies in Australia (Lever-Tracy and Quinlan 1988; Castles 1991).

There are at least two reasons to expect to find immigrants in the United States more concentrated in specific industries or occupations, but even these underlying causal factors cannot easily be tapped in the census microdata. One reason is that the greater urban concentration of immigrants in the United States might mean that larger proportions of them live in ethnic concentrations within urban areas, and the resulting intensification of ethnic social networks might facilitate the formation of ethnic workplace concentrations. Residential location has in fact been used to measure the existence of the enclave economy in some studies. However, residential locations within urban areas are not measured in the microdata. Another possible factor affecting ethnic concentrations in labor markets is the level of unionization, which could affect the employment of immigrants across categories of jobs. Not only are Canadian and Australian unions more powerful than those in the United States, but they might also have been more receptive to immigrant workers. Unfortunately, information about union membership is not available in any of the three censuses, so a direct assessment of the comparative impact of unions on immigrants is not possible. It may be speculated that the relation between unions and immigrants is more positive where unions are stronger. The weaker U.S. unions are not oblivious to immigrants as potential recruits but might often respond defensively because of the potential that immigrant labor has to undermine the earnings position of established groups (Rosenblum 1973; Parmet 1981; Collomp 1988; see also Delgado 1993). DeFreitas's (1988) and Borjas's (1987) research suggests that immigrants in the United States are in fact in a competitive position relative to the dominant native-born White group, although this impact may be limited by the specific industrial concentrations of immigrants and by the fact that it is the Black native-born who are more vulnerable to immigrant competition.

The stance of Canadian unions toward immigrants might have been more positive, but there are no data with which to compare the relative success of U.S. and Canadian unions in organizing immigrants. In a reanalysis of Reitz's (1990) survey data for Toronto, minority group immigrant males of recent arrival in nonprofessional or nonmanagerial occupations were as likely to be union members as were the native-born, though this was less true of immigrant women. The rate of union membership for such males in the "majority Canadian group" (persons of English, Irish, or Scottish background whose families had been in

Canada at least three generations) was 34.2 percent, compared to 37.7 percent for Black West Indian immigrant men, 24.4 percent for Chinese, and 53.5 percent for Portuguese. The corresponding figures for women were 23.1 percent for the majority Canadian group, 24.5 percent for Black West Indian immigrant women, 27.5 percent for Chinese, and 17.0 percent for Portuguese.[9] By way of explanation, women in Toronto are more often unionized in the professional occupations, and relatively few recent immigrant women are employed in such jobs.

Australian unions historically have responded very positively to immigration. As discussed in Chapter 3, they have supported a strong immigration policy in return for acceptance of immigrant entry into unions. This was the case, at least, for Italian and Greek immigrants, who have often worked in the auto industry and in other mainstream employment sectors. Unions have had less success with more recently arrived groups, many from Asia, as Bertone and Griffen (1992) have shown. However, obstacles are also apparent (Quinlan and Lever-Tracy 1990).

Even if immigrant labor market concentrations are greater in the United States and less in Canada and Australia, the magnitude of any effect is unknown. Research has supported the labor market stratification perspective by focusing on disadvantaged labor market locations of immigrants. It has shown that recent minority immigrants in all countries tend to be overconcentrated in jobs which are low-paying and where working conditions are often poor and hours unattractive, with very limited prospects for career advancement. Often, they work in particular industries in highly competitive, low-wage sectors, such as textiles, and in particular factories or workplaces within such industries. However, we know little about the extent to which settings in which there are high levels of immigrant segmentation put immigrants at a greater disadvantage than settings in which comparable immigrants experience less segmentation. Even when labor market concentrations of immigrants are shown to lead to wages which are lower than expected based on measured human capital such as years of education, it may be that immigrants who work in these jobs often do not have the qualifications for other employment; thus, their low wages and lack of career prospects might reflect at least to some extent a lack of human capital (see Borjas 1990). To explain why immigrant earnings are low in these jobs, competitive labor market theorists also point to more subtle deficiencies in immigrant qualifications, such as the possibility that foreign education or experience may be poor or not relevant to present job requirements (Borjas 1985, Chiswick 1986).[10] In short, immigrant concentration in poor jobs does not mean that the jobs themselves are the source of disadvantage. Such concentration could be a descriptive fact without explanatory significance. The research has shown that immigrants have a distinctive labor market *loca-*

tion, but it has not clearly demonstrated that labor market structure itself is the cause of that location. Labor market stratification theory in general remains controversial for such reasons, as described in Chapter 1.[11]

Union effects on immigrants may apply even when they are not necessarily traceable to specific sectors. Research on the impact of unionization in general has suggested that its effects are not at all limited to specific unionized workplaces or narrowly circumscribed industries. Rather, the largest effects come when unions become institutionalized powers within broad labor market sectors. Where unions become institutionalized, wage effects for both unionized and nonunionized workers have been demonstrated in a time-series analysis of union and nonunion sectors of the U.S. workforce by Rubin (1986). On a cross-national basis, those countries with stronger union movements have tended to adopt a 'corporatist' approach to employment which includes benefits for workers across diverse labor market segments, while countries with weaker unions have adopted a 'dualist' approach that increases labor market segmentation and inequality (Goldthorpe 1984). This finding supports the speculation that greater unionization in Canada or Australia could affect immigrants by determining the overall earnings distribution as much as by affecting wage rates for specific occupations or industries in which immigrants are concentrated.[12]

Immigrant self-employment, and the ethnic enclave economy, could alter the impact of labor markets for employment. Light (1972) has suggested that minority businesses might provide immigrants with opportunities outside the mainstream workforce, freeing them from disadvantages they might otherwise experience (see also Light and Rosenstein 1995). Wilson and Portes (1980) suggest that specifically in Miami, with its extremes of rich and poor, Cuban immigrants in self-employment have escaped the poverty to which they otherwise might have been exposed. Thus, the self-employment option could weaken any expected contextual effect which might have been expected based on labor market structure. Immigrants who are self-employed tend to earn more than their employed counterparts, net of easily measured human capital endowments such as education and work experience. Hence, very high rates of self-employment might affect the overall entry-level earnings for the group. Lower entry-level earnings for immigrants in the United States might be offset also by opportunities for self-employment within the ethnic-enclave economy.

However, it seems doubtful that the self-employment option moderates the entry-level immigrant earnings hierarchy much. The reasons are several. First, cross-national variations in opportunities for self-employment are small, as was seen above. In fact, immigrant self-employment has been a focus of interest in Canada (Reitz 1990, Razin and Langlois

1996) and Australia (Castles 1991; Collins 1995) as well as in the United States. Second, where self-employment opportunity is greater, it affects the native-born as well as immigrants. In the first years following the arrival of immigrants, in fact, opportunity for self-employment may be among the circumstances putting immigrants at a disadvantage. The native born have a head-start in accumulating location-specific resources for entrepreneurship. Third, even at best, only small minorities of immigrants in fact become self-employed. Again, this is particularly true for the most recently arrived groups, since it takes time to establish businesses. In the U.S. urban census sample, among males, only two recent immigrant groups have rates of self-employment higher than that of native-born non-Hispanic Whites: 10.0 percent. The rate for Koreans is highest, at 23.5 percent. The other above average group is the recently arrived Cubans, but at 11.8 percent they are barely more often self-employed than mainstream persons. Recently arrived Chinese men have a self-employment about the same as the mainstream rate—10.3 percent. Many immigrant groups have *lower* rates of self-employment: Indians (7.8 percent), Blacks (3.4 percent), Filipinos (2.7 percent), Vietnamese (2.2 percent), and Mexicans (2.1 percent).

More important, while self-employment boosts earnings in all groups, the group-to-group hierarchy of earnings is virtually the same for the self-employed as for those who are otherwise employed. Those groups whose employment earnings are relatively high also have relatively high self-employment earnings. Those groups whose employment earnings are relatively low also have relatively low self-employment earnings. This duplication of the earnings hierarchy for the self-employed probably occurs because the resources required for success in self-employment—financial and human capital, including ethnic resources—mirror those required for success in employment. Hence, the impact of self-employment on that hierarchy is very small. The result is that the inclusion of the self-employed alters the earnings hierarchy very little.[13]

Overall, it seems reasonable as a first approximation to estimate labor market effects on immigrant entry-level earnings by focusing on the earnings distribution itself and ignoring (for the moment) differences in the earnings hierarchies due to differences in the value of human capital or differences in specific labor market concentrations of immigrants.

Overall Earnings Distributions and Immigrant Earnings

Estimates of the impact of cross-national differences in the earnings distribution on immigrant entry earnings in the 93-city labor force sample are presented in Table 5.5. The methodology[14] used for these estimates is based on the assumption that cross-national differences in the coefficient

TABLE 5.5 Estimated Effects of Earnings Distributions on Cross-national Differences in the Entry-Level Earnings of Immigrants in Urban Labor Force, by Origins and Gender, ca. 1980

U.S.-Canadian Comparison

Origins and Gender	Relative Mean Earnings (Observed: Tables 2.2, 4.5)			Estimate Based on U.S. Workers with Canadian Earnings Distribution[1]			Estimate Based on Canadian Workers with U.S. Earnings Distribution[2]		
	United States	Canada	Difference	United States	Canada	Difference	United States	Canada	Difference
Men									
White	0.90	1.00	-0.10	0.91	1.00	-0.09	0.90	1.00	-0.10
Chinese	0.63	0.77	-0.14	0.66	0.77	-0.11	0.63	0.75	-0.12
Other Latin American	0.55	0.71	-0.16	0.58	0.71	-0.13	0.55	0.69	-0.14
Black	0.54	0.70	-0.16	0.57	0.70	-0.13	0.54	0.68	-0.14
Women[3]									
White	0.44	0.50	-0.06	0.44	0.50	-0.06	0.44	0.49	-0.05
Chinese	0.40	0.48	-0.08	0.41	0.48	-0.07	0.40	0.47	-0.07
Black	0.39	0.46	-0.07	0.40	0.46	-0.06	0.39	0.44	-0.05
Other Latin American	0.32	0.42	-0.10	0.33	0.42	-0.09	0.32	0.40	-0.08

(continues)

TABLE 5.5   (continued)

U.S.-Australian Comparison

Origins and Gender	Relative Mean Earnings (Observed: Tables 2.2, 4.5)			Estimate Based on U.S. Workers with Australian Earnings Distribution[4]			Estimate Based on Australian Workers with U.S. Earnings Distribution[5]		
	United States	Australia	Difference	United States	Australia	Difference	United States	Australia	Difference
Men									
White	0.90	1.00	-0.10	0.93	1.00	-0.07	0.90	1.00	-0.10
Asian	0.75	0.84	-0.09	0.83	0.84	-0.02	0.75	0.77	-0.02
Women[6]									
White	0.44	0.65	-0.21	0.45	0.65	-0.20	0.44	0.66	-0.22
Asian	0.47	0.64	-0.17	0.48	0.64	-0.16	0.48	0.64	-0.16

[1]Mean earnings for U.S. groups have been raised to reflect the smaller Canadian coefficient of variation, by reducing the difference from the mean by the ratio of coefficients: 0.708/0.765 = 0.925.

[2]Mean earnings for Canadian groups similarly have been lowered to reflect the larger U.S. coefficient of variation.

[3]For women, a method similar to that used for men is employed, except using coefficients of variation measured among women. Thus, the U.S. groups have been raised to reflect the smaller Canadian coefficient of variation, by reducing the difference from the mean by the ratio of coefficients: 0.706/0.771 = 0.916. However, women's coefficients reflect variations around the overall mean for women; in the adjustments, this overall mean, and the gender difference, is assumed to remain constant.

[4]Mean earnings for U.S. groups have been raised to reflect the smaller Australian coefficient of variation, by reducing the difference from the mean by the ratio of coefficients: 0.537/0.765 = 0.702.

[5]Mean earnings for Australian groups similarly have been lowered to reflect the larger U.S. coefficient of variation.

[6]For women, a method similar to that used for men is employed, except using coefficients of variation measured among women. Thus, the U.S. groups have been raised to reflect the smaller Australian coefficient of variation, by reducing the difference from the mean by the ratio of coefficients: 0.570/0.771 = 0.739. However, women's coefficients reflect variations around the overall mean for women; in the adjustments, this overall mean, and the gender difference, is assumed to remain constant.

Sources: See Table 5.3.

of earnings variation affect each person in proportion to his or her earnings deviation from mean earnings. In other words, we assume that the position immigrants in the United States might have within the Canadian or Australian earnings distributions can be estimated by appropriately "squeezing" the American distribution. Estimates for men and women are prepared on a gender-specific basis. That is, males and females are assumed to work in totally separate labor markets, and gender-specific earnings distributions are used in the adjustment. The adjustment also assumes that relative earnings of males and females remain unchanged (the position of females is nevertheless expressed in relation to the native-born White male benchmark).

In Table 5.5, the first three columns show observed entry-level earnings for selected immigrant groups, and cross-national differences (U.S.-Canadian in the top panel, U.S.-Australian in the bottom panel). The second set of three columns shows how the relative position of U.S. immigrant groups would compare to that of their counterparts in Canada (top panel) or Australia (bottom panel) if the overall U.S. earnings distribution was similar to the Canadian or Australian (in terms of the coefficient of variation). The third set of three columns reverses the comparison, showing how the relative positions of Canadian or Australian immigrant groups would compare to those of their U.S. counterparts if the overall Canadian or Australian earnings distributions were similar to the U.S. distributions.

The impact of the earnings distribution in the Canadian-U.S. comparison is significant but moderate in size. If the U.S. male earnings distribution, with its 1980 standard deviation of 0.765 of mean earnings, were squeezed down to a standard deviation of 0.708 of mean earnings, which was the corresponding situation in Canada (these figures are from Table 5.3), while preserving the earnings hierarchy, the impact would be to raise the relative earnings of recent immigrant groups falling below the mean income. The lower the group's position in the United States, the greater the benefit of reducing earnings inequality to the Canadian standard.[15] White male immigrants would move up from 90 percent of native-born White male earnings to 91 percent, Chinese male immigrants would move up from 63 to 66 percent, "other" Latin American male immigrants from 0.55 to 0.58 percent, and Black male immigrants from 54 percent to 57 percent. Given that the actual relative position of the three groups in Canada was 100 percent, 77 percent, 71 percent, and 70 percent, respectively, it may be inferred that the difference in earnings distributions in the two countries accounts for about a tenth of the greater earnings disadvantage in the United States for the White immigrants, and about a fifth of the greater earnings disadvantage for the minority groups.

Adjusting the position of Canadian immigrant groups to reflect a U.S. earnings distribution has a slightly smaller effect. This is because immigrant groups have a higher entry-level status in Canada and the impact of earnings variations is greatest for persons farther from the mean. For White immigrant males in Canada, entry-level earnings are on par with those of native-born White Canadian men, so there is no effect of altering the earnings distribution at all. These immigrants earn the same mean income regardless of how overall earnings vary around that mean. Other immigrant groups in Canada are affected, but less so than their counterparts in the United States. The impact of the earnings distribution thus interacts with other determinants of low earnings, such as the skills gap. Where the immigrant skills gap is greater and entry-level earnings are lower, a wider earnings distribution magnifies and compounds the resulting disadvantage.

For immigrant women in the United States, the impact of shifting to the Canadian earnings distribution moves in the same direction but is estimated to be smaller. The smaller effect arises because although the coefficients of earnings variation for men and women are of about the same magnitude, the earnings of immigrant women do not fall so far behind those of native-born White women (in percentage terms) as do the earnings of immigrant men behind those of native-born White men. The U.S.-Canadian difference in female earnings distributions accounts for about one-tenth of the lower entry levels for minority immigrant women in Canada, and for less than one-tenth for White immigrant women.

The substantially more egalitarian earnings distribution observed in the 1981 Australian data has a more dramatic estimated effect on the relative earnings of immigrants there compared to the United States (see the bottom half of Table 5.5). Recent White male immigrants would find that they move up from 90 percent of native-born White male earnings to 93 percent (rather than 91 percent as in the Canadian comparison). For recent Asian immigrants, reducing U.S. inequality to Australian levels would raise the relative earnings of recent Asian immigrant men in the United States from 75 percent to 82 percent. This is over three-fourths of the cross-national difference in immigrant entry levels. On the other hand, the relative position of Asian immigrant women is little affected by the overall earnings distribution, because on average, Asian immigrant women in both countries have earnings close to the average for native-born White women.

In sum, the cross-national differences in overall earnings distribution are estimated to account for varying proportions of the observed differences in the earnings of specific minority origins groups. The impact of overall earnings inequality on White immigrant groups is less because White immigrants enter closer to mean earnings in all countries. The impact on minority immigrant men explains about one-tenth of the lower entry levels in the United States compared to Canada, and nearly three-fourths of the lower entry levels in the United States compared to Australia. The impact on immigrant women is estimated to be less if we assume no change in relative male-female earnings differentials, mainly because earnings disadvantages of immigrant women relative to native-born White women are less in percentage terms. Other determinants of immigrant entry-level earnings, such as the skills gap, interact with the impact of extreme earnings inequality. They compound each other in driving down the earnings of newly arrived immigrants. The labor market effect is very real and substantial, and should be considered as among the most important reasons for lower immigrant standing in the United States. This is true regardless of whether the impact ultimately is traced to specific sources such as immigrant concentrations in labor market segments or is found to exist for immigrants across specific labor market niches. The size of the effect makes the effort to pinpoint its source more compelling.

Interurban Variations in Labor Markets

The analysis of the effects of interurban variations in labor markets within the United States on immigrant earnings can be far more detailed because of the better measures available. We can examine effects of overall earnings distributions, and we also can look at specific labor market segments. In the latter case, we can examine not only the location of immigrants within segments but also the impact on immigrants of the size of the segments. Furthermore, we can take account of the self-selection effects of labor markets on where immigrants live as well as the impact of labor markets directly on immigrant earnings. This analysis takes us well beyond what has been done in previous analyses and might provide a better perspective from which to interpret cross-national labor market effects.

Regional differences are one of the most prominent features of U.S. labor markets. Industrial restructuring, declining unionization, and greater earnings inequality are all associated with regional differences and regional change, including the flight of jobs from the "rust belt" and "frost belt" regions of the north and northeast to the "sun belt" of the south and southwest. As old industries declined, new industries rose, often in new areas and with new employment arrangements.

Immigrants have been attracted to a variety of regional labor market systems. Some have been attracted to the restructured urban economies of the northeast—New York, in particular, but also Boston and other cities; others have flocked to the expanding and rapidly changing economies of the south and west, including Miami, San Francisco, and Los Angeles. Labor demand is one of the common denominators here, and labor market structure seems less relevant. Rates of unionization, for example, vary widely among these immigrant cities. Some cities, such as

New York and San Francisco, remain relatively highly unionized, while others, such as Miami, have very weak labor movements. The cities which do *not* attract immigrants in the United States, even those which have enjoyed fairly healthy economies and strong labor demand, also vary widely in terms of labor market structure. Minneapolis–St. Paul is one of these economically healthy low-immigration cities, and it is relatively unionized; Atlanta is an economically healthy low-immigration city and is relatively ununionized. Perhaps contrary both to human capital theory and to segmented labor market theory, lack of labor market regulation—and associated extremes of high and low earnings—is not a source of demand for immigrants within the United States. Yet we might still ask what the effects of this labor market variation are on immigrants. What is the impact of local labor market structures on immigrants? What is the relation between local labor market structure and educational polarization identified in Chapter 4? Does labor market structure explain any of the effect of such polarization?

Regional labor markets also differ in Canada, but less so. And more importantly, all three of the major immigration centers in Canada—Toronto, Montreal, and Vancouver—are relatively highly unionized environments compared to the United States. This suggests that at the urban level, the Canadian-U.S. labor market differences might actually have a greater impact on immigrants than appears in the national data. Meltz's (1989) comparison of union "densities" in Canada and the United States showed that while unionization is higher in Canada, the regional differences within countries are nearly as dramatic as are the differences between them. In his study for 1982, union densities in parts of the industrial U.S. northeast—New York and Michigan states, for example—were actually higher than those in Ontario, though not as high as in British Columbia. However, it remains true that in Canada, the urban areas with greatest immigration tend to be those with high levels of unionization. Hence, from the standpoint of immigrants, there might be less effective labor market variation in Canada than in the United States.

In Australia, there is relative regional uniformity in matters of labor market structure, as in other matters affecting immigrants. Union influence, income inequality, and labor market structures all tend to be comparatively uniform. Hence, labor market structures are not expected to have an effect on immigrant earnings within Australia. Furthermore, because labor market options are less varied, they might have less impact on settlement decisions regarding Australia.

Again the pattern emerges of diversity in the United States, less in Canada, and least in Australia. How, if at all, do these labor market patterns help account for interurban and cross-national differences in immigrant entry?

The Interrelationship of Labor Market Characteristics in the United States

A range of specific labor market structures have been measured for U.S. cities. To capture labor market segmentation, three variables are included: lack of unionization (based on data from Freeman and Medoff 1979), the size of the low-level or labor-intensive services (retail trade, personal services, and entertainment and recreational services), and the size of the "peripheral industries" sector as defined by Oster (1979; see above). DeFreitas's measure of immigrant-intensive industries also has been applied.[16] The impact of postindustrialism, or the "global cities" phenomenon, is measured in the proportion of professional and managers in the urban area. Finally, a measure of overall earnings inequality based on the coefficient of variation in earnings also is included. Mean years of native-born education are added to show the relation of labor market structures to "education cities" examined in Chapter 4, and the proportion of immigrants shows how these various dimensions are related to immigrant settlement. The matrix of intercorrelations is presented in Table 5.6.

It is immediately obvious that labor market polarization is not more prevalent in the education cities. There is a substantial independence of the educational levels of the native-born workforce, the institutional sector examined in Chapter 4, and measures of labor market polarization measured here. Occupational structures in education cities include high proportions of persons in professional and managerial occupations ($r = 0.81$). However, these labor markets are *not* characterized by larger low-end labor market segments. They actually have somewhat smaller peripheral industries ($r = -0.36$) and virtually no difference in the size of the low-level service sector (-0.06). High-education cities do have more immigrants ($r = 0.62$), however, and hence more employment in immigrant-intensive industries ($r = 0.15$). Note that cities with larger low-end labor market sectors broadly defined are not particularly attractive to immigrants ($r = 0.03$).

Education cities, and cities with a high proportion of managers and professionals, do have greater earnings inequality ($r = 0.28$ and 0.10, respectively). However, as Nelson and Lorence (1985) also found, this effect occurs mainly because earnings are boosted at the top end, not because there is a polarized labor market with substantial service-sector or other employment generated at the bottom. In fact, both high levels of education and high proportions of managers and professionals in an urban area are *negatively* associated with the size of the low-level service sector ($r = -0.06$, and -0.20, respectively) and the size of the peripheral industry sector ($r = -0.36$ and -0.42, respectively). The fact that they are less

TABLE 5.6 Matrix of Intercorrelations[1] Among U.S. Urban Area Characteristics, 1980

Urban area Characteristics[2]	1.	2.	3.	4.	5.	6.	7.	8.
1. Mean Years of Education of White Native-Born Men	1.00							
2. Proportion in Managerial or Professional Occupations	0.81	1.00						
3. Earnings Inequality	0.28	0.10	1.00					
4. Size of Low-Level Service Sector	-0.06	-0.20	0.49	1.00				
5. Low Union Density	0.20	0.29	0.61	0.31	1.00			
6. Size of Peripheral Industries	-0.36	-0.42	0.23	-0.01	0.18	1.00		
7. Size of Immigrant-Intensive Industries	0.15	-0.05	0.36	0.11	-0.12	0.30	1.00	
8. Proportion of Immigrants	0.62	0.24	0.38	0.03	-0.06	-0.05	0.55	1.00

[1]In the United States, the 79 urban area (i.e., SMSA) characteristics were measured across the entire 5 percent A-File sample of the urban labor force aged 16–64; N = 2,832,668 across all urban areas. An exception is Mean Years of Education of White Native-Born Men, which was measured in sample data as described in Table 4.7. These measures were then applied to the labor force sample used in most of the analysis of immigrant earnings, namely, White native-born and recent immigrant men with earnings over $100. Thus, N = 170,649 for this table of intercorrelations.

[2]For further description of the measures, see Chapter 5, p. 177.

Sources: See Table 5.3 and Chapter 1, note 14.

unionized (r = 0.20 and 0.29, respectively, with low unionization) reflects professional and managerial employment. Education cities do not have sharply polarized labor market structures.

A lack of occupational or labor market polarization in immigrant cities runs counter to the global cities hypothesis of Saskia Sassen. Sassen argued that labor market restructuring toward higher skills and professional-managerial employment generates personal service jobs, which in turn attract immigrants. She suggested, however, that these jobs might not show up in official data such as census data: "The expansion of the advanced service sector . . . generates an increase in the category of very high income workers whose lifestyles, in turn, generate a demand for low-wage workers. Many of these jobs fall outside any of the major industry counts, not so much because they involve illegal immigrants, but because they are part of that expanding category usually referred to as 'off-the-books jobs'" (Sassen 1988, 158).

Sassen continued with a number of examples: "Part of the goods and services produced in the underground economy circulate through the modern sector of the economy that caters to these high-income lifestyles: the preparation of specialty and gourmet foods, the production of decorative items and luxury clothing and other personal goods, various kinds of services for cleaning, repair, errand-running, etc." (Sassen 1988, 158).

Even if these jobs are "off the books," they do not necessarily go unreported in census data. Certainly the labor-intensive service jobs identified in these census data are very poorly paid. Even for native-born Whites, overall earnings in these jobs average $6600 (35 percent) below the mean for men, and $4000 (45 percent) below the mean for women (the figures are in U.S. dollars, for 1980). More important, Sassen's claim that the high-end labor market sector explains why these industries arise in New York and not in Detroit seems to have missed the difference between the effect of labor market stratification and labor market growth. Our data suggest that what distinguishes the New Yorks from the Detroits is both higher labor demand in New York and the associated presence of immigrants. Unskilled immigrants are indeed attracted to cities with high-end employment. However, as we found in Chapter 4, the flow of immigrants to education cities is related to high labor demand in general. Large immigrant communities tend to have lower educational levels, most likely due to selective effects of networks and chain migration. These findings fit more closely with the work of Waldinger (1984) and Bailey (1987), who suggested that in these instances, immigrant labor supply generates specific demand, rather than the other way around (see also Noyelle 1987, 117).

This interpretation, that polarized labor markets do not attract more immigrants, in no way evaluates the quality of the employment obtained by immigrants. The question of how satisfactory are the employment arrangements for immigrants has little to do with the question of whether immigrants come to fill demand created by an affluent, professionalized, native-born workforce, as Sassen had suggested, or whether they are attracted by a dynamic economic environment and then fill various specific jobs which may be created because of their presence, as our data would seem to indicate. The interrelationship of supply and demand is one question; immigrant exploitation is another. Immigrant-intensive industries do arise in the education cities, indicating that patterns of concentration and potential exploitation do arise. But as DeFreitas (1988) had pointed out, these are a rather ad hoc group of industries, in which immigrant labor proves useful to employers. The jobs arise as employers take advantage of the presence of an immigrant workforce unable to bargain for higher wages.

The question is, what labor market structures are associated with earnings inequality and also attract immigrants? Four low-end employment sectors are related to overall earnings inequality. These include nonunionized jobs in general (r = 0.61), labor-intensive services (r = 0.49), immigrant-intensive industries (r = 0.36), and peripheral industries (r = 0.23). Of these, the relation of earnings inequality to unionization stands out most sharply. As Meltz (1989) pointed out—and the AFL-CIO casebook *A Tale of Two Nations* agrees—the regional pattern is linked to state legislation, particularly "right to work" laws.[17]

However, the matrix of correlations in Table 5.6 shows that the three major low-end labor market structures—low-level services, peripheral industries, and low union densities—are *not* related to whether immigrants are attracted. The best answer to the question of what structure both leads to inequality and is associated with more immigrants is the immigrant-intensive industries of DeFreitas. It is the heavy concentration of immigrants in particular industries that deserves special attention.[18] If other dimensions of low-end labor market structure are independently related to immigrant inequality, it may be because of their impact on wage standards generally rather than because of an impact on immigrants in particular. These sectors drive down wages and affect immigrants and other vulnerable workers, creating inequality for both.

The variability of earnings inequality in the United States, and its independence from attractiveness to immigrants, can be seen in Table 5.7. The table presents the coefficients of variation for all 93 urban areas across the three countries.[19] It shows, first, that not only are wage disparities highest in the United States, less in Canada, and least in Australia, but the laissez-faire U.S. pattern is also reflected in greater variation in the degree of inequality among urban areas. In the three most inegalitarian *categories* of urban areas (two left-hand columns), all are found in the United

TABLE 5.7 Earnings Inequality in Urban Area Labor Force, in the United States, Canada, and Australia, ca. 1980

0.750+	Coeff. of Var. (N)	0.650–0.699	Coeff. of Var. (N)	< 0.650	Coeff. of Var. (N)
Miami	0.835 (24455)	Nassau	0.697 (38117)	Toledo	0.648 (9577)
Orlando	0.789 (10553)	Omaha	0.696 (10496)	Syracuse	0.643 (9438)
Memphis	0.785 (10838)	Indianapolis	0.695 (18212)	Seattle	0.641 (17085)
West Palm Bch.	0.776 (7038)	Richmond	0.693 (10510)	Albany	0.641 (10733)
Ft. Lauderdale	0.774 (13660)	Hartford	0.693 (10988)	Pittsburgh	0.640 (30997)
Tampa	0.773 (19439)	San Francisco–		Toronto	0.639 (19263)
Fresno	0.765 (6332)	Oakland	0.685 (50576)	Calgary	0.630 (3618)
San Antonio	0.764 (15139)	Oxnard–Ventura	0.684 (7330)	Rochester	0.626 (14294)
San Diego	0.763 (27170)	Kansas City	0.682 (21317)	Buffalo	0.626 (16345)
Greensboro	0.751 (11272)	Salt Lake City	0.679 (12418)	Detroit	0.625 (57953)
Dallas	0.750 (50496)	Philadelphia	0.679 (65582)	New Brunswick	0.605 (9590)
		St. Louis	0.679 (23110)	Youngstown	0.603 (6871)
0.700–0.749	*Coeff. of Var. (N)*	Louisville	0.678 (32145)	Montréal	0.597 (15296)
New Orleans	0.749 (16263)	Cincinnati	0.676 (19999)	Jersey City	0.589 (7753)
Los Angeles–L.B.	0.748 (109285)	Northeast PA	0.675 (7032)	Edmonton	0.588 (3867)
Oklahoma	0.746 (13026)	Minn.–St. Paul	0.675 (33163)	Québec	0.582 (3000)
Nashville	0.744 (13113)	Chicago	0.671 (107233)	Ottawa–Hull	0.580 (4388)
Austin	0.743 (8319)	Sacramento	0.671 (14206)	Winnipeg	0.574 (3292)
Charlotte	0.742 (10807)	Portland	0.669 (18441)	Vancouver	0.574 (6851)
Norfolk	0.742 (12458)	Riverside–S.B.	0.668 (20419)	Gary	0.569 (8787)
Birmingham	0.739 (10978)	Columbus	0.668 (16413)	Flint	0.554 (7677)
Tucson	0.738 (6845)	Washington, D.C.	0.667 (53146)	Hamilton	0.548 (3000)
Tulsa	0.736 (10520)	Baltimore	0.666 (33325)	Brisbane	0.533 (3303)
Jacksonville	0.733 (10233)	Akron	0.662 (9372)	Melbourne	0.521 (9228)
Atlanta	0.731 (32511)	Allentown	0.660 (10319)	Perth	0.516 (2901)
Newark	0.731 (29811)	Milwaukee	0.659 (21272)	Sydney	0.512 (11012)
Phoenix	0.728 (21299)	Dayton	0.656 (11906)	Adelaide	0.488 (2974)
Honolulu	0.727 (13147)	San Jose	0.655 (21391)		
Greenville	0.727 (9611)	Cleveland	0.654 (28145)		
New York	0.724 (125899)	Grand Rapids	0.653 (8712)		
Wilmington	0.717 (5984)	Springfield	0.652 (7531)		
Long Branch	0.711 (7045)				
Raleigh	0.710 (9285)				
Denver	0.707 (26418)				
Orange Co.	0.706 (31613)				
Providence	0.704 (13755)				
Houston	0.700 (48884)				
Boston	0.700 (43650)				

The index of inequality is the coefficient of variation, the standard deviation of earnings divided by the mean. For this table, the measure has been applied to the full-time, full-year labor force.

Sources: See Table 5.3.

States. Coefficients of variation for U.S. cities range from a high of 0.835 in Miami, and include 0.763 for San Diego, 0.750 for Dallas, 0.748 for Los Angeles, and 0.724 for New York. Cross-nationally, the average of the coefficients of variation for the United States is near 0.7, compared to less than 0.6 in Canada, and just above 0.5 in Australia. The range of variation is nearly twice as great in the United States as in Canada, and twice in Canada what it is in Australia. This can be measured by calculating the standard deviation of the coefficients of covariation. This figure is 0.053 for the United States, 0.029 for Canada, and 0.016 for Australia.

Table 5.7 also shows that a number of important immigrant destination cities in the United States have less earnings inequality: San Francisco-Oakland's earnings variation index is a comparatively low 0.685, Chicago's is 0.671, and San Jose's is 0.655. By contrast, however, all nine Canadian cities are in the most egalitarian group, with coefficients of variation within a much narrower range: 0.639 in Toronto, 0.597 in Montreal, 0.574 in Vancouver, and down to 0.548 in Hamilton. The five most egalitarian cities are all Australian. All have coefficients of earnings variation in the range 0.488 to 0.533.

The pattern of interurban variation in unionization rates in all three countries is very similar, as the data in Table 5.8 (from the 1970s) clearly show.[20] While unionization rates are low in the United States, at only 22.7 percent, the standard deviation of these rates is a high 9.6 percent. Unionization rates are higher in Canada, at 42.3 percent on average, but the range of variation as measured by the standard deviation is less, 4.6 percent. Finally, the unionization rates are highest in Australia, 50.7 percent on average for the five cities, and the standard deviation is only 1.2 percent.

Most importantly, unionization rates in an urban area are a very strong negative predictor of earnings inequality in the United States. The correlation coefficient for the relation between the unionization and earnings inequality across the 79 U.S. cities is r = –0.71. Unionization rates thus account for about half of U.S. interurban variation in inequality. Perhaps related to the greater strength of unions nationally in Canada, not only is the local variation less, but the link between local unionization rates and local earnings inequality is less strong. Very likely this reflects a pattern whereby stronger labor movements establish labor standards which benefit both union and nonunion employees. This leads to an expectation for a more egalitarian labor force regardless of local conditions and the specific local power base for unions.

The relation between local equality and local union rates in Canada is only r = –0.37, indicating that local unionization rates account for only about 15 percent or less of local variations in inequality. In Australia, with its national industrial relations system, local unionization rates are quite similar across the country and have little if anything to do with lo-

TABLE 5.8   Relation Between Earnings Inequality and Union Density in the Urban Areas of the United States, Canada, and Australia, 1980

Country	Coefficient of Variation in Earnings, Urban Areas[1]	Union Density, Urban Areas (Percent Union Members)	
		All Workers	Production Workers
United States (N = 79)			
Mean	0.695	22.7	35.0
S.D.	0.053	9.6	13.4
r	–	–0.71[2]	–0.68[2]
Canada (N = 9)			
Mean	0.584	42.3	46.1
S.D.	0.029	4.6	5.1
r	–	–0.37	–0.37
Australia (N = 5)			
Mean	0.514	50.7	55.8
S.D.	0.016	1.2	1.3
r	–	+0.64	+0.64

[1]Figures are from Table 5.7. In these data, men and women are combined. Average coefficients of variation for men are: U.S. 0.641, Canada 0.590, and Australia 0.514. Average coefficients of variation for women are: U.S. 0.547, Canada 0.472, and Australia 0.432.
[2]$p < 0.001$.
Sources: See Table 5.3; for union data see Chapter 5, note 20.

cal conditions affecting earnings inequality (which, again, does not vary much, in any case). In effect, labor markets in Australia operate as if there is one national labor market, rather than local labor markets. This reflects a strong institutional base for collective determination of wage rates in Australia.

Labor market polarization characterizes a number of U.S. cities, mainly due to variations in unionization but also to some extent related to other dimensions of labor market stratification. These labor market variations are quite independent of educational polarization, and they should be examined in terms of their impact on immigrant settlement and earnings determination, quite apart from the effects of high native-born education examined in Chapter 4. The wide variation in U.S. labor market structures provides an opportunity for further comparative analysis and generates a higher-resolution picture of the differences among the three countries in the entry-level earnings of immigrants.

Selective Effects of Urban Labor Markets

To assess selective effects of urban labor markets, two regression analyses have been performed within each ethnic-origin group. One examines how local labor markets affect the educational levels of immigrants who settle in an area. Specifically, it estimates the effects that overall earnings inequality, plus the size of key urban labor market structures—high-end professional and managerial employment, peripheral industries, low-end service jobs, and immigrant-intensive industries—have on immigrant educational levels. Where sector size effects arise, it is presumably because immigrants are attracted to work within the respective labor market segments. The second regression analysis estimates this implied effect on immigrant sector of employment.

The first regression analyses, for effects of labor market characteristics on the skill levels of immigrants in particular groups, are presented in Table 5.9. The regression analysis within each group includes a control for the size of the specific immigrant group in the urban area, which was shown in Chapter 4 to affect immigrant education. The results provide some support for both competing labor market theories—for human capital, which predicted positive effects, and for stratification, which predicted negative effects. Significantly, however, the effects are different for European-origin and non-European racial minority immigrant groups, and this fact lends additional support to the stratification theory.

First, let us look at the effect of greater overall inequality and greater high-end professional and managerial employment, in the first two columns of Table 5.9. These variables have significant effects in attracting the better-educated native-born White workers, but have only weaker and less consistent effects in attracting the more highly skilled immigrants. Most of the regression effects for both men and women are either insignificant or negative. The significant positive effects are for White immigrants, Other Latin American immigrants (many of whom might also be White), and Filipino and Chinese immigrant men and women. The reason for the mostly nil or negative effects may be that increased job opportunities at the top end are irrelevant to the immigrant labor market in most groups. These immigrants—Blacks, Mexicans, Cubans, and some Asian groups—are unlikely to be professionals or managers.

Table 5.10 confirms this interpretation by showing how labor market structures affect the actual employment of immigrants. In this analysis, each industry variable is tested in a separate regression equation, and education is included as a control variable so that we may see how sectors affect immigrant employment beyond considerations related to job qualifications. Where high-end employment is more substantial, immigrants from most groups are unaffected. Their employment is elsewhere. The

TABLE 5.9 Effects[1] of Labor Market Structure and Origin-Group Size on Years of Education of Recent Immigrants in the U.S. Urban Labor Force, by Origins and Gender, 1980

Origins	Earnings Inequality	Professional and Managerial Occupations	Low-End Employment Sectors			Origin Group Size (Log)	(N)
			Low-Level Service	Peripheral Industry	Immigrant Intensive Ind.		
Native-born White	0.032 (2)	0.123 (2)	-0.006 ns	-0.027 (2)	0.027 (2)	n/a	(112218)
Recent immigrants:							
White	-0.056 (2)	0.164 (2)	0.202 (2)	0.092 (2)	-0.090 (2)	0.006 ns	(10567)
Black	-0.097 (2)	0.034 ns	-0.092 (2)	0.012 ns	-0.023 ns	-0.124 (2)	(4985)
Chinese	-0.074 (2)	0.086 (2)	0.049 (4)	0.101 (2)	0.006 ns	-0.264 (2)	(3470)
Filipino	0.067 (3)	0.132 (2)	-0.213 (2)	0.158 (2)	-0.158 (2)	0.065 (3)	(3094)
Asian Indian	-0.059 (3)	-0.003 ns	-0.047 ns	-0.057 (4)	-0.033 ns	-0.163 (2)	(3049)
Korean	0.002 ns	-0.044 ns	-0.074 (4)	-0.001 ns	0.016 ns	0.010 ns	(2105)
Vietnamese	0.036 ns	0.068 ns	-0.035 ns	-0.046 ns	0.056 (4)	0.022 ns	(1570)
Japanese	0.017 ns	-0.030 ns	-0.186 (2)	-0.033 ns	-0.029 ns	-0.120 (3)	(1117)
Other Asian	0.069 ns	-0.006 ns	-0.151 (2)	-0.026 ns	-0.054 ns	-0.058 ns	(1102)
Mexican	-0.015 ns	-0.013 ns	-0.048 (2)	-0.107 (2)	-0.007 ns	-0.038 (2)	(15049)
Cuban	0.096 ns	-0.027 ns	-0.024 ns	-0.043 ns	0.011 ns	-0.158 (4)	(1869)
Other Latin American	0.045 (4)	0.099 (2)	0.020 ns	0.030 ns	-0.022 ns	-0.170 (2)	(7079)

Sector Size

Men

(continues)

TABLE 5.9 (continued)

Origins	Earnings Inequality	Professional and Managerial Occupations	Low-End Employment Sectors			Origin Group Size (Log)	(N)
			Low-Level Service	Peripheral Industry	Immigrant Intensive Ind.		
Women							
Native-born White	0.023 (2)	0.091 (2)	−0.016 (2)	−0.054 (2)	0.036 (2)	n/a	(80107)
Recent immigrants:							
White	−0.056 (2)	0.142 (2)	0.267 (2)	0.071 (2)	−0.105 (2)	0.053 (2)	(6608)
Black	−0.114 (2)	0.009 ns	0.040 ns	−0.009 ns	−0.036 ns	−0.026 ns	(4308)
Chinese	−0.026 ns	0.128 (2)	0.076 (2)	0.112 (2)	−0.004 ns	−0.226 (2)	(2763)
Filipino	0.086 (2)	0.080 (2)	−0.210 (2)	0.137 (2)	−0.082 (2)	0.064 (2)	(3759)
Asian Indian	−0.014 ns	−0.108 (3)	−0.077 (4)	−0.129 (2)	−0.021 ns	−0.142 (2)	(1677)
Korean	−0.013 ns	0.073 (4)	−0.035 ns	0.119 (2)	0.011 ns	0.097 (2)	(1911)
Vietnamese	0.003 ns	−0.014 ns	−0.067 ns	−0.051 ns	0.018 ns	0.132 (2)	(1104)
Japanese	−0.044 ns	−0.020 ns	−0.116 ns	0.103 ns	−0.045 ns	0.132 (4)	(479)
Other Asian	0.005 ns	−0.018 ns	−0.140 (3)	0.064 ns	0.055 ns	0.127 (3)	(663)
Mexican	0.008 ns	−0.030 ns	−0.029 ns	−0.108 (2)	−0.101 (2)	−0.021 ns	(5798)
Cuban	−0.117 ns	−0.085 ns	0.068 ns	−0.145 (4)	−0.025 ns	−0.009 ns	(1534)
Other Latin American	0.071 (3)	0.032 ns	−0.020 ns	−0.009 ns	−0.036 ns	−0.172 (2)	(5033)

[1]Standardized regression coefficients for effects of six urban area characteristics on immigrant years of education; separate regression for each origins-gender group.

[2]$p < 0.001$.

[3]$p < 0.01$.

[4]$p < 0.05$.

Sources: See Table 5.3.

TABLE 5.10   Effects of Labor Market Sector Size on Immigrant Employment in the U.S. Urban Labor Force, with Years of Education Controlled, by Origins and Gender, 1980

	Sector Size and Areas of Employment			
	Professional and Managerial Occupations	Low-End Employment Sectors		
Origins		Low-Level Service	Peripheral Industry	Immigrant-Intensive Ind.
Men				
Native-born White	0.044 [2]	0.043 [2]	0.079 [2]	0.076 [2]
Recent immigrants:				
White	0.056 [2]	0.088 [2]	0.077 [2]	0.084 [2]
Black	0.022 ns	0.054 [2]	0.053 [2]	0.076 [2]
Chinese	−0.013 ns	0.007 ns	0.042 [4]	0.041 [4]
Filipino	−0.001 ns	0.120 [2]	0.045 [4]	0.013 ns
Asian Indian	−0.015 ns	0.086 [2]	0.090 [2]	0.072 [2]
Korean	0.010 ns	0.086 [2]	0.090 [2]	0.072 [2]
Vietnamese	0.097 [2]	0.036 ns	0.102 [2]	0.176 [2]
Japanese	0.050 ns	0.142 [2]	0.026 ns	0.028 ns
Other Asian	0.018 ns	0.049 ns	0.146 [2]	0.085 [3]
Mexican	0.014 ns	0.043 [2]	0.107 [2]	0.198 [2]
Cuban	0.021 ns	0.001 ns	0.078 [2]	−0.041 ns
Other Latin	0.032 [3]	0.030 [4]	0.088 [2]	0.094 [2]
Women				
Native-born White	0.008 [4]	0.050 [2]	0.079 [2]	0.054 [2]
Recent immigrants:				
White	0.047 [2]	0.127 [2]	0.065 [2]	0.067 [2]
Black	0.008 ns	0.038 [4]	0.069 [2]	0.046 [3]
Chinese	−0.010 ns	0.157 [2]	0.019 ns	0.044 [4]
Filipino	−0.062 [2]	0.114 [2]	0.030 ns	−0.004 ns
Asian Indian	−0.024 ns	0.051 [4]	0.101 [2]	0.069 [3]
Korean	−0.029 ns	0.172 [2]	0.157 [2]	0.013 ns
Vietnamese	0.046 [2]	0.020 ns	0.096 [3]	0.119 [2]
Japanese	0.068 ns	0.159 [2]	0.048 ns	0.047 ns
Other Asian	−0.060 ns	0.055 ns	0.085 [4]	0.018 ns
Mexican	−0.003 ns	−0.006 ns	0.053 [2]	0.088 [2]
Cuban	0.039 ns	0.072 [3]	0.153 [2]	0.033 ns
Other Latin	0.015 [2]	0.144 [2]	0.144 [2]	0.068 [2]

[1]A separate regression equation has been estimated for each origins-gender group and industrial sector, with years of education as a control variable throughout. The N's for this table are the same as in Table 5.9.
[2]$p < 0.001$.
[3]$p < p.01$.
[4]$p < 0.05$.
Sources: see Table 5.3.

exceptions again are White immigrants (whose employment pattern here parallels that of the native-born Whites), Vietnamese, and Other Latin Americans.

Borjas had suggested that greater inequality and high-end employment opportunities in the United States ought to have positive selective effects and boost immigrant skill levels. We can see that this doesn't really happen for most groups. Borjas's data came mainly from his analysis of migration between the United States and Canada, most of which would have been by Whites. Our data are consistent with his findings for Whites, but they also suggest a difference between White and non-White immigration. Patterns of U.S.-Canadian migration may not be a good model for immigration from the Caribbean, Asia, Africa, and Latin America. The high-end employment sector might create positive selective effects mainly for White immigrants, such as for Canadians moving to the United States, or for Europeans. They appear not to have the same effects for Black, most Asian, and non-White Latin American immigrants.

Urban areas with the greatest overall earnings inequalities also are not more attractive to the best-educated immigrants in most cases (the exceptions being Filipinos and Other Latin Americans). In fact, the pattern is more often the other way around. Again, this does not support the human capital interpretation of Borjas. Immigrants may correctly perceive that at least in the short term, the high incomes possible at the top end in certain cities will not be for them. In a few instances, inequality actually attracts the *less* educated immigrants. This is consistent with the segmentation theory, suggesting that immigrants may be attracted to low-end employment opportunities.

Now we look directly at effects of specific low-end sectors (proceeding from Table 5.9 to Table 5.10). Labor market segmentation theory suggests that the prevalence of low-end employment attracts less-educated immigrants, because they are found working in these low-end jobs. The data provide some support for this theory, but the effects are particular to specific industries and specific minority immigrant groups. A larger low-end service industry sector attracts better-educated White immigrants, but attracts less-educated minority immigrants in six of eleven instances for men, and in three of eleven instances for women (refer to Table 5.9). And unlike the case for the high-end employment, larger low-end service employment does in fact more often lead to employment in that sector for many minority immigrant groups (Table 5.10).

It would be a mistake to exaggerate this segmentation effect on recruitment, however. Of the six negative selective effects of larger low-level service sectors—for Filipino and Other Asian men and women; for Black, Japanese, Korean and Mexican men; and for Asian Indian women—the *actual employment effect* of those industries is r = 0.120 for Filipino men,

0.114 for Filipino women, 0.142 for Japanese men, but only 0.054 for Black men, only 0.043 for Mexican men, and only 0.051 for Asian Indian women, and is insignificant in other cases, such as Other Asian men and women. So even for these cases it is difficult to establish a clear and consistent scenario whereby a larger low-end service sector attracts less-skilled immigrants who are then employed in those sectors.

On the other hand, it could be important that the White immigrants are among the clear exceptions. In fact, for them, the larger low-level service industries have the opposite effect of leading to higher levels of education rather than low. It appears possible that as predicted by segmentation theory, the selective effects of industrial structure operate differently for the White groups than for the minorities.

Although there are negative selective effects of larger peripheral industries and immigrant-intensive industries, these are less consistent than the negative effect of origin-group size. The regressions show statistically significant negative selective effects of larger peripheral industries only for 5 of 24 cases (Asian Indian men and women, Mexican men and women, and Cuban women), and negative selective effects of immigrant intensive industries also only for 5 of 24 cases (White and Filipino men and women and Mexican women). There are positive effects in some cases, too—for example, the effects of peripheral industries on the educational levels of the Chinese and Filipinos. By contrast, the net negative selective effect of group size is significant in half of the cases, 7 of 12 for men, and another 3 of 12 for women.

In sum, the selective effects of labor market structure are weak and inconsistent, but they tend to support human capital theory for White immigrants and segmentation theory for racial minorities. Where there are selective effects of labor market structures and inequality, they tend to be negative, at least for minority group immigrants. At the same time, networks of chain migration, and other factors associated with immigrant community characteristics, have selective effects which are at least as strong as the effects of labor market structure, and most often, stronger.

Earnings Effects of Urban Labor Markets

The analysis of low-end labor market segments on immigrant earnings involves three issues: the extent of segmentation along the three dimensions measured, the earnings effect of employment *location* within one of the low-end segments, and the effect that the *size* of the segment in a particular area has on immigrant earnings. A separate analysis examines the impact of the *overall earnings distribution* on immigrants. Earnings distributions can be, and often are, related to sector sizes, but might have quite independent effects on immigrant earnings.

Each question addresses the issue of labor market structure differently. The distinction between an effect of location within a segment, and an effect of the size of the segment itself, is crucial to our concern with the comparative perspective. Our earlier discussion suggests that both may be important. However, while labor market location is a dramatic feature of immigrant groups, variations in sector size and in earnings distributions must be important for labor market structure to be of significance in explaining interurban (or cross-national) differences in immigrant status. Even if immigrant earnings are lower as a result of working within certain labor market segments, it does not automatically follow that immigrant earnings are lower where such sectors are larger. When we look at effects of sector size, it is possible using regression analysis to relate any effects to the location of workers within that sector. The separate analysis of overall earnings distribution enables us to capture the effects of all structural variables that might affect earnings. An additional advantage is that the effect of earnings distributions is more readily related to cross-national differences.

Earnings Effects of Low-End Labor Market Locations

Two issues are examined: first, the extent of concentration of immigrant groups in particular industrial sectors, and second, the extent to which those working in such sectors suffer earnings disadvantages as a result.

Table 5.11 shows the proportions of immigrants working in each low-end sector, compared to native-born Whites, by origin group and gender. Instances of statistically significant concentrations of immigrant groups compared to native-born Whites are indicated in bold type. Some groups are overconcentrated in labor-intensive service industries (particularly recent Chinese and Korean immigrant men, and recent Korean and Japanese immigrant women), and some are overconcentrated in peripheral industries (particularly recent Mexican immigrant men, also recent Mexican, Cuban, and Other Latin American immigrant women, and recent Chinese immigrant women). What is most striking, however, is that *all* recent immigrant groups, both men and women, are substantially and significantly concentrated in immigrant-intensive industries. Of course, to some extent this is an artifact of measurement, immigrant-intensive industries having been defined as those in which immigrants are concentrated. It is nevertheless remarkable the extent to which such concentrations exist, and the fact that all groups are affected. Among men, against a benchmark of 35.1 percent of native-born Whites who work in industries classified as immigrant intensive, for recent immigrants anywhere, between 51.8 percent (for Filipinos) and 71.9 percent (for Chinese) work in those same industries. And whereas 44.4 percent of native-born White

TABLE 5.11 Concentration[1] of Immigrants in Low-End Employment Sectors in the U.S. Urban Labor Force, by Origins and Gender, 1980

Origins	Low-Level Service Industries		Peripheral Industries		Immigrant-Intensive Industries	
	Percent Employed[2]	Difference from Native-Born White[3]	Percent Employed[2]	Difference from Native-Born White[3]	Percent Employed[2]	Difference from Native-Born White[3]
Men						
Native-born White	16.5	–	26.0	–	35.1	–
Recent immigrants:						
White	**20.4**	**3.9** [4]	**30.0**	**4.0** [4]	**55.1**	**20.0** [4]
Black	16.4	–0.1 ns	26.9	0.9 ns	**54.1**	**19.0** [4]
Chinese	**40.7**	**24.2** [4]	14.4	–11.6 [4]	**71.9**	**36.8** [4]
Filipino	14.6	–1.9 ns	18.0	–8.0 [4]	**51.8**	**16.7** [4]
Asian Indian	14.5	–2.0 ns	18.7	–7.3 [4]	**62.2**	**27.1** [4]
Korean	**30.7**	**14.2** [4]	20.7	–5.3 [6]	**57.6**	**22.5** [4]
Vietnamese	18.1	1.6 ns	21.9	–4.1 ns	**61.5**	**26.4** [4]
Japanese	19.7	3.2 ns	14.0	–12.0 [4]	**59.6**	**24.5** [4]
Other Asian	**24.4**	**7.9** [5]	20.8	–5.2 ns	**60.7**	**25.6** [4]
Mexican	**20.2**	**3.7** [4]	**44.8**	**18.8** [4]	**65.4**	**30.3** [4]
Cuban	**21.8**	**5.3** [6]	**34.7**	**8.7** [5]	**54.8**	**19.8** [4]
Other Latin American	**22.2**	**5.7** [4]	**32.8**	**6.8** [4]	**64.0**	**28.9** [4]
Women						
Native-born White	24.4	–	11.4	–	44.4	–
Recent immigrants:						
White	22.5	–1.9 ns	**21.5**	**10.1** [4]	**64.0**	**19.7** [4]
Black	24.9	0.5 ns	11.4	0.0 ns	**60.9**	**16.5** [4]
Chinese	24.5	0.1 ns	**29.7**	**18.4** [4]	**73.5**	**29.1** [4]
Filipino	13.6	–10.8 [4]	10.8	–0.6 ns	**67.4**	**23.0** [4]
Asian Indian	12.9	–11.5 [4]	12.1	0.7 ns	**66.6**	**22.2** [4]
Korean	**33.7**	**9.3** [4]	**20.2**	**8.8** [4]	**74.9**	**30.6** [4]
Vietnamese	22.8	–1.6 ns	15.7	4.3 ns	**65.0**	**20.6** [4]
Japanese	**41.1**	**16.7** [5]	15.2	3.9 ns	**66.2**	**21.8** [4]
Other Asian	27.5	3.0 ns	15.1	3.7 ns	**72.3**	**27.9** [4]
Mexican	23.3	–1.2 ns	**39.1**	**27.7** [4]	**79.1**	**34.7** [4]
Cuban	19.2	–5.3 ns	**32.1**	**20.8** [4]	**69.3**	**24.9** [4]
Other Latin American	27.2	2.8 ns	**31.5**	**20.1** [4]	**76.7**	**32.3** [4]

[1]Instances of statistically significant concentrations of minority group immigrants to native-born Whites are indicated in bold type.

[2]N's for each percentage are as in Table 5.9.

[3]The statistical significance of the difference between an immigrant group and native-born Whites is the significance of immigrant origins as a predictor of employment sector in regression equations, with native-born Whites as the reference group.

[4]$p < 0.001$.

[5]$p < 0.01$.

[6]$p < 0.05$.

Sources: See Table 5.3.

women work in industries classified as immigrant intensive, for recent immigrant women, between 60.9 percent (for Blacks) and 76.7 percent (for Other Latin Americans) work in those same industries. Clearly, immigrant concentrations in labor markets must be identified and studied in a finely graded classification. Broad designations such as "labor-intensive services" or "peripheral industries" capture only a few of the specific locations of immigrant workers.

Next, we ask how these labor market locations of immigrants affect their relative earnings. What is the net earnings effect of location in a marginal industry sector within each immigrant group? And what impact does this industrial location have in explaining the observed entry-level earnings for the group relative to the native-born Whites? To answer the first question on the earnings effect of industrial location, we estimate regression effects of industrial location on earnings, net of human capital endowments, separately for each origins group and gender. Metric effects are presented in Table 5.12, in the first of the pair of columns shown for each of three types of industrial sector.[21]

All three of the marginal employment locations are associated with low net earnings in at least some groups, though the extent varies. Labor-intensive service work is done by those lacking in job skills, but the pay is low even in relation to qualifications. In the regression results, for native-born Whites, labor-intensive service job earnings, net of human capital, are $1800 (10 percent) lower for men, and $1900 (21 percent) lower for women. In all immigrant groups, work in the labor-intensive service sector also is associated with lower net pay, and often the disadvantage is substantially greater than it is for native-born Whites. Peripheral industry jobs sometimes represent an earnings disadvantage net of human capital, but the extent is highly variable by group. These jobs are not a disadvantage for native-born Whites, for White immigrants, and for certain other immigrant groups, but they are for others. Concentrations in immigrant-intensive industries present a larger disadvantage for more groups. Net of human capital, recent immigrants of White, Black, Chinese, Japanese, Mexican, and Other Latin American origins among men, and Chinese, Mexican, and Other Latin American origins among women, suffered earnings deficits associated with employment in immigrant-intensive industries.

The impact that these industry-location effects have in lowering earnings of an immigrant group relative to native-born Whites depends not only on the size of the industry-location effect, but also on the extent of the group's concentration in the specific sector compared to the native born. To evaluate this overall impact, we must consider earnings determination processes across groups, not just within groups. We are concerned with the extent to which low earnings of particular immigrant

TABLE 5.12   Effects[1] of Low-End Employment Sector Location on Entry-Level
Earnings of Immigrants in U.S. Urban Labor Force, by Origins and Gender, 1980

	Low-Level Service		Peripheral Industry		Immigrant-Intensive Ind.	
	Effect of Sector Location[2]	Impact on Relative Earnings[3]	Effect of Sector Location[2]	Impact on Relative Earnings[3]	Effect of Sector Location[2]	Impact on Relative Earnings[3]
Origins	$ Net	$, Difference	$ Net	$, Difference	$ Net	$, Difference
Men						
Native-born Whites	−1855 [4]		736 [4]		−265 [4]	
Immigrant origins:						
White	**−3050** [4]	**−154**	223 ns	−102	**−1457** [4]	**−710**
Black	−1833 [4]	182	−270 ns	−212	**−687** [4]	**−277**
Chinese	**−3102** [4]	**−655**	1151 [6]	−19	**−1248** [4]	**−821**
Filipino	−2081 [4]	196	605 ns	−89	712 [6]	463
Asian Indian	**−2599** [4]	**−111**	−650 ns	−278	1450 [4]	1365
Korean	**−2550** [4]	**−449**	−877 ns	−317	198 ns	259
Vietnamese	−2466 [4]	382	821 [6]	118	−397 ns	316
Japanese	**−7608** [4]	**−1173**	**−4801** [4]	**−825**	**−3299** [4]	**−2043**
Other Asian	**−2522** [4]	**−170**	92 ns	−137	1026 ns	686
Mexican	**−1490** [4]	130	223 [6]	−102	**−1077** [4]	**−528**
Cuban	−1907 [4]	209	475 ns	65	−39 ns	−63
Other Latin American	−1391 [4]	204	25 ns	−160	**−579** [4]	**−251**
Women						
Native-born Whites	−1913 [4]		669 [4]		−294 [4]	
Immigrant origins:						
White	−1684 [4]	163	181 ns	−2	81 ns	221
Black	−1879 [4]	120	**−552** [6]	**−144**	−254 ns	−24
Chinese	−1605 [4]	40	−354 ns	−273	**−619** [6]	**−546**
Filipino	**−2620** [4]	**−66**	−454 ns	−140	924 [4]	758
Asian Indian	**−2293** [4]	**−32**	**−1809** [5]	**−288**	1662 [4]	1297
Korean	**−1327** [4]	**−53**	−473 ns	−158	221 ns	294
Vietnamese	−1391[4]	238	433ns	−27	180 ns	327
Japanese	−598 ns	253	−736 ns	−176	−737 ns	−213
Other Asian	−1957 [4]	6	394 ns	−33	619 ns	498
Mexican	−892 [4]	418	39 ns	5	−341 [6]	28
Cuban	−782 [6]	372	**−806** [5]	**−186**	58 ns	39
Other Latin American	−1131 [4]	250	87 ns	−22	**−402** [5]	**−118**

[1]Instances of a significant negative effect which reduces relative earnings are in bold type.
[2]Metric regression coefficients for the effect of industrial location, with human capital controls, based on separate equations for each group (from Equation 5.1; see note 21 in text; N's are as in table 5.9).
[3]The difference in metric coefficients for effects of immigrant status net of human capital, in two equations across the sample, with and without industrial location and immigrant group interactions (from Equations 5.2 and 5.3; see note 22 in text).
[4]$p < 0.001$.
[5]$p < 0.01$.
[6]$p < 0.05$.
Sources: see Table 5.3.

groups are statistically explained when account is taken of the effect of their industrial location.

In Table 5.12, the second of the pair of columns for each industrial sector contains figures representing, for each immigrant-origin group, the difference made by removing the industrial-location effect from the earnings determination equation.[22] The earnings determination equations here are those for the entire sample, to show the position of each immigrant group relative to the native-born White benchmark group. The difference made by removing the industrial-location effect represents the extent of overall earnings disadvantage accounted for by employment in the low-wage sector (considering both the extent of such employment and its wage rate for the group compared to other groups). The industrial-location effect includes a direct effect of industry location across all groups. It also includes an interaction term to reflect the effect which is specific to the immigrant group. It was apparent in Table 5.11 that the industrial location effect is highly group specific. Group specificity of effects may arise from group-specific patterns of concentration within industries. For example, when both immigrants and native-born may be located in a particular industry, native-born group members may tend more often to be employed as managers or skilled workers while immigrant group members may be concentrated in lower levels of employment.

The findings in the second of the pairs of columns in Table 5.12 show that the impact of industrial location on immigrant earnings varies considerably. Bold type is used in the table to call attention to instances where a negative sector effect actually reduces the relative earnings of group members. However, the following generalization holds: Nearly every immigrant group is negatively affected by location in at least one type of low-end employment sector. Among men, recent White and Chinese immigrants are negatively affected both by concentration in labor-intensive services and in immigrant-intensive industries. A number of other Asian groups also are negatively affected by concentrations in labor-intensive services. Japanese immigrant men are negatively affected by concentrations in all three types of sectors (although overall, Japanese immigrant men are not disadvantaged and earn comparatively high incomes). Black immigrant men are negatively affected by their concentration in immigrant-intensive industries. Mexicans and Other Latin Americans are negatively affected by concentrations in peripheral and immigrant-intensive industries. Among men, only Filipinos, Vietnamese, and Cubans are not significantly affected.

Among women, there also are negative impacts. Recent White immigrant women are not significantly affected. However, Black, Asian Indian, and Cuban immigrant women are negatively affected by concentrations in peripheral industries; Chinese and Other Latin American women by concentrations in immigrant-intensive industries; and Filipino, Asian Indian, and Korean women by concentrations in labor-intensive services. Vietnamese, Japanese, and Other Asian women are not negatively affected by industrial location. The earnings of Mexican immigrant women are lower in labor-intensive services and in immigrant-intensive industries, but the overall effect on their earnings is not strongly negative. One reason for this effect is that Mexican immigrant women were not concentrated in labor-intensive services. Another is that the negative effect of employment in immigrant-intensive industries, compared to the earnings in other sectors, was not as strong in this group as in some others.

Clearly, not every instance of immigrant low-end industrial concentration leads to substantial negative impacts on immigrant earnings. What is required is *both* substantial concentration and a substantial negative location effect. Chinese immigrant men are substantially concentrated in labor-intensive industries, and the effect of that location is substantially negative. Hence, for Chinese immigrant men, the resulting location impact on earnings is substantial: -$655 is about 11 percent of the overall net earnings disadvantage for the group. A similar situation exists for recent Korean immigrant men, both concentration and a negative earnings effect, and the resulting impact of -$449 represents 7 percent of the overall net earnings disadvantage. For Japanese women, in contrast, there is substantial concentration in this sector but without a statistically significant earnings effect. Hence, there is no negative earnings impact of this location for Japanese immigrant women.

Concentration in immigrant-intensive industries is virtually universal for immigrant groups, but net negative earnings effects are not. So an overall negative impact is found only in those cases of negative earnings effects: for White, Black, Chinese, Japanese, Mexican, and Other Latin American immigrant men, and for Chinese and other Latin American immigrant women. The negative impact of employment in immigrant-intensive industries is greater for Mexican men than for Mexican women, because although both are heavily concentrated, the negative effect on earnings is greater for the men. The effect of such employment for Blacks is less than for some of the other groups, because although particularly for men the earnings in this employment sector are low, the extent of concentration is somewhat less.

The findings underscore the fact that even immigrant-intensive industrial locations vary considerably in their specifics and may not always represent disadvantage. In some cases—Asian Indian immigrant men and women may be cited as an example—the impact of concentration in immigrant-intensive industries appears to be significantly positive on the earnings position of the group. Both men and women are represented in such industries at over 20 percent above the level for native-born Whites, and the earnings effect of such location is +$1450 for men and +$1660 for women. Hence, the net positive impact is a substantial amount relative to total earnings (particularly for the women).

The size of these industrial-location impacts are moderate. Rarely are net negative impacts more than 10 percent of overall disadvantage net of human capital. However, conclusions should await an analysis in which we have examined the impact of sector size and overall earnings distributions, not just industrial location. For, as was noted above, if there are location effects but not structural effects, then labor market structures might merely be associated with low earnings rather than actually causing them.

Earnings Effects of Sector Size

If unregulated labor markets produce greater inequality, particularly for socially vulnerable groups such as immigrants, then the degree of regulation should matter. The hypothesis is suggested that the size of the low-end employment sector may be an important variable. The larger the size of the labor-intensive service sector, or that of peripheral or immigrant-intensive industries, the greater the likelihood that immigrants will be employed in these sectors and that these sectors will have a negative effect on their earnings position relative to other groups. Therefore, we ask: Do labor markets with larger low-end industrial sectors lead to lower entrance earnings for immigrants?

The answer will come from an earnings determination analysis in which sector size is introduced as an independent variable. We also want to know whether the effect of sector size on the earnings of an immigrant group is related to concentration of the group within the industrial sector. So we need two equations, one including sector size but not individual location, and the other with both sector size and individual location.[23] Results are reported in Table 5.13. Sector size is expected to matter particularly in two circumstances: where larger sector size attracts immigrant employment, and where location in the sector reduces immigrant earnings. These cases are highlighted in boldface in the table. There are 14 such instances of theoretically expected effects in the table, involving most immigrant groups: Blacks, Chinese, Koreans, Japanese, Other Asians, Mexicans, Cubans, and Other Latin Americans.

The findings cast very serious doubt on the importance of sector size. The effect of sector size is significantly negative in only one of the 14 cases in which an effect is expected, that of White immigrant men in immigrant-intensive industries. Furthermore, even in this case, *the negative effect of sector size is not substantially explained by the location of immigrants within the sector* (because the sector size effect is only slightly reduced by

TABLE 5.13   Effects[1] of Labor Market Sector Size in an Urban Area on the Entry-Level Earnings of Immigrants in the U.S. Urban Labor Force, by Origins and Gender, 1980

| | Sector-Size/Origins Interactions for: | | | | | |
| | Low-Level Service[2] | | Peripheral Industry[2] | | Immigrant-Intensive Ind.[2] | |
Immigrant Origins	$, Net of Human Capital	$, with Location Controlled	$, Net of Human Capital	$, with Location Controlled	$, Net of Human Capital	$, with Location Controlled
Men						
White	**54** ns	**69** ns	108 ns	114 ns	**−142** (3)	**−131** (3)
Black	141 ns	137 ns	192 ns	201 ns	**81** ns	**85** ns
Chinese	**401** ns	**384** ns	156 ns	155 ns	**106** ns	**113** ns
Filipino	209 ns	202 ns	84 ns	87 ns	50 ns	47 ns
Asian Indian	616 (3)	645 (3)	84 ns	101 ns	−33 ns	−50 ns
Korean	**21** ns	**23** ns	−17 ns	−9 ns	−7 ns	−10 ns
Vietnamese	150 ns	131 ns	326 ns	320 ns	176 ns	171 ns
Japanese	−1207 (3)	−977 (3)	434 ns	462 ns	**355** ns	**370** ns
Other Asian	**242** ns	**239** ns	202 ns	208 ns	63 ns	52 ns
Mexican	−153 ns	−149 ns	204 (3)	205 (3)	9 ns	**30** ns
Cuban	96 ns	82 ns	166 ns	164 ns	−71 ns	−76 ns
Other Latin American	161 ns	151 ns	141 ns	147 ns	1 ns	**4** ns
Women						
White	40 ns	57 ns	47 ns	49 ns	38 ns	34 ns
Black	51 ns	40 ns	36 ns	46 ns	−11 ns	−12 ns
Chinese	100 ns	133 ns	58 ns	61 ns	**82** ns	**88** ns
Filipino	−180 ns	−160 ns	151 ns	157 ns	−50 ns	−52 ns
Asian Indian	118 ns	119 ns	−17 ns	7 ns	−8 ns	−21 ns
Korean	**−21** ns	**−2** ns	145 ns	161 ns	28 ns	26 ns
Vietnamese	138 ns	113 ns	−5 ns	−4 ns	44 ns	40 ns
Japanese	52 ns	43 ns	104 ns	112 ns	201 ns	201 ns
Other Asian	−73 ns	−94 ns	25 ns	26 ns	20 ns	18 ns
Mexican	−10 ns	−30 ns	27 ns	28 ns	11 ns	11 ns
Cuban	17 ns	1 ns	**66** ns	**80** ns	−97 ns	−102 ns
Other Latin American	−3 ns	4 ns	18 ns	18 ns	**−33** ns	**−33** ns

[1]Instances of theoretically expected effects based on overconcentration in marginal sector (from Table 5.11) and negative location effect reduced immigrant earnings (from Table 5.12) are in bold type.

[2]The table reports metric regression coefficients for the effects of sector size, with human capital controls; within gender groups, each column is a separate regression. Left column from Equation 5.4; right column from Equation 5.5. See note 23 in text.

[3]$p < p.05$.

Sources: see Table 5.3.

including sector location in the equation). What the data suggest is that while immigrants are concentrated in industrial locations where they have very low earnings, in areas where such sectors are small and immigrants are not located in them, their earnings are low anyway. In effect, immigrant location in disadvantaged sectors is a *reflection* of disadvantage, but *not a cause*. Immigrant disadvantage is often greater in certain employment sectors, but the analysis shows that where these sectors are smaller, immigrants are employed elsewhere and are disadvantaged regardless. Therefore, the disadvantage is not primarily or even partly attributable to the number of jobs available only in sectors such as low-end services or in particular industries.

The analysis has been repeated with the size of union membership as the sector size variable. The results are the same but have not been reported here because we do not have data on individual union membership and cannot relate sector size to individual employment location.

Impact of Earnings Distribution on Immigrants

Even if sector size does not affect immigrant earnings, it may be that labor market structures affect immigrants by virtue of the way they shape the entire earnings distribution. Earlier in this chapter, the cross-national effect of overall earnings distributions was estimated. What impact does interurban variation in earnings inequality have on the entrance earnings of immigrants?

The impact of earnings inequality should be assessed independently of the actual occupational location of immigrants, because theoretically, it would reflect the effect of any feature of labor markets which produce greater inequality. These are not necessarily structural locations, but may arise, for example, from employment legislation affecting employment in all sectors. The regression equation used in the analysis contains a term for earnings inequality, the coefficient of earnings variation (divided by 10, to highlight effects of differences roughly equal to the cross-national differences of 0.1). We are also interested in how earnings inequality affects those at different levels of education, so a term representing the interaction between earnings inequality and education is included.[24]

In Table 5.14, the negative metric coefficients for the impact of earnings inequality indicate that overall mean earnings are lower where there is more inequality. This may reflect the fact that fewer persons benefit from union wages in those areas. Of more immediate interest is the interaction between inequality and education. Where there is more inequality, education has a stronger effect on earnings, at least for men. Persons with higher levels of education benefit from inequality; those with less education are the ones who suffer. An increase in the coefficient of earnings variation of

TABLE 5.14 Effects of Earnings Inequality in an Urban Area on the Entry-Level Earnings of Immigrants in the U.S. Urban Labor Force, by Origins and Gender, 1980

	Men				Women			
	$, Basic Equation[1]	w/Earnings Inequality[2]	Difference[3]	Percent[4]	$, Basic Equation[1]	w/Earnings Inequality[2]	Difference[3]	Percent[4]
Intercept	-1744 (6)	-1830 (6)			-26 ns	-44 ns		
Human capital								
Years of education	1440 (6)	1449 (6)			710 (6)	711 (6)		
Yrs. of educ. squared	68 (6)	69 (6)			45 (6)	45 (6)		
Years of experience	1185 (6)	1182 (6)			306 (6)	306 (6)		
Yrs. of exp. squared	-19 (6)	-19 (6)			-5 (6)	-5 (6)		
Hours	127 (6)	130 (6)			147 (6)	147 (6)		
Language knowledge	2490 (6)	2387 (6)			761 (6)	747 (6)		
Immigrant origins								
White	-1363 (6)	-1285 (6)	-78	5.7	-486 (8)	-476 (8)	-10	2.1
Black	-6176 (6)	-5937 (6)	-239	3.9	-799 (7)	-704 (8)	-95	11.9
Chinese	-6178 (6)	-6076 (6)	-102	1.7	-1430 (6)	-1421 (6)	-9	0.6
Filipino	-6867 (6)	-6715 (6)	-152	2.2	-305 ns	-251 ns	-54	17.7
Asian Indian	-5544 (6)	-5506 (6)	-38	0.7	-323 ns	-286 ns	-37	11.5
Korean	-6152 (6)	-5999 (6)	-153	2.5	-1022 (7)	-991 (7)	-31	3.0
Vietnamese	-5764 (6)	-5659 (6)	-105	1.8	-1112 (8)	-1097 (8)	-15	1.3
Japanese	1997 (8)	1806 ns	191	(5)	-1397 ns	-1506 ns	109	(5)
Other Asian	-5366 (6)	-5211 (6)	-155	2.9	-965 ns	-884 ns	-81	8.4
Mexican	-2136 (6)	-1671 (6)	-465	21.8	-718 (7)	-502 ns	-216	30.1
Cuban	-4343 (6)	-3769 (6)	-574	13.2	-1509 (6)	-1196 (8)	-313	20.7
Other Latin Am.	-4171 (6)	-3918 (6)	-253	6.1	-1288 (6)	-1190 (6)	-98	7.6
Inequality effects								
Inequality		-1313 (6)				-210 (6)		
Education/inequality interaction		147 (6)				19 ns		

(continues)

TABLE 5.14 (continued)

	Men				Women			
	$, Basic Equation[1]	w/Earnings Inequality[2]	Differ-ence[3]	Percent[4]	$, Basic Equation[1]	w/Earnings Inequality[2]	Differ-ence[3]	Percent[4]
Origins/inequality interactions								
White		-182 ns				-20 ns		
Black		967 ns				-149 ns		
Chinese		792 ns				186 ns		
Filipino		-329 ns				-1110 ns		
Asian Indian		439 ns				671 ns		
Korean		-999 ns				-442 ns		
Vietnamese		367 ns				33 ns		
Japanese		3144 ns				1137 ns		
Other Asian		-163 ns				-777 ns		
Mexican		335 ns				-561 ns		
Cuban		936 ns				-170 ns		
Other Latin American		687 ns				-183 ns		
(N)		(167274)				(115743)		

[1]From Equation 5.2; see note 22 in text.
[2]From Equation 5.6; see note 24 in text.
[3]Difference between effect of immigrant origins with and without urban-area earnings inequality in the equation; i.e., the part of the effect of immigrant origins due to urban-area earnings inequality.
[4]Percent of effect of immigrant origins due to urban-area inequality.
[5]Group not disadvantaged in net earnings.
[6]p < 0.001.
[7]p < 0.01.
[8]p < 0.05.

Sources: See Table 5.3.

0.1, roughly equivalent to the difference between the United States and Canada, or between Canada and Australia (and equivalent to the difference between Los Angeles, 0.748, and Miami, 0.835, or between Detroit, 0.625, and New York, 0.724; see Table 5.7), results in a $147 increase in the yield of an additional year of education for men, significant in relation to the total value of a year of education (based on the main effects of education in the regression). For women, a more inegalitarian earnings distribution increases the effect of a year of education by only $19.

The education/inequality interaction means that for male immigrants with less education, those in more inegalitarian labor markets have relatively lower entrance earnings. The size of this effect might be appreciated as follows. Overall in the United States, for males at mean educational levels, a one-year education gap with the native-born resulted in 7.7 percent lower relative earnings ($1440/$18,646). Where the coefficient of earnings variation is greater by 0.1, the same one-year education gap results in 8.5 percent lower relative earnings ($(1440+147=1587)/$18,646). For recent Black immigrant men, the education gap was 1.3 years, so the expected effect is larger, about 8.7 percent. In other words, the greater earnings inequality would lead to entrance earnings for Black immigrants which are 1.0 percent lower than where earnings inequality is less. For Chinese males, the education gap was 0.3 years, so the expected effect of greater inequality is less than for Blacks.[25] However, the findings should be interpreted in light of the fact that the education gap also varies greatly among urban areas. Where the education gap is greater, the impact of the earnings distribution is also expected to be greater.

The interaction terms between earnings inequality and immigrant origins in Table 5.14 are all insignificant. This means that beyond the effects related to educational levels, earnings inequality has no consistent impact on the relative position of specific immigrant groups. The impact of inequality is felt across the board and is unrelated to conditions affecting specific groups, such as distinctive occupational or industrial locations. Hence, the lack of significant interactions between inequality and immigrant origins is consistent with the finding that sector size does not affect immigrant earnings. Labor market structure affects recent immigrant groups because of its effect on the overall earnings distribution, and because of the fact that more inequality is a greater disadvantage to all those lacking in labor market resources.

The importance of the earnings distribution in explaining immigrant inequality for specific groups also can be appreciated by comparing the direct effect of immigrant status, where only human capital is in the equation, with its effect when variables related to the earnings distribution are added. The difference reflects the impact of the earnings distribution. In Table 5.14, the differences are presented in the third column (dollar figures) and fourth column (percentage of overall disadvantage), for immigrant men and women. The differences show that the earnings distribution is indeed significant for groups experiencing an education gap with the native-born, particularly for Mexicans, Cubans, and Other Latin Americans, but also for Blacks and Whites. It is less significant for Asians. The earnings distribution explains 3.9 percent of net earnings disadvantage for Blacks, and fully 21.8 percent for Mexicans. The analysis also suggests that the earnings distribution may be important for specific groups of women, though these effects were not statistically significant. Black, Mexican, and some Asian immigrant women appear to be negatively affected by greater earnings inequality.

The earnings distribution is a labor market measure which can be applied to urban areas in each country because it is not dependent on the industrial or occupational coding. The above analysis has been repeated for Canada and Australia, though tables are not presented here. Variations in earnings inequality in Canada and Australia are less than in the United States and do not have the effect of increasing the value of education. Earnings inequalities are greatest in Toronto and Calgary, and less in Québec and Montréal, and yet in the latter cities, education is more strongly related to earnings. In Australia, the metric impact of variations in earnings inequalities are actually significant statistically, perhaps reflecting the greater relative importance of the education determinant in Australia (one year of education increases earnings by 9.2 percent , compared to 8.5 percent in Canada, and 7.7 percent in the United States), in turn a reflection of the greater scarcity of education and perhaps of the greater labor market regulation. In both Canada and Australia, for different reasons, variations in inequality have little impact in increasing inequality for immigrants with lower than average educational levels.

Summary

Interurban comparisons add importantly to our knowledge of the effects of labor market structures on immigrant employment and earnings. Nationally, or in any one urban area, immigrant concentrations in marginal industrial locations are associated with lower net earnings. However, when the interest is in comparative labor market structures, the interurban comparisons show that larger low-end industrial sectors do not produce correspondingly greater immigrant inequality. Instead, we find that greater overall earnings inequality, associated with lack of unionization, leads to lower earnings levels for recent immigrants, particularly those with the greatest skills gap with the mainstream workforce. In effect, labor market structures affect immigrants not by obliging them to work in particular kinds of jobs but rather through their effect on the overall distribution of earnings. A wider overall distribution works against the efforts of immigrants to establish an economic foothold.

Conclusions

Less regulated labor market structures, such as are more prevalent in the United States, appear to have a significant impact in lowering the entrance statuses of immigrants, particularly minority group immigrants. Cross-national estimates suggest that earnings distributions may explain up to one-third or more of the differences in entry-level status of specific immigrant groups compared among the United States, Canada, and Australia. The same effect can be seen also in the interurban analysis within the United States. Inegalitarian labor markets and those with larger low-end employment sectors attract less skilled immigrants. The poorly paid jobs at the bottom end of the economic ladder, often rejected by mainstream workers, may appear to immigrants to offer an opportunity to find an employment niche. However, a greater overall gap between rich and poor leads to lower immigrant earnings, quite apart from considerations of skill levels.

The impact of earnings distributions no doubt has roots in labor market structure and should therefore be called a structural effect. It is very likely linked to union density, for example. However, at least in the interurban analysis within the United States, it does not appear to be systematically related to particular structural *locations* within labor markets. Although some of these locations are associated with lower earnings for some groups, it is the overall distribution of earnings which affects the extent of earnings inequality for immigrant groups. The most important earnings effects of labor markets occur because of the impact that labor markets have on the overall earnings distribution, rather than because of the location of immigrants in specific labor market sectors.

How large is the effect of labor markets compared to that of educational institutions or the immigration selection and settlement process? Given the substantial attention given to labor markets in the existing research on immigration, it is perhaps surprising that the effects of labor markets are comparatively small. Whereas educational differences accounted for as much as one-half or more of the cross-national differences in immigrant entry-level earnings, and these are compounded by interurban extremes, the labor market effects may explain about one-third. In our concluding chapter we return to the question of the relative impact of different institutional sectors, and the implications for racial hierarchy and for social policies.

Earnings inequalities are increasing in all three countries, and the entry-level earnings of immigrants can be expected to decline as a direct consequence. This trend raises the hurdles for newcomers, increasing the challenge of establishing a viable foothold in a new land. It also increases the challenge for the host society seeking to ensure that opportunities for economic contribution and assimilation remain open.

In the next chapter, we consider how government intervention offsets the impact of earnings inequalities, and the consequences of cross-national differences on the economic prospects for immigrants.

6

The Welfare State

How does the welfare state in each country affect the economic situation for immigrants? One might expect that cross-national differences in social welfare institutions would magnify economic differences due to labor market outcomes, since they reflect many of the same values and priorities. The U.S. welfare state is weaker and less interventionist than its counterparts in Canada and Australia. The U.S. approach to social welfare reflects the same individualistic orientation which pervades its labor markets and other institutions. Help for the poor, in the form of income redistribution through progressive taxation and targeted social assistance, is relatively minimal. By contrast, while Canadian and Australian social safety nets may not be as generous as the European standard, they are more effective antipoverty programs. So immigrants as potentially disadvantaged persons might be expected to benefit more in Canada and Australia than in the United States.

However, things don't quite work out that way, because other factors come into play. A comparison of studies of welfare use by immigrants in each country, reviewed below, shows *greater* welfare use by immigrants in the United States, and *less* in Canada and Australia. This difference apparently applies not only to the poorest U.S. immigrants from Mexico but also to immigrants of other non-European origins. Immigrants in all groups use welfare more frequently in the United States. The reason, evidently, relates to their lower earnings levels. Lower average immigrant earnings in each immigrant group in the United States mean that larger proportions of these immigrants run into economic difficulties. Compared to their counterparts in Canada or Australia, immigrants in the United States more often experience serious problems of economic adjustment, and they more often fall into poverty. Hence, immigrants in the United States more often are forced to rely on welfare assistance, less generous though that assistance may be.

This chapter reviews evidence about two aspects of the immigrants/welfare issue. The first relates to the description of cross-national differences in social welfare as an institution. To estimate the size and impact of these differences, comparative data from the Luxembourg Income Study are used to measure income redistribution due to progressive taxation and government cash transfer payments. The second aspect relates to welfare eligibility and use by immigrants in each country. Since immigrants in specific groups have lower earnings in the United States, they may more often fall into the categories of eligibility for welfare benefits such as means-tested social assistance. Obviously, welfare eligibility directly impacts the actual patterns of welfare use by immigrants in each country. Studies on this question are available for each country and can be examined in comparative perspective.

These two sets of variables—differences in the size of welfare state income redistribution, and differences in welfare eligibility of immigrants—are potentially offsetting in their impact on immigrants. The purpose of the chapter is to provide a preliminary assessment of the variables involved, based on comparative data from existing sources.[1] The analysis draws on data collected during the late 1970s and 1980s, to provide ballpark estimates for the impact of welfare at that time. Our conclusions reinforce the importance of the findings of the previous chapters on immigrant earnings and extend them by placing a primary area of policy response in comparative context. Policy issues are raised not only for the United States but also for Canada and Australia, and these will be returned to in the final chapter.

Comparative Social Welfare and Taxation

The minimalist U.S. approach to social welfare is one of the clearest instances of American exceptionalism, and an obvious expression of the extent of American attachment to individualist values. Virtually every analysis of social welfare from a comparative perspective has emphasized this fact (Skocpol 1992; Lipset 1996, 71–75; Day 1997, 4–11). Americans are most likely to accept inequality as legitimate (Evans and Kelley 1993), and as contributing to national economic prosperity (Lipset 1996, 73). Lipset refers to the United States as an "outlier," an extreme statistical exception, in this regard.

The point of contrast is the European tradition of social democracy and broader rights of citizenship (Korpi 1989), and in this context, Canada (Johnson et al. 1994) and Australia (Saunders 1994) may lie between the two extremes, reflecting a blended mixture of New World individualism and Old World social democracy. The neoconservative thrust in recent decades has reduced the size of the welfare state in all three countries, but the cross-national differences remain. Opposition to social welfare cuts in Canada (see, for example, McQuaig 1993) are directed specifically at maintaining a traditional difference with the United States. The Australian debate similarly takes place within a different context of options and minimum standards.

Specific Cross-national Policy Differences

The specific policies included under the rubric of social welfare may vary in their redistributive impacts. Some government expenditures have a greater redistributive impact than others. Hence, Korpi (1989) is right that aggregate expenditures on social welfare, or total public sector employment, are not good indicators of societal commitment to the alleviation of poverty. For example, most pension payments go to the middle class, not the poor. Comparative analysis shows that aggregate expenditures on all government transfers which include publicly funded old-age pensions as well as unemployment benefits and social assistance to the poor have not differed in a systematic way among the three countries.[2]

Programs with the most redistributive impact, unemployment insurance and social assistance, were compared in detail for the United States and Canada in 1986 by Blank and Hanratty (1993). Both countries have unemployment benefits schemes which are similar in that they are designed to offset earnings losses arising from unemployment and to smooth the transition to a new job. The programs differ mainly with regard to specific conditions of eligibility and benefits, with the United States offering the weakest protections. Table 6.1 presents 1991 OECD data showing the rates at which overall benefits for unemployment replaced prior incomes from employment in the United States, Canada, and Australia (OECD 1991, 199–227). Both Canada and Australia have offered income replacement over longer periods of time, and in most cases at higher rates, than has the United States. The differences between Canada and Australia are less clear cut. However, Canada offers higher replacement rates in the first year and lower rates in subsequent years, at least for persons with dependent spouses.

In the area of assistance to the poor, programs differ more substantially in structure. The United States targets poor families with children for cash benefits (Aid to Families with Dependent Children, AFDC, replaced in 1996 by a more restricted program called Temporary Assistance for Needy Families, TANF); federal assistance to other poor persons is limited to food stamps (vouchers). Canada provides broader assistance to the poor at the provincial level, with federal programs to assist families with children not being means tested. Australia provides, in addition to unemployment benefits, a pension for those unable to work due to medical reasons. It also provides a family allowance, which is not means tested (Saunders, 1994).

TABLE 6.1 Unemployment Benefits for Different Family Types and Lengths of Unemployment, ca. 1989

A. Summary of Unemployment Insurance and Assistance Benefits

| | Type of Benefit | Employment Record Required | Maximum Benefit Duration | Initial Relation to Earnings | Initial Gross Replacement Rate at Average Production Worker Levels of 1988 Earnings | | |
					Single	With spouse At Work	Dependent
United States	Unemployment Insurance	20 weeks	26 weeks	Proportional	50	50	50
Canada	Unemployment Insurance	27 weeks	50 weeks	Proportional	60	60	60
Australia	Guaranteed Income	None	Indefinite	Fixed	24	0	43

B. Average Annual Replacement Rates for Continuous Spell of Unemployment

| | Single Person | | | | With Spouse At Work | | | | Dependent | | | |
| | Years | | | | Years | | | | Years | | | |
	1	2	3	4	1	2	3	4	1	2	3	4
United States	25	0	0	0	25	0	0	0	25	0	0	0
Canada	59	23	23	23	58	0	0	0	59	37	37	37
Australia	24	24	24	24	0	0	0	0	43	43	43	43

Sources: (Panel A) OECD 1991, 201; (Panel B) OECD 1991, 233.

Redistributive Impact of Government Transfers and Taxation

The redistributive impact of government transfers can perhaps best be measured on a comparative basis using the Luxembourg Income Study comparative data base.[3] This use of survey data has the additional advantage of tapping into the impact of progressive taxation. Atkinson et al. (1995, Chapter 7) show that across 13 OECD countries, the redistributive impact of government transfers and taxation is, as a general rule, inversely related to their size. In countries like Sweden and the Netherlands, where government transfers constitute a large proportion of incomes (figures for the early 1980s were 28.5 and 35.0, respectively), such transfers have relatively little redistributive impact. The United States, Canada, and Australia all lie at the opposite extreme, where government transfers constitute only about 10 percent of incomes. The redistributive impact of transfers in these countries is much greater. Nevertheless, the data clearly indicate substantial differences in redistribution among these three countries.

Table 6.2 shows how transfers and taxes together alter the distribution of earnings (and other sources of market income) for persons in each of the three countries, and at two points in time. The data include the total samples in the LIS data, and the income data are based on "adult equivalent incomes." "Adult equivalence" refers to an adjustment for family composition, to reflect effective incomes for individuals assuming a within-family sharing formula.[4] A detailed examination of the impact of various assumptions about such sharing shows that specific comparisons of relevance here are not substantially affected.[5]

Let us consider, first, transfer incomes. In the United States, for the poor whose incomes were below 50 percent of the median, transfers added 64.7 percent to market income in 1979, dropping to 59.8 percent in 1986. By contrast, for the poorest persons in Canada, transfers added 95.3 percent to market income in 1981 and 90.3 percent in 1987. And in Australia, transfers represented a much larger addition to the incomes of the poor, adding 175.5 percent in 1981, rising to 204.3 percent by 1985. In 1985, transfer payments effectively tripled incomes for the poor in Australia.

For the near poor, those with market incomes higher than 50 percent of the median but less than 70 percent, the cross-national differences in transfer payments also are significant. In 1981, transfer payments boosted market incomes by 51.9 percent for the near-poor group in Australia (52.2 percent in 1985), 33.5 percent in Canada (39.6 percent in 1987), but only by 20.3 percent in the United States (19.9 percent in 1986). For income groups above the 70-percent-of-median level, differences in the impact of transfer payments are far less. The impact of these income adjustments through transfers did not change substantially during the early 1980s.

TABLE 6.2   Income Redistribution Due to Transfers and Tax in the United
States, Canada, and Australia, by Percentage of Median Equivalent Income
Groups, ca. 1980 and 1986

Country, Year, and Percent of Median Equivalent Gross Income	Transfers (as Percent of Market Income)	Tax (Rate as Percent of Market Income Plus Transfers)	Net Redistribution (Disposable Income as Percent of Market Income)	Transfers (as Percent of Market Income)	Tax (Rate as Percent of Market Income Plus Transfers)	Net Redistribution (Disposable Income as Percent of Market Income)
A. United States		1979			1986	
< 50	64.7	−7.8	51.9	59.8	−15.6	34.9
≥ 50; < 70	20.3	−11.9	6.0	19.9	−11.9	5.6
≥ 70; < 100	8.7	−15.3	−7.9	8.6	−15.9	−8.7
≥ 100; < 150	4.9	−20.3	−16.4	5.5	−19.5	−15.1
≥ 150	2.9	−26.4	−24.3	2.7	−25.8	−23.8
B. Canada		1981			1987	
< 50	95.3	−2.1	91.2	90.3	−10.2	70.9
≥ 50; < 70	33.5	−7.0	24.2	39.6	−9.3	26.5
≥ 70; < 100	12.1	−12.4	−1.8	15.5	−15.4	−2.3
≥ 100; < 150	5.7	−15.9	−11.1	7.2	−19.1	−13.3
≥ 150	2.7	−18.7	−16.5	3.1	−22.9	−20.5
C. Australia		1981			1985	
< 50	175.5	−2.2	169.4	204.3	−1.0	201.2
≥ 50; < 70	51.9	−8.2	39.5	52.2	−6.6	41.4
≥ 70; < 100	9.6	−17.1	−9.1	9.8	−14.8	−9.3
≥ 100; < 150	4.9	−21.7	−17.8	4.9	−17.9	−18.0
≥ 150	2.0	−27.4	−25.9	1.7	−22.5	−27.9

Source: Calculated from Atkinson, et al., 1995, Appendix 7, tables A7.1 and A7.2; based on
Luxembourg Income Study. Redistribution of adult equivalent market income into disposable income. Market income includes employment and self-employment earnings, property
income, and other private market income, based on household income data. Market income
plus transfers, minus tax, equals net disposable income. The equivalence scale adjusts
household income based on family size, by dividing by the square root of family size. Income groups are based on gross income adjusted for family size.

Income tax systems are more progressive in Australia and Canada than
in the United States, reinforcing the cross-national differences in the redistributive effects of government transfers. Table 6.2 reports tax rates on
gross incomes (market incomes plus transfers) by income groups. The
cross-national differences apply both to the poor and to the near poor, to
all persons whose equivalent income level was less than 70 percent of the
median. Tax systems in Canada and the United States appear to have become significantly less progressive during the early 1980s.

The net effect of transfers and taxes in altering market incomes is shown in Table 6.2, again by income groups. It is very clear that the redistribution toward the poor and near poor is substantially greater in Australia than in Canada, and substantially greater in Canada than in the United States. The trend over time is affected more by trends in taxation than by trends in program transfers. Both Canada and the United States moved toward a somewhat less redistributive system during that period, while Australia moved in the opposite direction, toward greater income redistribution. These comparative data provide compelling confirmation that cross-national differences in the welfare state as an antipoverty institution are sizable. While the U.S. welfare state does redistribute income toward the bottom end, the Canadian and even moreso the Australian welfare states are far more interventionist in this regard. In effect, these two countries have more effective antipoverty programs.

The same data may be examined from the point of view of the amounts of money involved relative to a fixed standard, rather than to incomes at each level. Atkinson et al. (1995) looked at the figures standardized as percentages of overall median incomes, rather than as percentages of personal (market) incomes. This provides a measure of how incomes at various levels of the income hierarchy are altered in dollar terms. Table 6.3 presents this information. The income groups used in this table are income quintiles (rather than income groups relative to the median incomes, as in Table 6.2). For the poorest quintile in the United States, transfers raise incomes by 13.2 percent of median equivalent incomes. The government then took some money back in the form of taxation, representing 3.5 percent. The net effect of government intervention for this bottom quintile is still positive: 9.7 percent. For the poorest in Canada, transfers are higher, and taxes lower, so the net positive effect on earnings is 14.9 percent of median incomes. In Australia, the number is 21.4 percent.[6]

To get a better sense of the relative impact of these differences, consider how a person whose income was, say, 40 percent of the median (and would be in the lowest income quintile) would be affected by government intervention in each country. An American in that situation would, on average, experience an income boost from 40 percent of the median to nearly 50 percent of median, just at the poverty level. A Canadian counterpart would move beyond this level to about 54 percent of median income, and in Australia he or she would move to over 60 percent of median income. These data reinforce the significance of cross-national differences in the antipoverty impact of the welfare state.

For the persons just above the poorest quintile, there are also cross-national differences. In the United States, those in the second-from-the-bottom quintile were net losers. In 1979, for example, although they re-

TABLE 6.3   Income Redistribution Due to Transfers and Tax in the United States, Canada, and Australia, as Percent of Median Equivalent Income, by Income Quintile, ca. 1980 and 1986

Country, Year, and Quintile of Equivalent Gross Income	Average Transfers	Average Tax	Net Redistribution	Average Transfers	Average Tax	Net Redistribution
A. United States		1979			1986	
Bottom	13.2	–3.5	9.7	13.7	–5.9	7.8
2	9.4	–10.7	–1.3	9.9	–10.5	–0.6
3	7.8	–20.5	–12.7	8.0	–21.3	–13.8
4	6.5	–34.8	–28.3	8.2	–34.5	–26.3
Top	7.6	–71.2	–63.6	7.1	–80.6	–73.5
B. Canada		1981			1987	
Bottom	16.6	–1.7	14.9	18.3	–4.5	13.8
2	11.5	–8.8	2.7	15.0	–11.0	4.0
3	9.0	–15.8	–6.8	11.9	–20.1	–8.2
4	7.1	–24.4	–17.3	9.2	–30.9	–21.7
Top	6.1	–44.0	–37.9	7.5	–57.8	–50.3
C. Australia		1981			1985	
Bottom	23.1	–1.7	21.4	22.5	–1.1	21.4
2	12.0	–12.1	–0.1	13.8	–12.2	1.6
3	7.2	–24.2	–17.0	8.1	–26.2	–18.1
4	6.7	–37.1	–30.4	7.3	–38.9	–31.6
Top	5.0	–74.5	–69.5	4.5	–82.5	–78.0

Source: Atkinson, et al., 1995, Chapter 7, Table 7.6, p. 107 (transfers data); Table 7.4, p. 106 (tax data); based on Luxembourg Income Study. Income groups are based on gross income adjusted for family size. Net redistribution is calculated here by taking average transfers (as a percent of median equivalent income), and subtracting average tax (also as a percent of median equivalent income). Hence in this case net redistribution reflects the average change in income due to transfers and taxes. Note the difference with Table 6.2.

ceived 9.4 percent in the form of transfers, they paid out 10.7 percent in taxation, so that in the end they experienced a net loss of 1.3 percent. The loss was less in 1986—0.6 percent. In Canada, those in the second quintile from the bottom were beneficiaries of government intervention in both time periods, though less so than those in the bottom quintile. In Australia, those in the second-from-the-bottom quintile were virtually unaffected in 1981, losing 0.1 percent, but they were net beneficiaries in 1985.

The three-country transfer payment data reported in Tables 6.2 and 6.3 include both old-age pensions (social security in the United States, old age security and national pension plans in Canada, and old age pensions in Australia)and payments specifically targeted at lower income groups. It is of interest to examine transfer payments separately for the nonelderly, to see cross-national differences specifically for the working-age populations not affected by old-age pensions. Table 6.4 shows average transfers as a percent of median equivalent income for persons with below median incomes, distinguishing those under 60 years of age from those 60 and over. U.S. transfer payments are most heavily targeted toward the elderly, leaving nonelderly Americans with relatively less. Therefore, it turns out that the largest cross-national differences are for the nonelderly group. Transfer payments for the low-income nonelderly were between 10 and 12 percent in Canada and Australia, compared to 6 and 7 percent in the United States. Furthermore, during the early 1980s, when these transfer payments to low-income persons were increasing in all three countries, the increases were larger in Canada and Australia.

These results from Atkinson et al. are the most comprehensive data from the LIS, arguably the most reliable source for cross-national comparisons of transfers and taxes,[7] but it is worth mentioning that they are fully consistent with previous analyses of the same LIS data set as well as with other comparative data. McFate (1991), using LIS data analyzed by Smeeding and Rainwater (1991), showed that whereas the U.S. tax and transfer system together did not lift any households out of poverty, in Canada it lifted between 18.3 percent (1981) and 20.1 percent (1987) of poor households out of poverty. Percentages for five European countries were even higher, up to 62 percent in the Netherlands.

Bradbury (1993, 20) presented LIS data on the wages of the full-time, full-year male workforce, before and after taxes. Inequality measured by the Gini index (see Chapter 5, note 3) declined less for the United States than for either Canada or Australia. For the United States, the pre-tax Gini of 0.286 declined to 0.256; for Canada, the Gini of 0.234 declined to 0.196; and for Australia, the Gini of 0.196 declined to 0.167.

And finally, Phipps (1995, 62) used the same LIS data to examine poverty rates based on earnings before and after transfers, for the United States, Canada, and Australia (plus Sweden). The analysis did not include the impact of taxation, which Atkinson et al. found very significant for the U.S.-Canadian-Australian comparison. In the 1979–1981 period, transfers reduced the poverty rates by 20.7 percent in Australia (from 39.1 percent to 18.4 percent), 17.5 percent in Canada (from 33.8 percent to 16.3 percent), and 15.7 percent in the United States (from 35.9 percent to 20.2 percent). In the 1985–1986 period, transfers reduced the poverty rates by 18.1 percent in Australia, 20.4 percent in Canada, and 17.2 per-

TABLE 6.4   Average Transfers as a Percent of Median Equivalent Income, in the
United States, Canada, and Australia, for Persons with Median Income, by Age,
ca. 1980 and 1986

Country/Year	Total	Under 60	60 and over
A. United States			
1979	10.5	6.7	24.2
1986	10.8	6.9	26.0
B. Canada			
1981	13.2	10.2	24.9
1987	15.9	12.1	30.3
C. Australia			
1981	15.3	11.3	30.6
1985	16.2	12.9	30.2

Source: Anthony B. Atkinson, Lee Rainwater, and Timothy M. Smeeding, (1995,
107). Income Distribution in OECD Countries: Evidence from the Luxembourg Income
Study. Paris: Organization for Economic Cooperation and Development. Copyright © 1995 OECD. Reproduced by permission of the OECD. Income groups are
based on gross income adjusted for family size.

cent in the United States. The poverty gap was also reduced by more in
Australia, less in Canada, and least in the United States.

In a separate study of Canada and the United States only, Blank and
Hanratty (1993) used the 1987 Current Population Survey from the United
States, and the 1987 Survey of Consumer Finances for Canada, to measure
poverty rates before and after transfers for one particular low-income
group—namely, single parents. Overall, before transfers, they found
poverty rates (using U.S. definitions) were lower in the United States, at
15.4 percent, than in Canada, at 17.5 percent. However, posttransfer
poverty rates were 13.5 percent in the United States, but only 11.8 percent
in Canada. Hence, transfers boost 5.7 percent out of poverty in Canada,
but only 1.9 percent in the United States. For single parents, Blank and
Hanratty (1993, 203, 205) showed that differences in social assistance and
unemployment insurance produce important effects on cross-national differences in income levels and poverty rates. Many single parents are poor
in both countries, slightly more so in the United States. Single parents in
the United States earned 37.9 percent of the average family earnings, and
45.1 percent in Canada. After transfers, the incomes of single parents in
the United States rose to 46.0 percent of average family income, while rising to 56.9 percent of average family income in Canada, 3.7 percent more
than in the United States. This works out to an income increase for single
parents of 19.5 percent on the average in the United States, compared to
26.6 percent in Canada. In terms of poverty rates, based on pretransfer

earnings, the poverty rate for single parents was 50.5 percent in the United States and 46.6 percent in Canada, a difference of 3.9 percent. The posttransfer poverty rate for single parents in the United States was 45.3 percent compared to only 32.3 percent in Canada, a difference of 9.1 percent. Government transfers bring about a 10.3 percent reduction in the poverty rate for single parents in the United States, and a 30.7 percent reduction in the poverty rate for single parents in Canada.

In sum, and taking all these data together, it is clear that there are substantial U.S.-Canadian-Australian differences in the welfare state, differences with implications for any low-income group such as recent immigrants. Welfare as an institutional sector would be expected to increase and exaggerate the cross-national differences in the economic well-being of low-income immigrants. Where the welfare state is more generous to the poor, then if immigrants take advantage of the welfare state to the same extent as others, those with low earnings from employment or self-employment will find that their relative economic position is less negative. On a cross-national basis, this factor would be expected to *increase* differences in the economic status of low-income immigrants. However, we also know that immigrants from all groups in the United States earn less and are at greater risk for poverty. They may more often be eligible for welfare. So to measure the actual impact of welfare on a cross-national basis, we have to look at actual welfare use by immigrants. That is the subject of the following section.

How Are Immigrants Affected?

Even though the social safety net in the United States is weaker, its impact in ameliorating the situation of immigrants has been very significant because a larger proportion of those in specific groups—especially in particular cities—are in economic need. The more generous government policies toward the poor in Canada and Australia will be expected to apply less to immigrants, because fewer of them are in fact poor. There is a complicating factor to consider here. Immigrants often do not use welfare benefits for which they are eligible. This also has been found in each country. So we have to consider the question of the comparative impact of welfare programs on immigrants very carefully.

A series of U.S. studies, by Tienda and Jensen (1986), Jensen (1988), Borjas and Trejo (1991, 1993), and Borjas (1994b) used census data to show that immigrants do in fact draw upon at least some parts of the social safety net more often than do the native born.[8] There is higher use of welfare (social assistance including AFDC, SSI, and general assistance from any level of government, and not including UI or social security) by immigrants compared to native born. For example, in 1980 data, Jensen (1988) found (see Table 6.5, panel A) that while public assistance was received by 6 percent of

TABLE 6.5   Welfare Recipience by Immigrant Origins, in the United States, Canada, and Australia, Various Dates

A. United States, 1979

Origins	Mean Earned Income	Poverty Rate	Public Assistance Recipience Rate	Mean Public Assistance Income
Native white	$20,180	0.06	0.06	$2,514
Immigrants, Total	17,136	0.14	0.10	3,146
White	17,956	0.07	0.05	2,856
Black	16,165	0.18	0.11	2,850
Asian	22,855	0.12	0.10	3,067
Hispanic	14,192	0.24	0.18	3,313

B1. Canada, 1985

Origins	Incidence of Family Receipt of Social Assistance
Native	0.10
Immigrants	
before 1956	0.07
1956–1965	0.05
1966–1970	0.03
1971–1975	0.04
1976–1980	0.06
1981–1985	0.06

B2. Canada, 1990

Origins	Incidence of Family Receipt of Social Assistance
Native	0.09
Immigrants	
before 1956	0.07
1956–1965	0.06
1966–1970	0.05
1971–1975	0.08
1976–1980	0.09
1981–1985	0.07
1986–1990	0.10

C. Australia, 1989

Origins	Proportion of Working Age Population Receiving Any Pension or Benefits
Native	0.105
Immigrants	0.115
European birth	0.125
Americas birth	0.075
Asian birth	0.119
African birth	0.073
Oceania birth	0.081

Sources: U.S. data are from Jensen 1988, 55; Canadian data are from Baker and Benjamin 1995, 656; and Australian data, from Whiteford 1992, 26.

families headed by native-born Whites, it was received by 10 percent of families headed by immigrants. Welfare use was concentrated among minority group immigrants, including Blacks and Asians as well as Hispanics. Welfare was received by 11 percent of Black immigrant families, 10 percent of Asian immigrant families, and 18 percent of Hispanic immigrant families (see also Tienda and Jensen 1986, 377; and Borjas 1994, 5). Borjas and Trejo (1991, 198) found a lot of variation among specific origin groups

Borjas and Hilton (1996) analyzed the Survey of Income and Program Participation (four waves over the period 1984 to 1991) and concluded that the use of welfare by immigrants is numerically larger if noncash program participation is included, such as food stamps, Medicaid, and housing subsidies. They found that 21 percent of immigrant households used some kind of assistance, compared to 14 percent of natives.

The Canadian and Australian research has generally found the reverse, namely lower rates of social assistance use by immigrants. In Canada, several studies show consistently that immigrants consume money transfers such as unemployment insurance and social assistance (welfare) at rates lower than is the case for the general population (Akbari 1989, Baker and Benjamin 1994 and 1995, Lui-Gurr 1995). Baker and Benjamin (1995) used the Canadian Survey of Consumer Finances for 1986 and 1991, and found that for social assistance (see Table 6.5, panel B), rates of utilization were about 9 to 10 percent for families headed by native-born Canadians, between 3 and 7 percent for various cohorts of immigrant families in 1985, and between 5 and 10 percent for various cohorts of immigrant families in 1990. Their analysis showed similar patterns for use of unemployment insurance.

Baker and Benjamin did not distinguish immigrants by specific origins, but inferences in this regard seem reasonable based on the fact that welfare use in 1985 by immigrant populations that arrived in Canada after 1971 was between 4 and 6 percent overall, which is only as high as welfare use by White immigrants in the United States, about half the U.S. rates for Black and Asian immigrants, and one-third the U.S. rate for Mexican immigrants. The 1990 Canadian rates for immigrants from the 1970s were higher, but these may not be comparable to American rates for a decade earlier. It is clear that the pattern for immigrants in Canada departs substantially from that found in the United States, even on a group-specific basis. Baker and Benjamin explicitly compared their results with those of Borjas and Trejo, and they concluded that whereas for Canada, "immigrants have lower participation rates in Unemployment Insurance and Social Assistance than natives," these "results for Social Assistance contrast with U.S. evidence that the raw entry participation rates of many immigrant cohorts exceed the native rates" (Baker and Benjamin 1995, 650).

Australian welfare use by immigrants may be similar to what is found in Canada. Whiteford (1992) used administrative statistics from the Department of Social Services, examined in relation to Australian Bureau of Statistics data on the total population in 1989. He estimated that most birthplace groups are less likely to receive social security payments (invalid pension, service pension, sole parent and widows pension, age pension, unemployment benefit, sickness benefit, special benefit, and family allowance supplement), compared to the native born (see Table 6.5, panel C). The overall average (11.5 percent for the working-age population, ages 15–64 for males, and ages 15–59 for females) is somewhat greater than for the native-born Australians (10.5 percent). However, his age-adjusted figures for European origins showed lower rates of receipt of benefits for all groups except those from Yugoslavia. Some groups of Asian refugees had very high rates (Lebanese, 24.2 percent; Vietnamese, 19.6 percent).

If immigrants in specific origin groups in the United States receive welfare more than natives, while whose in Canada and Australia receive welfare at the same rates or less, then the implication is clearly that the welfare state as an institutional sector actually to some extent *reduces* cross-national differences in immigrant status that result from labor market outcomes. The welfare state is weaker in the United States, but the smaller expected effect on recent immigrants is offset by their higher rates of welfare eligibility and need.

Many studies show that immigrants tend to underuse welfare. That is, immigrants use welfare less often than one would expect on the basis of need. This can be seen in Jensen's data, reported in Table 6.5. Whereas the rate of public assistance recipience for the native-born population is roughly equal to the poverty rate, at 6 percent, the rate of recipience for immigrant groups is in every case below the poverty rate—in fact about 30 percent less. This is true for White, Black, Hispanic, and Asian immigrants in 1979. Jensen suggested several general reasons for lower utilization: the fact that immigrants are risk-takers, they rely on friendship and kin networks, and they may want to avoid the social stigma because they are seeking social approval. Often it has been found that the rate of welfare use increases with length of time in the country. Borjas and Trejo call this an "assimilation effect." Using the 1970 and 1980 public use census microdata samples, they found that the use of welfare is higher for the newer immigrant groups and for immigrants who have been in the country longer. Baker and Benjamin (1995, 658) also found an assimilation effect for Canada.

Underutilization of welfare by immigrants in the United States means that the effect of the U.S. welfare state in offsetting immigrant poverty and improving the status of immigrants in the United States compared to

Canada or Australia is somewhat limited. Still, the fact that immigrants in the United States use welfare more than those in Canada or Australia confirms that the differential eligibility effect is important.

Conclusions

In comparative perspective, the U.S. welfare system reflects a more individualistic approach with fewer benefits for the poor, making it more difficult for immigrants who fall into poverty to qualify for any welfare support. Despite this, welfare payouts to immigrants are actually more frequent in the United States than in Canada or Australia, so that the system actually reduces immigrant inequality compared to these other countries. This is true partly because of poverty among the Mexicans, but not only for that reason; the higher rates of welfare utilization for immigrants appear to hold true for other minority immigrant groups also.

This finding is important in the context of our previous findings (in Chapter 3) of higher educational levels among immigrants in specific groups in the United States. What it seems to suggest is that the welfare burden of immigrants is in fact as much imposed by the institutional environment as by the characteristics of immigrants themselves. Despite *higher* levels of education of immigrants from all sources in the United States, the institutions of that country assign them *lower* status, and *so much so that they more often fall into poverty and require reliance on the welfare system.* The so-called welfare burden in these cases turns out to be a burden imposed by U.S. institutions on immigrants, rather than a burden imposed by immigrants on the United States. It is these mainstream social institutions which in effect assign immigrants to poverty status. This fact is made clear when we see that immigrants in Canada and Australia, who are in fact less well educated, turn out to have lower rates of poverty and lower reliance on their more generous welfare systems.

These findings obviously point toward the need for further study, to probe details on a group-specific basis, and in individual cities. It is also important to examine how other institutions, such as the family, may help immigrants offset conditions imposed by the institutional environment. It is also of great importance to examine how the changing institutional environment is altering the rates at which immigrants are assigned to poverty in each of the three countries. In this regard, and in line with findings from previous chapters, it is expected that these changes are most rapid in Canada. This is because education has changed most rapidly in Canada, and it is the educational institutions which have been most powerful in altering the labor market environment.

Changes to the welfare system are also important, including the recent welfare reforms in the United States. These changes should also be examined in comparative context. If reductions in welfare benefits for immigrants who are poor have their intended effect, then in the cross-national comparison, welfare institutions may increase the differences in immigrant status. Of course, Canada and Australia are reducing welfare benefits, too. Still, their systems remain more generous than those in the United States and have not yet singled out immigrants for reductions. However, if institutional change leads to declining status for immigrants in Canada and Australia, producing higher rates of immigrant poverty, then their welfare use may be expected to rise. This could create political pressures to reduce immigrant access to such support, parallel to what has happened in the United States. Yet it may be unlikely that either country will experience the extremes of the political responses in the United States, because neither will have groups with poverty rates comparable to those of the Mexican group in the United States. For this reason, the immigration issue is unlikely to create the same pressures on the welfare system in those countries.

PART 3

Conclusions
and Policy Issues

7

Compounding Institutional Forces that Shape Immigrant Economic Success

This study has shown how an array of mainstream social institutions, including education, labor markets, and social welfare, have shaped the relative economic success of the first cohort of 'new immigrants' in U.S., Canadian, and Australian cities following policy reforms of the 1960s. Census data reveal that immigrants from similar backgrounds have entered the economic hierarchy at substantially lower levels in the United States, particularly in the larger immigration-destination cities, than have their counterparts in either Canadian or Australian cities. Each national and urban immigrant destination has a distinctive social-institutional environment, which in effect assigns immigrants to their place in society. Those specific institutional structures, which have been associated with the strongly individualistic character of American society, produced markedly lower entry-level earnings for immigrants in that country and particularly in its high-immigration cities.

These findings make clear that the economic success of immigrants is not only a function of factors outside a society which determine the composition of immigrant flows—border control, refugee needs, or the immigration market in general—nor is it determined entirely by specific differences in the selectivity of immigration policy. To a very significant degree, immigrant success is also shaped by the structure of the host society's own mainstream institutions. Where institutions have been structured in more individualistic patterns, immigrants encounter greater obstacles to a realization of their economic potential. The evidence here focuses on the critical initial years of entry, which set the primary parameters for the entire process of immigrant integration to follow.

These institutional forces create problems for immigrants because they tend to compound and magnify the adversities inherent in the process of migration and adjustment to a new environment. By the same token, the implications are most negative for racial minority immigrants. Previous research shows us that immigrants of non-European-origin to societies dominated by European-origin populations very often have entry-level earnings which are substantially lower than would be predicted based on their observable skills. Research also shows that these racial minority immigrants move up in the economic hierarchy more slowly than immigrants from Europe. Why this is the case is debated; one key issue is the extent to which racial discrimination is involved. What matters here is that these minority immigrants start lower and struggle longer than White immigrants. Institutional structures do not cause these difficulties, but they do determine the significance of their consequences. In settings where the native born accumulate more extensive educational credentials, where labor market disparities are greater, and where social redistribution is less progressive, the impact of low entry tends to be magnified. The negative consequences are not only economic but also social, cultural, and ultimately political, and not only for immigrant groups themselves but for the entire society.

Our findings on each institutional sector are summarized in concluding sections in each relevant chapter. Here the implications are developed in two ways. The first is to spell out the nature of the institutional effects which have been identified, including the compounding or value-added aspect of relations among institutions. And second, institutional changes now under way are considered, to indicate how these may be affecting immigrant entry-level status in each country. While the pace and direction of these changes varies, the general direction has been toward greater institutional individualism, increasing the potential for low immigrant entry-level status. At the same time, the progressive globalization of economic activity, one of the forces often cited as underlying institutional change, also ensures that global migration will continue and even accelerate. This points toward a coming crisis of immigration, forcing policy choices which are the subject of the next and final chapter.

Compounding Institutional Effects

The institutional effects on immigrant entry-level earnings can be thought of in terms of a sequence of compounding effects, summarized in Table 7.1. Effects produced in one institutional sector may be compounded by effects in others which follow in the sequence. For example, if native-born educational levels are higher, then the implications are magnified where earnings inequalities are greater and income redistribution less extensive. The scenario for immigrants in the United States is the following: The relatively laissez-faire immigration policy lowers immigrant skill levels; immigrants encounter a native-born population which

TABLE 7.1 Compounding Effects of Institutions on Immigrant Entry-Level Earnings

Institution	National and Urban Institutional Comparisons		Effects on Immigrants	Specific Comparisons	Changes Under Way: 'Globalization'
I. Immigration Policy	U.S. emphasis on family reunification Canada and Australia select on occupational criteria	= = >	Lower immigrant education; possible effects on areas of settlement	Somewhat higher immigrant education in United States (despite effects of selection); lower immigrant education levels in high-immigration urban areas	U.S. attempts to control illegal immigration; Canada maintains growth policy with enhanced selection; Australia reduces immigration levels
II. Education	Higher education of native-born in United States, particularly in key United States 'education cities'	= = >	Greater immigrant skills gap	Greater immigration skills polarization in the United States; 'Education cities' are high-immigration areas, raising local skills polarization	Canada upgrades education to United States levels; Australia upgrades more slowly
III. Labor Markets	Greater earnings inequalities in United States, particularly in less unionized cities; (not related to native–native-born education)	= = >	Lower entry-level earnings	Lower immigrant entry-level earnings in the United States, particularly in and in less unionized cities	Deregulation and increased inequality in all countries, particularly United States and Australia
IV. Taxation; Social Welfare	Less income redistribution in United States; greater poverty	= = >	Greater immigrant poverty and welfare use	Greater immigrant poverty and welfare use in the United States despite less generous welfare system (and higher immigrant skills)	Welfare cuts in all countries; specific cuts to immigrant benefits in United States

has built up a massive store of educational credentials as competitive resources; immigrants' difficulties in establishing an economic foothold are compounded by unregulated labor markets, more extreme earnings inequality, and a comparatively weak and deteriorating social safety net. The extent of this compounding depends on the interrelations among the various components of the institutional system. Generally, each component of the U.S. institutional system produces compounding effects which magnify inequality and lower immigrant entry-level status.

The institutional compounding is even more extreme at the urban level because of educational polarization. Those urban areas with the highest native-born educational levels have, for reasons explicated in Chapters 3 and 4, often attracted immigrants with the lowest educational levels. However, labor market polarization is rather independent of this pattern, which limits the compounding effect. Educational polarization affects cities like New York and San Francisco; labor market polarization is more relevant in less-unionized cities, Miami being the principal example of an immigration city in this category.

Our empirical analysis has focused on particular immigrant origin groups which are represented cross-nationally, mainly Blacks and Asians, especially Chinese. However, the institutional effects are felt in all groups, including the Mexicans within the United States. The Mexicans are very strongly affected by the skills gap, which is largely due to selective processes. However, the very high rates of poverty and welfare dependence among Mexican Americans also derive in part from the compounding effects of U.S. educational and labor market institutions.

For immigrant women, compounding institutional effects come in addition to the initial impact of gender inequality itself. That is also an institutionally determined variable, of course. Where the relative earnings of women are lower, the initial earnings of immigrant women are reduced correspondingly, so the compounding effects of the other institutional forces begin at that point. By far the lowest earnings of any immigrant group included in this study were for minority immigrant women in highly individualistic institutional settings.

Implications for Previous Comparative Analyses

An institutional-systems approach helps point toward revisions required in previous analyses, which have tended to focus on only one institution or on a limited range of institutions. One approach, represented in the work of George Borjas, emphasizes immigration policy and the political control of immigration selection. Our approach modifies and extends his in four ways: (1) It confronts the very limited capacity of immigration policy to determine the composition of the immigrant population; (2) it explains various ways in which immigration policy is governed by its institutional environment; (3) it recognizes the much farther reaching impact that the institutional environment itself has in shaping the fate of immigrants; and (4) it reveals the urban dimension of the impact of institutions (possibly including immigration policy) on cross-national differences in immigrant entry. It is not that immigration policy is irrelevant or unimportant. Rather, other dimensions of society have critical effects on outcomes of interest. As a method of understanding immigrant entry-level status and consequent impacts of immigration, an approach which focuses only on immigration policy is very incomplete. It is also likely to prove of very limited use in changing the impact of immigration on society.

The analysis here also suggests revisions to a second approach to immigration, one which focuses almost entirely on labor market institutions and structures as determining the relative degree of immigrant integration. This approach argues that the ascendance of corporate interests favors the recruitment of immigrants as sources of low-cost labor and allows their exploitation in marginal employment sectors. The findings here suggest that (1) labor market institutions are only one source of immigrant inequality, not necessarily the most powerful; (2) their initial impact on newly arrived immigrants occurs mainly as a result of the overall distribution of earnings rather than the concentration of immigrants in particular labor market segments; and (3) the impact of other institutional sectors, particularly educational institutions, is to a very significant degree independent of labor market structures. These conclusions were supported both in the interurban comparisons within the United States and those conducted cross-nationally.

A particularly influential version of the segmented labor market analysis applied to immigrants has been Saskia Sassen's discussion of the global city. In a global city, corporate superelites supposedly have a heightened capacity to exploit immigrants in personal services, a capacity arising from their extreme affluence and their global reach, which frees them from the constraints of national boundaries and governments. This study has confirmed that there is indeed a pattern whereby less-educated immigrants are clustered in the biggest U.S. cities and those with highly educated economic elites. However, it turns out that the reasons for this polarization pattern are different. Two important points of revision are required. First, the educational polarization lying behind the extreme inequalities in larger U.S. cities is a function of general economic expansion and attendant labor demand. It is unrelated to the presence of elites with any specific economic role, to expanding markets for personal services, or to any other commonly measured dimension of labor market segmentation. Second, heightened immigrant inequality in leading cities is not an inevitable feature of mass immigration in the global economy.

To the contrary, despite the fact that immigration plays an even larger role in the economic strategies of Canada and Australia and of their leading cities than it does in the United States, polarization applies much less in Canada, and not at all in Australia.

The analysis here suggests that the link between global economic change and the recruitment and entry levels of immigrants is more complex and multi-institutional than suggested by Sassen's global cities discussion. Global change has been a force for restructuring in a range of institutional domains, including education, labor markets, social welfare, and immigration policy. It has affected not only the United States but also Canada and Australia, with effects on immigrant standing that are felt in different ways over time. We will return to this issue later in this chapter and the next.

John Porter's *Vertical Mosaic* hypothesis about Canadian-U.S. differences, and the implications of parallel comments on Australia by the Birrells, encompass several institutions, but they also require revision for reasons related to institutional changes. Porter associated the underdevelopment of education in Canada with the use of immigration to bring in highly skilled professionals and managers from the United States and the United Kingdom. Both immigration and education have changed dramatically. Since the immigration reforms of the mid-1960s, Canadian immigration became more selective, and the educational levels of immigrants rose substantially. The influx of less-educated European immigrants from Italy and Portugal slowed, and there was a shift toward non-European immigration sources. A Canadian middle class that was once highly accessible to well-educated Americans and Britons became, at least in terms of formal qualifications, comparably accessible also to Blacks and Asians.

Meanwhile, however, the Canadian educational system also changed, in ways which eventually will offset these trends. Expansion, particularly at the postsecondary level, is rendering the middle class in Canada once again less accessible to newcomers. A 'vertical mosaic' is being re-created. In Australia, by contrast, educational change is less dramatic, and the Australian middle class remains more accessible to newcomers than either the Canadian or American.

Explaining Effects of the Institutional System

In a general way, institutional effects reflect a broad cultural pattern. In each of the four institutional domains, the U.S. institutions which are found to contribute to the potential for lower immigrant entry levels may be characterized as reflecting the value of individualism. The link between individualism and inequality arises from the fact that individualism emphasizes equality of opportunity, which implies a relative disregard for equality of outcomes. In an individualistic environment, individuals attempt to accumulate resources for competition which are not shared collectively except within families. Those who lack such resources encounter a significant disadvantage, and inequalities arising within one institutional domain become compounded by disadvantages in others.

Institutional sectors are, however, far from equal in their relevance to cross-national differences in the experiences of immigrants. The differences may be explained at least in part by reference to the specific nature of the institutions themselves and their relations to other institutions.

Immigration policy responds to a whole series of social and economic forces, which limit its capacity to focus on one specific objective, such as skill selectivity. The international position of Canada and Australia, and increasing global economic interdependence, has led both countries to pursue population growth through immigration, as a means to secure a more prominent global economic role for themselves. Larger immigration programs may force an increased emphasis on the employability of immigrants, but they may also by the same token force a reduction in the capacity to select only the most highly skilled. And in the context of high immigration, periodic reductions in immigration levels, such as Canada implemented in the mid-1980s and Australia has implemented more recently, actually tend to reduce skill levels, at least in the short term, because of the priority which tends to be given to the family-class applicant backlog. And these reductions cannot be maintained over the longer term without compromising the larger economic objective of population growth.

In the United States, on the other hand, immigration is comparatively marginal to primary economic goals, which has led to the family-reunification emphasis in immigration policy. This comparative marginality also may favor immigrant concentration in a few cities, particularly among those who are less educated. U.S. efforts to increase the skill levels of immigrants have entailed increases in the total numbers of immigrants, but given the lack of public support for immigration, there is little movement in this direction.

Increasingly the view has been expressed that political institutions may not contribute much to the control of global migration, for example in the recent collection of essays by Cornelius et al. (1994), and there is substance to this view. Hoerder (1996) suggests provocatively that the entire global sweep of human migration over several centuries has been influenced mainly by social and economic forces, and that the relatively recent creation of the nation-state seems to have played mainly a facilitative role. Political institutions may make decisions which are largely a reflection of the same social and economic forces which drive migration in any case. Hence, there is only a weak social basis for an autonomous role for immigration policy.

The great power of education as an autonomous force boosting native-born credentials and affecting immigrant entry-level status may be attributable to several reasons. First, education is fundamental to individual life chances, which drive individual educational aspiration. Educational expansion in the United States has responded not only to the progressive increase in educational requirements in a postindustrial economy but also to a distinctively American value placed on individualism and the pursuit of the 'American Dream' through occupational mobility. Second, educational credentials are accumulated by individuals, who retain them as portable assets throughout the life course. Aggregate native-born educational levels therefore change only slowly, mainly with replacement over the course of generations. In addition, they may reach extreme high levels in particular attractive locations within a society because of the option of interurban mobility. Third, and as important, these changes in the native-born population are remote from the processes determining educational credentials in the immigrant applicant pool, and the interurban mobility decisions of the native-born population are very different from the chain-migration processes affecting specific immigrant urban areas of settlement.

Labor market effects are weaker, for reasons which may be related to the nature of its processes of institutional change. The most salient labor market attribute affecting immigrant entry-level earnings is overall earnings inequality. Variations in earnings inequalities reflect an institutional force strongly related to the power and influence of organized labor. Where unions are more powerful, earnings inequalities are less, there is less poverty, and immigrant entry-level earnings tend to be closer to the mean. Where unions are less powerful, inequalities are greater, there is more poverty, and the entry-level earnings of immigrants are lower. This pattern is relevant to the cross-national differences. Canada remains more extensively unionized and has less inequality, and until recently, Australia has had the most-regulated labor markets and the least resulting inequalities. The pattern also contributes to the diversity of immigrant entry-level earnings among U.S. cities. However, as mentioned, the most extreme inequalities which result from labor market disparities do not apply in a global city like New York nearly as much as in less strategic places like Miami and San Diego.

Labor market concentrations for immigrants have little or no impact on entry-level earnings, but effects may appear over time, as the lower career earnings trajectories of entry-level jobs becomes more apparent. The consequences of jobs-without-a-future obviously appear when that future does in fact arrive. Previous studies show that 'new' immigrants have lower earnings trajectories than previous immigrants from European sources, and labor market concentrations may be among the reasons. Whether these effects exist could be decided by means of a cohort-specific follow-up analysis of earnings as related to locations in specific labor market segments.

Overall, labor market differences are less powerful than educational differences as factors affecting immigrant entry level status. Increases in the accumulation of educational credentials by the native-born workforce create obstacles mainly for newcomers. Labor market disparities, on the other hand, cannot affect immigrants without also affecting the native-born workforce as well. This domestic impact may help keep these disparities in check.

Even when immigrants become concentrated in completely separate labor market niches, these may change quickly, or they may dissolve as quickly as they are formed. For example, a new immigrant group may become employed in the personal service sector, but this pattern of employment is by no means fixed. The very marginality of such employment may mean that shifting labor market conditions lead to rapid changes in the specific employment sectors of immigrants. This may explain why stereotypical jobs for immigrants are far less institutionalized than gender segregation in work, the so-called 'pink ghetto.' The existence of immigrant jobs such as security guard or convenience-store attendant represent a less powerful institutional force than does the existence of gender-specific employment, such as secretary or receptionist. The less well-formed boundaries for immigrants in the labor market may be a reason why immigrant concentrations have less effect on immigrant earnings than gender segregation has on the earnings of women.

Cultural underpinnings of inequality may also help explain the relative importance of education and labor markets for immigrants. Inequalities related to educational skills have a powerful legitimacy because of a presumed positive relationship of education to economic productivity. This legitimacy of education as a source of inequality holds across societies, even where there are significant differences in absolute levels of education. This legitimacy also no doubt explains why most analysts examine immigrant inequalities 'net' of education and other human capital. Virtually any inequality due to human capital tends to be regarded as acceptable and unproblematic. On the other hand, inequalities affected by collective action and political pressures of workers' organizations tend to be regarded as having less legitimacy because of a presumed negative relation to productivity; sometimes they are even called unproductive. Whatever the economic implications of union action, which is debated, the claim to legitimacy is often the politically weaker consideration of fairness. Hence there may be less ideological 'room' for variations in inequality due to union action as opposed to inequalities of human capital.

Cross-national differences in the welfare state and income redistribution tend to reinforce the patterns of inequality arising in other institutions. For this reason, it might have been expected that the weakness of the U.S. welfare state would compound the inequalities for immigrants there. However, rates of immigrant poverty are significantly higher in the United States, so immigrant welfare use is actually higher there. The welfare state in the United States has served partly to offset the inequalities generated by other institutions. At the same time, the political reaction has been to limit this effect by favoring the disallowance of welfare payments specifically to immigrants. This points toward the weakness of the welfare state as an institutional force maintaining cross-national differences. Political forces act quickly on social policy, bringing divergent trends arising in this particular institutional sector into line with patterns generated in other institutions.

National and Urban Impacts of Institutional Systems

Urban institutional diversity is far greater in the United States than in Canada or Australia, a fact which seems to run counter to the political decentralization of the latter two countries. One reason may be population size. The United States has a very large number of urban concentrations, allowing for greater economic specialization. Most large Canadian and Australian cities are capitals of political regions, imposing a greater degree of uniformity of function. American institutional individualism also may again play a role. While the federal government has vast economic powers in the United States, there may be fewer pressures there for national standards in education, labor markets, or social welfare compared to Canada or Australia.

Each institutional sector has a different pattern of impact on urban areas. An immigration policy emphasizing family reunification could encourage the concentration of less-skilled immigrants in specific cities because of selective, family-based chain migration, as has been suggested. Educational credentials can become unevenly distributed across cities because of internal migration generated by reasons only partly economic and including matters related to culture, lifestyle, or social milieu. Though these build up over time, they represent comparatively current conditions. Earnings disparities, on the other hand, arise from even earlier historical patterns in the development of the labor movement, of which the main power base remains in the urban northeast as a legacy of an earlier era of expansion of industrial manufacturing.

It would be fascinating, but it is not possible here to examine interurban differences in welfare state impacts in each country. Our hypothesis would be that as in the other institutional sectors, interurban differences would be far greater in the United States than in Canada, and that Australia would present a fairly uniform picture from place to place. In the United States, national standards for the social safety net do not exist to the same extent as in the other countries.

In comparative research on immigration, clearly it is of critical importance to combine national and urban levels of comparison. A national comparison that ignores urban variations may fail to identify important sources of cross-national difference in the impact of immigrants. A comparison of urban areas that ignores the national situation may fail to identify national institutional differences which effect the particular urban areas.

Macroinstitutional Discrimination?

An institutional system with negative outcomes for a particular social group might be judged discriminatory, but only if the institutional arrangement cannot be justified by the larger purposes of economic productivity. In Chapter 1, it was noted that the concept of institutional discrimination is normally applied to very specific organizational practices, for example, height requirements for security personnel, which could have the effect of excluding from consideration persons in a group which tended to be short in stature. Such a practice would constitute institutional discrimination if the height requirement could not be justified as essential to the adequate performance of the particular job.

We might apply the same criterion to macro-level institutional structures such as educational systems, labor markets, and the welfare state. If they have negative outcomes for specific groups such as minority immigrants, and if the specific structures cannot be justified by economic objectives, they could be considered discriminatory.

This points directly toward one of the central issues of our time, namely the economic rationale for institutional individualism. This issue goes far beyond the scope of this book. Here it is sufficient to simply point to the issue, and indicate that it is a topic of ongoing research (e.g., Persson and Tabellini 1994). Individualistic institutions promote competition and individual responsibility, which unarguably contribute to economic objectives. At the same time, individualistic institutions generate social inequalities, and if these inequalities become so severe that those at the bottom end, or their children, become unable to mount a competitive effort, or if they create a divisive political climate which undermines commitment to collective objectives, then economic objectives may be undermined. There may be an optimal median, though it is far from clear what that median may be. Hence the issue of macroinstitutional discrimination cannot yet be answered.

The question can be posed regarding the specific institutions and inequalities investigated here. That institutional individualism generates extreme inequalities for certain racial minority immigrant groups is one of the empirical findings of this study. The investigation has been motivated by a concern about the social, cultural, and political implications of such inequality as well as by its economic consequences. These implications, and their repercussions for society in general and its economic performance in particular, depend in part on the discriminatory character of specific institutional frameworks.

Institutional Change and the Future of Immigration

Two contemporary trends linked to global economic change seem to point almost inevitably toward a growing crisis in immigration on the horizon. Across most industrial societies, there has been a pattern of change in recent decades toward more individualistic and market-driven institutions. Unions have lost clout in labor markets, educational levels rise as individuals prepare themselves for more intensive job competition, and there has been reduced funding for social services—including not only the welfare state but also education, forcing tuition increases if not outright privatization at the crucial postsecondary level. All these trends produce lower immigrant entry-level status. At the same time, global economic integration also ensures the continued and in fact increasing importance of immigration. The logic of these two developments—continued immigration, and institutional changes producing more inequality for immigrants—seems inescapable. In the future, immigration seems destined to produce escalating problems of racial inequality in advanced industrial societies.

But institutional change occurs at different rates in different institutions and in different locations, so the potential effects on immigrant entry must be carefully examined. Rising educational standards in the United States have lowered the entry-level earnings of immigrants, exposing them to the most severe effects of increased earnings polarization. Aggregate investment in educational institutions is a factor of which the impact on immigrants is felt only slowly as young cohorts emerging from schools and universities enter the labor market and proceed through the age-graded occupational hierarchy. Changes in those investments have an impact which is delayed by one or more decades. In the comparison of Canada and the United States, the dramatic changes in relative educational levels stand out as the most important difference affecting immigrants. Educational institutions and educational credentials in Canada are moving toward the U.S. model, creating increased immigrant inequality in Canada. The increase in the supply of highly educated workers in Canada has been so rapid, in fact, that it has at least temporarily suppressed wage levels (Freeman and Needels 1993). However, the impact on new immigrants has been profound nonetheless.

A preliminary analysis of the 1991 Canadian census shows that while immigrant cohorts arriving in the 1980s were better educated than the ones that arrived in the 1970s, they fell further behind an even better educated native-born workforce. Partly as a result, the entry-level earnings of these immigrant cohorts are very substantially lower than those of the one arriving in the 1970s. For example, whereas Black immigrant males earned 70 percent of the native-born White males' earnings in Canada for the cohort of the 1970s, for the 1980s cohort, the figure declined to 56 percent. Whereas Chinese immigrant males earned 77 percent of the native-born White male earnings for the cohort of the 1970s, for the 1980s cohort, the figure declined to 69 percent. The impact of educational change in Canada will accelerate, as better-educated, native-born Canadians move to their peak earning years. Entry-level earnings of immigrants in Canada will converge with those in the United States. By contrast, educational change has occurred more slowly in Australia, and entry levels of immigrants there are expected to remain higher.

The implications of trends in earnings polarization are also very clear. First, increased earnings inequality in all countries implies progressively lower entry levels, particularly for those immigrant groups who already have low entry levels. Labor markets in the United States and Australia especially are likely to exert substantial downward pressure on the entry-level earnings of immigrants. Increases in inequality in the United States have been significant in terms of the size of the cross-national differences. There, this impact is increased by the compounding effect of the larger immigrant skills gap. In Australia, potentially the most dramatic changes are coming from the restructuring of labor market institutions. Recent changes toward market deregulation have been very rapid. An institutional sector previously cited as having smoothed the path of economic integration of immigrants is undergoing a thorough restructuring. Consequences for immigrants may be significant. The experiences of women in Australia and New Zealand may be a useful point of comparison. Earnings of women have been comparatively high in both countries, attributable in part to the national wage arbitration system. The rapid restructuring of this system in New Zealand seems to have undercut the position of women in a very significant way, reflected in declining earnings relative to men. Parallel trends for immigrants may become visible in the future. The comparatively less disadvantaged position of immigrant women in Australia may change. The magnitude of all these effects on immigrants will be less in Australia, however, because of less compounding. The higher relative educational levels of the immigrants

236236

236236

236236

236236

236236236

236236

236236236

236236

means that their earnings will remain closer to the mean. In Canada, so far, earnings polarization has been less dramatic, but the compounding effect of the educational skills gap will increase.

Substantial restructuring of the social safety net is more recent in all three countries. The trend is toward a weaker welfare state and less progressive income redistribution. Only in the United States have immigrants specifically been targeted, undoubtedly related to the higher rates of poverty in particular immigrant groups. As inequalities for immigrants grow in Canada and Australia, pressures on their welfare states can be expected to increase correspondingly.

Linking these institutional trends to economic globalization surrounds them with an aura of inevitability which can be misleading. The requirements and consequences of globalization are by no means completely known. At the same time, the prospect for crisis in the future of immigration suggests that policy choices must be made, and it is to this need that we turn in the next chapter.

8

Policies for Migration in a Global Economy

In his provocative discussion of problems facing American society, the French economist and businessman Michel Albert offers what I believe is a fairly conservative assessment, namely that "Immigration could well turn out to be *the* subject of political debate in most of the developed nations in the twenty-first century" (Albert 1993, 5, his emphasis). The analysis here is in complete agreement; and it points toward the reasons. In this final chapter, I want to consider some of the policy choices which will be faced. Not everyone will draw the same policy implications from the analysis presented in the previous chapters. However, the choices of how to respond to migration in the new global economy cannot be evaded, and their importance demands some discussion to indicate the scope of the issues.

The policy responses to immigration lie in three general areas: migration policy, the integration and treatment of immigrants within institutions, and the basic design of mainstream social institutions. Each of these has practical options for individual countries that require consideration. There are also obvious difficulties, however, and this forces consideration of a fourth option: that of global economic development. In a global economy, where national sovereignty is eroding, it is increasingly necessary to consider global responses to all questions, including that of migration. This approach would address the forces that were earlier classified, perhaps too neatly, as exogenous to any one immigrant-receiving society, and would attempt to alter the global context of migration. We will consider each of these possibilities in turn.

Migration Policy

There has been a reliance on immigration policy to select those immigrants who are most clearly economic assets to a receiving society. The findings of this study suggest that immigration control is very limited in its capacity to affect immigrant entry-level earnings. Perhaps this means there has been an overemphasis on immigration policy, taking the form of urgent attention to border controls in the United States, the meticulous fine-tuning of immigration selection criteria in Canada, reductions in immigration in Australia, and a prominent debate over the potential for refugee fraud everywhere.

An analysis of the market for migration might well show that Canada and Australia are probably at the limit of their capacity to attract skilled immigrants. They have already been more selective in the past, and yet the United States gets the better-educated immigrants. The new U.S. legislation may well mean that the United States will now be taking a larger share of the best-educated potential immigrants. Past experience also illustrates that increasing the educational levels of immigrants usually means selecting *more* immigrants, not fewer.

A main policy issue has been the family-reunification component of immigration, but this has proven less susceptible to control. The image of immigrant selection is that it is similar to a hiring process: Individuals are selected as necessary for a specific purpose. The reality is that immigrants come in families. Each immigrant selected for economic reasons not only brings his or her family but also generates somewhere between three and four subsequent family-class applications, on average. Year-to-year fluctuation in the proportion of family-class immigrants does not alter this fact. The only way to control family-class immigration is either to deny more of these applications when they are made or else to introduce family ties into the initial immigrant-selection criteria. The first of these options has been difficult to implement politically and may deter desirable immigrants from applying. The second has never been discussed, at least not publicly. (Selecting immigrants on the basis that they lack families, or that all of their family members are highly skilled, may be discounted as either impractical or undesirable.)

Reliance on immigration policy to address the new racial diversity and declining entry-level earnings among immigrants is also a poor response for other reasons. Foremost among these reasons is that closing the door on the 'dark stranger' places a strain on race relations within any society. It cannot solve interracial problems. The 1960s debate over race relations and immigration policy in the United Kingdom certainly illustrated this fact. When the long-established principle of free movement within the Commonwealth was confronted by the new economic possibility of mass migration to Britain, the principle was quickly abandoned. The ensuing debates clearly damaged domestic race relations, and progressive race relations legislation was sometimes offered as a quid pro quo for further immigration restrictions. Yet any improvements in domestic race relations arising from antidiscrimination measures in employment were surely offset by the negative impact of immigration restrictions (Reitz 1988a).

Immigration controls basically represent government intervention in a market-driven process of international labor mobility. For the present, the complete lifting of migration controls to let the market operate freely is advocated only in limited international situations, such as within the European Community. Few have argued that the United States, Canada, or Australia (apart from its relation to New Zealand) are ready for such moves. The reasons are not complicated: They relate to extreme global economic inequality, and its strong correlation with race and culture. On the other hand, declining immigrant entry levels within immigrant-receiving societies, and expanding economic pressures for migration, may create pressures toward increasing restrictions on international labor mobility.

Increased immigration control not only represents a political liability and is unlikely to have a major effect, it also runs counter to the processes of progressively more open markets and economic change. It is unlikely to be sustained over the long term. As the capacity of national governments to control economic events declines, labor migration is one component and ultimately will be affected. Perhaps the future ultimately will see a transition to international regulation of international labor migration.

Promoting the Integration of Immigrants Within Institutions

The finding that social institutions *other* than immigration policy have great importance in assigning immigrants their place in society has one broad implication for policy. It is that attempts to improve the economic role of immigrants cannot be made solely through concern with immigrant selection. Rather, greater attention should be given as well to processes of immigrant integration within various other institutional sectors.

It is worth reflecting here on the fact that before the immigration reforms of the 1960s, and in particular before the adoption of points-based immigrant selection in Canada and Australia, immigrants were considerably less educated relative to the native born—and yet large-scale immigration was considered a great, even a phenomenal, success. The reason is fairly clear. These immigration programs brought immigrants from Europe who found a much easier time integrating themselves within the institutions of society. This easier integration has many indicators, the most important undoubtedly being higher immigrant levels of earnings in relation to education. The success of immigration today also depends on successful integration of immigrants within institutions. What is different today is simply that this integration has been less successful. Given that the declining entry-level earnings of immigrants are tied to broad institutional changes unlikely to be quickly reversed, and that immigration is likely to continue, policy cannot escape the question of integration within institutions.

There is already a lot of policy in the labor market area. In policy for managing diversity, for example, or dealing with ethnic or racial inequality, the emphasis is on removing barriers to discriminatory treatment. We ask: Is a firm open to minorities? Are antidiscrimination laws strong enough? Despite intense controversy over the facts of employment discrimination against racial minorities, governments have proven strangely reluctant to inquire more fully into these facts, using available methods. The opportunity to invest resources in a definitive and reliable empirical assessment of the extent of such discrimination is rarely taken. Even the small steps toward international standards for the measurement and assessment of discrimination against migrant and ethnic minority workers taken by the International Labour Office in Geneva (ILO 1997; Bovenkerk 1992) could be more strongly supported than they are. Perhaps there is a justifiable fear of the truth: that conclusive evidence of discrimination will generate pressures for decisive action. This could expose the interests of different components of the population, potentially translating racial economic polarization into political polarization, or making it worse.

Immigrants may be assisted in adjusting to labor markets in their new countries of residence first of all by ensuring that their existing qualifications are adequately recognized. It makes little practical sense to insist on the selection of highly educated immigrants and then to have their qualifications disregarded by prospective employers. Of course, often employers have no way of evaluating credentials acquired in far-off and unfamiliar lands. A more cosmopolitan and tolerant attitude helps, but it does not solve the problem of deciding just what foreign credentials actually mean. Again, modest investments could make a difference (cf. Australia 1982; Iredale 1988). Our developing global information highway ought to prove useful here, recognizing an increasingly global labor market.

One issue that must be dealt with in each country is access of immigrants to an effective wage determination process. In the United States, the union movement still attempts to target immigrant groups for organizing, an important opportunity for growth in the future. The same is true in Canada and Australia. Canadian unions often pay lip service to equity issues, but largely ignore the integration of immigrants. In Australia, the traditional corporatist approach that labor has taken toward immigration has given way in the context of current restructuring. These issues require attention because it is in the interest of all workers to ensure that immigration does not compromise the wage determination system.

Also, a good social investment would be additional educational opportunities for immigrants. In North America, employers frequently invest in orientation for new employees as a way of ensuring the most rapid return on the human capital investment they are making. A similar principle may apply to the orientation of new immigrants. For many, this includes language training, but it may also include primer courses on local labor markets and providing the opportunity to adapt foreign professional experience to a new location. Many immigrants' economic success may founder because of a simple lack of knowledge of the "ropes" in their new society. This includes the need to ensure the availability of remedial educational opportunities at all levels, so the tools are there to pursue educational opportunities. European-style job training and apprenticeship programs could be important. This has long been a weakness of the educational systems in the United States and Canada. Existing programs require credible evaluation and monitoring, with successful efforts disseminated internationally.

Perhaps as important is to ensure that the mainstream educational system meets the needs of the second immigrant generation. When the children of immigrants experience difficulties in school, a high drop-out rate should be taken as a danger signal, alerting policymakers to the possibility that the school system may not be responding adequately to the needs of immigrant children.

The question of immigrants and welfare has generated a storm of controversy in the United States, and is debated in Canada and Australia as well. Many resent immigrant use of welfare even on a level justified by their economic circumstance. Yet social assistance may be nowhere as effective as among immigrants attempting to adjust to a new society. Social welfare programs are necessary when people fail to find adequate employment and cannot support themselves adequately. If immigrants are greeted as a resource for the future, where human capital investments have already been made and a reservoir of work experience exists, then expenditures to ensure a successful integration process may make excellent public policy sense. And yet, while studies in the United States and Canada have found that immigrants initially underuse social welfare, attributable to their lack of assimilation into society, a main policy response has been to decry their use of welfare at all.

The policy backlash against immigrant welfare use surfaced first in California, where the large illegal immigration population has created resentment and a perception that immigrants represent a social burden. Proposition 187, passed by public ballot in November 1994, prohibited illegal immigrants from having access to social services, even including public education. Implementation of this measure has been opposed by those fearing dire social consequences if educational opportunities are denied to the children of any substantial population group, whatever their legal status. But the federal welfare reforms of 1996 included actions directed against even legal immigrants, reducing their access to food stamps and Supplemental Security Income. These welfare measures face court challenges as representing an unconstitutional form of discrimination, and as a denial to individuals of the benefits of programs to which they contribute taxes. Meanwhile, President Clinton has worked to reinstate at least some of the reduced welfare support for legal immigrants, arguing that "we must restore basic health and disability benefits when misfortune strikes immigrants who come to this country legally, who work hard, pay taxes, and obey the law. To do otherwise is simply unworthy of a great nation of immigrants." Restoring welfare benefits to immigrants will be an uphill political struggle because public sentiment seems to be running so strongly the other way. There now appears to be, ingrained in the public mind, an image of newly arrived immigrants as likely to seek a public handout. This is the same perception which lies behind calls for more restrictive immigration rules. Imposing welfare restrictions on immigrants is seen as forcing greater self-reliance, deterring undesirable immigrants, and of course, reducing government deficits.

In Canada and Australia, where immigrants are less often poor, the debate over immigrants on welfare has not reached the intensity it has in the United States. No specific public policy measures have been aimed explicitly at immigrants. In Canada, the Reform Party has been most vocal in favoring more restrictive immigration and in advocating reductions in social welfare, with increased user fees for public services such as health care. But attempts by some Reform members to link immigration to the abuse of welfare has received scant attention by elected governments. In Australia, the charge that "large numbers of migrants live entirely on the public purse and contribute nothing to the nation" has been repeated by Blainey (1990), whose previous book sparked a debate about immigration in the early 1980s. In a similar vein, M.P. Pauline Hanson and her One Nation party have raised the issue of welfare use by minorities (including aboriginal peoples). Despite the political rhetoric, however, policy responses have been muted.

The welfare issue has been addressed by asking how immigrants' economic contribution may justify any welfare costs. Attempts to perform cost-benefit calculations for immigrants[1] often ignore some of the most valuable contributions of immigrants. No credible methodology for this cost-benefit analysis has been developed. An adequate methodology should surely take account of the fact that for immigrants, primary and secondary education has been paid for by others. Families have already been formed, life goals set, and often children also partly raised and educated. These are significant assets that immigrants bring with them. The cost-benefit analysis should also include the contribution of immigrants to the economic diversity and international connections that exist in an urban center. It should not measure the contribution of immigrants only by their individual earnings, or the taxes paid on those earnings, particularly if by doing so, immigrant contributions are undervalued by discriminatory experiences or other forms of institutional disadvantage.

From a comparative standpoint, there is real irony in the U.S. situation. To a significant extent, as we have shown in previous chapters, the comparatively low earnings—and hence higher rates of poverty—of many immigrant groups in the United States are not primarily a consequence of different immigrant characteristics or of a less selective U.S. immigration policy. In most origins groups, immigrants to the United States are actually better educated than their counterparts in Canada or Australia. Rather, immigrants to a significant extent are assigned lower entrance status by the distinctively American structure of certain institutions, primarily those affecting education and labor markets. It is these institutional differences which have produced the lower immigrant earnings in the United States, and presumably the comparatively higher rates of poverty and of welfare use. The irony lies here, because rather than immigrants imposing a burden on society, at least from a comparative perspective, it seems more appropriate to say that U.S. institutions have imposed a substantial burden on immigrants. And despite this, the U.S. policy response has been to reduce welfare eligibility, in effect imposing an additional institutional burden on those immigrants. Such measures will further exaggerate the cross-national differences in immigrant status and further hamper the successful integration of immigrants into American society.

Policies for Institutional Change and the Challenge of Global Competitiveness

While these and other issues of institutional accessibility, such as whether social services are accessible to cultural minorities, are important, the findings of this study suggests that gains from addressing diversity mean little if they are followed—as experience suggests that they often are—by offsetting institutional changes. The importance of the institutional dimension of inequality is that our discussion of policy for racial or ethnic diversity ought to include the overall design of institutions.

Redesigning basic institutions in response to problems they create for immigrants may seem impractical or far-fetched. To the contrary, more credibility has been given to the idea of redesigning welfare and social services to make them *less* accessible for immigrants. But it may nevertheless be worth at least considering the reasons behind institutional structures and changes, as much as the characteristics of immigrants themselves, as ways of affecting their economic success.

Because of its power as an institutional force in earnings allocation, the most important adjustments may be possible in relation to education. However, although native-born education clearly creates obstacles for immigrants, it is very difficult to consider its reduction for that reason. Educational expansion cannot be considered macroinstitutional discrimination, if the economic or other social benefits of education are obvious. Of course, 'credentialism' and 'educational inflation' are bad words, but they have not been seriously considered in educational planning. Probably few would argue, for example, that Australia should curtail investment in education, in order to maintain higher entry-level earnings for immigrants. Educational investments are simply too important to be made in relation to immigration planning. While the emphasis in education for the United States and Canada today is on cutbacks, even in this environment, few want to reduce the total amount of education. Instead, the pressure is to get the same (or more) education more cheaply. Furthermore, education is still seen as contributing to national economic productivity, even if to some extent the demand for education is not dictated strictly by economics.

Still, the findings of this study present an opportunity to ask: What does our investment in education cost, and what are its benefits? Even more critically, what is the optimal level of investment in education for an industrial society? Is there any limit to the expansion of education, and if so, what is it? Economic analysis virtually universally accepts that a year of education represents valuable human capital, based on employers' willingness to pay. Yet we have pointed to several reasons why employers may base hiring and promotion decisions on education quite apart from the relevance of specific educational credentials to productivity, and to many reasons why individuals will want to acquire more education even beyond the job opportunities that it opens up. There are as yet no hard economic data indicating that the more educated are more productive in all the jobs where they are better paid, or identifying the optimal level of investment in education for economic productivity.

The overall structure of access to educational institutions is changing. In Canada, the trend today is toward more privatized education, meaning the introduction of private schools at the elementary and secondary-school levels as well as increased user fees (higher tuition) at public universities. These trends are bound to create a greater gap between high-quality opportunities at the top end and deteriorating quality standards elsewhere as resources are withdrawn from low-level educational institutions by advantaged groups. In a more stratified educational system, quality improvements at the top lead to increased barriers for groups lacking the resources to participate at those top levels. They have to settle for the lower standards elsewhere. In this respect as well, Canadian trends in education are moving toward the U.S. model. This may be more true in education than in any other institutional sector.

In labor markets, the move in most countries is toward a degree of deregulation of labor markets, to address the issues of competitiveness. As labor markets are restructured, individuals experience dislocation, and the quality of available jobs may change. Granting minorities equal access to jobs, while replacing those jobs with others at low wages, contributes little to equity. Virtually every employer wrestles with this issue.

Concerning labor markets or institutional design generally, the broadest policy question today is, what is the optimal degree of institutional individualism? One argument is that institutional change toward more individualistic institutions is required by a broader phenomenon of globalization. Proposals are made to respond to the challenge of globalization by pursuing individualistic policies such as privatizing public services including education, deregulating labor markets, and reducing the social safety net. Globalization includes several components, any or all of which may promote individualism. One, certainly, is economic. Increased international trade and competition are forcing the restructuring of institutions along individualistic, market-driven lines, as part of an effort to increase national competitiveness. Another is political. The expansion of international activity of all kinds, including—but not restricted to—the economic, has led to the decline of nation-states as decisionmaking units and centers of power. To the extent that collectivist institutions—including governments as well as private organizations like unions—are rooted in national societies, the expanding international dimension weakens the base for collectivist action, giving way to greater individualism. Global migration itself may weaken national identities and the bonds between individuals and national collectivities.

The appropriateness of specific institutional changes in response to global trends should be decided on their merits, not ideology or slogans. The requirements of globalization impinge on different societies in different ways, at different points in time. Greater individualism is not an all-purpose remedy for every institution in every industrial society regardless of their institutional starting point. After all, moves toward greater individualism in the United States in response to global economic competition have occurred despite the fact that American society was already more individualistic than all of its competitors.

The political appeal of individualism goes well beyond the question of competitiveness. If individualism creates inequalities, then its economic benefits will be more readily perceived by those most favorably placed within the hierarchy of inequality. The advancement of individualistic institutions in many industrial societies may be one important reason for the trend toward substantially increased economic inequalities, and the increasing gap between the rich and the poor. This redistribution of wealth from bottom to top has led to questions about whether those at the top may promote institutional change as a private interest. Global economic competition could be used by affluent and powerful groups within societies as an excuse to promote institutional changes which redistribute wealth in their own direction.

Although those promoting individualism often call for freer markets and the absence of state intervention, they are not entirely opposed to all nonmarket interventions. Rather, contemporary individualism seems to favor the family as the institution for the nonmarket allocation and reallocation of wealth, rather than any broader institution, such as the state. What appears to be individualism may be little more than a claim for preservation of an existing market advantage which can be shared with one's own family—which of course means one's own social class. Those who oppose provision for collective economic welfare in the form of quality public education and low-cost university tuition, health care, and so on often are those who know that they already have the resources to provide these services for themselves and their children. They often greet the issue of maintaining commitment to the collective welfare with the question of how to pay for it—always a question as much about social distribution as about the absolute levels of economic resources in a society. If institutional change is partly an outcome of struggles among interest groups as much as a response to progressive globalization, then the pattern of change over time can be expected to depend on how this issue plays itself out in the political and social struggles within particular countries. Michael Piore's *Beyond Individualism* (1995) grapples with these issues.

In a global environment, perhaps the larger challenge is that of finding a basis for social cohesion. The merits of individualism may be offset if increased inequality undermines the capacity of individuals to act together for collective goals, including but not restricted to the economic. Globalization, including global migration, may lead to a declining sense of social cohesion. As a society becomes more diverse, the question arises whether the sense of the collectivity is being undermined, so that any provision for the collective well-being in any institutional sector seems less like providing for 'us' and more like providing for 'them.' The political appeal of individualism to diverse groups may arise in part from a desire to reduce any obligations to persons perceived as outside one's own social group.

It is important to recognize that migrant source countries are part of the global system undergoing change. These changes are exogenous to the forces under study here and cannot be considered in detail. However, the capacity to influence economic development on a global scale should not be overlooked as a policy factor affecting global migration. Change may affect the newer source countries, but economic development has occurred more rapidly for some than for others. Economic development in Europe, and the creation of a European labor market, drastically changed that source for immigration to North America or Australia, not only reducing it, but shifting its emphasis to the more highly skilled. Internal migration in Europe has been far less than anticipated, partly because the basic economic similarity of the societies makes migration unattractive. Progress toward a reduction in global inequality could have a similar impact on global migration in the future.

Notes

Chapter One

1. The proportion intending to work at all was somewhat higher in Canada. In 1972, for example, the proportion intending to work was 46.7 percent in Canada, and 40.9 percent in the United States. These figures were declining somewhat over time in both countries. The data on intention to work in highly skilled occupations cannot be compared directly because the "professional" category in U.S. data is broader than the same category in the Canadian data. Nevertheless, the data on year-to-year trends in each country reveal potentially important information about the effect of policy. In Canada, the proportion of immigrants classified as intending professional occupations rose from 12.1 percent in 1956–1961 to 23.5 percent in 1962–1967—*before* the introduction of the points system. The fact that the proportion was higher in later years (it rose to 30.7 percent in 1968 and to 32.3 percent in 1969 and then fell slightly, reaching 26.8 percent in 1972) suggests that other factors might be more important than the points system in determining immigrants' skill levels. In the United States, the proportion of those intending professional employment was 17.4 percent over 1953–1965, before the new policy, and increased from 24.6 percent in 1966–1968 to 31.9 percent in 1971 and 31.1 percent in 1972. It appears that the trend toward increasing skill levels was somewhat independent of the major policy changes.

2. Immigrant skills rose over the period 1961 through 1976 in the United States. Keely and Elwell state: "The proportionally smaller contributions to the workforce from Europe and the Americas were also contributions of less-skilled workers. The converse was true of Asia, Africa, and Oceania. Their proportional contributions to the workforce were greater, and they were of a higher occupational level" (p. 198).

3. The U.S. census measures years of schooling. The Canadian census measures years of various types of schooling, including elementary, secondary, university, and nonuniversity schooling. The Canadian measure might be more inclusive than the U.S. one, if the U.S. census question does not always capture vocational schooling. Thus, there might be an upward bias in the Canadian measure. See Duleep and Regets (1992, 426).

4. In recent publications, Borjas has introduced the argument that immigration policy nonetheless has a skill-selective effect by shaping the mix of immigrant origins, although he recognizes that policy does not necessarily affect the skill levels of immigrants from particular points of origin. However, even this origins-mix effect on immigrant skills is highly doubtful. The issue is reviewed in Chapter 3.

5. For most immigrants from the third world, Borjas' conclusions are based on a regression analysis including many variables and a number of source countries, but (of course) only the three destination countries. The inference that the less positive selection of immigrants to the United States would have been more positive except for the policy change of the late 1960s is based only on a control for the periods before and after the policy change.

6. In Australia, in 1990, two polls showed an average of 56 percent thinking that immigration should be reduced, 32 percent thinking it was about right, 8 percent thinking it should be increased, and 4 percent uncertain (Gott 1990, 127). The Australian Morgan Gallup for May 1992 showed that the proportion who thought there were too many immigrants was 68 percent (see also Gott 1990, 127). It is interesting that the Australian polls showed more positive attitudes when the term 'migrants' was used instead of 'immigrants.' These Australian results are comparable to findings in the United States and Canada. In a series of similar polls in the United States, the proportion of Americans wanting immigration reduced went up from 33 percent in 1965 to 61 percent in 1993 (*New York Times,* June 27, 1993, 1, 16). In Canada, various sources at about the same time placed the proportion of Canadians thinking there was too much immigration in the range between 53 and 66 percent (see Reitz and Breton 1994, 77–78).

7. The Australian, Canadian, U.S., and other field surveys of discrimination are compiled by the International Labor Office in Geneva and described by Bovenkerk (1992). The Australian results (Riach and Rich 1991) are similar to the Canadian (Henry and Ginzberg 1985) and U.S. (Turner, Fix, and Struyk 1991) findings (see Reitz and Breton 1994, 82–83, for a detailed comparison of the Canadian and U.S. data).

8. The number of anti-Semitic incidents recorded by the B'nai B'rith in each country is roughly in proportion to population size, and if anything, somewhat higher than expected in Canada and Australia based on the U.S. benchmark. For example, in 1991, the Anti-Defamation League of B'nai B'rith in the United States recorded 1,879 anti-Semitic incidents; the same year, the League for Human Rights of B'nai B'rith in Canada recorded 251 such incidents, more than expected based on a 10:1 population ratio. The number recorded by the B'nai B'rith Anti-Defamation Commission in Australia was 207 in 1993 and 227 in 1994, rising rapidly in recent years. These numbers, again, are more than expected given total population ratios.

9. As Heckman and Hotz (1986) put it, "we have no *a priori* knowledge of the functional relationship between income and [say] education." The same can be said of any other human capital measure. In their critique of dual labor market theory, the two disputed the "assumption that the true functional form of the earnings equation under the hypothesis of no dualism is known." As they explained: "Since nothing in economic theory implies that workers with three years of schooling need to be half as productive as workers with six years of schooling (and indeed may even perform different tasks in the market), we have no *a priori* knowledge of the functional relationship between income and education. The same can be said for the relationship between income and any other productive attributes. Since no simple relationship is necessary between measured schooling (or work experience) and human capital, similar remarks also apply to human

capital earnings models." (p. 528) This is really an argument against drawing any conclusions about discrimination from any labor force data that do not explicitly measure productivity (which might not be possible).

10. In the United States, a June 1965 Gallup poll showed 33 percent wanting less immigration, 39 percent wanting the same amount, and 7 percent wanting more, with 21 percent undecided. A March 1977 poll showed an increase in opposition to 42 percent, with 37 percent wanting the same amount, and again 7 percent wanting more, with 14 percent undecided (*New York Times,* June 27, 1993, 1). In Canada, a June 1975 Gallup poll showed 39 percent wanting less immigration, 43 percent wanting the same amount, and 10 percent wanting more, with 8 percent unsure (*The Gallup Report,* July 2, 1975). In Australia, a Gallup poll in 1970 showed 38 percent saying there were too many immigrants, 45 percent saying that immigration was about right, and 12 percent wanting more, with 5 percent unsure (Gott 1990, 138). These are roughly similar results in the three countries.

11. Canada since 1970, and later Australia, have promoted 'multiculturalism' policies, but majorities in all three countries favor assimilation. In one poll, in the United States 51 percent favored immigrant groups being "encouraged to change their distinct culture and ways to blend in with the larger society" rather than maintaining their distinct cultures; a larger 61 percent in Canada felt the same way (Reitz and Breton 1994, 27–28). In Australia, the traditions of 'White Australia' reflect racism, and the debate occasioned by the book by Geoffrey Blainey *All for Australia* (1984) brought the issue of race again to the surface. However, Australians' attitudes toward minority cultures do not seem markedly different from those of Canadians or Americans. For example, in 1977, a poll showed that 54 percent thought migrants should "be encouraged to fit into the Australian community as soon as possible" rather than maintaining their own culture. By 1981, the proportion rose to 65 percent (Birrell and Birrell 1987, 283).

12. The numbers of refugees vary from year to year in all countries, but the following numbers illustrate the pattern. In the five-year period between 1980 and 1984, the United States admitted 534,492 refugees (INS *Statistical Yearbook* 1986, Table 4), about 0.2 percent of its 1980 population. In the same period, Canada admitted 101,568 refugees, about 0.4 percent of its 1981 population (*Immigration Statistics,* 1987; see also Zolberg 1992, 104). Australia admitted 89,222 during the same period, about 0.6 percent of its 1981 population (Collins 1991, 262).

13. In the U.S. data, the file supplied complete information only for County Groups, but in most cases these could be assigned unambiguously to an SMSA. In the relatively few cases where County Groups were split between SMSAs, or between SMSAs and nonmetropolitan areas, these units were assigned to an SMSA on the basis of the location of the majority of their population. See also Tienda and Lii (1987, 148).

14. The *1980 US PUMS A-file* contains data on 2,832,668 persons residing in one of the 79 urban areas with a population greater than 500,000, between the ages of 16 and 64, and in the labor force. Of these, 2,085,992 were native-born, non-Hispanic Whites. Given this very large number, a 10-percent subsample was drawn, yielding 119,813 men and 88,409 women. Immigrants in the sample who had arrived between 1970 and 1980 numbered 68,476 men and 45,246 women. A fairly significant number of White immigrants not born in Europe were excluded

from the analysis. Approximately 6 percent of the sample had annual earnings of less than $100, and these also were excluded from the analysis. (A supplementary sample of 19,876 native-born Blacks also was retained.) The *1981 Canadian PUST Individual File* contains data on 112,941 persons residing in one of the 9 urban areas with a population greater than 500,000, between the ages of 16 and 64, and in the labor force. Of these, the native-born Canadians of European origins (regarded here as comparable to the native-born, non-Hispanic, White Americans) numbered 45,930 men and 35,200 women. Immigrants in the sample who had arrived between 1970 and 1980 numbered 4,805 men and 3,735 women. Immigrants of European ethnic origins who were born neither in Europe nor in the United States were excluded from the analysis. Again, approximately 6 percent of the sample had annual earnings of less than $100, and these were excluded from the analysis. The *1981 Australian Persons Sample File* contains 40,335 persons residing in one of the 5 urban areas with a population greater than 500,000, between the ages of 16 and 64, and in the labor force. For the native-born of native-born parents (the Australian comparison group for native-born, non-Hispanic, White Americans), a 25-percent subsample was drawn containing 4,013 men and 2,709 women. Immigrants in the sample who had arrived between 1970 and 1980 numbered 1,999 men and 1,395 women. A significant number could not be identified in terms of race based on the data, and they were excluded from the analysis. Approximately 5 percent of the sample had annual earnings of less than $100, and they also were excluded from the analysis. Further details on the measurement of origins are provided in Chapter 2. In each data file, samples of immigrants who had arrived before 1970 also were drawn for occasional use.

Chapter Two

1. Because our primary concern is with relative levels of earnings, earnings are measured in the local currency of each country.

2. For males, Blacks are 14.2 percent, Mexicans 2.5 percent, Asians 0.9 percent, and other Latin Americans 0.4 percent, for a total of 18.1 percent. For females, Blacks are 18.1 percent, Mexicans 2.3 percent, Asians 1.0 percent, and other Latin Americans, 0.4 percent, for a total of 21.8 percent.

3. A complete analysis of how immigrant status is affected by the presence of non-White native-born groups is an important issue, but it is beyond the scope of this study. However, some discussion of the issue is included below, and there are relevant data in Tables 2.1 and 4.4.

4. The group labeled "White (other)" has a somwhat lower status. It is analyzed separately because these individuals indicated that they were born in Asia, Africa, or Central or South America (which includes the Caribbean), and thus they do not fit the normal conception of the European immigrant.

5. Puerto Rican migrants, many of them in New York, are not included in this analysis, which includes only immigrants from outside both the United States and its territories (including Puerto Rico).

6. Neither the Canadian nor the Australian census identifies Whites as a racial group. The Canadian census identifies European ethnic origins. White immigrants in Canada are those of European ethnic origins who were not born in Asia,

Africa, or Central or South America (including the Caribbean). In Australia, White immigrants were considered to be European-born immigrants whose parents both were born in Europe.

7. To some extent, this comparison might be affected by differences in origins *within* the Chinese group. Chinese-origin immigrants to Canada more often come from Hong Kong, while those to the United States more often come from Taiwan or the mainland. However, given the consistency of the cross-national differences across origin groups, it seems reasonable to presume that these differences within the Chinese group do not account entirely for the cross-national differences in entry-level earnings. We can return to this issue when we examine interurban variations within the United States, which also to some extent might be influenced by differences in origins within origin groups.

8. The definitions of these units are roughly comparable among the three countries, with the exception that very large urban conglomerations in the United States, mainly in New York and Los Angeles, are represented by a number of separate SMSAs (these have become Consolidated Metropolitan Statistical Areas, or CMSAs, in the 1990 census).

9. Newark and Jersey City are included within the boundaries of the 1990 New York CMSA, Orange County and Oxnard-Ventura are included in the 1990 Los Angeles CMSA, and San Jose is included in the 1990 San Francisco–Oakland–San Jose CMSA.

10. Correlations between population size ca. 1980 and the proportion of recent immigrants are 0.48, 0.48, and 0.40 for the United States, Canada, and Australia, respectively; correlations between unemployment rates ca. 1980 and the proportion of recent immigrants are –0.14, –0.78, and –0.20, respectively.

11. At the same time, there were an array of smaller cities in both countries that were chosen by very few Blacks. The five Canadian cities with fewest Black immigrants represented almost 30 percent of the urban population but had only 10 percent of Black immigrants. The 44 American cities with the fewest Black immigrants represented about the same proportion of the urban American population and also had only 10 percent of Black immigrants. So the greater concentration of Black immigrants in the United States applies mainly to the largest cities.

12. As in earlier tables, the N's in the table refer to the sizes of the specified origin groups, but the accuracy of the statistics on entry-level earnings depends on the sample sizes of both the origin groups and the dominant groups. All of the origin groups reported have samples of 100 persons or more; the size of the dominant group sample is not reported but is substantially larger in each case.

Chapter Three

1. The landmark change in U.S. immigrant policy was the Immigration Act of 1965 (sometimes referred to as the Hart-Celler Act), which were amendments to the 1952 Immigration and Nationality Act (the McCarran-Walter Act).

2. In 1980, separate legislative provision was made for refugees (1980 Refugee Act), so the numerically limited refugee category specified in the 1965 legislation was eliminated (with its numerical allotment transferred to one of the family-preference categories).

3. These data come from the U.S. Immigration and Naturalization Service, *Statistical Yearbook of the Immigration and Naturalization Service, 1986* (Washington, D.C.: U.S. Government Printing Office, 1989), Table 4.

4. Estimates indicate that many thousands of illegal immigrants enter the United States each year, with the total having reached several million as early as 1980. The census data examined below include both legal and illegal immigrants.

5. In the years immediately following the introduction of the points system in 1967, the numbers of immigrants fluctuated, but the sources rapidly shifted. In 1974, a year in which non-European immigration had reached new highs, the government issued a green paper reviewing immigration, preparing the way for a new Immigration Act in 1976. This Act formalized immigration principles and processes and authorized the government to set annual numerical targets for immigration. By 1979, refugee intake also was significantly expanded. Despite policy changes in Canada, numbers of immigrants continue much as before, with year-to-year fluctuations now set by Parliament, mainly in response to perceptions of economic needs. Numbers averaged across several years remain fairly constant (as the decennial data in Chapter 1 showed), at about 150,000 per year, perhaps 0.6 percent of population (compared to 0.4 percent of population in the United States). Starting during the Mulroney years and continuing despite an extended period of recession and high unemployment, immigration is at a comparatively high level, between about 200,000 and 250,000 per year, the latter figure being close to 1.0 percent of population. Thus, Canadian immigration numbers remain higher than those in the United States, even after taking the population size difference into account.

6. This function was first vested in the Department of Manpower and Immigration, later renamed Employment and Immigration, and currently, Citizenship and Immigration.

7. The Immigration and Naturalization Service is in the Department of Justice, and the Visa Office is located in the Department of State. The Department of Labor conducts the labor certification process as an adjunct activity.

8. *Globe and Mail,* January 1, 1993, p. A5.

9. In some years, live-in caregivers and retired persons are included among the independent immigrants.

10. On the other hand, Freeman and Betts (1992, 84) say that the limitation of the 1965 immigration reforms in the United States to family reunification, with only limited labor certification, was generally regarded as a "victory for the trade unions."

11. In Australia, employers also have shown interest in an expansionist immigration policy. This has been particularly evident even during the period following abandonment of the "White Australia" policy. "Employers whose sales growth was hooked to population expansion and State Governments, most of whom still gauged their success by their ability to attract industry and people to their respective States, were the main sources of pressure to maintain high immigration intakes" (Birrell and Birrell 1987, 86). The demand included both skilled and unskilled workers. But partly because of the lack of a skilled domestic workforce due to weaker educational and job training institutions, employers have also demanded immigration to offset shortages of skilled workers and trades-

men. In Australia, in the 1970s, this was evident throughout the heavy manufacturing and construction industries, which relied heavily on Southern European immigration.

12. Referring to differences in the levels of education of the Canadian and U.S. populations, Boyd stated that the more skills-oriented Canadian approach to immigration "ultimately reflects differences in the training and recruitment of manpower in the Canadian and U.S. economies." Referring to Porter, Boyd wrote that whereas the "underproduction of skilled manpower needed in an industrial economy is attributed to the absence of highly positive values about education; it also reflects previous successful reliance on immigration to provide the requisite highly trained manpower." . . . "The lack of internally generated highly qualified manpower means that in contrast to the economy of the United States, that of Canada is heavily dependent on the external training and recruitment of immigrants to meet its manpower needs" (Boyd 1976, 84–85).

13. "In the early 1960s, 72.1 percent of immigrants [to either Canada or the U.S.] who did not have a high school diploma migrated to the United States. By the late 1970s, this statistic was 86.9 percent, an increase of almost 15 percentage points. In contrast, in the early 1960s, 82.4 percent of immigrants with a college diploma chose the United States, but by the early 1970s, the fraction increased to only 89.0 percent, less than 7 percentage points" (Borjas 1993, 26). This shift, while significant, is not overwhelming.

14. Borjas's (1990, 209) statement about immigrants to both Canada and Australia having an average 13 years of education, one year more than immigrants to the United States, is attributed to 1980 and 1981 census data, but his own table on this point (Borjas 1988, 43), based on all immigrants in those respective censuses, shows that the average in all three countries was 11.7 years. The method of measurement we have used here differs slightly from that used by Duleep and Regets: In our summary for the Canadian education data, we do not count vocational education. Thus, the Canadian data do not have the upward bias observed by Duleep and Regets. As in Duleep and Regets, the census data here include education obtained after arrival.

15. The study by Sorensen et al. (1992) attempted to link categories of immigrants in the United States to ethnic concentrations in specific urban areas. While the data support the hypothesis at least for Asians, the measurement of ethnic concentrations seems to have been too crude to provide a proper test. In the Asian case, it would be important to measure specific Asian communities, since Korean communities, for example, are not a magnet for South Asian immigrants. The different Asian composition of immigrants in particular cities also creates another analytic problem, confounding the relation between employment categories and the education of immigrants. Chicago, for example, contains a relatively large proportion of employment-class immigrants and has large ethnic communities, seeming to contradict the negative community size effect hypothesis. However, Chicago happens to contain a mix of Asian immigrants that includes a large proportion of South Asians, for example, who have high average educational levels. Within groups, the impact of family-class immigration in lowering the educational levels of large ethnic groups in Chicago may nevertheless hold. In the case of Whites, the measure of ethnic concentration in the Sorensen et

al. data included all Whites and not just immigrants; the attraction of immigrant communities was very likely not captured at all in the measures. And the occupational preference categories are unimportant for Mexican immigrants.

16. Note that the community size variable was measured using data from men. It might be useful to provide a measure based on data from women, and also to reanalyze the community effect separately for married and single women.

17. Multivariate regression analyses (not presented in a table) enable us to examine how the educational levels of immigrants might be affected jointly by immigrant community size, the size of the urban area, and general labor demand. In the United States, all three variables are negatively correlated with immigrant educational levels. The regression shows that employment growth and the size of immigrant populations both are important determinants of immigrant educational levels, net of urban area size. In Canada and Australia, by contrast, urban characteristics are less strongly correlated with immigrant educational levels, and none are significant net of immigrant origins.

Chapter Four

1. Comparing 1980 census data for the United States with 1981 data for Canada and Australia, Borjas observed that higher educational standards in the United States compared to Canada or Australia exacerbated the immigrant skills gap in that country, with a direct bearing on the lower immigrant statuses. "Natives have only about eleven or twelve years of education in Australia and Canada, as compared to thirteen years in the United States. These differences in educational attainment, therefore, partly explain why immigrants in the United States have lower earnings (relative to natives) than immigrants in other countries" (Borjas 1990, 209).

2. Data are available by race in the United States, and by gender for all three countries. In the United States, there is a general convergence of female toward male educational levels, and of Black toward White levels, though a gap remains, particularly at the university level.

3. For the most recent years, the Canadian figures were substantially higher than those for the United States, but because of changes in the category definitions for Canada, these figures are not included in Table 4.1.

4. In the OECD data, Canadian scores on math proficiency tests for thirteen-year-olds were 62.0 (standard error = 0.6) compared to 55.3 for Americans (standard error = 1.0); see CERI (1992, Table R8[e], Chart D). Another comparative point of reference is the data from TIMSS, the Third International Mathematics and Science Study (Robitaille et al. 1996). The mean mathematics scores for Canadian students in grade eight were 527 (530, in Australia)—but only 500 in the United States; mean science scores for Canadian students in grade eight were 531, similar to 534 in the United States, both below the figure of 545 for Australia (CERI 1996, 71).

5. OECD data show a similar pattern. Across the entire population aged 25–64 in 1989, 81 percent of Americans, 71 percent of Canadians, and 57 percent of Australians had completed secondary education. Of Americans, 23 percent had university degrees, compared to 15 percent of Canadians (CERI 1992, 23).

6. Additional U.S. data show that the median number of years of school completed for all persons 25 years of age or over was 9.3 years in 1950, rising to 10.6 in 1960, 12.1 in 1970, 12.5 in 1980, and 12.7 in 1988. U.S. Bureau of the Census, *Statistical Abstract of the United States*, 1990, p. 133.

7. The private rate of return, which focuses on after-tax earnings but reduces costs by the extent of the public subsidy of education, is normally higher. In Canada, in 1961, the private rate of return to higher education was 19.7 percent, compared to 15.4 percent in the United States in 1969 (the social rate was virtually the same in 1969 as in 1959—10.9 percent). See Psacharopoulos 1985, 599–600.

8. The private rate of return for higher education in Australia in the same year was 21.1 percent, also higher than the 19.7 percent figure for Canada in 1961.

9. The White population in each country is the benchmark group for the analysis of racial inequality. Yet the native-born population includes other racial groups, notably Blacks in the United States. Given that Blacks have lower levels of education than Whites (in our urban labor force sample, a mean of 12.05 years for Black men compared to 13.49 for White men, and 12.57 years for Black women compared to 13.22 for White women), the inclusion of non-White groups in the United States would lower the native-born educational levels there. The mean years of education for native-born Americans from all racial groups is 13.24 for males, and 13.07 for females.

10. If D_j represents the earnings of person j, K represents the mean earnings of the benchmark group, and I_{ij} represents membership in immigrant group i, then:

$$D_j = K + a_i I_{ij} + d_j, \qquad \text{(Equation 4.1)}$$

where a_i represents the effect of membership in immigrant group i on earnings. The entry level of an immigrant group i would be represented by the ratio of a_i to K. If X_{kj} represent a vector of k human capital attributes of person j, and b_k represents the earnings effects of these variables, then:

$$D'_j = K' + b'_k X_{kj} + a'_i I_{ij} + d'_j, \qquad \text{(Equation 4.2)}$$

where a'_i represents the effect of membership in immigrant group i on earnings, net of human capital. The ratio of a'_i to K would represent the entry level of the immigrant group i if its human capital endowments match those of the benchmark population.

11. The measurement of education and work experience for immigrant groups ignores the question of whether these were acquired domestically (see Reitz and Sklar 1997). Quadratic terms for both education and work experience are included to take account of nonlinearity in the effects of these labor market resources. Hours of work are included as human capital, implying that measured regression effects are net of differences in hours. Language knowledge refers to English everywhere except in Montréal, where knowledge of either English or French is considered positive human capital, and in Québec, where French is considered the relevant language.

12. Note that earnings data given below for each country are in the respective national currencies. The comparisons of the earnings of immigrants relative to native born are unaffected by currency differences.

13. Borjas's analysis employed somewhat different human capital variables. The results of his analysis by immigrant origins (Borjas 1988, 50–54) is also comparable, when allowance is made for his reliance on birthplace to tap origins. The use of birthplace alone is extremely unreliable as an indicator of ethnicity or race.

14. Each equation contained both a linear and a quadratic term. The Australian earnings equation is close to linear, with only a slightly positive squared term. The observed earnings equations for both Canada and the United States have large and positive square terms, meaning that at the time of observation, the marginal value of an additional year of education was higher in both countries for those with more education. In each country, the rate of change of earnings with education can be calculated by evaluating the first derivative of the earnings equation with respect to education. The result can then be expressed as a percentage of mean earnings in the country. In Australia, for men in 1981, earnings levels rose with education at the rate of 9.2 percent per year, at the Australian mean educational level of 11.27 years. This rate rose only slightly at higher levels of education in Australia. For example, at 13.49 years of education, the U.S. mean, earnings levels in Australia rose with education at the rate of 9.5 percent per year. In 1981, in Canada, at the Canadian mean level of 11.87 years, earnings rose with education at the rate of 8.5 percent per year of education, a rate which increased to 9.9 percent at the U.S. mean of 13.49 years. In 1980, in the United States, the rates are 7.7 percent at 11.27 years (the Australian mean), 6.1 percent at 11.87 years of education (the Canadian mean), and 6.6 percent at 13.49 years (the U.S. mean).

15. We assume that immigrant recruitment is not affected by native-born educational levels. This assumption is examined in more detail later.

16. Generally, human capital endowments including education have greater benefits for the native-born Whites than for immigrant groups. Many of the education/immigrant-status interactions are significantly negative, particularly for men, in all three countries (results not included in a table).

17. Substantial changes in native-born educational levels might affect the labor market as well as the earnings determination process, as Freeman and Needels showed (1993, 128). This would be expected, given equal demand for highly educated workers and the observed differences in availability. The estimates in Table 4.6 can be recalculated, swapping education coefficients, to see how the labor markets in each country might be affected by changes in the supply of educated workers. The results do not depart from the figures in Table 4.6 by more than a percentage point. Hence, the basic conclusion that native-born educational levels explain half or more of the observed lower entry-level earnings of minority immigrant groups in the United States is unchanged.

18. The ranking of these cities is affected only a little by the restriction to Whites among the native-born males, not only because Whites are the largest group in most of the cities, but also partly because the ranking of educational levels of native-born minorities is similar.

19. It would be useful to repeat the above analyses but leaving out key cities, to see what impact they have on the analysis.

20. The size of the immigrant education gap opened up by rising native-born educational levels can be measured, in a regression equation estimating individual education, as the interaction between urban-area native-born educational

level and immigrant status. Let *e* represent individual years of education. The average native-born educational level in an urban area, *E*, will determine individual educational levels for the native born, obviously, but immigrant status will give rise to departures from this norm. Let immigrant status be represented by I_i, for *i* immigrant groups. The question is, as native-born education levels rise, what happens to immigrant education levels. The statistical interaction of *E* and I_i, or $E*I_i$ will capture the extent to which trends for the immigrant groups depart from those in the mainstream. So we are interested in the equation $e = K + aE + b_i I_i + c_i(E*I_i) + d$, where K is a constant, and d the error term. The coefficient **a** is expected to be unity, since it represents the relation between aggregate educational levels of the native-born Whites and individual educational levels for the same group. The b_i will reflect variation in the overall educational levels of a particular minority group relative to the native born. The main interest here is in the c_i, the interaction coefficient reflecting the extent to which educational levels in group *i* depart from the mainstream norm. The right-hand columns of Table 4.9 report c_i. Negative c_i represent a greater education gap in the high-education cities.

Chapter Five

1. A number of studies providing data on income or earnings inequality for scores of countries spanning various levels of development, as part of an interest in development-related issues, are less useful because of problems of comparability between data for individual pairs of countries. This may be particularly true of studies like those by Kuznets (1955, 1966) or Paukert (1973, used again recently by Persson and Tabellini 1994). Some such studies in any case use the Sawyer (1976) compilation as a primary source for OECD countries: Muller (1985, 1988), Hoover (1989), Simpson (1990), and Nielsen (1994). Muller added data from the World Bank's *World Development Report* (various years) and other sources, focusing on the upper tail of the distribution. Information contained in these sources is consistent with what is presented in the text here. Paukert used a data set on 56 countries, which included both the United States and Australia, but not Canada (elaborated from the 44-country comparison of Irma Adelman and Cynthia Morris [1971]). The data concerned personal income before tax, and found greater extremes of income at the bottom in the United States. The share of all income received by the bottom 20 percent of the distribution was 5.6 percent in the United States and 6.6 percent in Australia; the poor have about 18 percent more of the income in Australia than in the United States. The share received by the bottom 40 percent was 17.9 percent in the United States, and 20.0 percent in Australia. Overall, the Gini index for the United States was 0.34, and for Australia, 0.30.

2. Saunders, Stott, and Hobbes (1991) had previously used the Luxembourg data in a comparison focused on Australia and New Zealand.

3. The Gini index varies between zero and one, with zero representing a distribution in which everyone receives the same earnings, and one representing a distribution in which one person receives all earnings.

4. The standard deviation divided by the mean.

5. See also the graphic summary by Hills (1995, 68) for the Rowntree Foundation Report.

6. Other sources confirm that earnings inequality is greater in the United States, less in Canada, and least in Australia. Borjas (1988, 92), for example, calculated in 1980 and 1981 census data that the coefficient of variation of earnings among the native born in Canada is about 86 percent of what it is in the United States.

7. For example, the proportions employed in wholesale and retail trade and in restaurants and hotels in 1990 were 22.1 percent in the United States, 24.0 percent in Canada, and 24.9 percent in Australia (Godbout 1993, 13).

8. The indexes might be replicated in the two data sets, but given the limited nature of Reitz's data on one specific city, the result would not justify the effort.

9. These previously unpublished data are available on request.

10. Of course, these possibilities prove difficult to resolve, because when it is found (for example, by Treiman et al. 1986–1987) that immigrant disadvantage is indeed related to foreign education and experience, such findings could reflect discrimination against foreign education or experience. In general, the impact of any measured or unmeasured human capital endowments—including years of education or experience—might reflect credentialism, a form of institutional discrimination.

11. Rodriguez (1989), Ortiz (1990), and Santiago and Galster (1994) investigated the effect of labor market concentrations for Puerto Rican migrants in the United States. However, the impact on Puerto Ricans represents a long-term effect, parallel to the impact of industrial restructuring on the native-born Blacks who were the focus of Wilson's (1987) analysis. Here the question is whether these conditions apply to the entry-level earnings of relatively recent immigrants. This impact may be much smaller.

12. Rosenfeld and Kalleberg (1990) applied this perspective to a comparison of the position of women in two corporatist countries, Norway and Sweden, and two relatively dualist countries, Canada and the United States, and found only limited support. They argued that part-time work is encouraged as a policy to integrate family and work in Scandinavia, and has a major effect on the gender gap in income there. The authors note that while Canada is considered a dualist country, it reflects corporatist tendencies.

13. Even for Koreans and Cubans, the benefits of self-employment are small. As a result of self-employment, Korean male earnings are 3.0 percent higher than what they would be without the self-employment options; for Cubans, they are 1.0 percent higher. The position of both groups in the hierarchy of earnings is unchanged.

14. See notes to Table 5.5.

15. Recall that the effect of native-born education was proportionally greater for immigrant groups with higher entry levels, an opposite pattern.

16. I am grateful to Gregory DeFreitas for providing me with measures for his immigrant-intensive industries.

17. *A Tale of Two Nations* compares "right-to-work" states with other states and provides evidence not only on earnings but also on other indicators such as infant mortality, job fatalities, and health insurance. It argues that "right-to-work" laws depress both wages and living conditions.

18. The pattern whereby immigrants are most strongly attracted to cities with immigrant-intensive industries holds for every group identified in this study, and

is fairly strong (r > 0.40) for all groups except the Vietnamese (r = 0.20) and Asian Indians (r = 0.31). On the other hand, every group except the Cubans has a *negative* association with labor intensive industries: the relation to peripheral industries is mixed and is substantially positive only for Cubans (r = 0.53), Mexicans (r = 0.22), Koreans (r = 0.11), and Other Asians (r = 0.10). The groups which are larger in cities with a high proportion of professionals and managers are Vietnamese (0.41), Chinese (0.27), Whites (0.25), and Blacks (0.25).

19. This measure is based on the earnings distribution for all full-year, full-time workers, including both native-born and immigrants. The measure thus excludes part-time workers, a significant class of workers whose jobs are comparatively unregulated.

20. U.S. data are from Freeman and Medoff (1979, 167–168), drawn from the 1973–1975 May Current Population Survey. In those data, Dallas is averaged with Fort Worth, and mean value substitution has been used in the cases of northeast Pennsylvania, Raleigh, New Brunswick, Austin, and Long Branch. Canadian data are based on reports on union membership tabulated by Metropolitan Area (see Canada, Statistics Canada 1983, 40, Table 21), adjusted to include workers covered by collective agreements (using comparisons at the provincial level, with data on union membership drawn from Canada, Statistics Canada 1990, 42, Chart 1.25, and data on persons covered by collective agreements drawn from Canada, Statistics Canada and Employment and Immigration Canada 1990, 26, Table 1). Australian data refer to employees in the state in which the urban area is located.

21. The regression coefficients in the first of the pairs of columns in Table 5.12 are based on the following equations, one for each group and gender. If D^i_j is dollar earnings for individual j in group i, L^i_{sj} represents employment in labor market sector s, and m^i_{sj} are the earnings differences associated with employment in those sectors for members of the group, then for each of the i groups:

$$D^i_j = K^i + m^i_s L^i_{sj} + b^i_k X^i_{kj} + d^i_j, \qquad \text{(Equation 5.1)}$$

where X^i_{kj} represent k human capital endowments, and d^i_j is the error term. The estimated coefficients m^i_s are presented in the first of the pairs of columns in Table 5.12.

22. The numbers in the second of the pairs of columns in Table 5.12 are differences in the effect of immigrant origins on earnings in two equations, one of which contains only human capital controls, and the other including effects of industrial location. Let X_{kj} represent a vector of k human capital attributes of individual j, and let b_k represent the earnings effects of these variables. If I_{ij} represents membership in immigrant group i, then:

$$D_j = K + b_k X_{kj} + a_i I_{ij} + d_j, \qquad \text{(Equation 5.2)}$$

a_i would represent the effect of immigrant status on earnings net of human capital. In a second equation, we add the effect of industrial location. We include a direct effect m_s of location in sector s (represented by L_{sj}, and also in interaction effect m_{is}, to reflect the distinctive impact that industrial location may have for the particular group. The equation is:

$$D'_j = K' + b'_k X_{kj} + a'_i I_{ij} + m_s L_{sj} + m_{is}(L_{sj}{*}I_{ij}) + d'_j, \qquad \text{(Equation 5.3)}$$

The figures in Table 5.12 are the part of immigrant earnings disadvantages explained by industrial location, $a_i - a'_i$.

23. Let S_{ijs} represent the size of sector s as a proportion of the total labor force, for individual j in group i. Let n_s represent the effect of sector size on earnings in the mainstream, and n_{is}, the effect that the size of sector s has on the relative earnings of members of immigrant group i. The equation of interest is:

$$D_j = K + b_k X_{kj} + a_i I_{ij} + n_s S_{sj} + n_{is}(S_{isj}{}^*I_{ij}) + d_j. \qquad \text{(Equation 5.4).}$$

To examine the extent to which the n_{is} are explained by sector location, we add a sector location variation as in Equation 5.3 (previous note):

$$D_j' = K' + b'_k X_{kj} + a'_i I_{ij} + n'_s S_{sj} + n'_{is}(S_{isj}{}^*I_{ij})$$
$$+ m_s L_{sj} + m_{is}(L_{sj}{}^*I_{ij}) + d_j, \qquad \text{(Equation 5.5)}$$

The key question is the *difference* between n_{is} and n'_{is} in the two equations. This difference, $n_{is} - n'_{is}$ would reflect the importance of immigrant concentrations in low-end employment sectors as a reason for lower entrance earnings for immigrants in labor markets with larger low-end sectors. Both n_{is} and n'_{is} are reported in Table 5.13.

24. The relevant equation is similar to Equation 5.4, except that inequality in urban areas is used instead of sector size. We are concerned also with the interaction between human capital and earnings distributions. Let V_j be the earnings distribution in urban area in which individual j resides. The equation of interest is:

$$D_j = K + b_k X_{kj} + a_i I_{ij} + q V_j + q_k(V_j{}^*X_{kj}) + q_i(V_j{}^*I_{ij}) + d_j.$$
$$\text{(Equation 5.6).}$$

Here, q_k represents the way in which the effects of human capital attributes, such as education, change as the earnings distribution changes; q_i represents the group-specific effect of the earnings distribution on the earnings of immigrant group i.

25. For Mexicans, the education gap is much larger, 6 years, so the quadratic factor must be taken into account. The analysis indicates that for Mexicans, a year of education results in only $600 additional earnings.

Chapter Six

1. It would be possible to address the questions of this chapter using the type of census data analysis used in the previous chapters, but there are several dimensions of additional complexity. One dimension of complexity is that the impact of social welfare and taxation is properly evaluated at the family or household levels, rather than at the individual level where we have analyzed earnings. The family as an institution mediates the relation between labor markets and economic well-being, which is the target of government income transfer policies. It is very difficult to separate the analysis of welfare impacts from the analysis of family incomes. A second dimension of the complexity is the complexity of the welfare systems themselves. They have many different kinds of benefits, and these are targeted at different age groups and family types, differently in each country. This entire analysis is a rather large undertaking not attempted here.

2. According to Cameron (1986), the public sector is larger in Australia (government employment in 1982 was 25.4 percent of the labor force in Australia) than in Canada (19.9 percent) or the United States (16.7 percent). At the same time, Cameron's data show that aggregate government cash transfers have been greater in the United States, at 11.5 percent of GDP in 1980–1981, than in Canada (10.2 percent) or Australia (9.1 percent) (Cameron 1986). Two comparisons using Luxembourg Income Study data show that the aggregate size of government cash transfers, including unemployment benefits, old age security, and social assistance to the poor, constituted a slightly larger share of incomes in Australia than in Canada, and a slightly smaller share in the United States. Saunders (1994, 204) reported that as a percentage of gross family income ca. 1980, the percentages due to government transfers are 9.4 percent for Australia, 9.1 percent in Canada, and 8.0 percent for the United States. Atkinson et al. (1995, 106–107) reported that ca. 1980, average government transfers as a percentage of median equivalent income were 10.8 percent in Australia, 10.1 percent in Canada, and 8.9 percent in the United States. By about 1986, the figures had increased to 11.3 percent in Australia, 12.4 percent in Canada, and 9.4 percent in the United States. This shows that although the figures remained roughly similar, the increases were different in each country and larger in Canada, altering the cross-national order in ranking. More recent trends may continue to vary. Saunders (1994, 187) has also examined the impact of the "social wage," meaning the monetary value of public-funded social programs such as education and health care, and found it to be substantially larger in Australia and Canada than in the United States. The social wage increased net disposable incomes by 14.2 percent in Australia, 14.7 percent in Canada, and 13.0 percent in the United States. The redistributive effect of any of these government activities obviously varies.

3. There have been only a few attempts to compare trends in earnings inequality with overall trends in income inequality. One such effort is the one by Fritzell (1992) using successive waves in the LIS database. He compared Canada and the United States, finding that the trend toward greater earnings inequality was more marked in the United States. The coefficient of variation of earnings increased from 0.594 to 0.674 over the seven-year period between 1979 and 1986 in the United States; in Canada, this measure was close to the U.S. figure in 1981, 0.565, but increased only to 0.571 during the next six years up to 1987. However, he also found that in Canada, overall income inequality did not increase, a fact that was attributed to offsetting social transfers in Canada. Hills (1995) found that while during the 1980s earnings inequality increased faster in the United States and Canada than in Australia, overall *income* inequality increased fastest in Australia and less quickly in the United States, and actually declined in Canada. Australia ranked fourth in the trend toward greater inequality, behind New Zealand, the United Kingdom, and Norway.

4. Labor market outcomes are affected by the family as a social institution. Individuals who lose out in the labor market may be shielded from poverty because they live with family members who are more successful in finding adequate employment. In other words, the family is an institutional sector which affects economic well-being. The measurement of income distribution often takes account of family composition, recognizing that family interacts in various ways with welfare.

Income distribution studies often measure incomes at the family or household level
and then estimate impacts on individuals by taking account of the way that economic welfare may be distributed within the family or household unit. Family
composition and patterns of labor force participation within families differ across
the three countries (see Phipps 1995, 82). There are more single adults, both with
and without children in the United States, and more couples, particularly with children, in Canada and Australia. The analysis of Canada and the United States by
Blackburn and Bloom (1993) indicates different changes in family composition in
the two countries. Saunders, O'Connor, and Smeeding (1994) analyzed LIS data to
show that the earnings of female household members decrease inequality in
Canada and the United States but not in Australia. This confirms a point observed
in Atkinson et al. (1995, 100), that the proportion of income from husbands and
wives is different in different parts of the income distribution, and that at lower levels, the contribution is greater from wives in the United States and Canada than
those in Australia. This appears to be one major reason why in the comparison of
overall household income inequality, Australia is closer to Canada than is the case
for just earnings distributions. The family as an institution, or the way the family
responds to other institutions, appears to differ among the three countries, leading
to relatively greater inequality in Australia.

5. Buhmann et al. (1988) have shown that the choice of equivalence scales to adjust for family size and composition affect the relative levels and ranking of countries and groups for certain countries with respect to income inequality and
poverty. However, the analysis by Atkinson et al. (1995, 50–51) suggests that the
cross-national differences specifically for Canada, the United States, and Australia
are not affected enormously by the equivalence scales. See also Saunders 1994,
198–199. The theory of equivalence scales is developed in Coulter et al. 1992.

6. Note, however, that the effect of presenting the data in terms of income quintiles rather than income groups relative to the median is that we can no longer
talk of the poor and the near poor, since these are defined in terms of incomes relative to the median.

7. The OECD income study by Sawyer (1975) included pre- and posttransfer
figures, and pre- and posttax figures. These have been used by others to compare
welfare state impacts, despite the fact that at least regarding transfers, Sawyer
guarded against direct cross-national comparison. Van Arnhem and Schotsman
(1982, 290, 336) indicated that Sawyer's data show the redistributive effects of
transfers in Canada and the United States to be about the same. Regarding the tax
system, the Canadian system was somewhat more redistributive than the American, though the difference faded in the broader comparison across OECD countries. Van Arnhem and Schotsman also indicated that Sawyer's OECD data show
that the tax system increases equality of individual incomes in the United States
and Canada but not in Australia. The cross-national comparison may be least reliable for Australia. The Australian data for Sawyer's study came from a survey in
which the sample contained a number of systematic biases, including underrep-
resentation of one-person households and nonurban areas. The Sawyer data also
show that government transfers increase equality more in Canada than in the
United States. Hicks and Swank (1984), and Swank and Hicks (1985), reexamined
the same Sawyer data, making adjustments particularly in the Australian case.

They found that considering both tax and transfers combined, the percentage changes to the Gini index are 14.1 percent for the United States, 16.3 percent for Canada, and 20.3 percent for Australia (Hicks and Swank 1984, 269; Swank and Hicks 1985, 134). These results are consistent with the LIS data. Hicks and Swank did not discuss the comparability of the data sets.

8. Blau's (1984) results from the 1976 Survey of Income and Education included relatively few immigrants from the newer non-European groups, so they may be somewhat less relevant here. Furthermore, her analysis of transfer payments included not only welfare (public assistance, AFDC, and supplemental security income), unemployment compensation, and workers' compensation, but also old-age pensions (including social security, railroad retirement, and veterans' payments). Welfare use by persons of working age was not separately examined. Immigrants in this study were found to use transfers more, mainly because they are older. After age and other factors are held constant, immigrant families use less welfare, and only slightly more social insurance. Welfare payments were 59 percent lower than among comparable native-born families with male heads, and 57 percent lower than comparable families with female heads. For recent immigrants, lack of knowledge of English reduces total transfers because of lower probability of participating in social insurance programs.

Chapter Eight

1. There have been a number of studies in the United States and a few in Canada attempting to assess the overall fiscal impact of immigrants. This question is related to that of welfare use but is more complicated. Studies of the U.S. case have been reviewed by Rothman and Espenshade (1992). Simon (1984) attempted to take all services and taxes into account, to add consumption of other government tax-supported services such as education and Medicare, and to calculate net fiscal impact. Using the 1976 SEI, which does not capture some of the more recent groups of immigrants, he found that immigrants are a net plus. However, the net positive result may not apply to more recent immigrant groups, or to any specific immigrant group for which average earnings are not high. Furthermore, the inclusion of pensions and education means that the focus is not only on programs intended to be redistributive and the results are subject to significant age-distribution effects. Finally, any redistributive effects of taxes are not included, because everyone is assumed to have the same tax rate. The impact of immigrants on the public treasury consistently has been found to be positive. A Canadian study by Akbari (1989) was modeled on Simon's work, but because of differences in study design is difficult to compare with his. Akbari examined the net balance of taxes paid and public services used by immigrants and native-born Canadians, based on the 1981 Canadian census public use sample. Public services included the full range: education, health services, and transfer payments (Family Allowances, Unemployment Insurance, Canada/Québec Pension Plan, Old Age Security, Guaranteed Income Supplements, and other federal and provincial transfers). Even after 35 years in Canada, immigrants are a net benefit to nonimmigrants. Positive impacts also have been found in Australia (Neville 1990; Centre for International Economics 1992).

References

Adelman, Irma, and Cynthia Taft Morris. 1971. *An Anatomy of Patterns of Income Distribution in Developing Nations.* Part 3 of Final Report, Grant AID/csd-2236. Evanston, Ill.: Northwestern University.

Akbari, Ather H. 1989. "The Benefits of Immigrants to Canada: Evidence on Tax and Public Services." *Canadian Public Policy/Analyse de Politiques* 15, no. 4:424–435.

Albert, Michel. 1993. *Capitalism vs. Capitalism: How America's Obsession with Individual Achievement and Short-Term Profit Has Brought It to the Brink of Collapse.* New York: Four Walls Eight Windows.

Anderson, Grace. 1974. *Networks of Contacts: The Portuguese in Toronto.* Waterloo, Ont.: University of Waterloo Press.

Asher, Martin A., and Robert H. DeFina. 1997. "The Impact of Changing Union Density on Earnings Inequality: Evidence from the Public and Private Sectors. *Journal of Labor Research* 18, no. 3(summer):426–437.

Atkinson, Anthony B., Lee Rainwater, and Timothy M. Smeeding. 1995. *Income Distribution in OECD Countries: Evidence from the Luxembourg Income Study.* Paris: Organization for Economic Cooperation and Development.

Australia. Committee of Inquiry into Recognition of Overseas Qualifications (Fry Committee). 1982. *The Recognition of Overseas Qualifications in Australia.* 2 vols. Canberra: Australian Government Publishing Service.

Australia. Commonwealth Bureau of Census and Statistics. Various Years. *Official Yearbook of the Commonwealth of Australia.* Canberra: Australian Government Publishing Service.

Australia. Department of Immigration. 1979. *Australian Immigration: Consolidated Statistics.* No. 11. Canberra: Australian Government Publishing Service.

Australian Bureau of Statistics. Various Years. *Labour Statistics-Australia.* Canberra: Commonwealth Government Printer.

_____. 1984. *Census of Population and Housing, 1981: Persons Sample File, User's Guide for the Machine-Readable Data File.* Canberra: Australian National University Social Science Data Archives.

_____. 1985. *Labour Force Status and Educational Attainment, Australia.* Cat. no. 6235.0. Canberra: Commonwealth Government Printer.

_____. 1990. *Labour Force Status and Educational Attainment, Australia.* Cat. no. 6235.0. Canberra: Commonwealth Government Printer.

Bach, Robert L. 1978. "Mexican Immigration and the American State." *International Migration Review* 12, no. 4:536–558.

Bailey, Thomas. 1987. *Immigrants and Native Workers: Contrasts and Competition.* Boulder: Westview Press.

Bailey, Thomas, and Roger Waldinger. 1984. "New York Labor Market: A Skill Mismatch." *New York Affairs* (summer).

Baker, Michael, and Dwayne Benjamin. 1995. "The Receipt of Transfer Payments by Immigrants to Canada." *Journal of Human Resources* 30, no. 4:650–676.

_____. 1997. "Ethnicity, Foreign Birth, and Earnings: A Canada/U.S. Comparison." Pp. 281–313 in *Transition and Structural Change in the North American Labour Market,* edited by Michael G. Abbott, Charles M. Beach, and Richard P. Chaykowski. Kingston, Ont.: Queen's University, John Deutsch Institute and Industrial Relations Centre.

Bamber, Greg J., and Russell D. Lansbury, eds. 1993. *International and Comparative Industrial Relations: A Study of Industrialised Market Economies.* Second Edition. London: Routledge.

Bamber, Greg J., and Gillian Whitehouse. 1993. "Employment, Economics, and Industrial Relations: Comparative Statistics." Pp. 275–318 in *International and Comparative Industrial Relations: A Study of Industrialised Market Economies*, Second Edition, edited by Greg J. Bamber and Russell D. Lansbury. London: Routledge.

Barff, Richard, Mark Ellis, and Michael Reibel. 1995. "The Links Between Immigration and Internal Migration in the United States: A Comparison of the 1970s and 1980s." Working Paper Series no. 1. Hanover, N.H.: Dartmouth College, Nelson A. Rockefeller Center for the Social Sciences.

Bartel, Ann P. 1989. "Where Do the New U.S. Immigrants Live?" *Journal of Labor Economics* 7, no. 4:371–391.

Bell, Daniel. 1973. *The Coming of Post-industrial Society.* New York: Basic Books.

Berg, Ivar. 1971. *Education and Jobs: The Great Training Robbery.* Boston: Beacon.

Bertone, Santina, and Gerard Griffin. 1992. *Immigrant Workers and Trade Unions.* Canberra: Australian Government Publishing Service.

Bibby, Reginald W. 1990. *Mosaic Madness: The Poverty and Potential of Life in Canada.* Toronto: Stoddart Publishing Co.

Bills, David B. 1992. "The Mutability of Educational Credentials as Hiring Criteria: How Employers Evaluate Atypically Highly Credentialed Job Candidates." *Work and Occupations* 19, no. 1:79–95.

Birrell, Robert. 1978. "The 1978 Immigration Decisions and Their Impact on the Australian Labour Force." *Australian Quarterly* 50:30–43.

_____. 1984. "A New Era in Australian Migration Policy." *International Migration Review* 18:65–84.

Birrell, Robert, and Tanya Birrell. 1987. *An Issue of People: Population and Australian Society.* Second Edition. Melbourne: Longman Cheshire.

Bissoondath, Neil. 1994. *Selling Illusions: The Cult of Multiculturalism in Canada.* Toronto: Penguin Books.

Black, Don, and John Myles. 1986. "Dependent Industrialization and the Canadian Class Structure: A Comparative Analysis of Canada, the United States, and Sweden." *Canadian Review of Sociology and Anthropology* 23, no. 2:157–181.

Blackburn, McKinley L., and David E. Bloom. 1993. "The Distribution of Family Income: Measuring and Explaining Changes in the 1980s for Canada and the United States." Pp. 233–265 in *Small Differences that Matter: Labor Markets and Income Maintenance in Canada and the United States,* edited by David Card and Richard B. Freeman. Chicago: University of Chicago Press.

Blainey, Geoffrey. 1984. *All for Australia*. North Ryde, Australia: Methuen Hayes.

Blank, Rebecca M., and Maria J. Hanratty. 1993. "Responding to Need: A Comparison of Social Safety Nets in Canada and the United States." Pp. 191–231 in *Small Differences that Matter: Labor Markets and Income Maintenance in Canada and the United States*, edited by David Card and Richard B. Freeman. Chicago: University of Chicago Press.

Blau, Francine D. 1984. "The Use of Transfer Payments by Immigrants." *Industrial and Labor Relations Review* 37, no. 2:222–239.

Blishen, B. 1970. "Social Class and Opportunity in Canada." *Canadian Review of Sociology and Anthropology* 7:110–127.

Bloom, David, Gilles Grenier, and Morley Gunderson. 1995. "The Changing Labour Market Position of Canadian Immigrants." *Canadian Journal of Economics* 28, no. 4b:987–1005.

Borjas, George J. 1985. "Assimilation, Changes in Cohort Quality, and the Earnings of Immigrants." *Journal of Labor Economics* 3, no. 4:463–489.

———. 1987a. "Immigrants, Minorities, and Labor Market Competition." *Industrial and Labor Relations Review* 40, no. 3:382–392.

———. 1987b. "Self-selection and the Earnings of Immigrants." *American Economic Review* 77:531–553.

———. 1988. *International Differences in the Labor Market Performance of Immigrants*. Kalamazoo, Mich.: W. E. Upjohn Institute for Employment Research.

———. 1990. *Friends or Strangers: The Impact of Immigrants on the U.S. Economy*. New York: Basic Books.

———. 1991. "Immigration and Self-selection." Pp. 29–76 in *Immigration, Trade, and the Labor Market*, edited by John M. Abowd and Richard B. Freeman. Chicago: University of Chicago Press.

———. 1993. "Immigration Policy, National Origin, and Immigrant Skills: A Comparison of Canada and the United States." Pp. 21–43 in *Small Differences that Matter: Labor Markets and Income Maintenance in Canada and the United States*, edited by David Card and Richard B. Freeman. Chicago: University of Chicago Press.

———. 1994a. "The Economics of Immigration." *Journal of Economic Literature* 32, no. 4:1667–1717.

———. 1994b. *Immigration and Welfare, 1970–1990*. Cambridge, Mass.: National Bureau of Economic Research.

Borjas, George J., and Lynette Hilton. 1996. "Immigration and the Welfare State: Immigrant Participation in Means-Tested Entitlement Programs." *The Quarterly Journal of Economics* 61, no. 2:575–604.

Borjas, George J., and Stephen J. Trejo. 1991. "Immigrant Participation in the Welfare System." *Industrial and Labor Relations Review* 44, no. 2:195–211.

———. 1993. "National Origin and Immigrant Welfare Recipiency." *Journal of Public Economics* 50:325–344.

Bound, J., and G. Johnson. 1992. "Changes in the Structure of Wages in the 1980s: An Evaluation of Alternative Explanations." *American Economic Review* 82:371–392.

Bovenkerk, Frank. 1992. "Testing Discrimination in Natural Experiments: A Manual for International Comparative Research on Discrimination on the Grounds of 'Race' and Ethnic Origin." Geneva: International Labour Office.

Bowles, Samuel, and Herbert Gintis. 1986. *Democracy and Capitalism: Property, Community, and the Contradictions of Modern Social Thought.* London: Routledge and Kegan Paul.

Boyd, Monica. 1976. "Immigration Policies and Trends: A Comparison of Canada and the United States." *Demography* 13, no. 1:83–104.

_____. 1989. "Family and Personal Networks in International Migration: Recent Developments and New Agendas." *International Migration Review* 23, no. 3:638–668.

Boyd, Monica, John Goyder, Frank E. Jones, H. A. McRoberts, Peter C. Pineo, and John Porter. 1985. *Ascription and Achievement: Studies in Mobility and Status Attainment in Canada.* Ottawa, Ont.: Carleton University Press.

Bradbury, Bruce. 1993. "Male Wage Inequality Before and After Tax: A Six-Country Comparison." Kensington, Australia: University of New South Wales, Social Policy Research Centre.

Braverman, Harry. 1974. *Labor and Monopoly Capital.* New York: Monthly Review Press.

Breton, Raymond, Wsevolod W. Isajiw, Warren E. Kalbach, and Jeffrey G. Reitz, *Ethnic Identity and Equality: Varieties of Experience in a Canadian City.* Toronto: University of Toronto Press.

Briggs, Vernon M., Jr. 1984. *Immigration Policy and the American Labor Force.* Baltimore: Johns Hopkins University Press.

Brimelow, Peter. 1995. *Alien Nation: Common Sense about America's Immigration Disaster.* New York: Random House.

Browning, Harley L., and Joachim Singelmann. 1978. "The Transformation of the U.S. Labor Force: The Interaction of Industry and Occupation." *Politics and Society* 8, nos. 3–4:481–509.

Buhmann, B., L. Rainwater, G. Schmaus, and T. M. Smeeding. 1988. "Equivalence Scales, Well-being, Inequality and Poverty: Sensitivity Estimates Across Ten Countries Using the Luxembourg Income Study (LIS) Database." *Review of Income and Wealth* (June):115–142.

Burnet, Jean, Danielle Juteau, Enoch Padolsky, Anthony Rasporich, and Antoine Sirois, eds. 1992. *Migration and the Transformation of Cultures.* Toronto: Multicultural History Society of Ontario.

Burtless, G. 1990. "Earnings Inequality Over the Business and Demographic Cycles." In *A Future of Lousy Jobs?* edited by Gary Burtless. Washington, D.C.: Brookings Institution.

CERI (see Center for Educational Research and Innovation).

Cameron, David R. 1986. "The Growth of Government Spending: The Canadian Experience in Comparative Perspective." Pp. 21–51 in *State and Society: Canada in Comparative Perspective,* edited by Keith Banting. Toronto: University of Toronto Press.

Canada. Citizenship and Immigration Canada. 1993. *Citizenship and Immigration Statistics.* Ottawa: Supply and Services Canada.

_____. 1996. *Canada's Immigration Law.* Ottawa: Supply and Services Canada.

Canada. Dominion Bureau of Statistics. 1963. *1961 Census of Canada. Population: Schooling by Age Groups.* Cat. no. 92–577. Ottawa: Queens Printer.

Canada. Employment and Immigration Canada. 1983. *Immigration Statistics, 1981.* Ottawa: Minister of Supply and Services Canada.

_____. 1986. *Immigration Statistics, 1984.* Ottawa: Minister of Supply and Services Canada.

_____. 1989. *Immigration Statistics, 1987.* Ottawa: Minister of Supply and Services Canada.

_____. 1992. *Immigration Statistics, 1991.* Ottawa: Minister of Supply and Services Canada.

Canada. Manpower and Immigration. 1974. *The Immigration Program.* Ottawa: Information Canada.

Canada. Statistics Canada. Annual. *Canada Yearbook.* Ottawa: Minister of Supply and Services Canada.

_____. 1974. *1971 Census of Canada. Population: The Out-of-School Population.* Cat. no. 92–743. Ottawa: Information Canada.

_____. 1978. *1976 Census of Canada. Population: Level of Schooling, by Age Groups.* Cat. no. 92–827. Ottawa: Supply and Services Canada.

_____. 1983. *Annual Report of the Minister of Supply and Services Canada Under the Corporations and Labour Unions Return Act.* Part II, *Labour Unions, 1981.* Catalog no. 71–202. Ottawa: Minister of Supply and Services Canada.

_____. 1984a. *1981 Census of Canada. Population: School Attendance and Level of Schooling.* Cat. no. 92–914. Ottawa: Minister of Supply and Services Canada.

_____. 1984b. *1981 Census of Canada Public Use Sample Tapes User Documentation: Individual File (2% Sample) Codebook.* Ottawa: Statistics Canada.

_____. 1989. *1986 Census of Canada: Schooling and Major Field of Study.* Cat. no. 93–110. Ottawa: Supply and Services Canada.

_____. 1990. *Annual Report of the Minister of Supply and Services Canada Under the Corporations and Labour Unions Return Act.* Part II, *Labour Unions, 1988.* Cat. no. 71–202. Ottawa: Minister of Supply and Services Canada.

_____. 1993. *1991 Census of Canada: Educational Attainment and School Attendance.* Cat. no. 93–328. Ottawa: Supply and Services Canada.

Canada. Statistics Canada and Employment and Immigration Canada. 1990. *Canada's Unionized Workers: A Profile of Their 1986 Labour Market Experience.* Cat. no. 71–214. Ottawa: Minister of Supply and Services Canada.

Card, D., and W. C. Riddell. 1993. "A Comparative Analysis of Unemployment in Canada and the U.S." Pp. 149–189 in *Small Differences that Matter: Labor Markets and Income Maintenance in Canada and the United States*, edited by David Card and Richard B. Freeman. Chicago: University of Chicago Press.

Castells, Manuel. 1975. "Immigrant Workers and Class Struggles in Advanced Capitalism: The Western European Experience." *Politics and Society* 5:33–66.

Castles, Stephen. 1989. *Migrant Workers and the Transformation of Western Societies.* Occasional Paper no. 22. Ithaca, N.Y.: Cornell University, Center for International Studies, Western Societies Program.

_____. 1990. *Global Workforce, New Racism, and the Declining Nation State.* Wollongong, Australia: University of Wollongong, Centre for Multicultural Studies.

_____. 1991. *The Global Milkbar and the Local Sweatshop: Ethnic Small Business and the Economic Restructuring of Sydney*. Working Papers in Multiculturalism no. 2. Canberra, Australia: Department of the Prime Minister and Cabinet, Office of Multicultural Affairs.

Castles, Stephen, and Jock Collins. 1989. *Restructuring, Migrant Labour Markets, and Small Business*. Occasional Paper no. 16. Wollongong, Australia: University of Wollongong, Centre for Multicultural Studies.

Castles, Stephen, and Godula Kosack. 1985. *Immigrant Workers and Class Structure in Western Europe*. Second Edition. London: Oxford University Press.

Castles, Stephen, and Mark J. Miller. 1993. *The Age of Migration: International Population Movements in the Modern World*. New York: Guilford Press.

Center for Educational Research and Innovation (CERI). 1992. *Education at a Glance: OECD Indicators*. Paris: Organization for Economic Cooperation and Development.

_____. 1996. *Education at a Glance: Analysis*. Paris: Organization for Economic Co-operation and Development.

Centre for International Economics. 1992. *Immigration and the Commonwealth Budget*. Canberra: Australian Government Publishing Service, Bureau of Immigration Research.

Chiswick, Barry R., ed. 1982. *The Gateway: U.S. Immigration Issues and Policies*. Washington, D.C.: American Enterprise Institute for Public Policy Research.

_____. 1986. "Is the New Immigration Less Skilled than the Old?" *Journal of Labor Economics* 4, no. 2:168–192.

_____. 1988. "Immigration Policy, Source Countries, and Immigrant Skills: Australia, Canada, and the United States." Pp. 163–206 in *The Economics of Immigration: Proceedings of a Conference at the ANU, 22–23 April 1987*, edited by Lyle Baker and Paul Miller. Canberra: Australian Government Publishing Service.

Clark, S. D. 1975. "The Post Second World War Canadian Society." *Canadian Review of Sociology and Anthropology* 12, no. 1:25–32.

Cohen, Robin. 1987. "The 'New' International Division of Labour: A Conceptual Historical and Empirical Critique." *Migration: A European Journal of International Migration and Ethnic Relations* 1:21–46.

Collins, Jock. 1991. *Migrant Hands in a Distant Land: Australia's Post-War Immigration*. Second Edition. Leichhardt, Australia: Pluto Press Australia.

Collins, Jock, Katherine Gibson, Caroline Alcorse, Stephen Castles, and David Tait. 1995. *A Shop Full of Dreams: Ethnic Small Business in Australia*. Leichhardt, Australia: Pluto Press Australia.

Collins, Jock, and Frances Henry. 1994. "Racism, Ethnicity and Immigration." Pp. 515–548 in *Immigration and Refugee Policy: Australia and Canada Compared*, vol. 2, edited by Howard Edelman, Allan Borowski, Meyer Burstein, and Lois Foster. Toronto: University of Toronto Press.

Collins, Randall. 1979. *The Credential Society: An Historical Sociology of Education and Stratification*. New York: Academic Press.

Collomp, Catherine. 1988. "Unions, Civics, and National Identity: Organized Labor's Reaction to Immigration, 1881–1897." *Labor History* 29:450–474.

Cornelius, Wayne A. 1989–1990. "Mexican Immigrants in California Today." Working Papers in the Social Sciences, vol. 5, no. 10. Los Angeles: University of California, Institute for Social Science Research.

Cornelius, Wayne A., Philip L. Martin, and James F. Hollifield, eds. 1994. *Controlling Immigration: A Global Perspective.* Stanford: Stanford University Press.

Coulter, F. A., F. A. Cowell, and S. P. Jenkins. 1992. "Equivalence Scale Relativities and the Extent of Inequality and Poverty." *Economic Journal* 102:1067–1082.

Cross, Malcolm, ed. 1987. *Racial Minorities and Industrial Change.* Cambridge: Cambridge University Press.

Daly, Anne. 1986. "Education and Productivity: A Comparison of Great Britain and the United States." *British Journal of Industrial Relations* 24(July):251–266.

Dawkins, The Hon. J. S. (Commonwealth Minister for Employment, Education, and Training). 1988. *Higher Education: A Policy Statement.* Canberra: Australian Government Publishing Service.

Day, Phyllis J. 1997. *A New History of Social Welfare.* Second Edition. Boston: Allyn and Bacon.

de Neubourg, Chris. 1985. "Part-time Work: An International Quantitative Comparison." *International Labour Review* 124, no. 5:559–576.

DeFreitas, Gregory. 1988. "Hispanic Immigration and Labor Market Segmentation." *Industrial Relations* 27, no. 2:195–214.

_____. 1991 *Inequality at Work: Hispanics in the U.S. Labor Force.* New York: Oxford University Press.

Delgado, Hector L. 1993. *New Immigrants, Old Unions: Organizing Undocumented Workers in Los Angeles.* Philadelphia: Temple University Press.

Devoretz, Don J. 1995. *Diminishing Returns: The Economics of Canada's Recent Immigration Policy.* Toronto: C. D. Howe Institute.

Dooley, Martin. 1985. "Changes in the Monetary Return to Education in Canada from 1971 to 1981: Some Preliminary Findings." In *Ontario Universities: Access, Operations, and Funding,* edited by D. W. Conklin and T. J. Courchene. Toronto: Ontario Economic Council.

_____. 1986. "The Overeducated Canadians: Changes in the Relationships among Earnings, Education, and Age for Canadian Men: 1971–1981." *Canadian Journal of Economics* 19(February):142–159.

Duleep, Harriet Orcutt, and Mark C. Regets. 1992. "Some Evidence on the Effects of Admissions Criteria on Immigrant Assimilation." Pp. 410–439 in *Immigration, Language, and Ethnicity: Canada and the United States,* edited by Barry Chiswick. Washington, D.C.: AEI Press.

_____. 1996. "Admission Criteria and Immigrant Earnings Profiles." *International Migration Review* 30, no. 2:571–590.

Etzioni, Amitai, and Paul Jargowsky. 1984. "High Tech, Basic Industry, and the Future of the American Economy." *Human Resource Management* 23, no. 3:229–240.

Evans, M.D.R. 1987. "Language Skill, Language Usage, and Opportunity: Immigrants in the Australian Labour Market." *Sociology* 21, no. 2:253–274.

Evans, M., and J. Kelley. 1986. "Immigrants' Work: Equality and Discrimination in the Australian Labour Market." *Australia and New Zealand Journal of Sociology* 22, no. 2:187–207.

_____. 1991. "Prejudice, Discrimination, and the Labor Market: Attainments of Immigrants in Australia." *American Journal of Sociology* 97, no. 3:721–759.

_____. 1993. "Legitimation of Inequality: Occupational Earnings in Nine Nations." *American Journal of Sociology* 99, no. 1:75–125.

Faist, Thomas. 1995. *Social Citizenship for Whom?: Young Turks in Germany and Mexican Americans in the United States.* Avebury, England: Aldershot.

Featherman, David, and Robert Hauser. 1978. *Opportunity and Change.* New York: Academic Press.

Foster, L., A. Marshall, and L. Williams. 1991. *Discrimination Against Immigrant Workers in Australia.* Canberra: Australian Government Publishing Service.

Freeman, Gary P., and Katharine Betts. 1992. "The Politics of Interests and Immigration Policymaking in Australia and the United States." Pp. 72–88 in *Nations of Immigrants: Australia, the United States, and International Migration,* edited by Gary P. Freeman and James Jupp. New York: Oxford University Press.

Freeman, Gary P., and James Jupp, eds. 1992. *Nations of Immigrants: Australia, the United States, and International Migration.* New York: Oxford University Press.

Freeman, Richard B. 1976. *The Overeducated American.* New York: Academic Press.

Freeman, Richard B., and James L. Medoff. 1979. "New Estimates of Private Sector Unionism in the United States." *Industrial and Labor Relations Review* 32, no. 2:143–174.

_____. 1984. *What Do Unions Do?* New York: Basic Books.

Freeman, Richard B., and Karen Needels. 1993. "Skill Differentials in Canada in an Era of Rising Labor Market Inequality." Pp. 45–67 in *Small Differences that Matter: Labor Markets and Income Maintenance in Canada and the United States,* edited by David Card and Richard B. Freeman. Chicago: University of Chicago Press.

Frisbie, W. Parker, and Lisa Neidert. 1977. "Inequality and the Relative Size of Minority Populations: A Comparative Analysis." *American Journal of Sociology* 82:1007–1030.

Fritzell, Johan. 1992. "Income Inequality Trends in the 1980s: A Five-Country Comparison." Luxembourg Income Study Working Paper no. 73. Stockholm: Stockholm University, Swedish Institute for Social Research.

Galster, George, and Anna M. Santiago. 1994. "Explaining the Growth of Puerto Rican Poverty, 1970–1980." *Urban Affairs Quarterly* 30, no. 2:249–274.

Gans, Herbert. 1962. *The Urban Villagers: Group and Class in the Life of Italian-Americans.* New York: Free Press.

Gardner, Robert W., and Leon F. Bouvier. 1990. "The United States." Pp. 341–362 in *Handbook on International Migration,* edited by William J. Serow, Charles B. Nam, David F. Sly, and Robert H. Weller. New York: Greenwood Press.

Godbout, Todd M. 1993. "Employment Change and Sectoral Distribution in 10 Countries, 1970–1990." *Monthly Labor Review* (October):3–20.

Goldthorpe, John H. 1984. "The End of Convergence: Corporatist and Dualist Tendencies in Modern Western Societies." Pp. 315–343 in *Order and Conflict in Contemporary Capitalism,* edited by John H. Goldthorpe. Oxford: Oxford University Press.

Gordon, David. 1972. *Theories of Poverty and Underdevelopment: Orthodox, Radical, and Dual Labor Market Perspectives.* Lexington, Mass.: Lexington.

Gornick, Janet C., and Jerry A. Jacobs. 1996. "A Cross-national Analysis of the Wages of Part-time Workers: Evidence from the United States, the United Kingdom, Canada, and Australia." *Work, Employment & Society* 10, no. 1:1–27.

Gott, Murray. 1990. "Leopard or Lizard? Immigration and the Political Science of Polled Opinion." Pp. 125–139 in *Australia and Immigration: Able to Grow?* edited by Michael Easson. Leichhardt, Australia: Pluto Press Australia, in association with Lloyd Ross Forum, Labour Council of New South Wales.

Granovetter, Mark. 1983. "The Strength of Weak Ties: A Network Theory Revisited." *Sociological Theory* 1:201–233.

Green, Alan G. 1995. "A Comparison of Canadian and U.S. Immigration Policy in the Twentieth Century." Pp. 31–64 in *Diminishing Returns: The Economics of Canada's Recent Immigration Policy,* edited by Don J. Devoretz. Toronto: C. D. Howe Institute.

Green, Alan G., and David A. Green. 1993. "Canadian Immigration Policy: The Effectiveness of the Points System and Other Instruments." Unpublished manuscript.

Gross, Edward, and John S. Western. 1981. *The End of a Golden Age: Higher Education in a Steady State.* St. Lucia, Australia: University of Queensland Press.

Grubb, W. Norton, and Robert H. Wilson. 1989. "Sources of Increasing Inequality in Wages and Salaries, 1960–1980." *Monthly Labor Review* 112, no. 4:3–13.

Harrison, Bennett, and Barry Bluestone. 1990. *The Great U-Turn: Corporate Restructuring and the Polarizing of America.* New York: Basic Books.

Hauser, Robert. 1980. "On 'Stratification in a Dual Economy': A Comment on Beck, Horan, and Tolbert, 1978." *American Sociological Review* 45(August):702–712.

Hawkins, Freda. 1971. "Canada's Immigration Reexamined." *Race Today* 3:369–371.

———. 1988. *Canada and Immigration: Public Policy and Public Concern.* Second Edition. Kingston, Ont.: McGill-Queens University Press.

———. 1989. *Critical Years in Immigration: Canada and Australia Compared.* Kingston, Ont.: McGill-Queens University Press.

Heckman, James J. 1979. "Sample Selection Bias as a Specification Error." *Econometrica* 47:153–161.

Heckman, James J., and V. Joseph Hotz. 1986. "An Investigation of the Labor Market Earnings of Panamanian Males: Evaluating the Sources of Inequality." *Journal of Human Resources* 21:507–542.

Henry, Frances. 1986. "Race Relations Research in Canada Today: A 'State of the Art' Review." Canadian Human Rights Commission Colloquium on Racial Discrimination, September 25.

———. 1994. *The Caribbean Diaspora in Toronto.* Toronto: University of Toronto Press.

Henry, Frances, and Effie Ginsberg. 1985. *Who Gets the Work? A Test of Racial Discrimination in Employment.* Toronto: Urban Alliance on Race Relations, and Social Planning Council of Metropolitan Toronto.

Hicks, Alexander, and Duane H. Swank. 1984. "Government Redistribution in Rich Capitalist Democracies." *Policy Studies Journal* 13, no. 2:265–86.

Hicks, N. L. "Education and Economic Growth." 1987. Pp. 101–107 in *Economics and Education: Research and Studies,* edited by George Psacharopoulos. New York: Pergamon Press.

Hill, Peter J. 1975. "Relative Skill and Income Levels of Native and Foreign-Born Workers in the United States." *Explorations in Economic History* 12, no. 1:47–60.

Hills, John. 1995. *Inquiry into Income and Wealth.* Volume 2: A Summary of the Evidence. York, England: Joseph Rowntree Foundation.

Hing, Bill Ong. 1993. *Making and Remaking Asian America Through Immigration Policy.* Stanford: Stanford University Press.

Hjarnø, Jan. 1996. "Global Cities in Two Ways: A Comment on Saskia Sassen's Global City Hypothesis." Migration Paper no. 18. Esbjerg, Denmark: South Jutland University Press.

Hodson, Randy. 1986. "Modeling the Effects of Industrial Structure on Wages and Benefits." *Work and Occupations* 13, no. 4:488–510.

Hodson, Randy, and Robert L. Kaufman. 1981. "Circularity in the Dual Economy: Comment of Tolbert, Beck, and Horan." *American Journal of Sociology* 86:881–887.

———. 1982. "Economic Dualism: A Critical Review." *American Sociological Review* 47:727–739.

Hoerder, Dirk. 1996. "Migration in the Atlantic Economies: Regional European Origins and Worldwide Expansion." Pp. 21–51 in *European Migrants: Global and Local Perspectives,* edited by Dirk Hoerder and Leslie Page Moch. Boston: Northeastern University Press.

Hohl, Donald G. 1974. "Proposed Revisions of U.S. Western Hemisphere Immigration Policies." *International Migration Review* 8:69–76.

Holton, Robert, and Michael Lanphier. 1994. "Public Opinion, Immigration, and Refugees." Pp. 125–148 in *Immigration and Refugee Policy: Australia and Canada Compared,* vol. 2, edited by Howard Edelman, Allan Borowski, Meyer Burstein, and Lois Foster. Toronto: University of Toronto Press.

Holzer, Harry J. 1996. *What Employers Want: Job Prospects for Less-educated Workers.* New York: Russell Sage Foundation.

Hoover, Greg A. 1989. "Intranational Inequality: A Cross-National Dataset." *Social Forces* 67, no. 4:1008–1026.

Horan, Patrick M., Charles M. Tolbert, and E. M. Beck. 1981. "The Circle Has No Close." *American Journal of Sociology* 86:887–894.

Hunter, Alfred A. 1988. "Formal Education and Initial Employment: Unravelling the Relationships Between Schooling and Skills Over Time." *American Sociological Review* 53:753–765.

Hunter, Alfred A., and Jean McKenzie Leiper. 1993. "On Formal Education, Skills, and Earnings: The Role of Educational Certificates in Earnings Determination." *Canadian Journal of Sociology* 18, no. 1:21–42.

ILO (see International Labour Office).

Iacovetta, Franca, Michael Quinlan, and Ian Radforth. 1996. "Immigration and Labour: Australia and Canada Compared. *Labour/Le Travail* 38/*Labour History* 71:90–115.

International Labour Office (ILO). 1993. *World Labour Report 1993.* Geneva: International Labour Office.

———. 1997. *Combatting Discrimination Against (Im)Migrant Workers and Ethnic Minorities in the World of Work.* Information Bulletin no. 4. Geneva: International Labour Office.

Iredale, R. R. 1988. *Wasted Skills: Barriers to Migrant Entry to Occupations in Australia.* Sydney: Ethnic Affairs Commission of New South Wales.

Jaynes, Gerald Davis, and Robin M. Williams, Jr., eds. 1989. *A Common Destiny: Blacks and American Society.* Washington, D.C.: National Academy Press.

Jensen, Leif. 1988. "Patterns of Immigration and Public Assistance Utilization, 1970–1980." *International Migration Review* 22, no. 1:51–83.

Jiobu, Robert M. 1988. "Ethnic Hegemony and the Japanese in California." *American Sociological Review* 53:353–357.

Johnson, Andrew F., Stephen McBride, and Patrick J. Smith. 1994. *Continuities and Discontinuities: The Political Economy of Social Welfare and Labour Market Policy in Canada.* Toronto: University of Toronto Press.

Jones, F. L., and Peter Davis. 1986. *Models of Society: Class, Stratification, and Gender in Australia and New Zealand.* Sydney: Croom Helm.

Jones, Maldwyn Allen. 1992. *American Immigration.* Second Edition. Chicago: University of Chicago Press.

Jupp, James. 1991. *Immigration: Australian Retrospectives.* South Melbourne, Australia: Sydney University Press.

Kalleberg, Arne L., and Tom Colbjørnsen. 1990. "Unions and the Structure of Earnings Inequality: Cross-national Patterns." *Social Science Research* 19:348–371.

Keely, Charles B. 1979a. "The United States of America." Pp. 51–64 in *The Politics of Migration Policies: The First World in the 1970s*, edited by Daniel Kubat. New York: Center for Migration Studies.

_____. 1979b. *U.S. Immigration: A Policy Analysis.* New York: Population Council.

Keely, Charles B., and Patricia J. Elwell. 1981. "International Migration: Canada and the United States." Pp. 181–207 in *Global Trends in Migration: Theory and Research on International Population Movements*, edited by Mary M. Kritz, Charles B. Keely, and Silvano M. Tomasi. New York: Center for Migration Studies.

Kennedy, John F. 1964. *A Nation of Immigrants.* Revised and Enlarged Edition. New York: Harper and Row.

Klein, Sidney, ed. 1987. *The Economics of Mass Migration in the Twentieth Century.* New York: Paragon House.

Kochan, Thomas, Harry C. Katz, and Robert B. McKersie. 1986. *The Transformation of American Industrial Relations.* New York: Basic Books:

Korpi, Walter. 1989. "Power, Politics, and State Autonomy in the Development of Social Citizenship: Social Rights During Sickness in Eighteen OECD Countries Since 1930." *American Sociological Review* 54(June):309–328).

Krueger, A. O. 1968. "Factor Endowments and Per Capita Income Differences Among Countries." *Economic Journal* 78:641–659.

Kubat, Daniel. 1979. "Canada." Pp. 19–36 in *The Politics of Migration Policies: The First World in the 1970s*, edited by Daniel Kubat. New York: Center for Migration Studies.

Kumar, Pradeep. 1993. *From Uniformity to Divergence: Industrial Relations in Canada and the United States.* Kingston, Ont.: Queen's University, Industrial Relations Centre.

Kuznets, Simon. 1955. "Economic Growth and Income Inequality." *American Economic Review* (March):1–28.

_____. 1966. *Modern Economic Growth.* New Haven: Yale University Press.

Lemieux, Thomas. 1993. "Unions and Wage Inequality in Canada and the United States." Pp. 69–107 in *Small Differences that Matter: Labor Markets and Income Maintenance in Canada and the United States*, edited by David Card and Richard B. Freeman. Chicago: University of Chicago Press.

Lever-Tracy, Constance, and Michael Quinlan. 1988. *A Divided Working Class: Ethnic Segmentation and Industrial Conflict in Australia.* London: Routledge and Kegan Paul.

Li, Peter. 1988. *Ethnic Inequality in a Class Society.* Toronto: Wall and Thompson.

Light, Ivan. 1972. *Ethnic Enterprise in America.* Berkeley: University of California Press.

Light, Ivan, and Edna Bonacich. 1988. *Immigrant Entrepreneurs: Koreans in Los Angeles.* Berkeley: University of California Press.

Light, Ivan, Georges Sabagh, Mehdi Bozorgmehr, and Claudia Der-Martirosian. 1993. "Internal Ethnicity in the Ethnic Economy." *Ethnic and Racial Studies* 16:581–597.

Light, Ivan, and Carolyn Rosenstein. 1995. *Race, Ethnicity, and Entrepreneurship in Urban America.* New York: Aldine de Gruyter.

Lipset, Seymour Martin. 1989. *The Continental Divide.* Toronto: C. D. Howe Institute.

———. 1996. *American Exceptionalism: A Double-Edged Sword.* New York: W. W. Norton.

Lui-Gurr, Susanna. 1995. "The British Columbia Experience with Immigrants and Welfare Dependency." Pp. 128–165 in *Diminishing Returns: The Economics of Canada's Recent Immigration Policy,* edited by Don J. Devoretz. Toronto: C. D. Howe Institute.

Marginson, Simon. 1993. *Education and Public Policy in Australia.* Melbourne, Australia: Cambridge University Press.

Massey, Douglas S. 1990. "Social Structure, Household Strategies, and the Cumulative Causation of Migration." *Population Index* 56:3–26.

———. 1995. "The New Immigration and Ethnicity in the United States." *Population and Development Review* 21, no. 3:631–652.

Massey, Douglas S., Rafael Alarcón, Jorge Durand, and Humberto González. 1987. *Return to Aztlan: The Social Process of International Migration from Western Mexico.* Berkeley: University of California Press.

McFate, Katherine. 1991. *Poverty, Inequality, and the Crisis of Social Policy: Summary of Findings.* Washington, D.C.: Joint Center for Political and Economic Studies.

McQuaig, Linda. 1993. *The Wealthy Banker's Wife: The Assault on Equality in Canada.* Toronto: Penguin Books.

McRoberts, H. A., and K. Selbee. 1981. "Trends in Occupational Mobility: Canada and the U.S." *American Sociological Review* 46:406–421.

Meltz, Noah M. 1989. "Inter-state vs. Inter-provincial Differences in Union Density." *Industrial Relations* (spring).

Mills, C. Wright. 1951. *White Collar: The American Middle Class.* New York: Oxford University Press.

Model, Suzanne. 1985. "A Comparative Perspective on the Ethnic Enclave: Blacks, Italians, and Jews in New York City." *International Migration Review* 19, no. 1:64–81.

———. 1991. "Caribbean Immigrants: A Black Success Story?" *International Migration Review* 25, no. 2:248–276.

———. 1992. "The Ethnic Economy: Cubans and Chinese Reconsidered." *Sociological Quarterly* 33:63–82.

Moore, Thomas S., and Aaron Laramore. 1990. "Industrial Change and Urban Joblessness: An Assessment of the Mismatch Hypothesis." *Urban Affairs Quarterly* 25:640–658.

Morales, Rebecca. 1983. "Transitional Labor: Undocumented Workers in the Los Angeles Automobile Industry." *International Migration Review* 17, no. 4:570–596.

Morissette, R., J. Myles, and G. Picot. 1995. "Earnings Polarization in Canada, 1969–1991." Pp. 23–58 in *Labour Market Polarization and Social Policy Reform*, edited by Keith F. Banting and Charles M. Beach. Kingston, Ont.: Queens University, School of Policy Studies.

Muller, Edward N. 1985. "Income Inequality, Regime Repressiveness, and Political Violence." *American Sociological Review* 50(February):47–61.

_____. 1988. "Democracy, Economic Development, and Income Inequality." *American Sociological Review* 53(February):50–68.

Nelson, Joel I., and Jon Lorence. 1985. "Employment in Service Activities and Inequality in Metropolitan Areas." *Urban Affairs Quarterly* 21, no. 1:106–125.

Neville, John. 1990. *The Effect of Immigration on Australian Living Standards*. Canberra: Australian Government Publishing Service, Bureau of Immigration Research.

Nielsen, François. 1994. "Income Inequality and Industrial Development: Dualism Revisited." *American Sociological Review* 59(October):654–677.

Noyelle, Thierry J. 1987. *Beyond Industrial Dualism: Market and Job Segmentation in the New Economy*. Boulder: Westview.

Noyelle, Thierry J., and Thomas M. Stanback, Jr. 1983. *The Economic Transformation of American Cities*. Totowa, N.J.: Rowman and Allanheld.

OECD (see Organization for Economic Cooperation and Development).

Oaxaca, Ronald. 1973. "Sex Discrimination in Wages." Pp. 124–143 in *Discrimination in Labor Markets*, edited by Orley Ashenfelter and Albert Rees. Princeton: Princeton University Press.

Organization for Economic Cooperation and Development (OECD). 1991. *Employment Outlook 1991*. Paris: OECD.

_____. 1993. *Employment Outlook 1993*. Paris: OECD.

Ortiz, Vilma. 1991. "Latinos and Industrial Change." Pp. 119–132 in *Hispanics in the Labor Force*, edited by Edwin Melendez and Clara Rodriguez. New York: Plenum Press.

Oster, Gerald. 1979. "A Factor Analytic Test of the Dual Economy." *Review of Economics and Statistics* 61(February):33–59.

Parai, Louis. 1975. "Canada's Immigration Policy 1962–1974." *International Migration Review* 9:449–477.

Parmet, Robert D. 1981. *Labor and Immigration in Industrial America*. Boston: Twayne Publishers.

Patmore, Greg. 1991. *Australian Labour History*. Melbourne, Australia: Longman Cheshire.

Paukert, Felix. 1973. "Income Distribution at Different Levels of Development: A Survey of the Evidence." *International Labour Review* 108:97–125.

Persson, Torsten, and Guido Tabellini. 1994. "Is Inequality Harmful for Growth?" *American Economic Review* 84, no. 3:600–621.

Phipps, Shelley A. 1995. "Poverty and Labour Market Change: Canada in Comparative Perspective." Pp. 59–94 in *Labour Market Polarization and Social Policy Reform*, edited by Keith F. Banting and Charles M. Beach. Kingston, Ont.: Queens University, School of Policy Studies.

Pike, Robert M. 1988. "Education and the Schools." Pp. 255–279 in *Understanding Canadian Society*, edited by James Curtis and Lorne Tepperman. Toronto: McGraw-Hill Ryerson.

Piore, Michael J. 1979. *Birds of Passage: Migrant Labor and Industrial Societies*. Cambridge: Cambridge University Press.

_____. 1984. *The Second Industrial Divide: Possibilities for Prosperity*. New York: Basic Books.

_____. 1995. *Beyond Individualism*. Cambridge: Harvard University Press.

Piven, Frances Fox, and Richard A. Cloward. 1993. *Regulating the Poor: The Functions of Public Welfare*. Updated Edition. New York: Vintage Books.

Podder, N. 1972. "Distribution of Household Income in Australia." *Economic Record* (July).

Porter, John. 1965. *The Vertical Mosaic: An Analysis of Social Class and Power in Canada*. Toronto: University of Toronto Press.

Portes, Alejandro. 1987. "The Social Origins of the Cuban Enclave Economy of Miami." *American Sociological Review* 30(October):340–372.

_____. 1989. "Contemporary Immigration: Theoretical Perspectives on Its Determinants and Modes of Incorporation." *International Migration Review* 23:606–630.

_____. 1995. *The Economic Sociology of Immigration: Essays on Networks, Ethnicity, and Entrepreneurship*. New York: Russell Sage Foundation.

Portes, Alejandro, and Robert L. Bach. 1985. *Latin Journey: Cuban and Mexican Immigrants in the United States*. Berkeley: University of California Press.

Portes, Alejandro, and Ruben G. Rumbaut. 1990. *Immigrant America: A Portrait*. Berkeley: University of California Press.

Portes, Alejandro, and John Walton. 1981. *Labor, Class, and the International System*. New York: Academic Press.

Psacharopoulos, George. 1981. "Returns to Education: An Updated International Comparison." *Comparative Education* 17:321–341.

_____. 1985. "Returns to Education: A Further International Update and Implications." *Journal of Human Resources* 20, no. 4:583–604.

Putnam, Robert D. 1993. "The Prosperous Community: Social Capital and Public Life. *American Prospect* (spring):35–42.

Quadagno, Jill. 1994. *The Color of Welfare: How Racism Undermined the War on Poverty*. Oxford: Oxford University Press.

Quinlan, Michael, and Constance Lever-Tracy. 1990. "From Labour Market Exclusion to Industrial Solidarity: Australian Trade Union Responses to Asian Workers, 1830–1988." *Cambridge Journal of Economics* 14:159–181.

Razin, Eran, and André Langlois. 1996. "Metropolitan Characteristics and Entrepreneurship Among Immigrants and Ethnic Groups in Canada." *International Migration Review* 30, no. 3:703–727.

Reich, Robert B. 1991. *The Work of Nations: Preparing Ourselves for 21st-Century Capitalism*. New York: A. A. Knopf.

Reimers, David M., and Harold Troper. 1992. "Canadian and American Immigration Policy Since 1945." Pp. 15–54 in *Immigration, Language, and Ethnicity: Canada and the United States*, edited by Barry R. Chiswick. Washington, D.C.: AEI Press.

Reitz, Jeffrey G. 1977. "Analysis of Changing Group Inequalities in a Changing Occupational Structure." Pp. 167–191 in *Mathematical Models of Sociology*, edited by P. Krishnan. Keele, England: University of Keele.

———. 1988a. "The Institutional Structure of Immigration as a Determinant of Inter-racial Competition: A Comparison of Britain and Canada." *International Migration Review* 22, no. 1:117–146.

———. 1988b. "Less Racial Discrimination in Canada, or Simply Less Racial Conflict?: Implications of Comparisons with Britain." *Canadian Public Policy* 14, no. 4:424–441.

———. 1990. "Ethnic Concentrations in Labor Markets and Their Implications for Ethnic Inequality." Pp. 135–195 in *Ethnic Identity and Equality: Varieties of Experience in a Canadian City*, by Raymond Breton, Wsevolod Isajiw, Warren E. Kalbach, and Jeffrey G. Reitz. Toronto: University of Toronto Press.

Reitz, Jeffrey G., and Raymond Breton. 1994. *The Illusion of Difference: Realities of Ethnicity in Canada and the United States*. Toronto: C. D. Howe Institute.

Reitz, Jeffrey G., and Sherrilyn Sklar. 1997. "Culture, Race, and the Economic Assimilation of Immigrants." *Sociological Forum* 12, no. 2:233–277.

Reubens, Edwin P. 1987. "Benefits and Costs of Migration." Pp. 1–40 in *The Economics of Mass Migration in the Twentieth Century*, edited by Sidney Klein. New York: Paragon House.

Riach, Peter A., and Judith Rich. 1991. "Testing for Racial Discrimination in the Labour Market." *Cambridge Journal of Economics* 15:239–256.

Riche, Richard, Daniel E. Hecker, and John U. Burgan. 1983. "High Technology Today and Tomorrow: A Small Slice of the Employment Pie." *Monthly Labor Review* (November):50–58.

Robitaille, D. F., W. H. Schmidt, S. Raisen, C. McKnight, E. Britton, and C. Nicol. 1993. *Curriculum Frameworks for Mathematics and Science*. TIMSS Monograph no. 1. Vancouver: Pacific Educational Press.

Rodriguez, Clara E. 1989. *Puerto Ricans: Born in the U.S.A.* Boston: Unwin Hyman.

Rosenblum, Gerald. 1973. *Immigrant Workers: Their Impact on American Labour Radicalism*. New York: Basic Books

Rosenfeld, Rachel A., and Arne L. Kalleberg. 1990. "A Cross-national Comparison of the Gender Gap in Income." *American Journal of Sociology* 96, no. 1:69–106.

Rothman, Eric S., and Thomas J. Espenshade. 1992. "Fiscal Impacts of Immigration to the United States." *Population Index* 58, no. 3:381–415.

Rubin, Beth. 1986. "Class Struggle American Style: Unions, Strikes, and Wages." *American Sociological Review* 51:618–631.

Sanders, Jimy, and Victor Nee. 1987. "Limits of Ethnic Solidarity in the Enclave Economy." *American Sociological Review* 52(December):745–773.

Sassen, Saskia. 1988. *The Mobility of Labor and Capital: A Study in International Investment and Labor Flow*. Cambridge: Cambridge University Press.

———. 1988–1989. "New York City's Informal Economy." Working Papers in the Social Sciences, vol. 4, no. 9. Los Angeles: University of California, Institute for Social Science Research.

_____. 1990. "Economic Restructuring and the American City." *Annual Review of Sociology* 16:465–490.

_____. 1991. *The Global City: New York, London, Tokyo.* Princeton: Princeton University Press.

_____. 1994. *Cities in a World Economy.* London: Pine Forge Press.

Saunders, Peter. 1994. *Welfare and Inequality: National and International Perspectives on the Australian Welfare State.* Cambridge: Cambridge University Press.

Saunders, Peter, Inge O'Connor, and Timothy Smeeding. 1994. "The Distribution of Welfare: Inequality, Earnings Capacity, and Household Production in a Comparative Perspective." Discussion Paper no. 51. Sydney: University of New South Wales, Social Policy Research Centre.

Saunders, Peter, and Anthony King. 1994. *Immigration and the Distribution of Income.* Canberra: Australian Government Publishing Service, Bureau of Immigration and Population Research.

Saunders, Peter, Helen Stott, and Garry Hobbes. 1991. "Income Inequality in Australia and New Zealand: International Comparisons and Recent Trends." *Review of Income and Wealth* 37, no. 1(March):63–79.

Sawyer, Malcolm. 1976. "Income Distribution in OECD Countries." *OECD Economic Outlook: Occasional Studies* (July):3–36.

Schlesinger, Arthur M., Jr. 1992. *The Disuniting of America: Reflections on a Multicultural Society.* New York: W. W. Norton and Company.

Seward, Shirley B., and Marc Tremblay. 1989. *Immigrants in the Canadian Labour Force: Their Role in Structural Change.* Studies in Social Policy Discussion Paper 89, B2. Ottawa, Ont.: Institute for Research on Public Policy.

Shavit, Yossi, and Hans-Peter Blossfield, eds. 1993. *Persistent Inequality: Changing Educational Attainment in Thirteen Countries.* Boulder: Westview Press.

Shockey, James W. 1989. "Overeducation and Earnings: A Structural Approach to Differential Attainment in the U.S. Labor Force." *American Sociological Review* 54:856–864.

Simon, Julian L. 1984. "Immigrants, Taxes, and Welfare in the United States." *Population and Development Review* 10(March):55–69.

Simpson, Miles. 1990. "Political Rights and Income Inequality: A Cross-national Test." *American Sociological Review* 55(October):682–693.

Skocpol, Theda. 1992. *Protecting Soldiers and Mothers: The Political Origins of Social Policy in the United States.* Cambridge: Harvard University Press.

Smeeding, Timothy M., Michael O'Higgins, and Lee Rainwater. 1990. *Poverty, Inequality, and Income Distribution in Comparative Perspective: The Luxembourg Income Study (LIS).* New York: Harvester Wheatsheaf.

Smeeding, Timothy M., and Lee Rainwater. 1991. "Cross-national Trends in Income, Poverty, and Dependency." Paper prepared for the Joint Center for Political and Economic Studies, Conference on Poverty, Inequality, and the Crisis of Social Policy, September 19–20. Washington, D.C.: Joint Center for Political and Economic Studies.

Smith, Michael. 1990. "What Is New in the 'New Structuralist' Analyses of Earnings?" *American Sociological Review* 55, no. 6:827–841.

Sniderman, Paul, and Michael G. Hagen. 1985. *Race and Inequality: A Study in American Values.* Chatham, N.J.: Chatham House.

Sniderman, Paul, and Thomas Piazza. 1993. *The Scar of Race*. Cambridge: Belknap Press of Harvard University Press.

Sorensen, Elaine, Frank D. Bean, Leighton Ku, and Wendy Zimmerman. 1992. *Immigrant Categories and the U.S. Job Market: Do They Make a Difference?* Washington, D.C.: Urban Institute Press.

Steinmetz, George, and Erik O. Wright. 1989. "The Fall and Rise of the Petty Bourgeoisie: Changing Patterns of Self-Employment in the Postwar United States." *American Journal of Sociology* 94, no. 5:973–1018.

Swan, Neil, Ludwig Auer, Denis Chénard, Angélique dePlaa, Arnold deSilva, Douglas Palmer, and John Serjak. 1991. *Economic and Social Aspects of Immigration*. Ottawa, Ont.: Supply and Services Canada.

Swank, Duane H., and Alexander Hicks. 1985. "The Determinants and Redistributive Impacts of State Welfare Spending in the Advanced Capitalist Democracies." Pp. 115–139 in *Political Economy in Western Democracies*, edited by Norman J. Vig and Steven E. Schier. New York: Holmes and Meier.

Thomas, W. I., and F. Znaniecki. 1920. *The Polish Peasant in Europe and America*. Vol. 5, *Organization and Disorganization in America*. Boston: Richard G. Badger, Gorham Press.

Tienda, Marta, and Leif Jensen. 1986. "Immigration and Public Assistance Participation: Dispelling the Myth of Dependency." *Social Science Research* 15:372–400.

Tienda, Marta, and Ding-Tzann Lii. 1987. "Minority Concentration and Earnings Inequality: Blacks, Hispanics, and Asians Compared." *American Journal of Sociology* 93, no. 1:141–165.

Tilly, Charles. 1994. "The Weight of the Past on North American Immigration." Research Paper no. 189. Toronto: University of Toronto, Centre for Urban and Community Studies.

Touraine, Alain. 1971. *The Post-Industrial Society*. New York: Random House.

Treiman, Donald J., Vivian Lew, Hye-kyung Lee, and Thad A. Brown. 1986–1987. "Occupational Status Attainment Among Ethnic Groups in Los Angeles." Working Papers in the Social Sciences, vol. 2, no. 1. Los Angeles: University of California, Institute for Social Science Research.

Turner, Margery Austin, Michael Fix, and Raymond J. Struyk. 1991. *Opportunities Denied, Opportunities Diminished: Discrimination in Hiring*. Project Report. Washington, D.C.: Urban Institute.

UNESCO (see United Nations Educational, Scientific, and Cultural Organization).

United Nations Educational, Scientific, and Cultural Organization (UNESCO). 1975. *Statistical Yearbook, 1975*. Paris: UNESCO.

_____. 1985. *Statistical Yearbook, 1985*. Paris: UNESCO.

_____. 1993. *Statistical Yearbook, 1993*. Paris: UNESCO.

United States. Bureau of the Census. 1983. *Census of Population and Housing, 1980: Public-Use Microdata Samples Technical Documentation*. Ann Arbor, Mich.: Interuniversity Consortium for Political and Social Research.

_____. 1988. *Statistical Abstract of the United States: 1988*. Washington, D.C.: U.S. Government Printing Office.

_____. 1992. *Statistical Abstract of the United States: 1992*. Washington, D.C.: U.S. Government Printing Office.

_____. 1993. *Statistical Abstract of the United States: 1993.* Washington, D.C.: U.S. Government Printing Office.

United States. Department of State. Bureau of Security and Consular Affairs. 1972. *Report of the Visa Office*, Appendix B. Washington, D.C.: U.S. Department of State.

United States. Immigration and Naturalization Service. 1985. *Statistical Yearbook of the Immigration and Naturalization Service, 1981.* Washington, D.C.: U.S. Government Printing Office.

_____. 1989. *Statistical Yearbook of the Immigration and Naturalization Service, 1986.* Washington, D.C.: U.S. Government Printing Office.

van Arnhem, J. Corina M., and Geurt J. Schotsman. 1982. "Do Parties Affect the Distribution of Incomes? The Case of Advanced Capitalist Democracies." Pp. 283–264 in *The Impact of Parties: Politics and Policies in Democratic Capitalist States*, edited by Frances G. Castles. Beverly Hills, Calif.: Sage.

Verma, Anil, Russell Smith, Marcus Sandver, Kathryn Ready, Morley Gunderson, Lance Compra, and Richard P. Chaykowski. 1996. "Free Trade, Labor Markets, and Industrial Relations: Institutional Developments and the Research Agenda." Report of the IRRA NAFTA Committee. *Proceedings of the 48th Annual Meetings*, Champaign, Ill.: Industrial Relations Research Association.

Waldinger, Roger. 1984. "Immigrant Enterprise and the New York Garment Industry." *Social Problems* 32(October):60–71.

_____. 1989. "Immigration and Urban Change." *Annual Review of Sociology* 15:211–232.

_____. 1989. "Structural Opportunity or Ethnic Advantage? Immigrant Business Development in New York." *International Migration Review* 23, no. 1:48–70.

_____. 1996. *Still the Promised City? African-Americans and New Immigrants in Post-Industrial New York.* Cambridge: Harvard University Press.

Waldinger, Roger, and Thomas Bailey. 1989. "The Post-Industrial Service Economy and Its Impact on Immigrant Hispanics, Native Blacks, and Immigrant Asians." Paper presented at the 1989 ASA meetings in San Francisco.

Waldinger, Roger, and Mehdi Bozorgmehr, eds. 1996. *Ethnic Los Angeles.* New York: Russell Sage Foundation.

Waldinger, Roger, and Yenfen Tseng. 1992. "Divergent Diasporas: The Chinese Communities of New York and Los Angeles Compared." *Revue Européenne des Migrations Internationales* 8, no. 3:91–114.

Walters, Pamela Barnhouse, and Richard Rubinson. 1983. "Educational Expansion and Economic Output in the United States, 1890–1969." *American Sociological Review* 48:480–493.

Wanner, Richard A. 1986. "Educational Inequality: Trends in Twentieth-century Canada and the United States." *Comparative Social Research* 9:47–66.

Waters, Mary. 1994. "Ethnic and Racial Identities of Second-Generation Black Immigrants in New York City." *International Migration Review* 28, no. 4:785–820.

Waters, Mary, and Karl Eschbach. 1995. "Immigration and Ethnic and Racial Inequality in the United States." *Annual Review of Sociology* 21:419–446.

Whiteford, Peter. 1992. "Are Immigrants Over-represented in the Australian Social Security System?" Discussion Paper no. 31. Kensington, Australia: University of New South Wales, Social Policy Research Centre.

Wilson, Franklin D., and Marta Tienda. 1988–1989. "Ethnicity, Employment, and Migration." Working Papers in the Social Sciences, vol. 4, no. 10. Los Angeles: University of California, Institute for Social Science Research.

Wilson, Franklin D., Marta Tienda, and Lawrence Wu. 1991. "Racial Equality in the Labor Market: Still an Elusive Goal." Discussion Paper no. 91–33. Madison: University of Wisconsin, Center for Demography and Ecology.

Wilson, Kenneth L., and Alejandro Portes. 1980. "Immigrant Enclaves: An Analysis of the Labor Market Experiences of Cubans in Miami." *American Journal of Sociology* 86, no. 2:295–319.

Wilson, William Julius. 1978. *The Declining Significance of Race*. Chicago: University of Chicago Press.

_____. 1987. *The Truly Disadvantaged: The Inner City, the Underclass, and Public Policy*. Chicago: University of Chicago Press.

Wooden, Mark, Robert Holton, Graeme Hugo, and Judith Sloan. 1990. *Australian Immigration: A Survey of the Issues*. Canberra: Bureau of Immigration Research.

Wright, Erik O. 1979. *Class Structure and Income Determination*. New York: Academic Press.

Wright, Robert E., and Paul S. Maxim. 1991. "Changes in the 'Cohort Quality' of Canadian Immigrants." Paper presented at the Canadian Economics Association Meetings at Kingston. Ottawa, Ont.: Institute for Research on Public Policy (unpublished).

Zhou, Min. 1992. *Chinatown: The Socio-economic Potential of an Urban Enclave*. Philadelphia: Temple University Press.

Zolberg, Aristide R. 1992. "Response to Crisis: Refugee Policy in the United States and Canada." Pp. 55–112 in *Immigration, Language, and Ethnicity: Canada and the United States*, edited by Barry R. Chiswick. Washington, D.C.: AEI Press.

Index

immigrant populations in, 52, 53(table), 57, 58, 59–60(table)
skills polarization in, 144, 226
Scandinavia, part-time employment in, 260(n11)
Secondary education, comparative trends in, 107–109, 110–111, 112
Segmentation. *See* Labor market stratification
Self-employment, 161, 163, 169–170, 260(n13)
Self-selection, 23, 27
Self-sufficiency, immigration policies and, 87
Selling Illusions: The Cult of Multiculturalism in Canada, 4
Service industry, 231
employment in, 157, 158(table), 159
entry-level earnings and, 192–194, 195, 197(table)
immigrant concentration in, 190–192
See also Low-level services
Settlement programs, 36
Settlements. *See* Immigrant communities
Single parents, income redistribution and, 214–215
Sixth Preference immigrants (United States), 96
Skilled labor. *See* Labor, skilled
Skill levels, 255(n13,14)
determinants of, 256(n17)
effects of institutions on, 224, 226, 229
entry-level status and, 13–16
immigration policy and, 19–23, 88–97
labor market effects on, 184, 185–186(table), 188–189
origins-mix effects and, 93–95
settlement patterns and, 97–104
Skill selection, 19, 20–22, 23, 30, 69–70, 88
Australia immigration policy and, 40, 70, 79–83
Canadian immigration policy and, 40, 70, 74–79
cross-national differences in, 83
immigrant skill levels and, 89(table), 90–93, 95, 96, 97
origins-mix effects and, 94
racial discrimination and, 40
self-sufficiency and, 87
settlement patterns and, 98–101
in United Kingdom, 40
U.S. immigration policy and, 70–74
See also Points system
Skills gap. *See* Skills polarization

Skills polarization, 106, 120–123, 148, 256(n1), 262(n25)
in Australia, 146–147
in Canada, 145–146
compounding institutional effects on, 226
earnings inequality and, 227–228
in "education cities," 133, 138–139, 140
entry-level earnings and, 202, 203
interaction with earnings distribution, 174, 175
in U.S. cities, 140–145, 147
"Snapshot" surveys, 17
Social assistance. *See* Welfare
Social cohesion, globalization and, 246
Social democracy, welfare and, 206
Social entitlement. *See* Welfare
Social security, 213
Social services, 32
employment in, 159
See also Welfare
Social skills, education and, 118
"Social wage," 263(n2)
Social welfare. *See* Welfare
South Asian immigrants, 9, 13
Southeast Asian immigrants, 9, 13. *See also* Vietnamese immigrants
Southern European immigrants, 94, 255(n11)
Statistical variance, of earnings, 153
Statue of Liberty, 83
Status
race and, 15–16, 18
skill levels and, 13–16
See also Entry levels
Stone product industry, 165
Stratification. *See* Labor market stratification
Structured Selection Assessment System (Australia), 80
Superelites, in global cities, 227
Sweden, government transfers in, 209
Sydney (Australia), 52, 53(table), 56, 57, 58, 61, 62–63(table)

Taiwan, 253(n7)
A Tale of Two Nations, 260(n17)
TANF. *See* Temporary Assistance for Needy Families
Taxation
compounding effects of, 225(table)
effects on immigrants, 36
family institution and, 262(n1)
income redistribution and, 264–264(n7)
welfare and, 209–215
Technology, employment in, 157